Trials of Discipleship

TRIALS OF DISCIPLESHIP

The Story of William Clayton, A Mormon

James B. Allen

UNIVERSITY OF ILLINOIS PRESS

Urbana and Chicago

All photographs are courtesy of the Church Archives,
The Church of Jesus Christ of Latter-day Saints,
except those of William Clayton's wives, which are
courtesy of Paul Dahl.

This book is printed on acid-free paper.

Library of Congress Cataloging-in-Publication Data

Allen, James B.
  Trials of discipleship.

  Includes index.
  1. Clayton, William, 1814–1879.   2. Mormons—
Biography. I. Title.
BX8695.C35A78   1987   289.3′32′0924   [B]   86-11328
ISBN 0-252-01369-7 (alk. paper)

For Renée, Kristine, J. Michael,
Kathleen, Nancy, and Scott J.

CONTENTS

My interest in William Clayton began in the early 1970s, when I learned that one of his descendants, Mr. Comstock Clayton, had donated William's Manchester, England, diary to Brigham Young University and was anxious that it be published. I was asked if I had any interest in editing it and, after examining it, found that indeed I did. It had significance far beyond Clayton himself, for in actuality it provided an intimate account of Mormonism in early Victorian England. As branch president of The Church of Jesus Christ of Latter-day Saints in Manchester, Clayton was deeply involved with all the activities of the church as well as the personal lives of its members. Here was a fascinating portrait of a people, and nothing quite like it was available in print. Professor Thomas G. Alexander agreed to become co-editor of the project, and, with profuse editorial notes, it was finally published under the title *Manchester Mormons*.

But that was not the end for me. The insight Clayton's diary provided into the nature of early Mormonism was fascinating, and I wondered if a full biography could not do something similar for the whole period of his lifetime. As the story of a convert to the church who lived first in England, then in Nauvoo, and finally in Utah, it would demonstrate the varied problems and attitudes of particular places, as well as how things changed for the Mormons over time and in that way it would make a significant contribution to Mormon history.

This work, then, is more than a biography. In its expanded interpretive framework I hope it will catch the interest of Mormons as well as non-Mormons who seek greater insight into the nature of the Latter-day Saint community during the hectic years of the nineteenth century. Those who are familiar with Mormon history remember Clayton as a personal friend and scribe of Joseph Smith, the man who recorded the revelation on plural marriage, a journalist who left us one of the most intimate accounts of the epic crossing of the plains in 1847, author of that best-known of all Mormon hymns, "Come, Come Ye Saints," and compiler of the noteworthy *Latter-day Saints' Emigrant Guide*. But this volume is equally, if not more, concerned with Clayton the representative disciple: that is, with what his life has to tell us about the early Latter-day Saint community as a whole. This is not to imply that Clayton was fully typical of the ordinary Latter-day Saint, or even that large numbers shared all his attitudes and concerns. But in many important ways he was at least a representative Latter-day Saint of the "below-the-leadership" level. His problems were often community problems, his attitudes reflected those of many other Mormons, and his frustrations dramatically illustrate the diversity of frustrations that were possible inside the Mormon community. For this reason I use the term "representative disciple" rather than "typical Mormon." Clayton's life represents some of the possibilities in Mormon life and in that way helps us understand the whole community better. The theme of discipleship, then, provides a conceptual framework for this study.

No historian is totally free from bias, and at this point I should recognize my own. As I studied Clayton's life I saw success and failure, strength and weakness, inspiration and stumbling blocks, but out of it all came a genuine respect for the man that had an obvious effect on what I have written. At the same time, I have tried not to forget the warning implied in a comment made by a friend who criticized an early draft of one chapter in which I rationalized with great empathy some of Clayton's problems. "William's frailties make him loveable," my critic wrote, "but not worshipable." I hope I have adjusted the manuscript so that what comes out is respect without idolatry and a sympathetic presentation of important issues without historical distortion.

Let me also take the liberty of expressing a personal concern that, in part, arises from my being both a believing Mormon and a professional historian. The quest of the historian is not only for the "facts," but also for a sense of balance as one attempts to re-create the past. In the process, at least two troublesome temptations must be avoided, both of which can affect historians of religion all too easily. One is to erase from history everything but that which is pleasing or noncontroversial, and the other is to emphasize the sensational, the bizarre, and the negative because of their likely appeal to certain readers. Both tendencies tend to distort, and neither will ever provide the steady balance so essential to historical understanding. I have tried to do neither. Our heritage, to paraphrase Paul, is made up of many parts that, when "fitly framed together," should provide us all with a better perspective on what the past was all about.

Finally, I must recognize with deep appreciation the many people who helped in the preparation of this manuscript. The research for *Manchester Mormons* was invaluable here, and I thank Thomas G. Alexander for his willingness to let me adapt much of that material to this book. In addition to the people recognized in *Manchester Mormons*, I am grateful for the research assistance of Glenn V. Bird, Breck England, Jessie Embry, and Bruce and Julie Westergren. I also owe much to Leonard J. Arrington, former church historian and now director of the Joseph Fielding Smith Institute for Church History at Brigham Young University, who strongly encouraged me in this project. The late Elder G. Homer Durham, managing director of the Church Historical Department, as well as other administrators and staff members of that department provided me with invaluable help and cooperation in obtaining access to various papers and special collections. Dean C. Jessee, Ronald K. Esplin, Ronald W. Walker, Jan Shipps, David J. Whittaker, and Thomas G. Alexander were very generous in providing insights and suggestions at various stages in the writing, and Maureen Ursenbach Beecher, Leonard J. Arrington, Davis Bitton, Jan Shipps, and Richard Cracroft all read the manuscript and made valuable suggestions. I am grateful, too, for certain descendants of William Clayton who also read and commented on this work. I also appreciate the fine editorial contributions of Charles Vogel, who helped me prepare the final version of the manuscript for press, as well as the work of Marilyn Webb and her associates in the Faculty Support Center of the College of Family, Home and Social Sciences at Brigham Young University, who prepared the typescript. And I am especially grateful for the support and patience of my wife and children, to whom this work is most deservedly dedicated.

Orem, Utah
1986

"I Feel I Am Not My Own": A Preview of One Man's Discipleship

The twenty-five-year-old William Clayton had much to think about one day in January 1840. He had been a Mormon for little more than two years, yet in that time his life had totally changed. He had given up his work, left his wife and children with her parents, dedicated himself full time to church missionary and leadership duties, built up in Manchester one of the largest branches of the church in England, and was deeply involved in listening to all manner of personal problems and giving pastoral guidance to the Manchester Mormons. Having no income, he depended for his livelihood upon the good will of the people he served. All this suddenly overwhelmed him as he wrote to his friend and co-worker, Willard Richards, of his total commitment: "I feel I am not my own. I am bought with a price, even the blood of Jesus Christ, and as a servant I must soon give up my account. I desire and strive, brethren, to keep my account right with the Lord every day that I may meet him with joy. [James] Lea could get away from his master but I feel always in the presence of mine, and my desire is to live nearer still that I may be ready in the hour to give up my accounts."[1]

Clayton, it seems, had caught a spirit something like that Jesus of Nazareth required of his followers some eighteen centuries earlier. Jesus made harsh demands, though he also gave his disciples promises of great rewards. "If any man come unto me and hate not his father, and mother, and wife, and children, and brethren, and sisters, yea, and his own life also, he cannot be my disciple." The faithful were warned that they must count well the cost of their professed commitment, for "whoever he be of you that forsaketh not all that he hath, he cannot be my disciple." But the reward was worth the sacrifice: "Verily I say unto you, There is no man that hath left house, or parents, or brethren, or wife, or children, for the kingdom of God's sake, Who shall not receive manifold more in this present time, and in the world to come life everlasting." "My sheep hear my voice, and I know them, and they follow me; And I give unto them eternal life."[2]

The history of early Christianity is replete with examples of faithful disciples who endured the worst of trials. But they were far from perfect, and their discipleship often included struggles with things other than ostracism from unbelieving families or some kind of physical persecution. Such problems as temptation, fear, and personal weaknesses tested their faith and caused even the best among them at times to falter. The apostle Peter wept bitterly at his own weakness when he realized, on the morning of Jesus' trial, that he had thrice denied his Lord. Thomas doubted the Resurrection. The Christians at Jerusalem held "all things in common," but this test of discipleship was too much for Ananias and Sapphira. They held back on their donations, and when their deception was discovered they both fell dead. The apostle Paul complained of his personal "thorn in the flesh," which he identified only as "the messenger of Satan to buffet me, lest I should be exalted above measure." Exactly what the problem was is unclear, and it has been variously posited as an evil spirit, false apostles (Judaizers) who continually made trouble for Paul, or some kind of physical malady. Paul's attitude, however, was that his problem was a necessity, for without it he could too easily exalt himself unrighteously. Discipleship, then, is not perfection but rather a struggle for perfection, and in this struggle a person often must wrestle with himself even more than with others.

William Clayton's feeling of faithful servitude was the result not only of faith in Christ but also of his faith in the American prophet, Joseph Smith. As followers of Joseph Smith, Clayton believed, the Mormons were the true modern disciples of Jesus Christ, and they could expect the same trials and rewards. "Verily, it is a day of sacrifice," they were told, and "the Lord requireth the heart and a willing mind." "But blessed are they who are faithful and endure, whether in life or in death, for they shall inherit eternal life."[3] So far as Clayton was concerned, the struggle for his heart and mind had been won, and he was ready at that moment to go anywhere, do anything, and give up any comfort for the sake of the new American religion.

Like the early Christian disciples, however, William Clayton had his personal thorns in the flesh, and he frequently expressed disappointment and dissatisfaction with himself for letting them make him stumble. He often took stock of his life and recognized the need for improvement. "Gird up your loins, Fresh courage take, Our God will never us forsake," he wrote for his fellow pioneers in 1846, but this expression eventually took on deeper meaning for him than simply hope for getting across the plains. In a life filled with illness, financial problems, and other adversities, a sustaining faith was one thing. It was another thing, however, to examine one's own weakness in the light of what it meant to be a Saint. At times this proved to be Clayton's most grueling trial as he struggled to improve himself and sought fresh courage so far as the continuing possibility of his own salvation was concerned.

William Clayton's new faith was founded in the intensely revivalistic, restorationist environment of early nineteenth-century America. It was a time when many Americans were disillusioned with traditional Christianity, and in their search for a restoration of primitive Christianity some heard of, and believed in, Joseph Smith. He told his followers of his own youthful quest for religious certainty in 1820 and of his personal vision of the Father and the Son that spring in a grove in western New York. He also told of his discovery and translation of an ancient American book of scripture, the Book of Mormon, and of the frequent appearance to him of various heavenly beings who restored certain ancient practices, knowledge, and authority. The Church of Jesus Christ of Latter-day Saints was the authentic restoration of the primitive church and, as announced at the beginning of its book of modern revelation, "the only true and living church upon the face of the whole earth."[4] The members called themselves Saints, which in itself was a fitting image of the restoration ideal.

In a way, the Book of Mormon was the visible symbol of the new church's break with traditional Christianity. Its mere existence proclaimed the idea that the canon of scripture was not closed, and Latter-day Saints accepted it as equally valid with the Bible. If, in places, the Bible was mistranslated, then the new scripture might even be more valid. Joseph Smith characterized it as "the most correct book of any on earth, and the keystone of our religion," adding that "a man would get nearer to God by abiding by its precepts, than by any other book."[5] All this gave nonbelievers fuel for their anti-Mormon fires, for anything that seemed to replace the Bible or challenge its finality seemed also anti-Christian. For the Mormons, however, the Book of Mormon was just what it purported to be: a "second witness of Christ," or a testimony to all that "Jesus is the Christ, the Eternal God, manifesting himself unto all nations."[6]

The exclusive nature of their faith was a weighty matter to believers like William Clayton and central to defining the nature of their discipleship.[7] New revelations and teachings of Joseph Smith gave them special knowledge, they believed, shared only by those who followed God's modern prophet. Such feelings only heightened their loyalty to the Kingdom and their willingness to follow the prophet no matter where he led them. There is nothing clearer in William Clayton's life than his absolute confidence that only through the gospel of Christ as taught by the Mormon church could the world be saved. He longed to share the message with the people of the world, but those who did not accept it were guilty, in his mind, of rejecting the Lord himself.

Equally important to Clayton was the fact that some things were taught so privately that at first not even all the Saints could share them. Plural marriage, the concept of eternal marriage, and the temple endowment were among them. When Clayton found himself far enough inside the prophet's confidential circle that he shared such private instruction, his devotion to Joseph Smith became even greater, and his ability to take on any new challenge was strengthened that much more.

This feeling of special identity added strength to Mormonism, but it also contributed to some problems. In a political and social climate that bred suspicion of any seemingly exclusivist group, especially if that group seemed to threaten traditional white Protestant values, the church could easily alienate itself from much of American society.[8] The Mormons revered the New World as a "chosen" land and the American Constitution as an inspired political document. They also considered themselves patriotic, loyal Americans, but they regularly found themselves at odds with the religious, social, and political norms in every state where the church established a gathering place.

Even at the beginning, Joseph Smith had alienated religious leaders, not so much by announcing that he had seen a vision, but by saying that the Lord told him that all the churches of the day were wrong.[9] Within a year after the church was organized, in 1830, Joseph Smith and most of his western New York followers moved to Ohio where they found refuge among recently converted Disciples of Christ

(Campbellites). Their economic hegemony in Kirtland, however, and the failure of the Kirtland bank caused tension with other citizens as well as dissension from within, and in 1838 Joseph Smith and most of the Ohio Mormons took refuge in the Mormon settlements in western Missouri. As early as 1831, that area had been divinely designated for the gathering of the Saints, the place for building the City of Zion,[10] and the Saints immediately began to acquire all the land they could. But conflict inevitably came, and the Mormons were brutally expelled from the state in the winter of 1838-39. They were welcomed with sympathy and open arms in western Illinois, and Nauvoo became the new gathering place, but within a few years tension mounted again. Fear of Mormon political domination gave rise to new questions about church-state relationships, and this, combined with certain new doctrines and practices, alienated the population and ended in the killing of Joseph Smith and the driving of the Mormons from Illinois. Under Brigham Young's leadership, in 1847, the symbolic Mormon Zion moved to the Great Basin. Even there, however, polygamy and church political influence caused constant conflict with the federal government. Until nearly the end of the nineteenth century, the Mormons seemed to remain continually at odds with the rest of American society.

All this presented a dual dilemma: one to the church as an institution, and another, of a little different sort, to individuals. As the church was continually hounded as both un- and anti-American, how best could it express what it considered to be its real identity within the larger culture to which it belonged? Equally important, how could an individual believer's search for personal identity within the church be reconciled with the need to suppress one's own desires—even, perhaps, one's own personality—for the good of the Kingdom? The problem could become complex when the church sometimes made demands that seemed to fly in the face of one's perception of his own self-interest. Becoming a disciple of Joseph Smith often meant leaving home and loved ones (sometimes as a family outcast), losing earthly possessions, enduring mockery and physical abuse, crossing an unfriendly ocean, and/or walking across a desert to join fellow followers in an unfamiliar home. In each case the choice was related to the group; once the decision to follow was made, then where one went and what one did was dictated by the interests of the Kingdom. Whatever the trials, it was the lot of the disciple to endure them patiently, knowing that a better day would come.

As an institution, Mormonism identified itself in several ways. One was in a unique form of restorationism. As Jan Shipps has recently observed for the scholarly world, Mormonism was not a typical restorationist movement, for it constituted an important blending of both Old Testament and New Testament religion.[11] In their own way, the Mormons of William Clayton's day knew that, for they emphasized certain Hebraic as well as Christian traditions. They believed not only that the primitive Christian church had been restored but also that the ancient blessings of Abraham and other Hebrew prophets were part of that restoration. The church was not only modern Christianity, but it was also modern Israel, and Abraham, Isaac, Jacob, and Moses played essential roles in the Mormons' understanding of their own place in God's scheme of things. Non-Mormons were gentiles, for they were not of the faith of Abraham.

The term "restoration of the gospel," then, meant that there was a clear continuity from the Hebrews through New Testament Christians to the Latter-day Saints. The Mormon priesthood, for example, was identified as the same as that held by Old Testament priests and prophets.[12] Even polygamy was justified, in part, as a restoration of ancient Israelite practice. Beyond that, the Mormons, like the children of Abraham and the disciples of the New Testament, considered themselves a covenant people. They had received a "new and everlasting covenant" that, to them, meant a new restoration of all old covenants, and these were eternal and everlasting in nature. Significantly, William Clayton sometimes closed his letters to other Saints with the phrase, "Yours in the E.C.," meaning "Yours in the Everlasting Covenant." This was his reminder that they all belonged to a new covenant community, latter-day Israel.

The restoration ideal was also an element in the apocalyptic fervor that became so visible in the life of William Clayton and other Mormon disciples. The unequivocal message of the early missionaries was that as emissaries of the restored church, they were taking the gospel of the Kingdom to the nations of the earth for the last time. As Orson Hyde wrote in his important missionary broadside, *A Timely Warning to the People of England,*

> The Lord has been pleased to send his holy angel from heaven to announce the joyful tidings to witnesses now living, that the time has come for him to set his hand the second and last time to gather the remnants of Israel; and with them the fulness of the Gentiles—

to establish permanent peace on Earth for One Thousand Years.
. . .

As John was sent before the face of the Lord to prepare the way for his first coming, even so has the Lord now sent forth his servants for the last time, to labour in his vineyard at the eleventh hour, to prepare the way for his second coming.[13]

Such proclamations were sent to kings and nations around the world.

All this led to an early internationalism, as Mormon missionaries went to all parts of the earth, and church offices were established in many countries, particularly those of Europe. At the same time, the message was that Zion would be built on the American continent and converts were urged to gather with the Saints in Zion—whether it was located at the moment in Missouri, Illinois, or Salt Lake City. Joseph Smith, however, also explained that the word Zion could actually mean three different things, depending upon its context: the New Jerusalem (located specifically in western Missouri), the whole of the American continent, or any place where a Zion people, the "pure in heart," were gathered.[14] With the latter definition, even those Saints who were unable to gather to America could be gathered with the "pure in heart" simply by joining the church and remaining faithful to their covenants. Mormonism thus established not only an identity between the destiny of America and itself but also an identity with the destiny of the world.

The Mormons were serious about these grand perceptions of their own destiny, and they were equally serious about their relationship to the man, or men, chosen to lead them into that destiny. In accepting Joseph Smith as the prophet of the restoration, they also accepted the proposition that "no one shall be appointed to receive commandments and revelations in this church excepting my servant Joseph Smith, Jun., for he receiveth them even as Moses."[15] What this meant was that Joseph Smith, or his successor in the prophetic office, was the final authority on matters of faith and doctrine. The army of Israel marched forth under one banner and with one objective: build the Kingdom. Satisfaction for the individual, at least as it appears in the life of William Clayton, was not unlike the self-satisfaction Puritans received from "knowing" they were among the "elect" of God. The comfort many embattled Mormons received from their "testimony" of Joseph Smith was in knowing that they were among the exclusive recipients of God's message to modern Israel.

The priesthood was especially significant in this pattern of devotion. Even though the church was hierarchical and authoritarian with regard to doctrine and general policy, its priesthood was available to every "worthy" male member. This, as much as anything else, gave male converts, at least, a sense of special worth, for they saw in it the power to exercise God's authority and thus be active officers in a very exclusive army of Israel.[16] William Clayton was not untypical, and his diaries and letters frequently reveal the personal satisfaction as well as the deep, often uncomfortable, sense of responsibility that came with his priesthood calling.

Joining the Mormon church was the most important turning point in William Clayton's life. It catapulted him immediately into a myriad of new activities and associations, took him to the United States, taught him completely new ideas, changed his attitudes toward marriage and other social customs, and, as he would constantly affirm, provided him with some deeply moving and soul-satisfying inner experiences that gave him a sense of well-being that he had never before thought possible. All these experiences and more suggest the richness that characterized the Mormon experience in the nineteenth century.

Clayton's life also suggests the enigmas involved in attempting to characterize a so-called faithful Saint. By most reasonable standards of the time, Clayton was faithful, but he also had his share of human frailties. How could someone with such deep faith in the wisdom of God, the rightness of his mission, and the positive outcome of whatever he was assigned to do sometimes retreat into periods of moroseness when he did not get the human recognition he thought he deserved? How does one explain the fact that even though most of his wives considered him a good husband so far as the system of plural marriage would allow, some of them divorced him? Why did he do some things that seem contrary to the mainstream of Mormon thinking and practice, such as using alcohol, showing an intense interest in the occult, or preaching some concepts that were not fully accepted among the rest of the Saints? Similar enigmas are part and parcel of the life of most people, and they are never completely explained, but in this study we will at least venture some informed speculation that might shed light on the many facets that made up the life of some nineteenth-century Mormon converts.

David Hackett Fischer has warned scholars against numerous fallacies in their writing,[17] three of which are especially relevant here.

One is a tendency to view individuals as "one-dimensional." Obviously this work will emphasize certain characteristics and themes, including the role of Clayton as a single-minded follower-of-the-leader. But Clayton was more than that, just as Mormonism was more than a religious, a political, a social, or any other kind of movement that could be characterized according to a single theme or model. At least some of Clayton's complexities will be illustrated here.

Another fallacy is that of the "universal" person, the assumption that "people are intellectually and psychologically the same in all times, places, and circumstances." Certainly this is not the case with Mormonism. While some beliefs and practices have characterized the church from the beginning, others have changed over time. For that reason, those who know something about modern Mormonism should not assume that Clayton, or any other disciple, was somehow out of the mainstream if he said or did things that are not characteristic of Mormons today. One must try, at least, to understand each generation in its own time, and according to its own perspectives, and not superimpose a present-day world view upon the past.

Finally, it is important to avoid the fallacy of the "mass" individual, the implication that anyone, including Clayton, was fully typical of anything. This is difficult, to say the least, for generalizations sometimes must be made, but they should fall far short of what Fischer calls "a species of false generalization in which an individual is puffed up like a balloon and mistaken for a class of individuals." Clayton was himself first and a Mormon second, even though, in his mind, he probably *should* have thought about it the other way around.

This study, then, provides an inside look at both the satisfaction and the stress, directly related to his faith, that a nineteenth-century Mormon could experience. It also illustrates something about the tough-mindedness that allowed at least some followers of Joseph Smith frequently to be disappointed and disillusioned yet maintain a seemingly unscathed commitment. In some ways William Clayton's story *was* the Mormon story: his values were wholly Mormon (or so he believed), his life patterns were those of many early converts, the church was a major factor in his most pivotal decisions, his chief pleasures were religious pleasures, and his major sorrows were, for the most part, direct results of his Mormon commitment. "I feel I am not my own," he wrote in 1840, and in that statement he reflected the highest ideal of the faithful Mormon convert.

NOTES

1. Clayton to Willard Richards, 28 Jan. 1840, Willard Richards Papers, Historical Department of The Church of Jesus Christ of Latter-day Saints, Salt Lake City, Utah, hereafter cited as Church Archives.

2. Luke 14:25, 33, 18:29–30; John 10:27–28.

3. Doctrine and Covenants of The Church of Jesus Christ of Latter-day Saints 64:23, 34; 50:5, hereafter cited as Doctrine and Covenants.

4. Ibid., 1:30. Two important articles dealing with the religious environment of early Mormonism are Gordon Wood, "Evangelical America and Early Mormonism," *New York History* 41 (Oct. 1980):359–86; Timothy L. Smith, "The Book of Mormon in a Biblical Culture," *Journal of Mormon History* 7 (1980):3–22.

5. Joseph Smith, Jr., *History of the Church of Jesus Christ of Latter-day Saints: Period I, History of Joseph Smith, the Prophet*, ed. B. H. Roberts, 6 vols., 2d ed. rev. (Salt Lake City: Deseret News, 1949), 4:461, hereafter cited as *History of the Church*.

6. See the title page of the Book of Mormon.

7. The leading article on the significance of the concept of exclusive authority in early Mormonism is Mario DePillis, "The Quest for Religious Authority and the Rise of Mormonism," *Dialogue: A Journal of Mormon Thought* 1 (Spring 1966):68–88. Another approach to the discontinuity between early Mormonism and the Christian churches of the time is suggested in John G. Gager, "Early Mormonism and Early Christianity: Some Parallels and Their Consequences for the Study of New Religions," *Journal of Mormon History* 9 (1982):53–60.

8. See David Brian Davis, "Some Themes of Counter-Subversion: An Analysis of Anti-Masonic, Anti-Catholic, and Anti-Mormon Literature," *Mississippi Valley Historical Review* 47 (Sept. 1960):205–24; Mark W. Cannon, "The Crusades against the Masons, Catholics, and Mormons: Separate Waves of a Common Current," *BYU Studies* 3 (Winter 1961):23–40.

9. See Neal E. Lambert and Richard H. Cracroft, "Literary Form and Historical Understanding: Joseph Smith's First Vision," *Journal of Mormon History* 7 (1980):31–42, for some insight into the various experiences of the time that were in some ways similar to Joseph Smith's. Visions and other spiritual experiences were not uncommon, but claims to exclusive divine authority were.

10. Doctrine and Covenants 57:1–3.

11. This idea is one of the themes in Jan Shipps's *Mormonism: The Story of a New Religious Tradition* (Urbana: University of Illinois Press, 1985).

12. See Doctrine and Covenants 84 and 107 for Joseph Smith's two major revelations on the priesthood.

13. Orson Hyde, *A Timely Warning to the People of England*, broadside, Church Archives. Although this broadside was first printed in Toronto, Canada, in 1836 under a different title, it was later reprinted both as a pamphlet and a broadside in England. It was one of the basic missionary tracts in England, and Clayton's missionary journal makes frequent reference to it.

14. See Doctrine and Covenants 52:1–3; 97:21; *History of the Church*, 6:318–19.

15. Doctrine and Covenants 28:2.

16. The experience of Parley P. Pratt was not untypical, and well illustrates the point. As a young man, Pratt searched for the primitive church and finally joined the most prominent primitivist movement of the day: Alexander Campbell's Disciples of Christ. "Here was the *ancient gospel* in due form," he wrote in his autobiography. "Here were the very principles which I had discovered years before; but could find no one to minister in." However, he said, he was still bothered by the lack of authority in the ministry—some evidence that the right to baptize and do other things had come directly from God. He was, then, a prime target for the Mormon message. He soon found himself doing missionary work in western New York, where he met the Mormon missionaries and was converted. The night after he was baptized, he wrote, "I was ordained to the office of Elder in the church, which included authority to preach, baptize, administer the sacrament, administer the Holy Spirit by the laying on of hands in the name of Jesus Christ. . . . I now felt I had authority in the ministry." (Parley P. Pratt, *Autobiography of Parley P. Pratt*, ed. Parley P. Pratt, Jr. [Salt Lake City: Deseret Book Company, 1938], 31, 42.) Pratt soon continued his missionary work, this time as a Mormon, and his quest was achieved in his satisfaction with the implications of that authority.

17. See David Hackett Fischer, *Historians' Fallacies: Toward a Logic of Historical Thought* (New York: Harper & Row, 1970), especially 200–209.

CHAPTER 1

Disciple from Penwortham

Thomas Clayton was a schoolteacher in Penwortham, England, and on July 17, 1814, his wife, Ann, proudly presented her husband with their first child, William. Every second or third year after that, for the next twenty-six years, she would present him with another, until the Claytons became the parents of fourteen children. Three of them died in infancy, but the rest lived to see their entire family uprooted from the soil of Lancashire and transplanted to America by the peculiar message and promises of the Mormon missionaries.[1]

The little village of Penwortham was located southwest of Preston, one of the major factory towns in the northern industrial county of Lancashire. In 1840, when Mormonism was beginning to blossom there, Preston had a population of over 49,000 people, while Penwortham boasted less than 1,400 in the township and 5,500 in the entire parish.

Little is known of William's early life in Penwortham, except that he was tutored by his father, was particularly gifted in music, and learned to play the violin. He became, in fact, a member of an instrumental group known as Ballou's Band. He was also a member of the Church of England, though he apparently found no particular interest in it. If and when he attended services, it was in the small, fifteenth-century St. Mary's church, said to be narrow, gloomy, and rather plain on the inside, though fairly attractive from the outside as it stood on a hill overlooking the valley of the River Ribble.[2] Young Clayton also developed an appreciation for fine craftsmanship and even, it is said, refused to carry a watch that would not run accurately. This may have been one manifestation of the meticulous, methodical nature that he revealed throughout his adult life. When Mormonism caught up with him, he was employed as a bookkeeper in a Penwortham factory.

Young William Clayton grew up during a time of rapid economic change. The population of industrial centers was growing as people flocked from the countryside in search of employment. The Claytons may have felt it providential that their family roots were in the Preston-Penwortham area, for at least they already had work before the great migration came pouring in. Penwortham's population apparently did not change much, but that of Preston more than doubled between the time Clayton was born and when the Mormon missionaries arrived twenty-three years later. During the next few years it grew even faster, at a rate of over 1,800 annually between 1838 and 1851. The principal employment was in Preston's fifty cotton-goods factories, though a few flax mills, three foundries, a machine shop, and a steam-powered sawmill also provided work. There were also other signs of the rapidly changing age. When Clayton was two years old, for instance, Preston became the first city in the United Kingdom, outside London, to install gas lighting. The Preston Gas Company was founded in 1815, and the following year it began providing service. Gas meters were not installed, however, until 1830.[3]

The River Ribble was about seventy miles long and on its way to the sea picked up the waters of the Hodder, the Calder, the Darwen, and the Douglas. Once known for its fine salmon fishing, the river itself succumbed, in part, to the realities of the new age as it became polluted by industrial waste along with Preston's sewage, and its fish life suffered accordingly. The river, nevertheless, was an important economic lifeline for the area, and vessels of up to 150 tons burden and twelve-foot draught could navigate its course to Preston to deposit and take on cargo. As young Clayton grew up, he could hardly help but observe such signs of the industrial age, for he must have crossed the Ribble frequently on the sturdy, five-arched stone bridge that spanned the river. Preston was only about a two-mile walk from Penwortham.

Young William might also have been intrigued with some of the amusements that characterized the area. Until 1830 a week of cock-fighting took place in Preston every year, and the Cockpit on St. John's place, near the parish church, was where that grisly sport took place. Though the rabble was not admitted to the arena, the masses showed their interest by crowding around the building during the fights and waiting for spectators to shout results down to them from the high, arched windows. The Cockpit was closed to fighting in 1830, and when the Mormon missionaries later came to town, they began renting it for preaching services. Clayton may even have seen a horse race during his young life, for this, too, was popular in Preston until 1833. Equally popular, at least into the 1820s, was the annual affair called the "trail hunt." About fifty dogs would scamper through the streets of Preston, following a strong smell set out for them and leading them directly to town hall. There the hunt would end in a general melee of men and dogs. Such activities were largely the province of the upper classes, but the common folk could hardly help but show an interest.

Ruth Moon, the oldest daughter of Thomas and Lydia Moon, also grew up in Penwortham, and she also eventually saw her entire family join the Mormons and move to America. Three years younger than William Clayton, she probably knew him from childhood. In any case, they fell in love and, on October 9, 1836, they were married in St. Mary's church in Penwortham.

The economic changes in the Preston-Penwortham area reflected the fact that Great Britain was enjoying the exhilaration of becoming the most important industrial nation in the world. Coal mines, iron mines, smelters, and factories had been booming for years, and English inventors were producing a seemingly unending stream of technological advances. British-manufactured goods could be sold more cheaply than those of almost any competitor, a fact that not only drove other nations from the market but also gave England the greatest commercial fleet in the world. The cotton mills of Lancashire clothed much of the world (including many Americans), and British capital soon began to build railroads in France and the United States. England was so far beyond the rest of the world in industrial capacity that by mid-century it would be dubbed "the workshop of the world."[4]

But the industrial revolution brought mixed blessings to William Clayton and his contemporaries. With industrialization came urbanization, human dislocation, unemployment, and a mass migration of workers from the countryside to factory towns such as Preston and Manchester. Overcrowded cities, low wages, long working hours, environmental pollution, filth, and disease within the heart of many manufacturing centers were all bad enough, but when high unemployment struck, the lot of workers was nearly unbearable. In spite of the wealth of the nation in general, large segments of its population, especially in the cities, led lives of poverty and great uncertainty as they were subject to the whims of the economic cycle.

Queen Victoria's early years were troubled times. Beginning in 1837 industry entered a severe, though temporary, period of depression.

Unemployment among the industrial workers soared, destitution hit many, and starvation was not uncommon. Between 1835 and 1842 the purchasing of goods in Manchester dropped by 40 percent, while in 1841-42 the unemployment rate in nearby Bolton was over 50 percent. When the Latter-day Saint Quorum of Twelve Apostles came to England for missionary work in 1840, they were struck with the pitiable conditions among the working classes and often wrote about it. Said George A. Smith, for example, "So many of the poor are begging that it would astonish the Americans. England is in distress and I pray the Lord for deliverance of the Saints from the coming ruins."[5] "The poor," wrote Wilford Woodruff, "are in as great Bondage as the children of Israel in Egypt,"[6] and Brigham Young declared with disgust that the factory owners "care little for their manufacturers, and have reduced the workers wage to almost the lowest extremity."[7] He was especially dismayed at the heavy taxes:

> Now after paying 2 or 3 shillings rent per week, 1/1 shilling for coal, beside taxes of *every kind*, we might say, for smoke must not go up the chimney in England without a tax, light must not come in at the window without paying duties, many must pay from 1 penny to 5 pence per week for water, and if we should attempt to tell all we should want a government list. . . . Add this to the tax on corn . . . and what is left but starvation, leaving out of account all seasonings, such as Peppers, Spices, and etc. which by taxation is four times the value it is in the United States. . . . The poor are not able to keep dogs, and if they were they would have to pay from 8 shilling to 1 £ per head per annum tax. There are taxes for living and taxes for dying, inasmuch that it is very difficult for the poor to get buried anyhow, and a man may emigrate to America to find a grave, for less money, than he can get a decent burial for in old England. We scarce recollect an article without a tax except cats, mice and fleas.[8]

The economic distress of the times began a great migration, not only from the countryside to the city, but also out of England itself. By the 1830s over 55,000 people annually were leaving the country, usually bound for Canada or the United States, and by mid-century the number jumped to over 250,000. Emigration agents, emigration propaganda, and a general attitude that emigration was good for the mother country were commonplace. Emigration was a sort of "safety valve" that siphoned off the worst effects of economic dislocation or discontent.

The importance of all this to Mormon history, and to the life of
William Clayton, is that it was among the urban, industrial workers
of England that the early American missionaries made most of their
converts. In 1840 nearly half the Mormon congregations in England
were located in industrial centers, and 61.5 percent of the total church
membership came from those areas.[9] The Mormon church in Britain
was in large part an urban church, and it was among the urban Saints
that William Clayton began his career as a Mormon and got his taste
of the responsibilities of leadership.

In July 1837, the year Queen Victoria ascended the throne, Mormonism arrived in England. It came with two apostles, Heber C. Kimball and Orson Hyde, and several other missionaries who had crossed
the Atlantic from America. These included Willard Richards of Mas-
sachusetts, Joseph Fielding (a Canadian Mormon who had originally
emigrated from England), John Goodson, Isaac Russel, and John Sny-
der.[10]

The message William Clayton and his fellow converts heard from
the American missionaries was voiced in powerful terms, calculated
in part to strike fear in the hearts of the people of England but also
to speak peace to their souls with the message of the restoration. All
about them the missionaries saw wickedness, and Orson Hyde, their
pamphleteer, used this as a springboard into their message. "God will
soon begin to manifest his sore displeasure to this generation, and to
your own country," he warned. Famine would strike, trade would be
cut off, war would arise on every side, and the rulers would be dismayed at their inability to avert calamity. Judgments were about to
be rained down upon all the ungodly of the earth, including those
preachers who perverted the ways of the Lord, "except they speedily
repent." Earthquakes, "strange things and fearful sights," and the sea
heaving beyond its bounds would all contribute to the tragedy of the
times. And why all this? Answered Hyde, "The apostasy of the church
is the prime cause of the earth being visited by the judgements of
God."[11]

Calamity, however, was not the main message of the missionaries
from across the ocean. They devoted more time to explaining the
restoration of the gospel and the hope for personal salvation that came
with it. Their leader, Heber C. Kimball, was a simple New England
potter, with little formal education. He was an effective speaker, nevertheless, with an infectious spirit that made him popular among the

common folk of Lancashire. "Simple, sincere, and personal," as he has been characterized by his biographer, Kimball had his greatest effect in intimate gatherings rather than in large public meetings. This likeable elder warmed his way into the hearts of many, and it was largely through his efforts that the foundation was laid for the growth of the church in England.[12]

The missionaries immediately ran into opposition, especially from certain ministers who accused them of "sheep stealing." One was James Fielding, brother of Joseph, who wrote in dismay to his brother: "I do not believe at all that you were sent of God to rend my little church to pieces. Were I to speak as 'plain' as you do I should boldly declare that it was not God but Satan as an angel of light sent you here."[13] On the other hand, many workers in the industrial communities of Victorian England found God in the Mormon message, and it was from among them that the bulk of the early converts came. The missionaries began their work in Preston, and by April 1838 they had netted over 400 converts in that city alone, and over 1,500 throughout the country.

One of the industrial workers who believed the American missionaries was William Clayton of Penwortham. Within three months after their arrival he was a member of the church. His wife, Ruth, was converted first, but when the young factory clerk finally made up his mind he acted with the quick decisiveness of a Saul who had just been struck with a sign while on the road to Damascus. Whatever happened on the night of October 21 so affected William that he allowed Heber Kimball to take him out to the River Ribble and baptize him at 11 P.M.

This was the first of a series of new beginnings for William Clayton, all related to his acceptance of the new American religion and his determination to follow its prophets, no matter where they led. The immediate change in his life was profound, for even though he was not at that moment called upon to leave his home or possessions for the sake of the gospel, it was his nature to throw himself wholeheartedly into preparing for whatever might come. Firmly convinced that the millennium was near, he was not about to be unprepared or to leave his neighbors without warning.

Clayton moved ahead rapidly, and in two months after his baptism he was ordained a priest in the Aaronic or preparatory priesthood order.[14] Less than four months later, on April 1, 1838, he was ordained

to the office of high priest and, with the approval of a church conference held in Preston, was set apart as second counselor in the British
Mission presidency.[15] The American apostles were returning home,
and it was necessary that they leave the work in the hands of a responsible presidency. Joseph Fielding was made president, and Willard
Richards became the other counselor. As the only new convert in the
group, the disciple from Penwortham had progressed at a unique pace
in gaining stature in the church and finding favor among its leaders.

When the American apostles left in 1838, the church in England
consisted of slightly over 1,500 converts. But the new mission presidency had a difficult task. Fielding, Richards, and Clayton not only
had to do missionary work, but they also found themselves facing
problems within the church itself and struggling simply to hold it
together. Even though Elder Kimball later reported that there were 800
or 900 people baptized between 1838 and 1840, the membership did
not actually increase. Some may have been converted too quickly, and
others may have become disillusioned when they did not find everything perfect among the Saints. Years later Joseph Smith's *History of
the Church* described the period as "a general time of pruning in
England. The powers of darkness raged, and it seemed as though Satan
was fully determined to make an end of the work in that kingdom."[16]

Clayton preached and proselytized in Penwortham, Longton, Preston, and nearby areas, but one can easily imagine his frustration as his
responsibilities unfolded. Totally committed to his new faith and, as
a member of the mission presidency, responsible for both holding the
church in England together and trying to expand it, he was still employed full-time as a clerk in a Penwortham factory. Who or what
suggested his next momentous decision is not clear, but by October
19 he had made it and acted upon it. He "quitted his temporal business
in England," the record says, "and gave himself wholly to the ministry."[17]

As the disciples of old were sent "without purse or scrip," so Clayton
took upon himself the burden of building up the Kingdom in England
with no apparent means of support. For the most part, the next two
years were spent in full-time church service, depending for his livelihood upon divine aid and the goodwill of the people among whom
he worked. In a sense, it was another new beginning.

But what about his family? He had a twenty-one-year-old wife and
a little daughter, Sarah, thirteen and a half months old. Moreover,

Ruth was pregnant with their second daughter, who would be born the following April. His only choice was to leave his wife and child with her mother, Lydia Moon, in Penwortham. He wrote them frequently over the next two years, but had little opportunity to visit. It was no easy sacrifice either for the young couple or for the mother. As Clayton wrote in his journal on February 12, 1840, while he was on one of his infrequent visits home: "My mother came this AM to say that she thought my wife was dissatisfied on account of my being from home and it was hard for Moon's to keep her and children."[18]

Almost immediately after entering a full-time ministry Clayton was assigned to Manchester, approximately fifty miles from Penwortham. It usually took him two and a half hours to make the trip by train. He was the first missionary to work in that city and his success was remarkable. By January 1840 he had built up a branch of 164 members, soon to become the second largest in England. It was exceeded only by Preston.

The city where Clayton spent most of his next two years was located in southeastern Lancashire. Some three-fifths of the nation's spinning and cotton weaving factories were located in that county, with over a hundred in the city of Manchester alone. Manchester, in fact, was the chief city of Lancashire, and its other industries included more textile works (such as flax and wool), chemical manufacturing, dyeing, brewing, coal mining, sawmills, iron works, hatmaking, and machine making. In 1840 the city had a population of 170,000, and nearly 70 percent of its workers were factory operatives. Parts of Manchester were attractive and appealing to live in. Apostle Wilford Woodruff called it "the metropolis of the manufacturing Districts in England" and "a beautiful borough," and after church offices were established on Oldham Road, Parley P. Pratt found his home and office comfortable.[19] The main industrial section of town, however, had problems. Most of its streets were small and narrow. The city's chief commercial arteries were its canals and railroads, on which coal, cotton, and other raw products were brought to factories by the boatload and carload. Smoke and other pollutants created both an unsightly and an unhealthy environment, and the houses lining the streets in the industrial section were usually of a uniform, drab architectural style.

At the very time Clayton arrived, Manchester was the scene of a number of important political and social reforms. The Chartists, who advocated reforms that would make the government more responsive to the people, were strong. So also was the Anti-Corn Law League, which eventually succeeded in repealing the taxes that the urban dwellers believed were the cause of high food prices. Manchester was also the home of Richard Cobden, an enlightened textile manufacturer and statesman who led the fight for Manchester's incorporation as a borough. The old manorial court system, he was convinced, simply could not respond adequately to the needs of a large industrial community. His efforts were rewarded with the incorporation of Manchester the same year William Clayton came to preach.

There were other reforms afoot that Clayton and his followers could easily relate to. A community mission established for the benefit of the poor promoted scripture reading, religious worship, and education. More important to the Mormons, the Manchester and Salford Temperance Society was formed in 1830 and began regular public meetings in 1835. By 1839 the society boasted twelve branch associations in the two communities and approximately 8,000 members. Because of the Mormon emphasis on refraining from spiritous liquors, the Mormon missionaries often were able to use local temperance halls for their preaching, and on occasion Clayton used the hall in Manchester.

Manchester also had problems with public health, sanitation, and general moral and economic well-being; all were associated in one way or another with its rapid industrialization.[20] A board of health survey in the 1830s revealed many poorly ventilated dwellings, numerous streets piled deep with refuse, many dwelling places in need of privies, and extremely crowded conditions (sometimes three or four families in a house) in tightly packed residential areas. In 1840 poverty was commonplace, half the babies were born in charitable institutions, crime was growing rapidly, and prostitution was rampant. When Apostle Woodruff visited there he commented with horror on the poverty he witnessed. "This morning," he noted on January 20, 1840, "about 3000 souls is flung out of employ at the factories because of the pressure of times & the lowering of the wages & they are standing in every corner of the Streets in groups counciling what to do, & there are at the present time (I have been informed) thousands of Souls almost in a State of utter starvation."[21]

On the other hand, the city was the home of a number of important charitable and educational institutions that helped make life better for some. These included a royal dispensary, a royal infirmary, several hospitals, a humane society, poor asylums, a number of elementary

schools, a college, a medical school, libraries, and certain scientific institutions.

It was a formidable challenge for the twenty-four-year-old Clayton to try to establish a branch of Mormonism in this industrial center. He proselytized, however, mainly among the working classes, and within six months he had converted about seventy people.[22] Among them was the Hardman family, who ran a boardinghouse at No. 2 Maria Street. Clayton himself eventually took up residence there, staying until he was released from his church assignment. Other early converts included James Bewshaw, a coachman, and his wife, Ellen, who were particularly kind in providing meals and other help for Clayton while he was in Manchester; and Robert Booth, whose wife, Ann, later received a remarkable vision foreshadowing the introduction of the doctrine of baptism for the dead.[23] There was also Sarah Crooks, a young working girl with whom Clayton became particularly good friends; Sarah Duckworth, an indigent woman who eventually ended up in a Manchester poor house; Elizabeth Holden, who poured out her soul to Clayton when she found herself in love with another convert, Arthur Smith, while she was still unsure whether her absent husband was dead or alive; and Henry Royale, who sometimes assisted in preaching and baptizing.

Many of Clayton's converts came from the Church of England, which claimed over half the people of Manchester who belonged to any church. Others were from prominent dissenting groups, such as the Methodists and the United Brethren. Perhaps as many as 80 percent of the Manchester Mormons were not married, and there were considerably more women than men.[24] Many of the women had migrated to Manchester to find work in the factories and were living in places like the Hardman boardinghouse. Most of these early converts were young, generally in their 20s or early 30s. Most were of the working class, and a number of them were suffering from severe financial problems as well as other anxieties. Over 62 percent of the 1840 membership soon migrated to America. Of the remainder, about half eventually left the church.

Clayton and the other two mission leaders soon found themselves spending a great deal of time dealing with the moral, spiritual, and economic welfare of the new converts. In July 1839 Heber C. Kimball wrote words of counsel from America. Their responsibility, he told the presidency, was to "feed the hungry, clothe the naked, and visit

the widow and the fatherless, and turn not the stranger away empty, feed thine enemy, do good to them that revile you and say all manner of evil, if it be false great is your reward in heaven."[25] They took the advice seriously.

By January 1840 Clayton was so impressed with the solemn magnitude of his calling that he decided to keep a record of it. On New Year's Day he began a missionary diary, which is now one of the most intimate and important accounts extant of life among the early British Saints. "Dei Gratia" (By the grace of God), he wrote, he intended impartially to record "all particular incidents and events which transpire," and he earnestly prayed for the ability to discern the truth in all cases with which he must deal.[26] Undoubtedly he expected his diary to be read by future generations, for it portrays in marvelous detail the concerns and problems as well as the brotherhood and spirituality felt among the Saints in Manchester. Most important, it reveals the tender, sensitive nature of young Clayton, and the firm yet selfless way in which he conducted his responsibilities as a Mormon leader in his native land. Typical entries: "I led this afternoon meeting and spoke on the necessity of the Saints dealing honestly with each other and showed the order of the church with regard to cases of poverty"; "Spoke to the saints about being faithful and praying"; "Her mother has been cross with her and etc. She wept much. I felt to weep"; "Prayed with little Ann and Sarah Isherwood"; "Had conversation with Mary Durrah. She says she cannot believe the testimony. She has long seen baptism to be a duty. She asked if God was no respecter of persons why had he not sent an angel sooner and etc. I talked a good deal to her. She wants to be baptized if she could believe—but she does not want to be a hypocrite. I told her she would be an L.D.S. She burst into tears and said if she thought she must not she would be miserable"; "Baptized Mary Durrah and Mary Johnson."[27]

Perhaps the most eloquent testimony to the good feelings the Saints in Manchester had for William Clayton was their willingness to give of their meager means to support him. It is unclear whether he paid for his lodging at the Hardman boardinghouse, but chances are that he did not. Clayton was deeply grateful for whatever kindness he received and, having no better way to repay, frequently recorded for posterity even the most simple kindnesses and gifts. He made note of not only where he took his meals but also when and from whom he received such gifts as cake, fruit, drinks, clothing, and money. On

Sunday, January 26, for example, he had breakfast at the Hardmans, then spent the day preaching. Two of the young women of the branch provided him with cocoa at the evening services, two people gave him money, and Sarah Crooks gave him oranges and raisins. He was back at the Hardmans for supper. On February 5 he told of having breakfast at the Hardmans and dinner at the Bewsher home, and during the day Sarah Perkins gave him a cup of red wine, five people gave him money for Willard Richards, Amby Sands gave him some "optical dye" for his baby daughter, and Sarah Crooks gave him some raisins, an orange, and some articles for his wife. Other gifts included figs, various drinks, cakes, "eggmilk," oysters, sweets, coach fare, various items of clothing, shoes, a comb, a new watch guard, repairs to boots and clothing, and a "smelling bottle." He even on occasion made note of taking water from his friends. The fact that he recorded these gifts with such regularity suggests not only his deep gratitude for the generosity of the Saints, but also his recognition that at times they could ill afford it. In some cases he tried to dissuade his friends from giving him money, but was unable to do so.

The religious ideas and practices of the Manchester Mormons in 1840 made up a fair amalgam, undoubtedly, of the whole British Mormon community. They knew little or nothing about the new ideas Joseph Smith would introduce in Nauvoo, which helps account for the fact that their religion was different in some ways from that of modern Mormonism. At the same time, there were certain central themes taught then that have remained constant over the years. They went something like the following: Joseph Smith was a prophet of God raised up to restore the ancient Church of Christ, the *only* true church on the earth; the Book of Mormon was a new witness for Christ; the essentials of salvation included faith in Christ, repentance, baptism by immersion for the remission of sins, and the laying on of hands for the gift of the Holy Ghost; the latter ordinance could be performed only by those holding the priesthood, which was exclusive to the church; Jesus Christ was literally the Son of God; the Resurrection of Christ was a literal reality, and his atonement provided not only for a real and universal resurrection of all mankind but also the opportunity for all people to be forgiven of their sins; individual salvation was dependent upon both faith and works—neither was efficacious without the other; the second coming of the Savior was imminent, and the church, or earthly Kingdom of God, was established to prepare a core of faithful

Saints to receive him when he established his millennial reign; the gifts of the spirit, including visions, dreams, healings, and speaking in tongues, may be freely expected among the Saints.

William Clayton preached of such things often. On Sunday, February 2, 1840, for example, he went to nearby Stockport where at a morning service he preached on the Resurrection, in the afternoon he talked about the problems of evil speaking, and that night he preached on the establishment of the Kingdom. The next week he preached in Manchester on the Resurrection, perfection, how to obtain the gifts of the spirit, putting on the armor of God, and charity. The faith of the Saints in Clayton's domain was a simple faith, more concerned with the fundamentals necessary to personal salvation and Christian living than with complicated theological disputations.

If there were differences "then and now" on these central themes, they were differences largely in emphasis. The details of Joseph Smith's First Vision, for example, were not widely discussed, being introduced in England only in 1840, but the simple belief that Joseph had received direct revelation and personal instruction from God was fundamental from the beginning. The millennium seemed more imminent then than now, and the Saints in Manchester seemed to expect more direct, personal communication from God than most do today. Clayton frequently mentioned dreams that had special meaning for him, and the spiritual gift of speaking in tongues seemed much more commonplace in 1840 than it does today.[28]

There were also practices that reflected basic differences in interpretation between 1840 and today, including those relating to the "Word of Wisdom." This important revelation, given to Joseph Smith in the temperance-laden environment of Kirtland, Ohio, in 1833, now stands as section 89 of the Mormon Doctrine and Covenants. It warned the Saints against the use of wine (except "pure wine of the grape of the vine, of your own make"), strong drink, tobacco, and hot drinks. It advocated moderation in eating meat and promoted the use of wholesome herbs and grains. Given "not by commandment or constraint, but by revelation and the word of wisdom, showing forth the order and will of God in the temporal salvation of the saints," it promised health and wisdom to those who would obey.

As interpreted today, the Word of Wisdom requires active Mormons to refrain from tea and coffee (these were the "hot drinks" of Joseph Smith's time), all alcoholic beverages, and tobacco. Violators are not dropped from church membership, but neither are they given prominent local church offices or allowed to participate in the sacred temple ceremonies. It took time, however, for the present policy to develop, so that in Clayton's day the Word of Wisdom was enforced somewhat less rigidly than today.[29] Nevertheless it was strongly preached, and often with the same warm fervor as other topics.

Some English temperance leaders, it seems, even believed that the Mormons made individuals teetotalers faster than they did, and for that reason it was not difficult for the missionaries to obtain temperance halls for their preaching services. Heber C. Kimball observed some years later that "as soon as they obeyed the Gospel they abandoned their excess in drinking."[30] The records show, however, that *complete* abstinence was not at first absolutely required. The emphasis was on avoiding excess, and in the cultural context of the time Mormon moderation was a great leap forward. In Clayton's case, for example, porter (a kind of beer) was given to him regularly by the Saints, and when he was ill they gave him even stronger beverages, but he was not accused by the apostles or the members of violating any rule. On May 27, 1840, Apostle Kimball stayed with Clayton at the Hardman home and that night Clayton had a sick spell. The brandy he was given to drink was probably as good a medicine as was available in Manchester and, he said, it "gave me ease." It appears that obedience to the Word of Wisdom in England in 1840 meant total abstinence from the use of tobacco, great moderation in the use of alcohol (its use for medicinal purposes was common, but drunkenness was clearly frowned on), and personal choice with regard to tea, coffee, or chocolate.

When illness struck, the Manchester Mormons quickly called in the elders of the church to anoint them with oil and pray for their recovery. The gift of healing was demonstrated regularly, as it is in modern Mormonism, but there were differences in the way the ordinance was performed. Today the consecrated oil is considered a symbol, not the healing agent, and the effectiveness of the ordinance depends upon the faith of the Saints as well as the will of God. The ceremony is performed by placing a drop of oil on the crown of the head, then "sealing" this anointing with an appropriate priesthood blessing. In earlier times at least some Saints thought of the oil itself as a kind of sacred healing agent, and it was common to anoint the afflicted part of the body directly or at times to take the oil internally. The Manchester Saints believed without question in the healing power of the priesthood, and their faith was rewarded frequently. There was some feeling among them, in fact, that members should not rely on physicians and medicine. On one occasion Clayton visited a house where there were three sick children, and the father had just arrived home with medicine from the dispensary. "They have scarce any faith," he wrote in his diary that night.

The Manchester Mormons, as well as some other English Saints, had another intriguing custom. They took seriously Paul's suggestion to the Romans that they "salute one another with a holy kiss,"[31] and often did so as they gathered for meetings. William Clayton frowned on the custom, recognizing that it could get out of hand and become offensive to some people, and as early as February 24, 1840, he advised the Saints to give up the practice. In April, however, it was still going on when George A. Smith, the only eligible bachelor among the Mormon apostles who had recently come from America, visited the Hardman boardinghouse. Soon several young ladies filled the sitting room to hear what the handsome young leader had to say, and one of them, whom Elder Smith described as "decidedly a little beauty," made a startling request. "Brother Smith," she coyly said, "we want a kiss of you," and her eyes "flashed like stars on a clear night." The apostle was taken aback, but he summoned up resolution enough to tell her that kissing was no part of his mission to England, and after that he was never regarded by the girls of Manchester as a ladies' man. He was dismayed that the English elders would teach that there was no harm in a "holy kiss," and particularly upset that the missionaries themselves were setting the example. "It required a very decided course both in Manchester and other places," he wrote later, "to prevent evil corruption growing out of this custom, which might have been firmly established had not the Twelve put it down."[32]

There were other differences of note. Reflecting the general religious practice of the times, the Manchester Mormons collected financial offerings in collection boxes during church services, something that quickly disappeared from the Mormon way of doing things. Members in transgression were required to confess their sins openly before the church. Church discipline, including excommunication and disfellowshipment, was decided upon by a branch council that included, at least in Manchester, both men and women. This was probably an aberration even at that time, for the basic pattern for church courts was promulgated as early as 1834, and it clearly excluded non-priesthood holders.[33] The only meetings Clayton attended were preaching services and council meetings, as opposed to the numerous other kinds of meetings that characterize Mormonism today. These and other things are all apparent in Clayton's Manchester diary and provide an important insight into the nature of the Mormon community he knew. He would see many changes in the next four decades.

Perhaps the most important event in this early period of Mormon activity in England was the mission of the Quorum of the Twelve Apostles. Arriving in two groups, one in January and the other in April 1840, the apostles immediately put new life into the church. They published the Book of Mormon as well as other church literature, began a mission periodical, the *Millennial Star*, expanded the work into areas not visited before, and appointed scores of new missionaries. In addition, William Clayton's friend and colleague, Willard Richards, was ordained an apostle, which brought to eight the total number of apostles in England. When all but one of the apostles left in April 1841, the membership in Britain had jumped to over 5,800, in addition to another 800 Saints who had emigrated.[34]

Clayton came in frequent contact with the apostles and had some significant experiences with them. He first met Wilford Woodruff, the most successful of all the apostles as far as baptisms were concerned, on Saturday, January 18, when Woodruff arrived in Manchester by train from Liverpool. Clayton was impressed, but so was Apostle Woodruff. "I had the happy privilege of taking Elder William Clayton by the hand," he wrote in his diary. "Elder Clayton is one of the presidents Council in England & a wise & worthy brother." A few days later he wrote to Richards that Clayton was "a man of wisdom and of God."[35]

Woodruff spent those nights in Manchester staying with Clayton at the Hardman house. "I rejoiced to see them," said Clayton of the apostle and the two missionaries with him. And well he might, for it turned out to be a particularly spiritual weekend. A branch member, the wife of James Lee, was ill and delirious—"possessed of a devil," as Woodruff described it. Clayton asked the church leader to visit the Lee home, believing, said Woodruff, that "apostles could do most anything in such a case." There Woodruff found a most distressing situation. Completely possessed, the woman was trying to tear off her clothes, and it took three men to restrain her. To add to the confusion, a number of Saints as well as several nonbelievers were gathered at the

home. This dismayed Woodruff. They had come to see a miracle
wrought, he observed, but his better judgment told him he should not
administer to her. After all, such "signs" were only for believers, and
Woodruff was always loathe to exercise his priesthood powers as a
show. Nevertheless, he said, because "Brother Clayton presided over
the branch, I joined him in administering to the woman." The administration consisted of anointing with consecrated oil and praying.
Elder Woodruff prayed and rebuked the evil spirits, and Clayton prayed
and rebuked the pain. They also had her drink some of the oil, then
washed her head with rum (a common practice at the time). At first
nothing seemed to work because, as Woodruff explained it, the influence of the unbelievers was too strong. But the skeptics soon left, and
at that point the apostle reported, "We laid hands upon her head, and
in the name of Jesus Christ I commanded the devil to come out of
her. The devil left, and she was entirely healed and fell asleep."[36]

The next day, Sunday, Clayton, Theodore Turley, and Woodruff all
preached to the Manchester Saints. Elder Woodruff was impressed with
the good spirit he felt in the congregation and especially with one
woman who said she had seen a vision of Jesus pleading with the
Father to "spare England one more year that the reapers might gather
the grain for the harvest was fully ripe." He was also impressed with
the faith of the Saints, for on that day he laid hands on twenty afflicted
persons, all of whom were healed. As he wrote in his journal, "The
Saints in England have great Confidence in God & His Servants &
their is so many apply for the laying on of hands that we need as
much faith as St. Paul had that at the touch of our garments or hank-
erchiefs that they might be healed."[37]

Tuesday, the day Woodruff left, was the highlight for Clayton. One
of the most personally rewarding experiences a faithful Mormon can
have is to receive his patriarchal blessing—a special blessing in which
he is told what branch of the House of Israel he belongs to and is also
given words of counsel and direction that can foreshadow his future
life. There was no patriarch in England until April 16, when Peter
Melling was so ordained, but in the meantime some of the apostles
gave such blessings themselves. On this day Woodruff laid his hands
on Clayton's head for just that purpose. So impressed was the young
missionary with the importance of the blessing that he recorded it in
his diary—not verbatim, but at least the essence of it:

Dear Brother William I lay my hands upon thy head [*two unclear lines*] I pray that he will give thee a token of his love towards thee by letting his spirit rest upon thee. O God, wilt thou give me the spirit of revelation at this time that [I may] pronounce thy blessing upon thy servant. Brother, thou art of the blood of Ephraim. Thou art one of the house of Joseph. Thou art one of those who will stand upon the mount Zion with the 144,000. God shall give thee great wisdom. He shall make thee a wise counciller to council the saints of God. Thy life has been hid up with Christ in God and thou hast known it not, and I seal thee up with eternal life and while thou remainst faithful no power shall prevail against thee nor be able to take thy life. The Lord shall yet give thee many souls in Manchester over whom thou shalt preside. God seal these blessings. &c. &c. &c.[38]

Certain phrases in this blessing—"Thy life has been hid up with Christ in God" and "I seal thee up with eternal life"—must have carried special meaning for the young disciple. In later years he may well have remembered them as foreshadowings of the sure promise of eternal life he received from none less than the prophet Joseph Smith himself.

A little over a month later Melling also visited Manchester and gave Clayton a second patriarchal blessing. Clayton was promised that he would have a good memory, that he would maintain strong faith in God, and that he would be the means of bringing hundreds and thousands to the truth. He was also told that he would "be preserved from the hands of wicked and ungodly men and should come forth in the kingdom of God."[39] It was blessings such as these that helped the Saints maintain their sense of a personal relationship with God and sustained them when the inevitable times of discouragement came.

Woodruff's promise that Clayton would be a wise counselor to the Saints must have struck a specially responsive cord. As branch president, he was caught up in a myriad of problems as he tried to help the Manchester Mormons smooth out their personal troubles. Two unusual cases say much about Clayton as a leader, as well as about the nature of the Mormon community itself in Manchester of 1840.[40]

Betsy Holden was the wife of John Holden, a British soldier who had not been heard of for three or four years. In her loneliness, she fell in love with Arthur Smith, a tailor, and the two wanted to be married. The Manchester Mormons, including Clayton, were dismayed, for without proof that her soldier husband was actually dead it seemed grossly improper for Betsy even to see another man, let alone marry him. Clayton counseled long and patiently with the young couple and was told by Betsy that they intended to break off their relationship. But the branch council was not so sure they meant it and on November 22, 1839, summoned Arthur to appear for a hearing. Clayton had no desire to cast blame on Betsy, for, as he wrote Willard Richards, "We know the natural weakness of woman." He finally suggested that it would be appropriate for her to give satisfaction to the church by making some sort of public statement. Distraught, Betsy was unable even to do this for, she told her church leader, it would almost break her heart.

Arthur, meantime, became so infuriated with church interference in what he considered a private matter that he began to withdraw himself from fellowship by refusing to take the sacrament. He rejected the counsel of the branch elders, even when Clayton threatened to disfellowship him, saying that he would wait until God personally told him what to do.

Even while this was going on, Smith gave Clayton and the branch another reason for concern. The incident seems petty today, but it suggests the seriousness with which the Manchester Saints took even small prerogatives. Sarah Duckworth was indigent, and as a deacon, Arthur was responsible for taking up the collections to help her. His authority seemed threatened when in his absence the branch proposed to collect some needed funds. The regular collection box should have been used, he complained, and the Saints were not following proper procedure. Clayton suggested that Smith take his complaint directly to the council, though by this time he was convinced that Smith "is not one with us."

If Smith could resent such a seemingly trivial intrusion on his rights, then the church's concern over his romance disturbed him even more. It is clear, however, that he was facing a trial of his discipleship not uncommon among the Mormons. Personal feelings went very deep, and many members found it difficult to accept church counsel in things they considered private or that appeared to be largely temporal in nature. Smith was apparently converted to the church in principle, but he found it hard to give unqualified obedience to church leaders whom he also knew as fallible men. Clayton would face the same challenge to his own discipleship in later years.

The other members of the mission presidency advised Clayton to take Smith's license from him—that is, strip him of his right to function in his church capacity. But before that happened both problems came before the branch council. Patiently Elder Clayton explained the emergency nature of the Duckworth collection, and Smith was reconciled. He asked for and received the forgiveness of the council. He also agreed to partake of the sacrament, but when a new debate flared up over Betsy, he refused to break with her. The council finally decided it had no choice but to take his priesthood office from him.

Clayton later discovered that Arthur and Betsy had been secretly married, against all counsel. There was seemingly nothing left to do but cut them off the church, which was done. The sequel, however, was heartwarming. Smith retained his respect for William Clayton— even weeping when Clayton did not refer to him as "brother." By May 1840 the couple were convinced that their marriage was illegal and, after taking care of proper legalities which presumably included having her first husband legally declared dead, had it performed again in Liverpool. In October, when Clayton was preparing to emigrate, Smith even went so far as to purchase cloth and cut out clothes for him. The Smiths also reunited with the church, and they later migrated to Utah where Arthur became a high priest and served nine years as a steward to Brigham Young.

A different kind of problem for William Clayton was that of James and Ann Lee. After his conversion to the church, Lee had been sent by his employer to Leicester, where there were no other Mormons. The Lees missed the fellowship of the church so deeply that they decided to leave Leicester and join the Saints at Manchester. But Lee's employer soon discovered their absence and followed them to Manchester trying to collect a debt that, he said, was still owing him.

Following good church practice, Clayton and the other mission leaders cautiously refused to allow James Lee to function in the priesthood until they could verify his church standing. In the meantime, Mrs. Lee became ill about a month after their arrival, which led to the delirium and miraculous healing recorded by Woodruff on January 18. The events that followed demonstrated the warmth and compassion that could exist among the Saints. The next day Clayton presented Lee to the members of the church, who freely forgave him of any transgressions (what they were is not clear) and offered him full fellowship with them. The Saints also made the next Sabbath a day of fasting and prayer in behalf of the Lees, in the hope of their full repentance. One outcome of requiring faltering Mormons to confess their sins before the body of the church was that the Saints then could demonstrate their brotherhood by assisting one another to overcome their problems. In this case the practice worked well, for the Lees were soon fully and happily integrated into the branch.

These examples are only representative of the many problems constantly confronting Clayton as he labored among the Mormons of Manchester. Family quarrels and petty jealousies, welfare cases and other financial difficulties, disagreements between branch members over finances and other matters, and unsaintly public conduct by a few branch members: all these were among the concerns he had to deal with. He worried deeply, worked long hours, came home weary and tired, and showed constant concern for the well-being of his little flock. "I feel to weep over her," he wrote as he dealt with the problems of one woman, and he was especially grieved when hard feelings arose between church members themselves. He made every effort to play the role of peacemaker, but sad notations regarding persistent disputes continued to appear in his daily journal. It should have been no surprise to the Saints to hear him preach on May 17 against "evil speaking and hard feelings," or on May 31 for him to use as his text I Peter, chapter 3, a scriptural passage that called for unity in the home and love and harmony among the disciples of New Testament times. Clayton was in a mood to call for the same thing among the Saints of the latter days.

Clayton had other concerns as a branch leader. Responsible for missionary work, he was anxious that the Saints maintain a good image before the public and do all they could to avoid antagonizing non-Mormons. He was critical of one missionary who spoke "too much about his works and other sects," and on at least two occasions he cautioned the elder against rashness in attacking other denominations. Missionaries, he believed, should "not speak of anything but the first principles," and they should set proper examples before the world in every way. Preaching the basic principles of Mormonism was, to him, more important than denouncing other faiths.

In spite of all of this, Clayton was not immune from criticism. Perhaps he seemed too harsh at times to some, for at least a few members of the branch were bitter toward him. One young woman called him an "abominable liar," though she later repented her charge, and certain Protestant missionaries called him one of the "worst devils that ever came from hell." Again, the reasons for criticism against him are not clear, but what is clear is that in spite of them he was held in high esteem by most of the Saints in Manchester.

Ironically, it was the women of Manchester who contributed to some of Clayton's most confusing frustrations. The possibility of a second marriage never seriously entered his mind until he heard about the doctrine of plural marriage from Joseph Smith in 1843, but a curious series of dreams in January 1840 at least seemed to foreshadow the possibility and undoubtedly caused some anxieties for him as well as his faithful wife. He dreamed that he took some ripe fruit home to Ruth but as he was leaving she ran up a hill and vanished. Later he dreamed that he was in a patch of ripe gooseberries at the home of some Penwortham friends and felt like a "single or unmarried person." About the same time two Manchester women dreamed that Clayton was at the Hardman home with one of his children, while another dreamed that his wife was dead or dying. Sarah Crooks, for whom Clayton even then was developing a special fondness, dreamed that one of the missionaries from America was joking about Clayton having a second wife, and the dream affected her so that she thought it might really be true.[41] One could read too much into this singular series of dreams, and nothing came of their dire implications, but the strange situation concerned Clayton enough that he wrote of it in his diary, even though he had no idea what to make of it.

Nothing ever seriously strained the relationship between William and Ruth, but his friendship with Sarah Crooks at least had the potential of doing so. He first mentioned Sarah in his diary on January 13, 1840, but it is clear that already he was well acquainted with her and that she was doing much to help him. On that day she gave him thirty shillings, twenty of which came from her own pocket and the rest from two other girls, to be used toward the purchase of a pair of trousers. Even though such donations from branch members were his only means of support, this time Clayton objected, for he felt these girls had done too much for him already. But, he dutifully recorded, "Sarah was grieved because I objected and said if I did not take it I must speak to her no more."[42] On several other occasions Clayton tried to refuse money from her, accepting only after she forcefully insisted.

The attachment between William and Sarah was more than a passing fancy. They frequently wrote letters to each other, went to meetings together, dined together, and stayed up late at night conversing with each other. As branch president, he helped Sarah and her friend, Rebecca Partington, find a place to live. The first place proved so unsatisfactory, however, that they finally moved into the Hardman boardinghouse. When Clayton left Manchester for a short visit with his family six days later, he had with him some money and a personal letter from Sarah. He got home that night, and the next morning wrote letters to several people, including Sarah Crooks and Alice Hardman. A week later he returned to Manchester and that night Sarah and Rebecca gave him his supper and Sarah washed his tired head with rum.

It is clear that this special friendship was open, and Clayton was careful to make it so. All the Saints in Manchester knew about it, and back home in Penwortham Ruth was fully aware of it. On occasion Sarah even gave Clayton various gifts for his wife and family. There is no evidence that their relationship ever went beyond the bounds of propriety.

As their friendship deepened, however, Clayton soon admitted to himself that the situation could easily develop into something more than he could handle. When he learned on February 27 that Sarah contemplated marriage, he suddenly found himself resisting the idea. "I don't want Sarah to be married," he confided in his journal. "I was much troubled and tempted on her account and felt to pray that the Lord would preserve me from impure affections. . . . I certainly feel my love towards her to increase but shall strive against it. I feel too much to covet her and afraid lest her troubles should cause her to get married. The Lord keep me pure and preserve me from doing wrong."[43] Caught in a war between his tender feelings for Sarah, on the one hand, and his love for his wife and his personal integrity, on the other, Clayton thus met another test of discipleship. This one was perhaps the most difficult of all, for it involved the temptations of the flesh that too often destroy both the reputation and the marriages of those who weaken. The attachment between Sarah and William caused inward struggles for both, but they avoided the obvious temptation.

Clayton did not spend all his time in Manchester, for on occasion he traveled to a conference or to meet some other church responsibility. One such occasion was a special conference in Preston, April 14-17, immediately after the second group of apostles arrived in England for their important 1840-41 mission. It was at this conference that Willard Richards was ordained an apostle and Wilford Woodruff reported on his phenomenal success in Herefordshire. Here the decision was made to pursue an ambitious publication program for the mission, and the apostles agreed to recommend that the gathering to America begin.

Clayton left Manchester at 2:45 on April 13, joining Wilford Woodruff and Hiram Clark on the train they had taken from Burslem that morning. He arrived at his mother-in-law's home in Penwortham that evening, where he found his family well. To his surprise, he also found Heber C. Kimball and Brigham Young there. The next day he attended a council meeting of the Twelve, though he apparently played no active role in it. It was enough for this young leader just to be with them. On the fifteenth the general meetings of the conference were held, and Clayton was made clerk of the conference. He was also the representative of the Manchester branch and could proudly report 240 members on the rolls. The next day Clayton spent the full day writing up the minutes of the conference. This was his first such experience, but it foreshadowed a task church leaders would give him regularly for many years to come.

That eight living apostles were in England so inspired and delighted Ruth Clayton's aunt, Alice Moon, that she made it a special cause for celebration. As the Preston conference ended the apostles were ready to scatter to their various fields of labor, but on April 17, the day before they left, all except John Taylor visited Alice's home in Penwortham. William Clayton and a few other Saints were also there, and Alice told them a story that made the arrival of the Twelve especially meaningful for her. Forty years earlier she had set aside a bottle of wine to be opened at her wedding, but in the rush of things she forgot about it. She then decided to save it for when her first child was born, but again it was forgotten. On other important occasions it was likewise passed over but, she believed, there was "something providential" in its preservation until that day. She then presented it to the apostles who accepted it and blessed it, and each person in the room had a glass.[44]

The next day Clayton returned to his duties in Manchester. That life still was not easy for him is seen in the fact that he had to "borrow" money from his wife to pay his coach fare. When he arrived he received a warm welcome from friends who gave him presents as well as food and drink, but he also began to hear more branch problems. He was

ill that night when he went to bed. Life was back to normal for the
disciple from Penwortham.

On July 6, 1840, an important conference was held in Manchester.
This was the end of Clayton's stewardship so far as England was concerned, but as he looked at the results of his past two years' work he
may have felt some justifiable pride. Manchester boasted 280 members—an increase of forty since the April conference. In addition, this
city had become a headquarters for the church in England, for here
Brigham Young had rented an office and was preparing to publish the
Book of Mormon, and Parley P. Pratt had been publishing the *Millennial Star* since April. Clayton was helping with the *Star*, as well as
with the forthcoming hymn book. The church's emigration program
was underway, and Clayton was already making plans for his family's
passage to America. So far as he was concerned the words Heber C.
Kimball wrote on April 17 were literally true: "The gospel is spreading,
the devils are roaring. As nigh as I can learn, the priests are howling,
the tares are binding up, the wheat is gathering, nations are trembling,
and kingdoms are tottering: 'men's hearts failing them for fear, and
for looking for those things that are coming on the earth.' The poor
among men are rejoicing in the Lord, and the meek do increase their
joy."[45]

At the conference Clayton was again chosen clerk. More important,
Joseph Fielding and his counselors were released from the mission
presidency, and Brigham Young, president of the Council of the Twelve
Apostles, became mission president. The new hymn book was approved and several men, including Clayton, volunteered for missionary
work. In spite of the fact that he had been so long away from family
and home, and in spite of the emotional stress that missionary work
and branch leadership had brought him, he could think of no more
necessary thing than to continue in his calling as a missionary to the
people of England.

The next day Clayton was assigned, along with John Needham, to
go to Birmingham as soon as his family left for America. He continued
to preach in the vicinity of Manchester for about two weeks and then
on July 23 returned to Penwortham to help his family get ready to go.
Before he left, some of the working girls in Manchester presented him
with their final gifts. Catherine Bates gave him a yellow silk handkerchief, and Elizabeth Dewsnup gave him a red one. Mary Wood gave
him a new satin stock (i.e., a cravat), and Sarah Crooks gave him

enough money for a new pair of boots. Ann Booth gave him four pence to remember her by, and Hanna Walker gave him a pocket handkerchief. "I feel it hard to leave the saints in Manchester," he wrote, "yet willing because it is for the best."[46] Five months later the convert-missionary was in Nauvoo, Illinois, remembering the friends he had left in Manchester, and he wrote a tender letter to them. "Many, many times have I pondered upon those happy times we spent in each other's company, & often my heart has filled when I have reflected upon those whom I have left behind. . . . I can feel stronger attachment to those I have left behind than any I have yet found. Give my love to all the saints. They have my love and prayers. I could rather weep than write about them."[47]

NOTES

1. See the Clayton family group sheets on file in the archives of the Genealogical Society of The Church of Jesus Christ of Latter-day Saints, Salt Lake City, Utah. See also Paul E. Dahl, *William Clayton: Missionary, Pioneer, and Public Servant*, 2d ed. (Provo, Utah: J. Grant Stevenson, 1964), for a rudimentary study of Clayton, and particularly for some aspects of his early life and family relations. Originally a Brigham Young University master's thesis, this work contains useful chronology but is unsatisfactory in dealing with issues and interpretations.

2. See Samuel Lewis, *Topographical Dictionary of England*, 7th ed., 4 vols. (London: S. Lewis & Co., 1848), 2:553–54.

3. Most of the information on Preston and Penwortham given here and following is from Lewis, *Topographical Dictionary*, 3:553–54, 610–11; and Anthony Hewiston, *History of Preston* (Preston: The "Chronicle" Office, 1883, republished by S. R. Publishers, 1969).

4. For an in-depth discussion of England in this era, see Asa Briggs, *The Age of Improvements* (London: Longsmans, Green and Co., 1959). See also John F. C. Harrison, *The Early Victorians* (New York: Praeger, 1971).

5. George A. Smith, "History of George A. Smith," 15 Feb. 1840, typescript, Church Archives.

6. *Wilford Woodruff's Journal*, ed. Scott G. Kenney, 9 vols. (Midvale, Utah: Signature Books, 1983–85), 1:405 (14 Jan. 1840), hereafter cited as *Wilford Woodruff's Journal*.

7. Brigham Young and Willard Richards to the First Presidency of the Church, 5 Sept. 1840, Brigham Young Papers, Church Archives.

8. Ibid.

9. James B. Allen and Thomas G. Alexander, eds., *Manchester Mormons: The Journal of William Clayton, 1840 to 1842* (Salt Lake City: Peregrine Smith,

1974), 13. See also James B. Allen and Malcolm R. Thorp, "The Mission of the Twelve to England, 1840–41: Mormon Apostles and the Working Classes," *BYU Studies* 15 (Summer 1975): 499–526. For an excellent study on the religious background of early converts, see also Malcolm R. Thorp, "The Religious Backgrounds of Mormon Converts in Britain, 1837–52," *Journal of Mormon History* 4 (1977):51–66.

10. For some details on this early mission to England, see Richard L. Evans, *A Century of "Mormonism" in Great Britain* (Salt Lake City: Deseret News Press, 1937); Heber C. Kimball, Orson Hyde, and Willard Richards, "Mission to England, or the First Foreign Mission of the Latter-day Saints," *Millennial Star* 3 (Apr. 1841):289–96; Stanley B. Kimball, *Heber C. Kimball: Mormon Patriarch and Pioneer* (Urbana: University of Illinois Press, 1981), 44–54; R. B. Thompson, *Heber C. Kimball, an Elder of The Church of Jesus Christ of Latter-day Saints: Giving an Account of His Mission to Great Britain, and the Commencement of the Work of the Lord in that Land* (Nauvoo, Ill.: Robinson and Smith, 1840); Orson F. Whitney, *Life of Heber C. Kimball, an Apostle: The Father and Founder of the British Mission* (reprint ed., Salt Lake City: Bookcraft, 1967).

11. Hyde, *A Timely Warning to the People of England*.

12. Kimball, *Heber C. Kimball*, 46–47.

13. James Fielding to Joseph Fielding, 27 Aug. 1838, Joseph Fielding Papers, Church Archives.

14. Dahl, *William Clayton*, 6. The priesthood in The Church of Jesus Christ of Latter-day Saints is a lay priesthood. It consists of two main divisions: the Aaronic, or lesser, priesthood, which includes the offices of deacon, teacher, and priest, and the Melchizedek, or higher, priesthood, which includes the offices of elder, seventy, and high priest. The office of high priest carries with it a presiding function.

15. *History of the Church*, 3:20.

16. Ibid., 3:162.

17. Ibid., 3:164; *Millennial Star*, 1:296.

18. Allen and Alexander, eds., *Manchester Mormons*, 98–99.

19. *Wilford Woodruff's Journal*, 1:407 (18 Jan. 1840); Parley P. Pratt to Brigham Young, 4 May 1840, in "British Mission," MS, Church Archives.

20. See Allen and Alexander, eds., *Manchester Mormons*, 15-16, and references cited therein.

21. *Wilford Woodruff's Journal*, 1:409 (20 Jan. 1840). See also entry of 19 Jan. 1840.

22. There are no precise figures available for this early period, but this estimate is arrived at by examining Manchester Branch, "Record of Members," Microfilm serial no. 13656, part 3, Genealogical Society of the Church. This particular record is current as of 1840. About seventy-two names on this record are listed as having been baptized between 1 Nov. 1838 and 30 Apr. 1839, and it is on this basis that the rough estimate above is made. Some baptized elsewhere could have moved in, but some baptized in Manchester could have left before the record was made.

23. See *Wilford Woodruff's Journal*, 1:475–77 (2 July 1840), for an account of this vision.

24. About 60 percent of the members brought in during the first six months were women; by mid-1840 this had jumped to nearly 77 percent.

25. Heber C. Kimball to Fielding, Richards, and Clayton, 25 July 1839, Fielding Papers.

26. Allen and Alexander, eds., *Manchester Mormons*, 1, 72 (19 Jan.), 83 (25 Jan.), 91 (1 Feb.), 106 (24 Feb.), 143 (19 Apr.), 146 (26 Apr.).

27. Ibid., 72 (19 Jan.), 83 (26 Jan.), 91 (1 Feb.), 106 (24 Feb.), 143 (19 Apr.), 146 (26 Apr.).

28. Clayton made several references in his journal to this practice. See Allen and Alexander, eds., *Manchester Mormons*, 95, 99, 157, 158, 162, 164, 165, 182, 199.

29. Throughout most of the nineteenth century, the Word of Wisdom was still not considered a "commandment" in the sense that it was a requirement for entering the church or for receiving certain privileges. How strongly it was preached or enforced actually varied from time to time, but it did not become a written requirement for receiving a recommend to enter the temple until the 1920s. For insights into the history of the Word of Wisdom, see Paul H. Peterson, "An Historical Analysis of the Word of Wisdom" (Master's thesis, Brigham Young University, 1972); Leonard J. Arrington, "An Economic Interpretation of the Word of Wisdom," *BYU Studies* 1 (Winter 1959):37–49; and the following articles in *Dialogue: A Journal of Mormon Thought* 13 (Autumn 1981): Lester E. Bush, Jr., "The Word of Wisdom in Early Nineteenth-Century Perspective," 46–65; Robert J. McCue, "Did the Word of Wisdom Become a Commandment in 1851?" 66–67; Thomas G. Alexander, "The Word of Wisdom: From Principle to Requirement," 78–88.

30. Whitney, *Life of Heber C. Kimball*, 152. "None of us [i.e., the missionaries]," Elder Kimball continued, "drank any kind of spirits, porter, small beer, or even wine, neither did we drink tea, coffee, or chocolate." This was somewhat of an exaggeration, however, for it is clear from the records that on occasion several of them partook of some of these items. The occasions were rare, however, at least so far as any documentary evidence is concerned, and Elder Kimball's statement well reflected the nature of their commitment and the image they were successfully attempting to portray.

31. Romans 16:16. It is interesting that in his revision of the Bible Joseph Smith changed this passage to read "Salute one another with a holy salutation."

32. George A. Smith, "My Journal," *Instructor* 82 (June 1947):321–22.

33. See Doctrine and Covenants 102.

34. Allen and Thorp, "Mission of the Twelve to England," 524–25.

35. *Wilford Woodruff's Journal*, 1:407 (18 Jan. 1840); Wilford Woodruff to Willard Richards, 3 Feb. 1840, Wilford Woodruff Papers, Church Archives.

36. As cited in Matthias P. Coweley, ed., *Wilford Woodruff, Fourth President of The Church of Jesus Christ of Latter Day Saints: History of His Life and Labors as Recorded in His Daily Journals* (Salt Lake City: The Deseret News, 1909), 114–15. See also *Wilford Woodruff's Journal*, 1:408; Allen and

Alexander, eds., *Manchester Mormons*, 71. Clayton, in *Manchester Mormons*, does not give nearly the detail that Woodruff does, though he mentions that "after washing her forehead with rum she appeared better and we left her."

37. *Wilford Woodruff's Journal*, 1:409 (19 Jan. 1841).

38. Allen and Alexander, eds., *Manchester Mormons*, 75.

39. Ibid., 156.

40. The two cases following are summarized from Allen and Alexander, eds., *Manchester Mormons*, 24–30, and appropriate citations are given there.

41. Ibid., 73.

42. Ibid., 69.

43. Ibid., 110.

44. Ibid., 141–42; Eldon Jay Watson, ed., *Manuscript History of Brigham Young, 1801–1804* (Salt Lake City: ca. Eldon Jay Watson, 1968), 71; Smith, "My Journal," 321.

45. Heber C. Kimball to the Saints of the United States, 14 Apr. 1840, in *History of the Church*, 4:115

46. Allen and Alexander, eds., *Manchester Mormons*, 168.

47. Clayton letter dated Commerce, 10 Dec. 1840, as copied by William Hardman, 26 Jan. 1840, Church Archives. Hardman apparently received Clayton's letter, with instructions to copy and circulate it.

CHAPTER 2

Emigration Homeward

William Clayton's deep affection for his mother-in-law may have suffered a small test on the morning of September 5, 1840. After months
of preparing his family, including Thomas and Lydia Moon, for emigration to America, he had taken them to the port of Liverpool and
spent the night with them on the ship *North America*. His plan was
to remain behind temporarily in order to fulfill what he considered
his most important mission at the moment: to go to Birmingham to
preach the gospel. But suddenly his mother-in-law, overwhelmed with
all the "toil and trouble" she saw ahead, began to weep. She wanted
Clayton to go with them and made her wishes known not only to her
son-in-law but also to Brigham Young and John Taylor. Probably out
of respect for her and all she had done for the church the past three
years, the two apostles consented. Clayton was stunned but, loyal
disciple that he was, changed his plans immediately. Three days later
he was on his way to America. It was another new beginning, and in
this case a mother-in-law's feelings not only changed a Mormon missionary's career but also may have affected some other important aspects of Mormon history.

It was not that Clayton did not have the emigration impulse—practically every British Mormon was caught up in that. America, after
all, was designated by revelation as the land of Zion, where modern
Israel should gather in the last days. Convinced that calamities would
soon overtake their nation, the British Saints were ready recipients of
the call to gather "home" with the Saints in Zion. Between 1840 and
1890 over 80,000 European Mormons migrated to America, about 55,000
of whom were from England alone.[1]

Though the "gathering" was a fundamental concept among the Mormons almost from the beginning, church leaders were reluctant to

preach it immediately among the European converts. First they must establish a solid membership base, firmly committed to the fundamentals of the faith; then they could encourage emigration. When the first missionaries left for England in 1837, Joseph Smith instructed them to "adhere closely to the first principles of the Gospel, and remain silent concerning the gathering, the vision, and the Book of Doctrine and Covenants, until such time as the work was fully established, and it should be clearly made manifest by the Spirit to do otherwise."[2]

Following this counsel, the American missionaries did not encourage the gathering, but many British Saints were eager to quit their homeland for the New World anyway. Some, no doubt, were caught up in the general emigration impulse that had taken hold among the working class, but the impulse was also a natural outgrowth of their reverence for the American prophet, and their desire to be where he was gathering the central body of the church. Even before the apostles arrived on their 1840 mission, many Saints were making their own preparations to emigrate. As a member of the mission presidency, Clayton was disturbed with their lack of respect for counsel. These Saints, he wrote Willard Richards, were "making ready for America without council and in their present state of religion [I] only feel to say if *they should go* as soon as they anticipate some of them will wish themselves back again."[3]

The problem drew very close to Clayton, for his wife's cousin, John Moon, was among those pressing for permission to leave. The matter was taken up with the mission president, Joseph Fielding, who soon instructed Clayton and his relatives that he did not feel it was the will of God for any elders or priests to leave without a definite call. At the same time, he did not totally discourage them. Seeming to anticipate what would happen very shortly, he wrote to Willard Richards, "We would if we were in their place, act as if we expected to go the coming summer, but we had no thought of that being the signal for the gathering to begin, nor have we had any instruction to give such a signal and till we do I will not be responsible for any thing that is or may be done about it. If any go they will not say that Brother or President Fielding gave his sanction to it."[4] Fielding was willing to allow the Moons and others to go to America if they would go as regular emigrants, rather than as Saints, but he also suggested that premature emigration might be a stratagem of Satan and that the desire to emigrate had led some Saints astray.

In April things began to change, and at a special conference on the fifteenth the apostles opened the door for approved emigration. All the Saints who wished to leave with church approval, they decided, must receive recommends from church leaders. At the same time they tried to give all classes equal opportunity by declaring that the wealthy Saints would not receive recommends unless they also assisted the poor.[5] Four months later the First Presidency of the church gave its official sanction to the beginning of emigration in a general address to the Saints throughout the world. "The work of the gathering spoken of in the Scriptures will be necessary to bring about the glories of the last dispensation," the faithful were told. Then, in what the British Saints must have considered a bit of an understatement, the church leaders observed, "It is probably unnecessary to press the subject on the Saints, as we believe the spirit of it is manifest, and its necessity obvious to every considerate mind; and everyone zealous for the promotion of truth and righteousness, is equally so for the gathering of the Saints."[6] The Saints from afar were at last being called to assist in building up the church in its new gathering place in Nauvoo, Illinois, and in building a new temple.

Some were too eager to wait for official approval, and on June 6 forty-one British Mormons, under the leadership of John Moon, sailed for America on the *Britannia*. On July 22, shortly after their arrival in New York harbor, Moon wrote to William Clayton and described the voyage. Invoking the Book of Mormon statement that America was a "choice land," reserved in part for the descendants of the ancient prophet Joseph, Moon expressed the typical emotion of an immigrant Saint when he wrote: "I feel myself glad to find my feet upon the land of Joseph after so long and tedious journey." Then, after describing his first sight of Long Island with its green trees and white houses, he said, "Such a beautiful sight I never saw. I did rejoice to behold the land of Joseph: Yea, I thought, it did pay for all the hardships which I had gone through."[7] Like many Saints to follow, John Moon and company did not consider themselves strangers in a strange land. They were only embarking upon a new career in a home that the Lord had preserved for them. Unfortunately, illness and financial difficulty caught up with the Moons and delayed their progress in that career. Instead of going on to Illinois, they were forced to spend the fall and winter in Pennsylvania, trying to find work and planning to join the Saints in Nauvoo the following spring.[8]

Clayton, meanwhile, was preparing for his own voyage, though he was not really aware of it at the time. Planning to send his family to America while he remained behind, he went home to Penwortham on July 23 and began winding up his affairs. August 27 was the scheduled date of departure, and there was much to do if the Claytons and the Moons were to gather together all they could take with them and dispose of everything else before they left. But he also missed his friends in Manchester, and a month later wrote to Brigham Young and Willard Richards: "Oh that I could send all the love I feel to my brethren and the Saints in M."[9]

The first few days in Penwortham were spent completing a task he had been assigned earlier: writing a history for Heber C. Kimball.[10] Clayton had drawn particularly close to Kimball—a friendship that endured for many years—and in the process the apostle recognized and took advantage of Clayton's writing skill. There was good reason. Any comparison of the handwriting, spelling, and general grammatical skills of the two men would demonstrate that Clayton clearly had the advantage. Possibly for this reason, as well as the fact that Kimball was so busy as a church leader, Clayton drew the task of preparing the apostle's history.

It is not precisely clear what particular history Clayton the ghost-writer was preparing, but it was probably the "History of the British Mission," which was later signed by Kimball, Orson Hyde, and Willard Richards and published in Joseph Smith's History.[11] This work contained an account of missionary work in England, beginning with Heber C. Kimball's arrival in 1837, to April 6, 1840. No doubt Clayton was writing it under Kimball's direction, and changes were probably made before it was published, but evidently the basic draft was completed by Clayton during this time of preparation. This was only a portent of things to come, for soon he would be called upon again not only by Kimball but also by other church leaders to keep their journals and perform other important clerical duties.

There was also much to do to make his family's emigration arrangements, and Clayton's activities during the next two months were probably typical of most Mormon disciples preparing to leave England for new homes on the other side of the Atlantic. On August 18, after deciding what could be taken and what must be left behind, the family had a public sale. "We are now almost empty,"[12] Clayton wrote the next day, and they seemed satisfied with their proceeds. At least they were not going penniless to America. The only thing they had trouble selling was John Moon's bass viol, which he had left with Clayton to dispose of, and Clayton finally had to leave it for John Melling to try to sell.

Then Clayton learned that the sailing date was postponed until September 4, for not all the Saints who wanted to go were quite ready. The spirit of the gathering had caught hold, and the church leaders in England were actively helping to arrange for passage, but it was no easy task to coordinate the activities of 200 Saints who must sell all the possessions they could not carry, arrange all their personal affairs, and make their way to Liverpool for embarkation. Clayton was relieved at the postponement, he said, "for we had hardly time to settle up our business by the 4 of September."[13]

In the meantime Clayton did more than make sailing preparations. He preached on occasion in Penwortham, noted with gratitude the continuing success of missionary work, and was even the target of an outburst of anti-Mormon sentiment. On the night of Saturday, August 29, some mischief-maker threw a note addressed to Clayton, along with another addressed to a Brother Whitehead, into Whitehead's shop. The note sarcastically suggested that Clayton and Whitehead preach a sermon from Ecclesiastes 10:1, which reads, "Dead flies cause the ointment of the apothecary to send forth a stinking savour: so doth a little folly him that is in reputation for wisdom and honour."[14] Though the notewriter signed himself a lover of the Mormons, he was clearly not their friend.

The sailing was delayed a second time, but finally, on September 4, Clayton and his family, with a company totalling twenty-six emigrating Saints, took their baggage by train from Preston to Liverpool. At that point they were suddenly confronted with a test of their bargaining abilities that many an emigrant at the bustling port of Liverpool probably failed. Clayton engaged a cart to carry their luggage from the train to the dock, agreeing to pay "1/1-1/2" (1 shilling and 1-1/2 pence). When they arrived at the dock, however, they had what Clayton called a "hard contest." A new man arrived, professing to be the owner of the cart and demanding 1/6. When Clayton refused to pay the inflated price, the man threatened to call the police and demanded an additional shilling. But Clayton was not to be taken in. "I told him that for his bad behavior I would not give him anything more than the bargain," he wrote, whereupon the cart owner grumbled for a while longer but finally "took it and went away in a rage." Several Saints, however, not anticipating such a problem, paid exorbitant prices for their cartage because they did not make firm agreements, as Clayton had done, before they engaged their porters.[15]

As the day closed, Clayton observed, "All the company was confused and busily arranging their boxes." The emigrants were not yet organized, but that night all who were there slept aboard ship or, as Clayton said, "We slept in the ship this night or *lay awake*." The unfamiliar surroundings, the uncomfortable wooden bunks, and the anticipation of what was to come undoubtedly kept most of them from sleeping much.

The next day, Saturday, September 5, Clayton's plans took a sudden new direction when his mother-in-law demanded that he go with them, and the church leaders agreed. The blow was twofold: not only would he be kept from his mission in Birmingham, for which some of the Saints had already raised money to help him, but also he might never see Manchester again, and many of his beloved converts there. This was too much, so even though he agreed to go with the emigrants he decided he must make one last visit to his friends. He left for Manchester immediately. When he arrived at 7:30 that evening, the generous Saints who had cared for him in sickness and in health for the past two years had one more chance to help. He was ill when he got there, slept at the Hardman house that night, and continued ill most of the next day. But the Manchester Mormons turned out in numbers to wish him farewell. Many came to the Hardman house to see him; some gave him money or food; Sarah Crooks gave him linen and cut it out for shirts; and Arthur Smith purchased some material for pants and cut out other clothing for him. The next day Jane Hardman gave him a watch guard, and Thomas Miller gave him a new hat. It was an emotional weekend among the Saints at Manchester, and as Clayton said, "Some of them wept much at parting."

Sarah Crooks was probably one of those who wept. So far as she knew, this was the last time she and William would ever see each other, for she had no immediate plans to emigrate herself. When William arrived at the Hardman home, Sarah and her friend, Rebecca Partington, were preparing to leave the boardinghouse that night. Something unpleasant was going on between the two, Clayton could tell, and, he wrote, "It almost broke my heart."

On Monday Clayton made his way back to Liverpool where his family and the other Saints were waiting aboard the *North America*. Still not feeling well, he was even more distressed when he found Willard Richards waiting at the ship. The newest apostle, it appears, disagreed with the others on the matter of Clayton's going to America and frankly told him so. "This gave me some trouble," Clayton wrote, in what was probably a classic understatement of his real feelings. But it was too late to turn back, and that night he joined in making ready for sailing the next day.

There were 206 Mormons aboard the *North America* when it was towed out of Liverpool on the morning of Tuesday, September 8, with Captain Alfred B. Lowber at the helm. The Mormons constituted perhaps a little more than half of all the passengers.[16] This included apostles Brigham Young, Willard Richards, and John Taylor, who came to see the Saints off and went with them about fifteen miles out to sea. At that point the steam-powered tugboat that had accompanied the *North America* turned back, and the apostles and two other Saints returned with it. The great Mormon emigration was fully underway: a few Saints had gone on their own; Moon's company of forty had arrived in New York; and another company of fifty Scottish Saints would leave a month later. Including Clayton's company, over 300 British Mormons arrived in America by the end of the 1840 season. Clayton's diary provides an intimate view of what was undoubtedly typical of many emigrant crossings of the 1840s.

William Clayton did not clarify how many family members he was responsible for as he sailed from the shores of England, but there were at least seven besides himself: Ruth and their two children, Sarah and Margaret; Ruth's parents, the elderly Thomas and Lydia Moon; and two of Ruth's sisters, Margaret and Lydia. In addition, Ruth was about one month pregnant. It is understandable that "old Lydia," as Clayton sometimes affectionately called his mother-in-law, was so insistent that he come.

One thing that distinguished Mormon emigrant companies from most others was that they were completely organized, with leaders chosen by church authorities. In the case of Clayton's group the organization took place while he was on the way to Manchester on September 5. Elder Theodore Turley, a returning American missionary, was placed in charge, with Clayton and five others named as counselors. Turley was an effective leader, and Clayton supported him thoroughly.

Crossing the Atlantic Ocean in 1840 may have been harder on Clayton than crossing the plains in America seven years later. The first day out seemed to set the pattern. Many of the passengers, including Clayton, had never been to sea and almost immediately became sick. Clayton was so ill, in fact, that when the apostles left the group to return on the steamer, he was unable even to send any letters with them. But that was only the beginning. The ship's mate came down to the steerage class compartment and told the passengers to fasten down all their boxes, for they expected to have a "good rocking." The "good rocking" came that night in the form of a heavy wind, and Clayton described the effect most vividly. "This was a new scene," he said. "Such sickness, vomiting, groaning and bad smells I never witnessed before and added to this the closeness of the berths almost suffocated us for want of air."

The gale continued for the next three days, nearly the whole company remained ill, and Clayton was confined to his bed most of the time. He was so ill, in fact, that he was not even aware of it when the ship twice came perilously close to a whirlpool. He was told about it later. "We were in great danger," he wrote with feeling, "but the Lord delivered us." On Friday night, September 11, one little girl became so frightened by the storm that she lost her senses, and on Sunday night, after the storm abated, she died. The next day her body was buried at sea.

This was only the first of several tragedies that suddenly tried anew the faith of Clayton and the emigrating Saints. Many of them continued ill, and at least three children were so seriously sick that the Saints lost hope for their survival. Elder Turley was distressed, for he believed that if they would only exercise enough faith the children would live. On September 18 he called the Saints together, spoke with great feeling on the subject, and asked them to express their feelings. One man replied that he believed the Holmes child would not recover, but Clayton responded sharply that he did not believe it was the will of God that they should lose one soul. Elder Turley agreed. This had a cheering effect upon the Saints, and "the power of darkness was in some degree banished." They prayed with the children, exhorted them to faith, but that night the Holmes child died. "This was a grief to our minds—but it was so," wrote Clayton, and the next day the body was sewn in canvas by the ship's crew and unceremoniously thrown overboard. Four more children were buried at sea before the voyage was over.[17]

Clayton remained ill throughout the entire voyage, and so did his mother-in-law and his wife. In addition, there were many problems with which all the Mormons had to deal, not the least of which were the close, uncomfortable quarters in steerage passage. If steerage in the *North America* was anything like other emigrant ships in the early 1840s, it consisted of one long room, no partitions, and a row of beds on each side. In some cases one berth accommodated five to eight persons, and privacy was nonexistent. One critical observer reported to a Parliamentary committee: "I have known cases of females who have had to sit up all night upon their boxes in the steerage, because they could not think of going into bed with strange men."[18] Sanitation facilities left everything to be desired, with no place to wash and even in some cases no toilet facilities. Laundering, if done at all, was done on the open deck with salt water, for fresh water was strictly rationed. Though a few Saints could afford second cabin, which provided separate compartments, the overwhelming majority in these early years were steerage passengers. In effect, the 200 Mormons aboard the *North America* had simply rented the steerage compartment, and this became at once their community home, their chapel, their washroom, and their sickroom for thirty-three days. The filth and the aroma that could accumulate under such conditions were enough to keep Clayton ill, and it was with some relief that he reported on September 19, after the death of a child, that "after the place was cleansed out gas was burned to sweeten the ship air and prevent disease."

Under such crowded, uncomfortable conditions it is not surprising that even among the Saints some friction occurred. On one occasion Elder Turley became disgusted with their lack of cleanliness, though perhaps it was not completely the Saints' own fault. On Monday, September 21, many were still too ill to move, but the steerage was becoming almost too filthy to bear. Turley preached a long sermon on cleanliness, probably reminding his charges that "cleanliness is next to Godliness," then went around to inspect the berths. To his disgust he found that some seasick Saints had not even undressed since they came aboard the ship. The filth he found in their clothes and bunks after they had been there for nearly two weeks was sickening and, as Clayton described it, "made the most awful smell when discovered almost too much to bear." Turley resolutely took it upon himself to drag some of them out of bed, undress and wash them, then order the entire place cleaned out. Little wonder that the sensitive Clayton remained ill nearly the entire voyage.

There were other sources of potential friction in this crowded emigrant ship. Each group or family tried to mark off its own living space by stacking its boxes in agreed-upon places. But with space at an absolute premium, even an inch or so could be precious. On one occasion Clayton "had words" with a woman and her family who, he believed, had trespassed on his space. "They are but one family and have two boxes out, we are two families and have but one," he complained. "I desired them to move one about four inches but they would not. She railed a little at me and used some hard words." Another problem came when some of the company accused Elder Turley of making a profit from the voyage—as much as a shilling a head for each of the Saints. Turley was, to say the least, disgusted with such petty charges but quickly produced all his bills and accounts to satisfy his critics that he had, indeed, used their money properly. He also took occasion to lecture them "for their hardness and unbelief." But these were only minor incidents, which could occur within any group suddenly thrown together under unusual pressures and conditions. The miracle, perhaps, is that they did not have more frequent and more serious problems with each other.

There were also confrontations with the crew and other passengers. At times the Mormons felt the captain was against them for having so many boxes, and they also had disagreements with the passengers in second cabin. Clayton and others became upset when five young women, three of whom were from Clayton's branch in Manchester, began associating too freely with the other passengers and members of the crew—even, reported one Saint, drinking wine with them. When Elder Turley asked them to stop, they were distressingly indifferent, telling their leader they could take care of themselves. All this antagonized the ship's crew who, as Clayton saw it, were angry with the Mormons "because we are unwilling that the sisters should be so familiar with the mates and sailors." It is understandable that the Mormon elders should try to maintain a sense of community and identity among the Saints, but to the average shiphand of 1840 it seemed to be an unreasonable exclusiveness.

On one serious incident Clayton and Turley took the side of the crew. The fresh water was disappearing too rapidly, and the crew suspected someone was stealing it. When the captain found Joseph Jackson arguing about it with some passengers in second cabin, he called him aside and asked if he would steal water. Jackson replied that he believed it right for the Mormons to take water, since many were suffering and the deaths of the children were partly caused by lack of water. The captain angrily ordered Jackson back down to steerage and threatened to keep him in chains for the rest of the voyage if he said anything like that again. Jackson became indignant and again told the captain that the Saints were suffering. It may have come to violence had not Clayton reprimanded his fellow Saints and got Jackson to hold his peace. After all, the water was probably being rationed fairly, and Clayton had no wish to demand special treatment for the Mormons.

The captain was not content, now that tempers had flared. Still angry, he told Jackson that it was all right for him to preach his religion as much as he liked, but he should say nothing more than that. Later he asked Turley if he understood the laws of mutiny, to which Turley replied that he did, as well as the laws concerning water. The captain informed Turley that if Jackson said anything more he would have him bound. "Yes, and I will help you," Turley responded.

Such actions on the part of a few Saints did not make it easy on the rest. Though Clayton was critical of the "peevish selfish actions of some of the second cabin passengers," he was also aware that the Saints were not totally blameless when frictions arose. "Many things are lost and nobody finds them," he complained on September 23. "Some are not saints who profess to be." Nevertheless, Clayton and Turley were determined to make the rest of the voyage as peaceable as possible.

Perhaps Clayton dwelt too much on the imperfections of the Saints, for these numerous irritations and disagreements did not hide the fact that the members of the *North America* migrating company were indeed *trying* to be good Saints. They held regular religious services, paid attention to nightly prayers, and were, for the most part, exemplary in their efforts to care for one another. In addition, they did not fail to observe the hand of God in their journey, and Clayton frequently gave thanks for it. One particularly exciting time came on September 22 when, about 11:00 A.M., the wood beneath the galley cook stove caught fire and burned through the deck. All morning the Saints had been longing for a wind, for the ship was becalmed, but at this Clayton became thankful that there was no wind for then the fire would have been terrible indeed. As soon as it was put out, a wind came up and the ship was underway again. "The Lord has been kind to us for which we feel thankful," wrote Clayton, "but not as much as we might."

On other occasions Clayton expressed similar gratitude. Even when complaining about the unsaintliness of some who professed to be Saints he said, "But considering our situation all things have passed off pretty well through the blessing of God." And on October 8 he wrote, "Last evening being my turn for prayer I felt to ask the Lord for a fair wind and I rejoice to see he has answered my prayers. The wind is very favourable near 10 mi. an hour. This is the third instance of the Lord answering my prayer for fair wind in a calm." There was no doubt in this disciple's mind that, in spite of their problems, they were indeed on the Lord's errand, and the Lord would see that they completed it.

Part of the Lord's errand was missionary work, and the Saints on the *North America* would not let that opportunity go by. Well into the night of October 5, for example, Elder Turley talked with the captain and several passengers about the ministrations of the angel Moroni to Joseph Smith. This was a sacred story to the Mormons, but Clayton commented sadly in his journal, "They treat it with disdain— especially the Captain." Such discussions occurred several times during that month at sea, though no one was converted. But aside from their unsuccessful preaching, and in spite of the problems caused by a few unexemplary Saints, the 200 Mormons must have left a positive image in the minds of some. When they reached America and were about to leave the *North America*, Captain Lowber was most friendly. He would like to bring another company of Mormons across the Atlantic, he said, and he even went so far as to ask more questions about their beliefs and inquire where the Saints met in New York City. Elder Turley answered his questions and introduced him to the local branch president. Captain Lowber probably never joined the Mormon church, but at least Clayton's company finally left him with positive feelings.

Uppermost in the minds of all the Mormons on the *North America* was to get to the new gathering place of the Saints, their new home. The depth of this feeling could be expressed no better than in the simple statement made by Clayton the day the fire broke out. "As soon as the bustle subsided," he wrote, "the wind began to blow and we were again on our way home." At least for this English disciple, "home" was no longer England. It was, rather, a place he had never seen—it was the settlement of Commerce, renamed Nauvoo, where the Lord had told the Saints to gather and where one day a sacred temple would herald the establishment of the Kingdom of God on earth. For William Clayton, "home" was where the Saints were gathered, no matter how new or strange the place.

As these Saints sailed homeward to Zion, it was only natural that they should want their own songs to express in their own peculiar way what they were doing. So it was that Clayton composed his first Mormon hymn—or at least the first one we have a record of. Though some would not call "Gentle Gale" a masterpiece, its verses clearly captured the longing for Zion that filled the hearts of the Saints on the *North America*:

1   With darkness long we've been o'erwhelm'd,
    Upon proud Britains land;
    But now the Lord has call'd us forth
    By his Almighty hand.
Chorus: Across the sea, we cheerfully go,
      Our kindred Saints to see,
      Blow gentle gale, fill every sail;
      And waft us over the sea.
2   God sent his servants from afar,
    This joyful news to tell;
    That we might all be saved from sin,
    And in his presence dwell.
      Across the sea, &c.
3   They told us that the Lord designed,
    Poor Zion to restore;
    And gather all her sons from far,
    That she might weep no more.
      Across the sea, &c.
4   Soon as the message we obeyed,
    And realized its power;
    To cross the mighty flood we then
    Were longing every hour.
      Across the sea, &c.
5   At length the time began to dawn,
    That we must haste away;
    And gather up for Zion too,
    To wait the perfect day.
      Across the sea, &c.
6   Sectarians breathed out their scorn,
    And said we soon should rue;

> But trusting to the word of God,
> We bade them all adieu.
> Across the sea, &c.
>
> 7   We gave our friends the parting hand,
> And relatives most dear;
> They poured their blessing on our heads,
> And drop'd the parting tear.
> Across the sea, &c.
>
> 8   But soon we hope to meet again
> With those we've loved before,
> And dwell with them on Zion's land
> In peace forever more.
> And now across the sea we go,
> Our kindred Saints to see;
> Blow gentle gale, fill every sail,
> And waft us over the sea.[19]

On October 7 the excited immigrants caught their first glimpse of America—Cape Cod. The next few days were frantic as the crew busily cleaned the ship and everyone made ready to arrive at New York harbor. On October 10 they had their first view of Long Island.

The next morning, Sunday, the *North America* was anchored between Ellis Island and Governor's Island, probably about a mile from the southern tip of Manhattan. An American doctor came aboard and, after examining them, pronounced the Saints fit to enter their new homeland. The ship then sailed farther into New York Harbor, and at exactly ten minutes after twelve Clayton, Turley, and Joseph Jackson set foot on American soil. Clayton was elated. The "superior neatness and tastely state of the buildings" impressed him, as did the large red apples they were able to buy for a cent apiece. The three went to the home of a church member for dinner, then to church services in Military Hall (probably the old U.S. arsenal), along with several other immigrants. Curiously, one of the first peculiarities Clayton noticed about the Americans at the service was "all the men and women . . . sitting cross legged and all the left leg over the right." He was not too tired to be observant.

The immigrants had taken thirty-three days to cross the ocean, and it would take them another forty-four to travel to western Illinois. They were eager to get underway. The next two nights were spent aboard the *North America* while Elder Turley made arrangements for a river steamer, the *Congress*, to take them up the Hudson River as far as the Erie Canal. On October 13 they took their leave of the ship and that night they slept aboard the *Congress.* With obvious pleasure at his sudden change of circumstances, Clayton noted in his diary, "I slept in best cabin."

Always a keen observer, the new immigrant was intensely interested in the sights and sounds of New York City and its surroundings. What a contrast from Penwortham, Manchester, and other cities he had known in England. "I felt struck," he said, "to see the horses and carts even to see the light harnesses and small carts and light loads drawn by them. The drivers all ride. The fruit is quite delicious to English people." As they left New York behind on October 14, he was impressed with the "white and very neat" buildings and with the "several spires towering towards the sky [which] bore a majestic appearance." When he awoke the next morning they were nearly a hundred miles up the Hudson, near the village of Catskill, and again Clayton was struck by the "beautiful white houses and banks on the river's side." He described the grainfields, pumpkin patches, farms, still more homes, and, he said, "in some places we saw fruit on the trees." For a young couple who had spent their lives in the industrial cities of England and had probably spent little if any time in the countryside, the pastoral scenes along the Hudson were something to marvel at. That night they stopped at Troy, where they would make ready for the trip along the Erie Canal.

Completed in 1825, the famous Erie Canal connected the Hudson River with Lake Erie, thus providing an all-water route from New York City to the rapidly developing western states in the Ohio valley. It traversed the broad, beautiful Mohawk valley and the passenger and freighting trade it carried soon made New York City the leading metropolis in America. It was the most convenient route west, and as Clayton and his companions boarded their horse-drawn canal boats they were only doing the same thing as tens of thousands of westering migrants both before and after them.

They engaged three boats, though at prices they all thought exorbitant, and at 3:45 on the afternoon of October 16 were on their way to Buffalo. Again Clayton was delighted with the scenery—the livestock, an aqueduct that he described as a "stupendous work," and the beautiful towns they passed. He was astounded at the engineering of the canal and described it in a letter to his friends in Penwortham. "The canal is upwards of 360 miles long," he wrote, "and is raised by a great number of locks. At the town of Lockport there are five locks together which raises the canal 60 feet. This is a stupendous work. After these locks the canal has been cut through a rock of solid stone upwards of a mile."[20]

The trip in the canal boat was fairly leisurely—calm water, no noise or pollution from a steam engine, and time to stop and gather fruit or buy groceries at shops along the way. Fresh milk, the immigrants happily discovered, could be purchased for four cents a quart. In addition, the owner of Clayton's boat was a religious man, so on Sunday the boat stopped and some of the Saints held their own prayer services. Some also took advantage of the time to do something they had not been able to do since leaving England: wash their clothes in fresh water.

The trip along the canal, though generally calm, was not entirely without incident. On October 20 it rained as they were passing Utica, and one of the horses slipped into the canal, nearly drowning. Such accidents were not uncommon, for Clayton heard that a little earlier a horse drawing another boat had actually drowned.

Clayton and Turley were on the last boat, the *Silver Arrow*, so on October 22 they took a faster packet to catch up with the others at Buffalo and make arrangements for the next part of the trip. The next day they reached Buffalo and met the other two boats. The passengers on the *J. D. Hawks* reported that three more children had died since the group separated. It was better aboard the second boat, the *Chawtauqua*, though provisions were running low. It was another two days before the *Silver Arrow* arrived.

Turley and Clayton, meanwhile, made arrangements for passage on a lake steamer, the *Wisconsin*, which would take them to the village of Chicago. The cost was $10 apiece, and at this point Turley began to worry about the poorest among his charges. He had been told that passage could be secured for half that price, and now he was afraid some would have to remain in Buffalo. They could not afford the rest of the journey at that price. Turley was "much cast down," Clayton said, at the thought of leaving them, and "almost heartbroke." But miraculously, Hiram Kellog, presiding elder at Kirtland, Ohio, showed up. He and Turley were old friends, and when Turley told him of the problem he immediately volunteered to take the whole company to Kirtland, where they would be more comfortable during the winter than in the rustic pioneer settlement of Commerce. They decided that all who wanted to, and could raise the money, would go on to Com-

merce, but the rest would go to Kirtland. There, in the shadow of the
first Mormon temple, they would spend the winter.[21]

The next day, Sunday, the *Silver Arrow* arrived in Buffalo. On Monday another disappointment came when it was discovered that the
captain of the *Wisconsin* had changed his plans and was not going to
Chicago. Those who planned to go on scurried to make other arrangements and finally booked passage on the *Illinois*. Three days later,
October 20, they said farewell to the families remaining behind and
were again on their way "home." The Saints who remained appeared
cheerful, but Clayton saw the disappointment in their eyes and felt
their sadness in his own heart. "Some was inclined almost to wish
they had not left England rather than be left short of Commerce," he
wrote. "We felt considerable at parting," he later reported, but he
added, "yet we knew that all was well. We have since seen that it was
right, they went to Kirtland."[22]

The water trip to Chicago took the immigrants the length of Lake
Erie, past Detroit, up Lake Huron, past Mackinaw Island, and down
Lake Michigan. They arrived at Chicago on November 4 and immediately rented teams and wagons to take them overland to the Rock
River. The company became separated, there were several of the usual
disagreements, and Clayton rented a house at Dixon, Illinois, for a
dollar a day until Turley and other stragglers could catch up.

A glimpse of some aspects of frontier life is seen in Clayton's description of what happened in and around Dixon. There was no fire-
place in the empty rented house, so they cooked out of doors. All the
way between Chicago and Dixon the settlers continually urged the
young women in the company to remain behind—suggesting a shortage
of women in these western settlements—and at Dixon the residents
wanted the entire company to settle down with them. In the empty
house Clayton and his companions had nothing to sleep on, so they
made their beds on the wooden boxes that held all their belongings.
Often, said Clayton, "the sides of a box made our bones ache, but,"
he assured his friends still in England, "the more we suffered the more
cheerful we appeared."[23]

At Dixon the group purchased a boat for $75, and within a few days
had it fixed up. On November 15 they loaded themselves and all their
boxes and pushed out into the Rock River. From there on they depended on the current to float them downstream to the city of the
Saints. They spent eleven days on the water, but each evening they

pulled into shore because the islands and the logs in the river made it treacherous at night.

The weather was becoming very cold, for it was late in the season, but the little company remained cheerful. On November 20 they went through the rapids that separated the Rock River from the mighty Mississippi. They were only about 130 miles from their destination, and Clayton said that simply entering the Mississippi "caused us to rejoice much." The next night, Saturday, they camped on the bank of the huge river and held a meeting. Elder Turley was deeply concerned, now that their journey was almost complete, that they have no ill feelings toward each other. It was a moving spiritual experience for all of them. Turley asked those who had quarrelled to forgive each other, and many Saints acknowledged their faults before the group and asked forgiveness. Then, as often happened in early Mormon meetings, some of them began to speak in tongues, and William Poole interpreted. "It was a time of rejoicing," Clayton recorded, as the Saints anticipated their arrival home.

Sunday night the group was at Burlington, Iowa, about thirty-five miles above the Mormon settlement, and in anticipation of their arrival the next day they bathed and changed their clothes. But the next day they only made it to within nine miles before they had to stop for the night. Tuesday, November 24, was the great day for Clayton. He seemingly could not wait to get there, for he and a few others decided to walk the nine miles to Commerce. They arrived at noon, and the first people they met were some Saints from Manchester who had arrived a week earlier. A committee had been formed to find accommodations for the new arrivals, and as soon as the boat arrived Clayton and his family took their luggage to a new but very small house on the banks of the Mississippi. At that point Clayton summarized in his journal the joy and relief that all the Saints must have felt as they arrived in the long-sought promised land, as well as their feeling that this strange and unfamiliar land was, indeed, their home. "Thus ended a journey of over 5000 miles having been exactly 11 weeks and about 10 hours between leaving Liverpool and arriving at our journeys end. We had been much exposed to cold weather and suffered many deprivations and disconveniences yet through the mercy of God we landed safe and in good health with the exception of 8 persons one of whom died soon after landing. We were pleased to find ourselves once more at home and felt to praise God for his goodness."[24]

The first night in the city of the Saints was spent at the home of Henry Moore, sleeping on the floor. The next day Clayton and his family together with three other families—fourteen people in all—moved into the house they had been temporarily assigned to. They made their beds of hay on the floor and were so cramped for space that they had to move their beds each morning. Under these crowded conditions William Clayton began to carve out a new life for himself among the gathered Saints in Nauvoo.

Clayton's emigration from his homeland would not be complete until he reported to his friends in England. He knew they would be both curious and anxious about many things, and on November 29, only five days after his arrival in Commerce, he wrote a lengthy report to Penwortham. On December 10 he wrote his friends in Manchester. The letters were similar in tone but each contained different details and the Saints in each town were instructed to transmit their letter to the Saints in the other. The excitement of arriving at a new home; the busy and difficult process of getting settled; the thoughts of a disciple on the journey just passed; and the advice of a now experienced emigrant to his friends back home—all were graphically portrayed in these two letters, which provided a fitting climax to the story of William Clayton's emigration.[25]

Clayton waxed eloquent in portraying the hardships of the journey, and his attitude toward hardship—that tribulation could only in the long run do him good—would be a keystone of his discipleship throughout his life. Living on new and different kinds of foods, alternately suffocating with heat aboard ship or freezing with cold, sleeping on boards and boxes, sleeping out of doors in severe weather: all this and more he detailed to his friends back home. "I once could not have believed that it was possible for me to endure the toils I have endured," he wrote to Manchester, "but to the praise of God be it spoken, all I have endured has never hurt or discouraged me, but done me good." So good, in fact, were the difficulties that he assured his eager readers that "we have been far more healthy and cheerful than when at home. . . . The Lord has preserved us from sickness . . . and we are now at our journeys end far more healthy and looking better than when we left England. I can assure you brethren and sisters that if you will be faithful you have nothing to fear from the journey." For his friends in Penwortham he told a story that would add emphasis to his point. As they had passed the rapids separating the Rock River from the Mississippi, some got out and walked, including Clayton's mother-in-law, "old Lydia" Moon, and her husband. The Penwortham Saints knew the Moons well and could therefore appreciate the fact that, "something like a young woman," Lydia picked up Clayton's daughter Sarah, who was "very fat and heavy" and started off at a quick pace. "I was considerably amused at this," he wrote, "but went to her relief. I mention this to show that the journey had done the old folks no harm."[26]

Should the Penwortham and Manchester Saints come to the New World? Clayton could have no other answer than an emphatic "yes!"— no matter what the trials. "The journey lies before you," he wrote to Penwortham, "and although it is impossible for pen to describe to you the difficulties you will have to endure you must come or suffer the vengeance of heaven as for my part I will say that if I were in England now and had experienced all the journey it would not in the least deter me from coming." He gave the Manchester Mormons both encouragement and realistic caution: "Stand firm by the truth like men and women, and be not afraid to come to this land, but don't for a moment suppose that all will be peace & ease when you get here. These are days of tribulations and we must endure our portion."

Clayton had also been confirmed in the hard lesson that tribulation would not always come from the outside, for even within the faith there were imperfections that must be dealt with. The immigrant company was mixed, he told the Saints in Penwortham, coming from various parts of the country and having different experiences in the church. "Some have been fed a little on strong food, others but newly baptized," he said, and all this together "has increased our troubles." In such company, he realistically observed, "You may naturally suppose many things would occur to try all parties. . . . We have not yet suffered sufficient to make us all of one mind and wherever you go you may expect fine men as men and not as angels, and man is naturally prone to evil as the sparks fly upwards." Such philosophical resignation to the reality of continuing differences among the Saints was another keystone of this British immigrant's faith, and one that he would often be reminded of throughout his life. Even in Nauvoo, he warned the Manchester Mormons, the Saints were not all perfect, but that was only to be expected. "There are some who are not good Saints and some very good ones. Joseph says, that when he is out preaching he always tells the people not to come here for examples, but to set them and to copy from the Savior who is our pattern. It is not until corn is gathered into the barn that thrashing and sorting commences."

What kind of country would the future immigrants be coming to, and what about the city of the Saints? Clayton's description of western Illinois was almost idyllic. The land, he told both groups, was "exceeding rich" and beautiful, with plenty of food in great variety. Peaches, citrus fruit, pumpkins, squash, and potatoes were all readily available, and he told them what prices they could expect to pay for sugar, honey, molasses, flour, cornmeal, and beef. The city, too, was full of promise. "Commerce, or rather Nauvoo," he reported to Manchester, "is a large city. The houses are built of wood and each house has an acre of land to it. There is space left for streets apparently from 10 to 15 yards wide. There are houses belonging to the saints for several miles round."[27]

All this philosophy and advice was interesting, but the Saints in Manchester and Penwortham probably found just as great, if not more, interest in the more pragmatic part of his letter to Penwortham. What should an emigrant take with him as he left England? Clayton's experienced advice no doubt reflected some stern realities of the emigration process in the 1840s, as well as something about life on the western frontier.

First, he told them, bring clothing from England, for it was "coarse and dear" in America. He advised the women to obtain either linen or cotton "trousers" and flannel petticoats, and the men to get a suit of cotton cloth. So far as footwear was concerned, he discouraged strong shoes with nails, and observed that all the men wore boots, which could be obtained in New York for sixteen shillings. "I have only seen 2 or 3 pair of shoes except Englishmen had them."

With regard to luggage, his advice was highly practical. He recognized that more luggage would mean more toil, but in the long run it would be worth the effort. The cost to carry it all to Nauvoo would be so much less than the cost of replacing what they left behind that it would be foolish not to bring everything possible. "We brought considerable of pots and I am glad we did for they will pay for carriage. They are scarce in this region." Their pots (apparently earthenware) had carried well, for they were packed in hay. Tools were of special importance, and Clayton was sorry he did not bring a set of joiner's tools. He also told the Saints to save all their working clothes (a most pragmatic suggestion for life on the frontier), but then added, almost

as if he suddenly wondered if all his cautions would discourage some
Saints, "But neither let clothes nor goods detain you from coming."

How to pack, of course, was of special interest. In Clayton's day an
emigrant's main problem was how to pack as much as he could, regardless of weight, into as many homemade wooden boxes as he had
space for. "You must make your boxes very strong," he warned the
Saints, "say inch boards well put together." They should be of such
a size that if needed, three would make into a bed, and he suggested
four feet long, two and a half feet wide, and two feet deep.

The Saints in England would also want to know firsthand about
Joseph the prophet. By then Clayton had met him, heard him speak,
and formed his own impressions. "If I were in England," he reported
in the Manchester letter, "I would raise my voice and testify that
Joseph is a man of God, which will roll forth unto the end of the earth
and gather together all the good there is on the earth." From that point
on the life of the English immigrant would be inextricably woven with
that of the Mormon prophet, and the influence would be profound.

NOTES

1. P. A. M. Taylor, *Expectations Westward: The Mormons and the Emigration of Their British Converts in the Nineteenth Century* (Edinburgh:
Oliver and Boyd, 1965), 146.

2. *History of the Church*, 2:492. It is not clear whether the vision referred
to was Joseph Smith's first vision, which occurred in the spring of 1820, or the
remarkable vision of the "three degrees of glory," which was given to Joseph
Smith and Sidney Rigdon in 1832 and now stands as Section 76 of the Doctrine
and Covenants. The latter is generally referred to in church literature as "The
Vision." In the early years of the church, Joseph Smith did not circulate his
account of the 1820 vision very widely, and it was not included in any church
publications or missionary literature prior to 1840. That year the first printed
account of the vision appeared in England, in a tract by Orson Pratt entitled
*An Interesting Account of Several Remarkable Visions and of the Late Dis-
covery of Ancient American Records*. On the other hand, the 1832 vision
contained some very advanced doctrines, and asking the missionaries to avoid
discussing it would be consistent with Joseph Smith's instructions that they
stick to preaching the "first principles." In addition, the fact that he did not
want them even to discuss the Doctrine and Covenants on this first mission
to England also strongly suggests that he had the 1832 vision in mind.

3. Clayton to Willard Richards, 30 Jan. 1840, Clayton Papers, Church Archives.

4. Joseph Fielding to Willard Richards, 25 Mar. 1840, Fielding Papers.

5. Whitney, *Life of Heber C. Kimball*, 278.

6. *History of the Church*, 4:185–86.

7. Clayton to Brigham Young and Willard Richards, 19 Aug. 1840, Young Papers. The major portion of this letter consists of Clayton's copy of a letter he had received from John Moon, dated New York, 22 July 1840.

8. Clayton to Edward Martin, 29 Nov. 1840, in *Heart Throbs of the West*, 5 (Salt Lake City: Daughters of the Utah Pioneers, 1944), 373–80; Clayton to the Saints at Manchester, 10 Dec. 1840, Clayton Papers. The Manchester letter is actually in the writing of William Hardman who, according to the note he penned at the end, received it from Clayton with instructions to copy it and send the copy to the Saints at Penwortham and Preston. Hardman noted to these Saints, "And from several pages in this letter I am led to infer that there is a letter at Preston or Penwortham which we are to see, if so, and you have got it, I can assure you we shall feel extremely grateful if you will favour the Saints in Manchester with a copy of it. May the Lord bless you all with unity and love and save you into his celestial kingdom is the prayer of your brother in the New & Everlasting Covenant. Wm. Hardman."

9. Clayton to Young and Richards, 19 Aug. 1840.

10. Allen and Alexander, eds., *Manchester Mormons*, 168.

11. *History of the Church*, 4:313–21. Another early account of Heber C. Kimball's mission is Thompson, *Heber C. Kimball*. Clayton may have had a hand in this volume also.

12. Clayton to Young and Richards, 19 Aug. 1840.

13. Allen and Alexander, eds., *Manchester Mormons*, 168.

14. Ibid., 169.

15. Ibid., 170–71. Unless otherwise noted, most of what follows respecting Clayton's voyage to America and arrival at Nauvoo is based on his diary account in *Manchester Mormons*.

16. P. A. M. Taylor suggests that an emigrant ship of 1840 would carry 300 or 400 passengers (see *Expectations Westward*, 176–79). Taylor provides some interesting material on the nature of such emigrant voyages. Another excellent and much more detailed treatment is David H. Pratt and Paul F. Smart, "Life on Board a Mormon Emigrant Ship," in the Proceedings of the World Conference on Records (Salt Lake City), 12-15 Aug. 1980, series 418, on file in the library of the Genealogical Society of The Church of Jesus Christ of Latter-day Saints. For some details on the *North America* and her sister ships of the Black Ball line, see Conway B. Sonne, *Saints on the Seas: A Maritime History of Mormon Migration, 1830-1890* (Salt Lake City: University of Utah Press, 1983), 49, 52, 70, 148-59. Clayton wrote the captain's name as Lower, but Sonne lists it as Lowber.

17. These included Mormon Harris, son of Paul and Jane Harris; the child of Elizabeth and William Poole; the child of a Brother and Sister Corbridge; and the child of a Brother Perry. P. A. M. Taylor has sampled records of Mormon transatlantic crossings, and from these it appears that Clayton's voyage was not unlike the others. Bad weather, broken masts, and shortages of food plagued many of them. Most of the emigrants, being poor, traveled in

steerage as did Clayton and his party. This meant cramped quarters, sickness, lack of privacy, and sometimes death. The British Passenger Acts, when they were enforced, seem later to have improved the problem of privacy (Taylor, *Expectations Westward*, 176–207).

18. Quoted in ibid., 178–79.

19. Thompson, *Heber C. Kimball*, 60.

20. Clayton to Martin, 29 Nov. 1840.

21. Kirtland, Ohio, was the first Mormon gathering place after Joseph Smith and his followers left the state of New York in early 1831. There were many sacred memories for the Mormons in Kirtland. Here the "law of consecration" had first been introduced, and in 1836 the sacred Kirtland Temple was completed. The temple was the first building for public worship to be erected by the Mormons, but it was also the place where special religious ordinances were introduced (foreshadowing the "endowment" ceremony introduced at Nauvoo), and where on one occasion the Savior and certain ancient prophets had visited and instructed Joseph Smith and Oliver Cowdery. It was small wonder that Clayton also longed to see Kirtland. As his group was traveling on Lake Erie, they stopped at Fairport to take on wood, and Clayton later reported to his friends, "We were then only about eleven miles from Kirtland. I had a great desire to go and see the house of the Lord, but could not" (Clayton to Martin, 29 Nov. 1840). The most recent and most complete treatment of the Kirtland era is Milton V. Backman, Jr., *The Heavens Resound: A History of the Latter-day Saints in Ohio, 1830-1838* (Salt Lake City: Deseret Book Company, 1983).

22. Clayton to Martin, 29 Nov. 1840.

23. Ibid.

24. Allen and Alexander, eds., *Manchester Mormons*, 201.

25. Clayton to Martin, 29 Nov. 1840, in *Heart Throbs*, and Clayton to the Saints at Manchester, 10 Dec. 1840, Clayton Papers. Unless otherwise noted, the quotations in the following description all come from these two letters.

26. Clayton to Martin, 19 Nov. 1840. Clayton says more about their good health in this letter, which is worth quoting. He was clearly trying to persuade his friends in Penwortham that hardships could not hurt them. "Old Thomas has not had one day bad health since we left England, except a little seasickness. Margaret Moon has grown so very fat that all her best dresses are very much too little, she has only one that she can wear the others she cannot get on. Yesterday I had to take my pen knife and cut her new shift sleeves (which her sister made) open for they had made her arms almost black. She is indeed a fat lump and has to keep going from house to house when she had time to sing for the saints. A hymn which I composed on the ship has to be sung almost every time she goes out. Brother William Poole is at work for a farmer about 10 miles from here. He is grown so fat that all his clothes are too little. His wife also is very healthy, fat and cheerful. She seems to be well and has lost her rheumatism. My wife and children are well at present. My youngest child has been poorly with her health. We are all about as merry as we dare be and would be glad to see you all here too."

27. Clayton to the Saints in Manchester, 10 Dec. 1840. Sugar and honey were 5 pence per pound, molasses 2 pence, potatoes 2 shillings per bushel, and flour 20 shillings per 200 pounds. Clayton also observed that the price of the best brandy in Nauvoo was 3 shillings per quart, and that "at any of the taverns you may pour your own glass of anything for about 2 pence." Drunkenness, however, did not seem to be a problem. As Clayton observed with satisfaction, "I have only seen about 3 drunken men since I arrived in America. I have heard of 3 I did not see." Clayton to Martin, 29 Nov. 1840.

CHAPTER 3

"Once More at Home"

"We were pleased to find ourselves once more at home." William Clayton and his English immigrant friends were fully convinced that in this fledgling American frontier community, dominated by a man named Joseph Smith, they would find all the happiness and fulfillment promised by the gospel. William's faith was more than rewarded as he was drawn into almost daily, close association with the prophet. It was not long, however, before any expectations he may have had for a life of peace and security were shattered by the economic and political realities of western Illinois.

When the first Mormons arrived in Illinois, the population was already a homogeneous lot, consisting of migrants from northern and southern American states as well as some European immigrants. The largest centers of population were in west central Illinois, though by 1840 the north was filling in rapidly. Chicago was beginning to boom, the river towns (Alton, Quincy, Jacksonville, Springfield, Peoria) were growing vigirously,[1] and land sales were flourishing. Certain speculators and politicians, however, saw some signs of economic stagnation as plans for a canal and a railroad system were not maturing. One way to forestall such a disaster, they believed, was to encourage continued large-scale immigration. When the Mormons began to arrive in early 1839, they were given a sincere and hearty welcome. But, like a runt that suddenly surpasses the growth of its brothers and sisters, the tiny settlement of Commerce soon became Nauvoo and, bursting its borders, was transformed in less than five years into one of the two largest cities in Illinois. The brother and sister cities were not enamored with the change.

Driven from Missouri because they seemed to threaten the political and social stability of that frontier state, the Mormons were aided generously in their resettlement in Nauvoo by the citizens of nearby Quincy. As they considered the future, however, some said it would be unwise to make another attempt at creating their own community or communities. Rather, they believed, they would have a better chance for peace if they simply scattered themselves among the population. Joseph Smith felt differently, and even before he arrived he began making plans for a grand new community of Saints. There would be several communities, in fact, but Nauvoo would be the queen, and the center of the Kindgom. On Sunday July 19, 1840, when Nauvoo was little more than a struggling collection of small wooden houses, shacks, and various temporary shelters, Joseph Smith gave a dramatic public discourse in which he proclaimed his vision of the future greatness of his city as well as all of western Illinois. As recorded by Martha Jane Knowlton, he boldly declared:

> Now let all who can cooly and deliberately dispose of their property come and give of their substance to the [poor?] that the hearts of the poor may be comforted and all may worship God together in holiness of heart. Come brethren come all of you. And I prophecy in the name of the Lord that the state of Illinois shall become a great and mighty mountain as [a] city set upon a hill that cannot be hid and a great that giveth light to the world. The city of Nauvoo als[o] shall become the greatest city in the whole world.
>
> . . . I now invite all liberall minded men to come up to Nauvoo and help to build up the city of our God. We are not greatly distressed, no nor ever will be. This is the principle place of gathering therefore let the brethren begin to roll in like clouds and we will sell you lots if you are able to pay for them, and if not you shall have them without money and without price.
>
> . . . Yea I prophecy that pleasure parties shall come from England to see the Mamoth and like the Queen of Sheba shall say the half was never told them. School houses shall be built here and High schools shall be established and the great men of the [earth] shall send their sons here to board while they are receiving their education among us. And even Noblemen shall crave the priviledge of educating their children with us and these poor Saints shall chink in their pockets the money of these proud men received from such as come and dwell with us.
>
> Now brethren I obligate myself to build as great a temple as ever Solomon did, if the church will back me up. Moreover, it shall not impoverish any man but enrich thousands. And I proph-

ecy that the time shall be when these Saints shall ride proudly over the mountains of Missouri and no Gentile dog nor Missouri dog shall dare lift a tongue against them but will lick up the dust from beneath their feet.[2]

When Joseph Smith delivered this stirring discourse, William Clayton was still in Manchester. If he had heard the prophet's grand projections, however, they would have stirred his soul with marvelous images of his own involvement in the glorious future of the Kingdom. Undoubtedly he heard similar predictions after he arrived four months later, and his pulse quickened with expectation. By that time there were Mormon settlements scattered throughout Adams and Hancock counties, as well as across the Mississippi River in Lee County, Iowa.

The situation, however, was fraught with potential problems. Non-Mormons became restless and suspicious as the Mormon population grew so rapidly that it soon threatened to overwhelm them. At the same time, both banks of the Mississippi were notorious for the "mean, rascally characters" who made up at least part of the population, and such people could only exacerbate any latent conflict. Finally, certain Mormon religious beliefs would eventually arouse opposition, as they had in Missouri.

The economy of western Illinois was highly speculative, and it was not difficult to purchase land on credit. Joseph Smith and other church leaders secured thousands of acres on both sides of the Mississippi. As a result, Joseph Smith became, among other things, a real estate agent, as he encouraged his followers to purchase and settle the lands he had gone in debt to obtain. Little did William Clayton suspect, as he entered Nauvoo so excitedly on November 24, that Joseph Smith's business activities would soon absorb a major part of his own time and become one of his contributions to building the Kingdom of God in America. Joseph Smith envisioned the Kingdom as much more than a spiritual, preaching institution. "Wherefore, verily I say unto you that all things unto me are spiritual," the Lord had said through him in 1830.[3] Clayton found that even the prophet of the Lord must spend most of his time on the secular, economic, political, and mundane realities of life, and much less time on such priestly and prophetic roles as administering church affairs, preaching doctrine, and receiving revelation.

What manner of man was Joseph Smith—the man who, from this moment on, had a more profound impact on Clayton's life than anyone he had ever known or ever would know?[4] The opinions of the time were, to say the least, varied: his contemporaries saw him as everything from charlatan and uneducated impostor to impressive enigma or inspired leader, and his followers loved and revered him as a prophet. Peter Burnett, who had been one of his attorneys during his recent Missouri difficulties, characterized the unique mixture in his personality and probably drew as balanced a view as any non-Mormon of the time. As he later wrote:

> You could see at a glance that his education was very limited. He was an awkward and vehement speaker. In conversation he was slow, and used too many words to express his ideas, and would not generally go directly to a point. But, with all these drawbacks, he was much more than an ordinary man. He possessed the most indomitable perseverance, was a good judge of men, and deemed himself born to command, and he did command. His views were so strange and striking, and his manner was so earnest, and apparently so candid, that you could not but be interested. There was a kind, familiar look about him, that pleased you. . . . He had the capacity for discussing a subject in different aspects, and for proposing many original views, even on ordinary matters. His illustrations were his own. He had great influence over others.[5]

If Joseph Smith was born to command, then the disciple from Penwortham was born to follow. Once he became acquainted with the Mormon prophet, his awe quickly turned to unwavering personal loyalty. He expected to have his faith confirmed, and what he saw in Joseph Smith did just that. "He is not an idiot," Clayton wrote his friends in Manchester as if to combat some vicious tale, "but a man of sound judgement, and possessed of intelligence which expands your mind and causes your heart to rejoice." The rest of his statement is a classic summary of what thousands of believing Mormons would say:

> He is very familiar, and delights to instruct the poor Saints. I can converse with him just as easy as I can with you, and with regard to being willing to communicate instruction he says "I receive it freely and I will give it freely." He is willing to answer any question I have put to him and is pleased when we ask him questions. He seems exceeding well versed in the scriptures, and whilst conversing upon any subject such light and beauty is revealed I never saw before. If I had come from England purposely to converse with him a few days I should have considered myself well paid

for my trouble. He is no friend to iniquity but cuts at it wherever he sees it and it is in vain to attempt to cloke it before him. He has a great measure of the spirit of God, and by this means he is preserved from imposition. He says, "I am a man of like passions with yourselves," but truly I wish I was such a man.[6]

Nowhere in the available papers is there even a hint that Clayton ever doubted the prophet or found cause to criticize him. His complete loyalty during Joseph's lifetime as well as his unwavering devotion to the prophet's memory in later years is only one example of the powerful influence the founder of Mormonism had on the lives of thousands of followers. There were over 30,000 of them by the time he died in 1844.

William Clayton was what Sidney Hook once characterized as the *"eventful* man" as opposed to the *"event-making* man" in history. Both types influence subsequent developments, but the *"event-making man,"* as described by Hook, is one whose "actions are the consequences of outstanding capacities of intelligence, will, and character rather than of accidents of history." Possessing a kind of greatness that involves an extraordinary talent, he appears at a "fork in the historical road" and increases the odds of success for the alternative he chooses by virtue of the "extraordinary qualities he brings to bear." The *"eventful* man," on the other hand, *does* influence subsequent developments, but in a way much like the brave young Dutch boy who kept his finger in the dike and saved the town—almost any passerby could have done it if he had the will to do so, but *he* became a hero because *he* was the one who was passing by and did it.[7] In Mormon history Joseph Smith was *the* "event-making man," for he was the one whose outstanding qualities largely created the direction Mormonism would go during his lifetime. Clayton became one of the exemplary "eventful men," as he faithfully followed his leader in absolutely everything and unhesitatingly put his finger in any crack in the dike that seemed to threaten the Kingdom. In practical terms, the "event-making men" would have little long-range impact without "eventful men" like William Clayton to support them.

But why did Clayton remain so steadfast when other converts with equally profound conviction sometimes drifted away? There is no fully objective explanation, but a few considerations are at least worth comment. At the heart of the matter was the continuing and permanent effect of whatever overwhelming spiritual experience persuaded him to ask for baptism at 11 o'clock at night. His conversion was genuine, he was convinced that the power of God had touched his soul, and the memory of that experience would not leave him. This the Mormons call "testimony," and one of its effects was to make it easy for the believer to accept as truth anything that came from the prophet.

Clayton's will to believe may have been enhanced by the fact that he was not, by nature, a seeker for high office, unlike some who later turned against the prophet. At the same time he relished close association with top leaders and received deep self-satisfaction from feeling that he was on the inside—that he always knew what was going on. He did not try to counsel the prophet (such a thought would have seemed almost blasphemously presumptuous to Clayton), especially when counsel was not sought. He was willing, rather, to take counsel and let it go at that. He found fulfillment in knowing he was thought well of, and perhaps the fear of even *seeming* disloyal helped stifle any tendencies toward open criticism.

Further, even though Clayton was a musician, a poet of sorts, and an avid reader, he was not by nature a philosopher or a speculator. His mind delighted in the specific and the concrete, which helps account for his success as a scribe and a clerk, but he was not given to the formulation of new ideas or the imaginative construction of philosophical concepts. As a secretary and scribe he recorded what he was told to record; as a diarist and historian he described what he saw around him, usually with skill and great descriptive power but seldom with any interpretive imagination; as a dispenser of ideas he was a follower and not a leader. Some disciples who possessed a certain inborn brilliance or speculative tendency could (and sometimes did) become disaffected from Mormonism, as their ruminations drew them away from the mainstream of Mormon thought. Clayton's training and basic personality led him to prefer simple, clear-cut instruction over abstract theorizing and to preach the doctrines of others rather than lead out in his own reflective metaphysical speculation.

It took a certain number of philosophers and imaginative formulators of ideas (i.e., people such as Joseph Smith, Sidney Rigdon, Parley P. Pratt, Orson Pratt) to build and lead the Mormon Kingdom, but it took many more ordinary people, like Clayton, to become the brick and mortar with which the Kingdom would be constructed. Such material provided resiliency and strength—the ability to bounce back after the storm, almost none the worse for wear. None of this explains

Clayton's character, but it at least suggests that his kind of discipleship, in combination with whatever other kinds there were, was necessary for the success of Mormonism.

Joseph Smith's impact on Clayton was immediate and had exactly the effect the English convert anticipated: it confirmed both his testimony and his optimism for the future. Five days after entering Nauvoo his family was still using boxes for furniture and sleeping on leaves, but he wrote to Edward Martin that "we are perfectly satisfied with the appearance of things here and we have abundance of proofs that Joseph Smith Junior is what he pretends to be viz a prophet of the most high God and this is the work of God and will roll forth to the ends of the earth." "Last night," he continued, "many of us were in company with Brother Joseph, our hearts rejoiced to hear him speak of the things of the Kingdom, he is an affectionate man and as familiar as any of us. We feel to love him much and so will you." Though he certainly expected some difficulties, Clayton was convinced that the future would go well. As if to foreshadow the famous hymn he composed a few years later, he remarked to his friend, "In fact and in short all is well."[8]

During the next few weeks Clayton heard Joseph preach in public twice, but he was also drawn to the attention of the prophet. As the new arrivals frequently attended "singing meetings," they were often asked to sing "Gentle Gale" for Joseph and others. This was the song Clayton wrote for the Saints aboard the North America, and it soon became popular in Nauvoo. To sing for the prophet was, for Clayton, the command performance most to be desired.

The Claytons were "at home" with the Saints and their prophet, but it was not ordained that they should settle down comfortably in the relative security of Nauvoo or that life should be easy for them. They soon began to inquire about land purchases and Joseph Smith's brother, Hyrum, told them that he had land to sell across the river in Iowa Territory for $3 an acre. Clayton was not sure what to do, for his objective was to settle with the Saints in Nauvoo. But there had been a settlement of Saints across the river since 1839, and the prophet's brother counseled them to go there. Other Saints counseled against it, telling William and Ruth that "the devil was over the river." The faithful disciple made up his mind to trust the Smiths. Hyrum, after all, was a counselor in the First Presidency of the church and another brother, William, was a member of the Quorum of the Twelve Apostles. Clayton finally purchased land from William on credit and agreed to pay by working on a Mississippi steamboat, in which William had an interest, and giving the apostle half his wages until the debt was cancelled.

The new year, 1841, then, brought another new beginning for the disciple from Penwortham, and one that reflected in a most fundamental way the potential personal impact of his religion. Indeed, there was something inspiring and dramatic, but at the same time incongruous, about an English bookkeeper in his twenties, with a wife and two small children, embarking on an adventure as a farmer on the unbroken Iowa prairie, hoping to pay for his farm by working on a Mississippi River steamboat. But the Mormon gospel wrought such changes in many lives.

On January 21, after purchasing a wagon, livestock, and some farm equipment, the young couple began moving their belongings across the frozen Mississippi. It took them four days, and after that life seemed to become a stream of unending disappointments. The little house they rented was so poorly ventilated that they could not long keep a fire indoors, which made the cold weather even more unbearable. They even had to cook their food out of doors. They were shocked at the low state of spirituality they found among the Iowa Saints, who were "having no meetings, full of envy, strife and contention and in a very bad state." When the weather moderated they began building their own log home, but on March 15 Clayton was sitting in his temporary house when he heard someone yelling that the new home was on fire. He hailed the driver of a passing wagon, who took him the half mile to the homesite. There he found a good neighborwoman who had carried water a quarter of a mile and was beginning to put out the fire. Clayton finished the job and found that the damage sustained to the house was not drastic. But they did lose a large rope and a pair of bed cords, which, he said, "in our circumstances was a considerable loss to us." That same day the fine hog they had "set much store on" to use for breeding purposes was mysteriously "cut" (i.e., castrated) after it had broken out and wandered away from home—"a sad grief to us," said Clayton.[9] But all this was only the beginning of troubles for the English bookkeeper-turned-farmer.

By this time Clayton undoubtedly was wondering whether it really was the will of the Lord that he should be in Iowa instead of Nauvoo. From the beginning the Mormon settlement there had been on shaky legal grounds, for Isaac Galland, a speculator of questionable character, had sold land to the Saints when his own title was unclear,[10] and this led to conflicting claims. Nevertheless, on March 20 Joseph Smith received a revelation in answer to the question, "What is the will of the Lord, concerning the Saints in the Territory of Iowa?" Clayton may well have been among the Saints who had asked this question. The answer, which was read in a general conference meeting on April 8, declared that those who were "essaying to be my Saints" should keep the Lord's commandments and prepare to build up cities to his name in the places appointed by Joseph Smith. Specifically with reference to Iowa, the revelation declared, "Let them build up a city unto my name upon the land opposite the city of Nauvoo, and let the name of Zarahemla be named upon it."[11] This was probably the answer Clayton wanted: it *was* God's will that they stay in Iowa, and the name *Zarahemla* simply made the point more dramatic. It came right from the Book of Mormon and referred to a magnificent city built by God's chosen people in ancient America. The symbolism was obvious.

On March 19 Clayton began planting seed, but on the twentieth, the day Joseph received the revelation about Iowa, his land title was challenged by a man named William Miller. He brought a constable with him who read a notice requiring Clayton to quit the land. Astonished, Clayton sought advice and even crossed the river to consult with Joseph Smith. Exactly what happened is unclear, but by April 2 Miller's claim had been settled, and Clayton was seemingly free to pursue his farming.

But times of trouble were not over. Fences were broken by cattle, crops were destroyed, and Clayton frequently became so ill he could not work. To add to it all, he was attempting not only to work on the steamboat, but also to invest in it, and that investment failed. The faith of the disciple was being sorely tried.

At the same time Ruth's third child was ready to be born, but even this happy event had minor problems. Time for delivery came on May 6, and Ruth wanted her mother to be there. Mother Moon, however, was on the other side of the river, in Nauvoo, so Clayton borrowed a skiff and rowed across "as hard as I could." Two hours later he returned with his mother-in-law, but Ruth had already delivered a healthy baby girl. At least there was one bright moment for the family.

There were also moments of deep spiritual satisfaction, though not in Zarahemla itself. In April Clayton attended the general conference of the church in Nauvoo. He was a member of the Nauvoo high priest quorum and thus sat with that quorum in a special place at meetings. He watched with pleasure an elaborate parade of the Nauvoo Legion and the laying of the cornerstone for the magnificent Nauvoo Temple. Clayton frequently went to Nauvoo on Sundays to hear Joseph Smith preach, and on May 9 the prophet expounded upon the doctrine of baptism for the dead.[12] Clayton had probably heard this doctrine before, but on that occasion he was so impressed that he and several others immediately went down to the river to act upon what they heard. It was a time of spiritual rejuvenation as many Saints renewed their own covenants through being voluntarily rebaptized, and then were baptized again in behalf of dead relatives. Clayton, too, rededicated himself to the service of God by being rebaptized, after which he was baptized in behalf of his grandfather Thomas Clayton, his two grandmothers, and an aunt.[13] It was times such as these, learning at the feet of the prophet and sharing spiritual experiences with the Saints, that helped keep Clayton's faith alive as he struggled for success in Zarahemla.

At the April conference Clayton heard the revelation read that commanded the building of Zarahemla and heard Joseph Smith make a comment that must have helped him reconcile his troubles with the will of God. The Saints were told that God's people were not immune from hardship, and the prophet reminded one man of the massacre at Haun's Mill, Missouri, as an example of what all of them might expect.[14] This was little comfort in a physical sense, but at least it suggested that because they were the Lord's people the Mormons should not expect always to have it easy. The difficulties were a demonstration of who the Saints really were as they tried to live apart from the world they were in. Such a thought actually provided a certain inner satisfaction for disciples like Clayton.

Sometime in August Clayton was particularly gratified when Joseph Smith inquired about his circumstances. "I told him" he wrote, "that [we] had not a privilege of having many things which we greatly needed," and soon after that he began receiving some welcome aid from the church.[15]

But Clayton was also severely ill with the ague, a form of malaria that produced alternate chills and fevers. Epidemics of the ague were common in western frontier communities, and in 1839 the Saints huddled at Commerce were struck by a particularly severe outbreak. That year Joseph Smith went among them administering to the ill and several miraculous healings were reported. The following summer, however, the epidemic was worse, and in 1841 it reached calamitous proportions. So many died that on one occasion Sidney Rigdon was forced to preach a "general funeral sermon" for them all.[16]

One of the casualties that year was Alice Moon, Ruth's aunt. Another, who died on August 17, was Henrietta Lucretia Patten Clayton—the baby girl who had been born to William and Ruth just three months earlier. She had been having chills for some time and suffered severely during the last two days. "When dead she was as pretty as I ever saw in my life," wrote the grief-stricken father. But, like the ideal disciple he was striving so hard to become, he let his faith at least mellow his sorrow. "This was a grief to us," he said, "but we afterwards saw the hand of God in it and saw it was best to be so during this time."[17] Very often during the remainder of his life this Mormon disciple would find such submissiveness a necessary ingredient of his faith.

As the summer wore on and the Claytons continued working their Iowa farm some of the crops matured, but more illness and other unforeseen problems delayed their harvest. In September a frost destroyed half of their potatoes. Severely ill, William tried to dig the rest but was unable to finish. Ruth and her younger sister, Lydia, completed the job and also harvested an acre and a half of corn. Finally, in mid-November, Clayton went to Nauvoo, evidently to seek counsel from the apostle who baptized him, Heber C. Kimball. The apostle advised him to move his family to Nauvoo, and on December 14 he did so. He was still sick and "occasionally shaking," but all he could find for his family to live in was a poorly built house in which they still suffered severely from the cold. So ended the English disciple's first year in the promised land.

When Clayton gave up farming in Lee County, Iowa, he was only anticipating by a few months the failure of the Iowa adventure. The revelation that Clayton heard at the April conference anticipated even more settlements in Iowa, specifically naming the town of Nashville, not far from Zarahemla, as one of them. Joseph Smith had grand hopes not only for building Nauvoo, but also for creating a kind of Mormon empire to the west, with Zarahemla as Nauvoo's sister city across the river. A stake was organized, and Clayton served first as a member of the high council and later as stake clerk.[18] However, Clayton was only one of many Mormon settlers in Lee County to be hounded by conflicting land claimants or to have difficulty with other Saints. In an effort to keep peace among brothers, the high council even voted to disfellowship anyone who took a brother before the law. The Iowa Saints also tried to keep the "law of consecration," a system of economic sharing attempted by the church in both Ohio and Missouri and based on the idea of selfless equality. But they were hardly perfect enough for that and the prophet instructed them to stop. Ultimately only about thirty houses were built in Zarahemla, and the stake was finally discontinued in 1842. Later Joseph Smith tended to blame the failure on problems with dishonest land speculators and in a public address on April 6, 1843, declared: "There is a chance in that place for every abomination to be practiced on the innocent, if they go, and I ask forgiveness of all whom I advised to go there."[19]

Clayton did not record his specific reaction to all this (or, if he did, it has not survived), but he was doubtless disappointed and dismayed. He was, after all, a witness to two distressing failures: his own efforts to become a self-sufficient farmer, and Joseph Smith's prophecy concerning Iowa. At the same time these early Mormons seemed to have a pragmatic attitude toward the fulfillment of such prophecy, and William Clayton shared it. It was an active, faithful pragmatism that compelled them to look at prophecy concerning their own future as a personal challenge. They were obligated to work to make the great things predicted by the prophet actually happen. But if they did not happen, this was no sign that the prophet was false. It was only a sign either that the Saints were not faithful and hardworking enough or, if they had done all they could, that the enemies of the church had prevented them from fulfilling their obligations. "Verily, verily, I say unto you," the Lord had told them through Joseph Smith in January 1841, "that when I give a commandment to any of the sons of men to do a work unto my name, and those sons of men go with all their might and with all they have to perform that work, and cease not their diligence, and their enemies come upon them and hinder them from performing that work, behold, it behooveth me to require that work no more at the hands of those sons of men, but to accept of their offerings."[20] William and Ruth *had* worked with "all their might" and with all they had, and it was probably with such thoughts filling their minds that they crossed the Mississippi again on that bleak day in December. If Zarahemla failed it would not have been *their* fault, and

if the prophecy failed it was not because *they* had not tried to bring
it to fulfillment.

If this was all simply another test of Clayton's discipleship, he rationalized the failures and still viewed Joseph Smith as the exemplar
rather than a scapegoat. Though he was caught up in the personality
of the prophet, his faith also went beyond the man himself. Trial,
sorrows, and failures were part of the process of building the Kingdom,
for the devil was also at work and he often won some battles. Clayton's
friends warned him of this before he went to Iowa, and his experiences
there proved it to him. But he had inexorable faith in the ultimate
victory of the Kingdom, and seemingly no amount of failure or disappointment could shake that.

Some may have called it stubbornness, doggedness, simple bull-
headedness, or even fanaticism. But whatever it was, for Clayton there
was no choice but to take the setbacks philosophically and go on to
the next challenge. Joseph Smith was the example, and when he was
languishing in prison in 1839 the Lord had responded to his prayers
for deliverance only by reminding him "Thou art not yet as Job!" He
also reminded the prophet of even greater tribulations to come, but
assured him that "if the heavens gather blackness, and all the elements
combine to hedge up the way, and above all, if the very jaws of hell
shall gape open the mouth wide after thee, know thou, my son, that
all these things shall give thee experience and shall be for thy good."[21]
It was exactly this philosophy that Clayton would cling to throughout
his life: no matter what the trials or disappointments, in the long run
they were for his benefit, and God would overrule all to that end.

Besides the fact that the devil was at work across the river, the
Zarahemla experience proved something else: farming was not for William Clayton. When he moved back to Nauvoo he would engage himself in more familiar pursuits: clerking, writing, recordkeeping—the
skills in which he knew he had great competence. It was a new beginning in an old direction, therefore, when Heber C. Kimball came
to him on the morning of February 10, 1842, and told him he must
report to Joseph Smith's office.[22] Willard Richards, Clayton's friend
and colleague from the British Mission, had been appointed recorder
for the Nauvoo Temple on December 13, but his workload was so
heavy that he needed an assistant. William Clayton received that assignment, which meant that he would be working regularly in the
counting room of Joseph Smith's new brick store on Water Street. In

June Willard Richards had to travel to the East, so on the twenty-ninth he turned over all the work of Joseph Smith's office to Clayton.[23] Finally, on the evening of September 3 the prophet called Clayton to him and said, "Brother Clayton, I want you to take care of the records and papers, and from this time I appoint you Temple Recorder, and when I have any revelations to write, you shall write them."[24] Nothing could be more satisfying to this well-trained clerk and scribe: he would be doing the work he was prepared for, and he would be in the constant company of Joseph Smith. Perhaps this time he had found his real home.

NOTES

1. For a general discussion of the western Illinois setting for the settlement of Nauvoo, see Robert Bruce Flanders, *Nauvoo: Kingdom on the Mississippi* (Urbana: University of Illinois Press, 1965), 13–22. Flanders's is still the best general history of Nauvoo, but see also David E. and Della S. Miller, *Nauvoo: The City of Joseph* (Santa Barbara and Salt Lake City: Peregrine Smith, 1974).

2. This excerpt is taken from the reproduction of Martha Jane Knowlton's journal entry in Dean C. Jessee, "Joseph Smith's 19 July 1840 Discourse," *BYU Studies* 19 (Spring 1979):390–94.

3. Doctrine and Covenants 29:34.

4. For the best recent full biographical assessment of Joseph Smith, see Donna Hill, *Joseph Smith: The First Mormon* (New York: Doubleday, 1977). Hill on pp. 6-10 summarizes some of the varied opinions of Joseph Smith. Hill's book provides a nice balance to Fawn M. Brodie, *No Man Knows My History: The Life of Joseph Smith*, 2d ed. (New York: Alfred A. Knopf, 1973).

5. Peter H. Burnett, *Recollections of an Old Pioneer* (New York: D. Appleton and Company, 1880), 66–67.

6. Clayton to the Saints at Manchester, 10 Dec. 1840, Clayton Papers.

7. Sidney Hook, *The Hero in History: A Study in Limitations and Possibilities* (London: Secker & Warburg, 1945), 108–9.

8. Clayton to Edward Martin, 29 Nov. 1840, in *Heart Throbs*.

9. Allen and Alexander, eds., *Manchester Mormons*, 202. A crossed out entry in the diary suggests that they suspected a member of the high council of the deed.

10. This is the traditional Mormon view of Galland, as well as the view generally accepted by scholars. A recent article by Lyndon Cook, however, presents a much more sympathetic view of Galland, and suggests that he was not the scoundrel that some writers have suggested. Cook shows that Galland was actually baptized and ordained an elder by Joseph Smith. Before long, however, he was estranged from the church, for reasons not clear. The matter

of clarifying land titles is still not fully resolved. See Lyndon W. Cook, "Isaac Galland—Mormon Benefactor," *BYU Studies* 19 (Spring 1979):261–84.

11. Doctrine and Covenants 125; *History of the Church*, 4:311. For more on the Iowa settlement and its failure, see Flanders, *Nauvoo*, passim; Andrew Jenson, *Encyclopedic History of The Church of Jesus Christ of Latter-day Saints* (Salt Lake City: Deseret News Publishing Co., 1941), 366–67, 971; "Records of Members and Minutes of the Branch Established in the Territory of Iowa 5 Oct. 1839," LDS Ward Records, Genealogical Society of the Church, microfilm.

12. The Mormon practice of baptism for the dead is based on the belief that the ordinance of baptism is necessary to salvation for everyone. Those who die without having a chance to accept the gospel in this life will hear it in the spirit world. The living, then, if authorized by proper priesthood authority, may perform baptisms by proxy for the dead. This does not automatically save the dead, but if they have lived righteous lives and then accept the teachings when they finally hear them in the world of departed spirits, the ordinance will be valid, as if they had been baptized themselves. See Doctrine and Covenants 127, 128, 138.

13. Allen and Alexander, eds., *Manchester Mormons*, 212.

14. Ibid., 200. The Haun's Mill massacre was a particularly brutal massacre of a small group of Mormons that took place on 28 Oct. 1838, as the Saints were being driven from Missouri (see James B. Allen and Glen Leonard, *The Story of the Latter-day Saints* [Salt Lake City: Deseret Book Company, 1976], 127). The revelation commanding the building of Zarahemla was originally given on 20 Mar. 1841 and is recorded in Doctrine and Covenants 25.

15. Allen and Alexander, eds., *Manchester Mormons*, 216.

16. For a comment on the extent of this epidemic, see ibid., 215–16.

17. Ibid., 215.

18. He was appointed to the high council on 24 Apr. 1841, and as clerk on 12 July (*History of the Church*, 4:352, 382).

19. Ibid., 5:336. For reading on the "law of consecration," see Leonard J. Arrington, "Early Mormon Communitarianism: The Law of Consecration and Stewardship," *Western Humanities Review* 7 (Autumn 1953):341–69; Leonard J. Arrington, *Great Basin Kingdom* (Cambridge, Mass.: Harvard University Press, 1958), chap. 1; Mario S. DePillis, "The Development of Mormon Communitarianism, 1826-1846" (Ph.D. diss., Yale University, 1960); Lyndon Cook, *Joseph Smith and the Law of Consecration* (Provo, Utah: Grandin Book Company, 1985).

20. Doctrine and Covenants 124:49.

21. Ibid., 121:10, 122:7.

22. Allen and Alexander, eds., *Manchester Mormons*, 214.

23. *History of the Church*, 5:49.

24. Journal History of The Church of Jesus Christ of Latter-day Saints, 23 Oct. 1842, Church Archives, hereafter cited as Journal History.

CHAPTER 4

William Clayton's Secular Nauvoo

Beginning early in 1842, William Clayton found himself involved in nearly every important activity of Nauvoo, but especially the private concerns of the prophet. For two and a half years, until Joseph's death in 1844, they were in each other's company almost daily. Writing letters, recording revelations, and performing important errands, Clayton became an intimate friend and confidant of the prophet. He kept the sacred "Book of the Law of the Lord," helped prepare Joseph Smith's official history (indeed, Clayton's personal journals became the source for many entries in that history), and kept various other books and accounts. He met regularly with the temple committee, was responsible for receiving tithes collected for building the temple, and kept all its construction records. In September 1842 he was appointed city treasurer, which required him to post a $1,000 bond, and on February 11, 1843, he was publicly elected to that office.[1] He also became recorder and clerk of the Nauvoo City Council, secretary *pro tem* of the Nauvoo Masonic Lodge, an officer of the Nauvoo Music Association, and a member of the committee responsible for erecting the Music Hall. He was present when the prophet announced or explained many new doctrines and practices, including plural marriage, and became a member of the secret Council of Fifty and of Joseph Smith's private prayer circle where the all-important temple ceremonies were introduced. In this unique combination of the secular and the religious, his life probably represents as well as that of anyone, other than Joseph, the totality of the Nauvoo experience.

Undeterred by the failure of Zarahemla, Clayton threw himself with a vengeance into the secular Nauvoo. At first he was probably awestruck at the thought of working in the prophet's office, especially when, on June 29, 1842, he learned he was to take it over completely.

But if he had visions of imminent, high-intensity spiritual activities, they were quickly adjusted to a down-to-earth awareness that most of Joseph Smith's daily life was concerned with the hard realities of the secular Kingdom. One of these realities was the land business, and only three days after his appointment the eager new clerk found himself riding around the city with his leader looking at lots. A week later the two of them were out on the Illinois prairie looking at more land and hoeing potatoes on Joseph Smith's farm.[2]

Joseph and William may have spent more time on real estate over the next two years than on any other single business item. Clayton was constantly looking at, showing, and selling property, meeting land agents,[3] and taking business trips for the prophet. On February 9, 1843, for example, Joseph Smith gave William a letter in which Joseph was told that a Mr. Walsh was willing to transfer to him some land that lay outside the city, upon proof that $500 had been deposited at Quincy. Three days later the prophet gave his clerk the full amount in gold and silver and sent him to Quincy. The trip took three days, in very cold weather, but Clayton deposited the funds and got the necessary receipt. Always ready to mix religion with business, he spent the evenings away from home in "interesting debate" and "pleasant conversation" on the gospel.[4]

The full extent of Joseph Smith's real estate activities may never be unravelled, but it is clear that he was one of the major land dealers in Nauvoo. This was one way to promote large-scale immigration as rapidly and orderly as possible. It also provided some personal income for the prophet, at least for a time. But equally important were the financial needs of the church, and as early as October 20, 1839, Joseph Smith became church treasurer and was given the power to set prices and sell lots. In January 1841 he was elected trustee-in-trust for the church, and soon his personal business affairs were almost inextricably mixed with those of the church.[5]

Joseph and William strongly urged new arrivals to purchase land from Nauvoo's most prominent agent—not just to help the prophet repay his heavy personal debts but also to provide funds for the work of the earthly Kingdom of God. Clayton felt deeply about this and in December 1843 said so as forcefully as he knew how in an article in the Nauvoo Neighbor:

> I feel it my duty to say . . . that there is in the hands of the trustee
> in trust, a large quantity of lands, both in the city and adjoining

townships in this county, which is for sale, some of which belongs to the church and is designed for the benefit of the poor, and also to liquidate debts owing to the church, for which the trustee is responsible. Some, also, is land which has been consecrated for the building of the Temple and the Nauvoo House.

If the brethren who move in here and want an inheritance, will buy their lands of the trustee in trust, they will thereby benefit the poor, the Temple, and the Nauvoo House, and even then only will be doing that which is their duty, and which I know, by considerable experience, will be vastly for their benefit and satisfaction in the days to come. Let all the brethren, therefore, when they move into Nauvoo, consult President Joseph Smith, the trustee in trust, and purchase their lands of him; and I am bold to say that God will bless them. . . .

We hold ourselves ready at any time to wait upon the brethren and show them the lands . . . and can be found any day, either at President Joseph Smith's bar-room, or at the Temple Recorder's office at the Temple.[6]

The economic problems facing the infant Mormon metropolis were not unlike those of other struggling frontier communities. It was difficult to obtain specie, and Joseph Smith sold too much land on credit and even at times practically donated it to the poor.[7] It was unusual for Clayton actually to receive cash, and this probably accounts for the satisfaction he seemed to feel when he wrote in his journal on July 31, 1843, that he had sold a hundred acres to Benjamin Meginess for $1,000 and that the purchaser had agreed to pay $800 cash and give a $200 note. Three days later Clayton received the down payment in specie and happily took the note for the rest.[8]

Joseph Smith's scribe was especially interested in the stream of European immigrants that poured into Nauvoo, mostly from England. When two boatloads arrived on April 12 and 13, 1843, he must have taken at least a moment to compare his own arrival a year and a half earlier with theirs. Instead of landing in New York and taking his circuitous route along rivers, canals, lakes, and over land, the new immigrants landed at New Orleans and from there took a river boat all the way to Nauvoo. The sight that greeted them was a far cry from the ramshackle community that greeted Clayton: brick homes were going up here and there, various businesses were operating, the temple was beginning to rise, and William could take any interested friends to Joseph Smith's brick store, where William worked in the second

story office. He could also take them to his own office—a small brick
building recently erected near the temple. More important, he had land
to sell, and he could, in all good conscience, take the new arrivals
around the city and its environs extolling the importance of buying
there and then, while the City of the Saints was in its growing stage.

On April 13 the immigrants were taken to the unfinished temple
where inside its slowly rising walls they were treated to a special religious service complete with choir music and a major address from
the prophet. William Clayton listened with interest as Joseph declared
that he would not address the new arrivals on doctrine but, rather, on
matters of temporal welfare. Clayton was well aware of the disparity
between rich and poor that characterized the Saints. He also knew of
Joseph Smith's not always successful efforts to sell at high prices to
the rich not only to make money but also to find means to help the
poor. Joseph's talk contained elements of all these concerns:

> I got away from my keepers in Missouri; and when I came to
> these shores, I found four or five hundred families who had been
> driven out of Missouri without houses or food; and I went to
> work to get meat and flour to feed them. The people were not
> afraid to trust me, and I went to work and bought all this region
> of country, and I cried out, "Lord, what wilt Thou have me to
> do?" And the answer was, "Build up a city and call my Saints to
> this place," and our hearts leap with joy to see you coming here.
> We have been praying for you all winter from the bottom of our
> hearts, and we are glad to see you. We are poor, and cannot do
> by you as we would; but we will do for you all we can. It is not
> expected that all of you can locate in the city. There are some
> who have money and who will build and hire others. Those who
> cannot purchase lots can go out into the country; the farmers
> want your labor. No industrious man need suffer in this land.
> The claims of the poor on us are such that we have claim on your
> good feelings, for your money to help the poor; and the church
> debts also have their demands to save the credit of the church.
> This credit has been obtained to help the poor and keep them from
> starvation, &c. Those who purchase church land and pay for it,
> this shall be their sacrifice.

Knowing that the immigrants would hear him accused of speculation
and of charging unjustly high prices, Joseph emphasized his dual role
as both entrepreneur and prophet:

Men of considerable means who were robbed of everything in the state of Missouri, are laboring in this city for a morsel of bread; and there are those who must have starved, but for the providence of God through me. We can beat all our competitors in lands, price and everything; we have the highest prices; and best lands, and do the most good with the money we get. . . . Suppose I sell you land for ten dollars an acre, and I gave three, four or five dollars per acre; then some persons may cry out, "You are speculating." Yes. I will tell how: I buy other lands and give them to the widow and the fatherless. If the speculators run against me, they run against the buckler of Jehovah. . . . I speak to you as one having authority, that you may know when it comes, and that you may have faith and know that God has sent me. . . .

Those who have money, come to me, and I will let you have lands; and those who have no money, if they will look as well as I do, I will give them advice that will do them good. I bless you in the name of Jesus Christ. Amen.[9]

The next day William Clayton and Joseph Smith rode out on the prairie with several immigrants, and about twenty acres of land were sold. Three days later Clayton thankfully began receiving hard cash from some of the immigrants, and two days after that he sold thirty acres more.

Joseph Smith was a good judge of character when he selected William Clayton to be his scribe, confidant, and land agent. But he was not always so perceptive, especially when someone played upon his natural sympathies. His predisposition toward trust and generosity created more than one disappointment for him.[10] A case in point was Joseph H. Jackson who for a time loomed as a possible successor to Clayton as the prophet's land agent. Perhaps this was one of the tests of faith so often experienced by the disciple from Penwortham, for the prophet almost replaced him with a scoundrel.

Jackson first appeared in Nauvoo in the fall of 1842 but left when someone, thinking him a Missouri spy, took a shot at him. He went to Carthage, became acquainted with several anti-Mormons, and in March returned to Nauvoo. Joseph Smith first met him on May 18, 1843, as he returned from a visit with Stephen A. Douglas in Carthage and found Jackson waiting at his home. Lying to the prophet, Jackson said that he was a Catholic priest, and two days later Joseph took him along as he rode out on the prairie with Clayton to look at land. Suddenly the prophet informed his clerk that in order to relieve him of the burden of selling lands he had appointed Jackson to take over. The new man, he said, appeared to be a "fine & noble fellow," but he was reduced in circumstances and Joseph felt disposed to hire him in order to "give him a chance in the world." For his part, Jackson promised Joseph and William that soon he would be baptized.[11]

Jackson, however, did not join the church, and before long his actions began to belie the prophet's first impression. Only three days after the ride on the prairie, Joseph had occasion to question one of his wives, Eliza Partridge, about the conduct of Jackson while Joseph was away, and he later told Clayton that "Jackson is rotten hearted." But even then the falling out was not immediate, and as late as December 29 Jackson was there when Joseph told of some of his early revelations. Jackson again declared that he was almost persuaded to unite with Joseph, to which the prophet replied: "I would that he were not only almost, but altogether." Eventually Jackson became an anti-Mormon of the worst sort, involving himself in conspiracies that led to Joseph Smith's assassination and even publishing an exposé of the church.[12] Jackson, it appeared from his own admission, had returned to Nauvoo only so he could win the prophet's confidence and then reveal to the world the "real designs and nature of his operations." He intentionally deceived the prophet, he later explained, for "the end justified the means," and in 1846 he published his exposé.[13]

Clayton was not replaced. Instead, he drew close enough to Joseph that when the prophet decided to transfer title of some of his lands in order to avoid having them taken away through lawsuits, he "appointed" Clayton to purchase some of it in his own name. William became highly protective of the prophet's land and on one occasion even stopped his Manchester friend, Arthur Smith, from cutting timber on Joseph's prairie property.[14] This did not mean that he always pleased the church leader. On January 2, 1844, for instance, he sold Willard Richards two lots for $500. For some reason, recorded but unexplained, this displeased the prophet and Clayton received a scolding. Joseph Smith, Clayton was learning, could scold, become angry, and make mistakes in judgment like any other human.

Real estate was not the only activity in which Clayton, as the prophet's scribe, participated. If Joseph Smith needed money, Clayton was sent to borrow it. On occasion he went to Carthage to pay taxes, he sometimes went on trips to obtain supplies, and he frequently spent time examining the books of various business ventures. One such venture was the little stern-wheeler, the *Maid of Iowa*, and on September 21, 1843, Joseph instructed Clayton to spend a month on this church-owned river boat regulating the books.[15] For personal reasons Clayton spent only a few days on the boat, but one of his greatest satisfactions was the fact that the prophet trusted him with such errands.

Clayton's errands also included acting as Joseph Smith's personal emissary in connection with various legal problems. A series of events from 1842 to 1844 illustrate these as well as the interesting variety of interrelated affairs he found himself involved in. They also reveal some significant personal attitudes and perceptions evolving in the mind of at least one devoted Mormon as he attempted to relate to the secular world of western Illinois.

Joseph Smith was frequently the object of arrest warrants, sometimes by Missouri officers attempting to have him extradited on various trumped-up charges, and other times on spurious Illinois charges. Often he had himself brought before the courts of the city of Nauvoo and, on writs of *habeas corpus*, released. One of Clayton's frequent tasks was to keep his leader informed of impending difficulties. On August 8, 1842, Joseph was arrested, along with Orrin P. Rockwell, for alleged complicity in the attempted murder of the former governor of Missouri, Lilburn W. Boggs. The Nauvoo municipal court quickly issued a writ of *habeas corpus*, and both Smith and Rockwell were released. The frustrated Missouri officers appealed to Governor Thomas Carlin, who had signed the arrest order, and Carlin immediately offered a reward for the apprehension of both men. Joseph went into hiding, and as he remained in seclusion over the next several weeks William Clayton was among those trusted friends who clandestinely visited him.

The record of those days reads almost like an adventure story. Joseph secretly crossed the Mississippi River to Zarahemla, and on August 11 sent word to Nauvoo that he wanted to meet a few trusted people, including his scribe, that night on an island. Sometime after dark William met Emma Smith, Hyrum Smith, William Law, Newel K. Whitney, George Miller, and Dimick Huntington near Joseph's store, then took a skiff to the island. After waiting patiently in the dark, they heard the sound of a skiff from the Iowa side, and Joseph, along with Erastus Derby, appeared. In a dramatic late-night council the small group of friends decided that the prophet should be taken up river, where he would continue to hide out. It was an emotional meeting for all of them, and five days later the prophet dictated his feelings to William Clayton in a long, tender soliloquy that captured the meaning of genuine friendship as well as anyone could. Said he, in part:

> My heart was overjoyed as I took the faithful band by the hand, that stood upon the shore, one by one . . . .
> I do not think to mention the particulars of the history of that sacred night, which shall forever be remembered by me; but the names of the faithful are what I wish to record in this place. These I have met in prosperity, and they were my friends; and now I meet them in adversity, and they are still my warmer friends. These love the God that I serve; they love the truths that I promulgate; they love those virtuous, and those holy doctrines that I cherish in my bosom with the warmest feelings of my heart, and with that zeal which cannot be denied. . . . They are my brethren, and I shall live; and because I live they shall live also.[16]

This was only one of several such clandestine visits.

It took both ingenuity and intrigue to keep Joseph's hiding place a secret. On the thirteenth Emma decided to go up river by carriage to see her husband. It soon became clear, however, that the sheriff was watching her every move. She walked to the Durphy home, therefore, leaving Clayton and Lorin Walker to take her carriage down the river, with the curtains open so everyone would know she was not there. Emma, meanwhile, eluded the sheriff, made her own way down the river, and boarded her carriage without being seen. She and her two escorts continued four miles down the river, turned out onto the prairie, drove around Nauvoo, and finally joined Joseph Smith at the home of Edward Sayers. Clayton, Emma, and Erastus Derby returned to Nauvoo the next day.

Two days later the prophet wrote his wife that he felt he must relocate, possibly in the pine country to the north, and asked her to come to him again. He also wanted William Clayton and Lorin Farr to come along and to bring "all the writings and papers, books, and histories, for we shall want a scribe in order that we may pour upon the world the truth, like the lava from Mount Vesuvius."[17] Obviously he expected to send some important teachings to the Saints from his hiding place, much like he had done while languishing in a Missouri jail in 1839, and Clayton was to be part of the process. His dependence on the scribe from Penwortham was growing.

Joseph did not go to the pine country but remained in an on-again-off-again hiding situation until December. Sometimes he felt he could return to Nauvoo with relative safety, and on August 19 he went home, under cover of night, to await the next crisis. It was not long in coming, for more Missouri officers were on their way. They kept their movements as secret as possible, but certain Mormons suspected who they were and wrote directly to Clayton, who was constantly in touch with the prophet and could deliver the warning. David S. Hollister wrote from Quincy on September 1, saying that the Missourians had two requisitions with them, one addressed to the governor of Illinois and the other addressed to the governor of Iowa. He suspected that the Iowa requisition was a ruse to throw the Mormons off guard, but he was unable to provide any certain information except that the enemy was "on the move." George Miller, writing from St. Louis on September 4, told Clayton that according to the proprietor of a St. Louis hotel, men had been there eight or ten days earlier boasting that they were on the way to Nauvoo to get Joseph Smith, alive or dead. The Hollister letter arrived on the morning of Saturday, September 3, and shortly after noon Deputy Sheriff Pitman and two other men arrived at Joseph Smith's home in Nauvoo. According to an account apparently written by William Clayton, the officers planned to arrive during the night, but somehow lost the road and became separated on the way from Quincy. Fatigued and "sore from riding," they nevertheless entered the house and found John Boynton, whom they began to question as to the prophet's whereabouts. Joseph was in another room eating dinner with his family, but Boynton, in the typical evasive fashion common among Joseph's friends, simply replied that he had seen him early that morning. The prophet, meantime, slipped out the back door, through the tall corn in his garden, and over to the home of Newel K. Whitney where he hid. At the same time Emma Smith confronted the officers, who admitted they had no search warrant but wanted to search the premises anyway. Realizing that the search would only delay them, thus giving her husband time to make good his escape, Emma graciously allowed it. Finding nothing, the Missourians left. About nine o'clock that night Joseph slipped out of the Whitney home and went to Edward Hunter's where he was warmly welcomed and where, wrote Clayton, "he can be kept safe from the hands of his enemies."[18]

Clayton was a firsthand observer of many such incidents, and they disgusted him thoroughly. Already his pen was smoldering with bitter denunciation of anyone who threatened his leader. "This is another testimony and evidence of the mean, corrupt, illegal proceedings of our enemies," he fumed, "not withstanding the Constitution of the United States" that contained guarantees against unreasonable search and seizure. "Yet these men audaciously, impudently and altogether illegally searched the house of President Joseph Smith even without any warrant or authority whatever. Being satisfied that he was not in the house, they departed. They appeared to be well armed, and no doubt intended to take him either dead or alive; which we afterwards heard they had said they would do; but the Almighty again delivered His servant from their bloodthirsty grasp."[19]

Joseph had escaped again, at least for the time being, and Clayton continued to do whatever he could to save his leader from further harassment. On September 17 he wrote a long letter to Governor Carlin "showing up," according to Joseph's history, "the Missouri persecution and my suffering in their true colors."[20] The letter is not extant, but one can imagine that it did not mince words in praising the prophet and denouncing his enemies.

That fall, with the help of the Mormon vote, Thomas Ford replaced Carlin as governor of Illinois, and on December 9 Clayton found himself one of a delegation of nine men leaving Nauvoo to visit the new chief executive in Springfield. Their task was to get Carlin's order for Joseph's arrest set aside. They arrived on the thirteenth and the next day, after consulting with Stephen A. Douglas and U.S. District Attorney Justin Butterfield, began making their plea. Ford sympathized with the prophet but was not sure of his authority to rescind the order. A few days of meetings and negotiations followed, and finally, after consultation with Douglas and six judges of the state supreme court, Ford decided on what amounted to a legal ruse as the most practical course of action. Joseph should voluntarily submit himself to arrest by a friend and come to Springfield. There the court would grant him a writ of *habeas corpus*, thus effectively forestalling the pending arrest by Missouri constables. Actually, three judges were ready to dismiss the case without a hearing, but the other three, together with Ford and Douglas, thought the *habeas corpus* procedure was the best way to assure the prophet's continuing freedom.

The plot had all the elements of a political intrigue, and Clayton understood its implications. He was impressed by Douglas's argument that since it had been said that Joseph had defied the laws of Illinois, this would be the surest way of satisfying the public mind and at the same time securing the governor from public censure. Clayton also recognized the obvious self-interest in the governor's actions, and his comment seemed reminiscent of Joseph Smith's denunciation of President Martin Van Buren, who had refused to intervene in behalf of the Mormons in Missouri for fear he should lose that state's vote. Ford, wrote Clayton, "appears to have the best of feelings towards Joseph but is unwilling as stated above to interfere *lest he should lose the confidence of his political friends.*"[21] But Clayton liked the plan, though he still feared the possibility that treachery somewhere along the line would result in Joseph being sent to Missouri. At this point the prophet's Masonic association seemed to pay political dividends, for Douglas assured Clayton that as a Mason, he believed there was not a particle of doubt that Joseph would be released immediately. The governor, Douglas said, had promised Joseph protection on his way to Springfield, and Douglas promised to see Ford personally and request a written authority for safe conduct.

On the seventeenth, at Clayton's request, the governor wrote a letter to Joseph explaining the plan. Butterfield did the same thing, and, armed with both documents, the delegation left for Nauvoo immediately. When the plan was presented to the prophet, he was delighted.

The scheme went off like clockwork. On the day after Christmas, Wilson Law arrested Joseph Smith, and Clayton was sent to Carthage to obtain a writ of *habeas corpus* to take Joseph before the Springfield court. The next day Clayton was with the prophet and his group as they started for Springfield to carry out the plan. The hearing began on January 4, and on January 6 William was among those who testified that on the day the attempt was made on Boggs's life Joseph was, indeed, in Illinois and not in Missouri. The trial concluded the same day according to the planned results, and that evening Clayton wrote gratefully in his journal: "We feel to thank the great God for thus delivering his servant from the power of the wicked and designing men."[22]

The first trip to Springfield, early in December, had another purpose, and one that was not completely fulfilled. Joseph Smith was chafing under the burden of heavy debt, much of which was a result of the church's financial crisis in Kirtland a few years earlier. Among other things, he had taken upon himself the obligation of paying certain debts even though they had been incurred for the benefit of the church. His financial situation in Nauvoo, moreover, was precarious partly because of his own initial land purchases and partly because he was so generous in granting credit to others. Joseph and other church leaders simply did not have enough cash flow to meet all the demands being placed upon them in 1842. The prophet had no intention of defaulting, but the pressures became so great that he finally decided to take advantage of the new Bankruptcy Act of 1841 and file for discharge, still planning to make full payment of all his debts when he was able.

At first Justin Butterfield opposed such action, partly because of Joseph's responsibilities as trustee-in-trust for the church. Shortly after Joseph's delegation arrived in Springfield, however, Hyrum Smith was actually discharged in bankruptcy and Butterfield himself consented to an "arrangement" whereby Joseph also could be discharged. So confident was William Clayton of the outcome that he wrote in his diary on his way home that "there is now nothing to prevent pres. Joseph [sic] discharge in Bankruptcy."[23] When Joseph later went to Springfield for the extradition proceedings, Butterfield represented him before the court and was apparently so impressed with the prophet's integrity that he became a permanent friend. Unfortunately, the bankruptcy issue was not settled before Joseph Smith was murdered.

William Clayton's journal entry for New Year's Day, 1843 (during the trip to Springfield), provides modern Mormons with one of their most oft-quoted statements from Joseph Smith. It also demonstrates Clayton's concern with recording the spiritual as well as the temporal as he made daily notes on what he saw and heard. As recorded by Clayton:

This A.M. we had a pleasant interview with Mr. Butterfield, Judge Douglas, Senator Gillespie & others. pres. Joseph stated to Mr. Butterfield the prominent points of difference in sentiment between the Latter Day Saints & sectarian viz: the latter are all circumscribed by some peculiar creed which deprives its members of the right of believing anything not contained in it; whereas the Latter Day Saints have no creed, but are ready to believe *all true principle* existing, as they are made manifest from time to time. He said further, that if any person should ask him if he was a prophet he should not deny it. As to deny it would give him the lie & then shewed from the Revelations of John that any man who has the testimony of Jesus has the spirit of prophesy &c.[24]

Four months of running and hiding while still attempting to conduct church and community business were wearing on the prophet as well as discouraging for his friends in Nauvoo. Shortly after his return to the city a day of fasting and thanksgiving was held, and on January 18 a group of close friends was invited to the Smith home for a grand dinner party. The list of guests included Lucy Mack Smith (Joseph's mother), Hyrum Smith, Brigham Young, Willard Richards, John Taylor, Orson Hyde, Wilford Woodruff, George A. Smith, Heber C. Kimball, the wives of these men, Eliza R. Snow, several other prominent citizens, and, of course, William and Ruth Clayton. The festivities began with the singing of two jubilee hymns written especially for the occasion, one by Wilson Law and Richards and the other by Snow. Joseph Smith distributed cards with the hymns printed on them. The conversation centered around the deliverance and at 2 P.M. the prophet and Emma began to serve dinner. It took four shifts, for their dinner table could not hold all the guests at once, and the Smiths had their own meal only with the last shift. The party broke up at 6 P.M. Wrote Clayton, "Truly it was a time of Jubilee; all hearts rejoiced."[25] But all the celebration must have been too much for his constitution, for he went home feeling ill and could not even attend the Masonic lodge meeting that evening, as Joseph did.

Clayton soon realized that Joseph's delivery was only a temporary reprieve. On the night of June 18, 1843, he was visiting at the home of a Sister Booth, along with Ruth and her sister, Margaret (who had only recently become his first plural wife). Suddenly William F. Cahoon rushed in, telling Clayton that Hyrum Smith wanted to see him at the temple immediately. Another writ was out for Joseph's arrest, but he was away with his wife and family, visiting Emma's sister, Elizabeth Wasson, who lived near Dixon. Clayton rushed to the temple where Hyrum met him and asked him to ride to Dixon immediately to warn Joseph. Clayton borrowed $120 for the trip, persuaded Stephen Markham to go with him, and rode swiftly out of town at midnight on Joseph Smith's favorite horse, Joe Duncan. The two riders covered the 190 miles in sixty-four hours, with very little rest along the way. It is not surprising that Joe Duncan was so jaded at the end of the trip that he could not be ridden for several days.[26]

Clayton and Markham found Joseph and Emma about halfway between Dixon and the Wasson home and delivered their message. They need not be alarmed, the prophet assured them, for his enemies could not hurt him. Nevertheless he prudently kept out of sight all day on June 22, even though he had agreed to preach at Dixon and many people turned out to hear him.[27] Clayton told Joseph that Hyrum wanted him to return home immediately, but Joseph thought it better to remain there a few days and see what happened.

The seemingly inevitable happened quickly. Already Joseph H. Reynolds, the sheriff from Jackson County, Missouri, and Constable Harmon T. Wilson of Carthage were in the area. They were disguised, however, passing themselves off as Mormon elders. On Friday morning, June 23, Clayton went into Dixon to find out what was happening. He must have been chagrined when he later discovered that he actually passed Reynolds and Wilson along the way without recognizing them. Perhaps he could have saved the prophet from arrest. But the two officers knew where Joseph was, for they had been told by his friends at Dixon who thought they were Mormons. They arrived at the Wasson home early in the afternoon, took Joseph by surprise, and after considerable abusive language and harsh treatment arrested him and tried to hurry him off to Missouri before anything could complicate their plans.

Clayton heard of the arrest from Markham and quickly began making arrangements for another writ of *habeas corpus*. Eventually, after a long series of complicated maneuvers, several writs were issued, and Joseph's captors were themselves arrested for using violence against him. In an almost comic-opera turn of events they were ultimately forced to take him to Nauvoo for a *habeas corpus* hearing where, of course, there was no question that Joseph would be released.

Clayton, meantime, set out to inform Hyrum and the others. He took a carriage to Rock Island and then a river boat to Nauvoo where he arrived on Sunday, June 25. As soon as they received the message, Hyrum Smith and Wilson Law called for volunteers to "rescue" the prophet. Some 300 men volunteered, and out of these around 120 were selected to go in two companies. One group boarded the *Maid of Iowa*, planning to stop any river boats in case Reynolds and Wilson had taken the prophet that way, and the other rode horseback toward Dixon.

No rescue mission was needed, however, and on June 30, leading his captors, Joseph made a dramatic, triumphal entry into Nauvoo. The poignancy of the day, especially as described by William Clayton, demonstrated the irresistible influence that was Joseph Smith's in the City of the Saints. Joseph himself sent a messenger ahead, who told his friends that his party would arrive about noon and that he wanted the band and as many citizens as possible to meet them. About 11 A.M. the band marched to the edge of town, followed by Hyrum and Emma Smith on horseback and a train of carriages a half-mile long carrying other prominent citizens. Clayton was there in a buggy, and about a mile and a half east of the temple they met Joseph Smith and his party, which included several men on horseback who had gone out on the rescue mission. As soon as they saw Joseph the people of Nauvoo began to cheer, whereupon Joseph left his buggy, mounted a horse, called for his wife and his brother and, holding hands, the three "wept tears of joy."

The band struck up "Hail Columbia" and the whole procession—horses, carriages, and crowds on foot falling in behind—marched slowly into the city. There the streets were lined with people on both sides, and with crowds cheering, guns firing, and cannons roaring, Joseph made his way to his home where an even greater crowd was waiting. There also he met his sixty-six-year-old mother, and, in describing the reunion, Clayton could not refrain from adding his own emotional editorializing to the scene. Joseph, he wrote, "repaired to her & with the welling tears rolling down his cheek kissed the parent who had so often been compelled to sorrow & suffer feelings of the most exquisite anguish to see her offspring hunted from place to place for his religious sake. Tears of joy bedewed her aged cheeks whilst she once more held him in clasped in her arms." His children also crowded around, and seven-year-old Fred exclaimed, "Pa, the Missourians won't take you away again, will they?" (Just a year earlier the same little Fred had amused the whole family by telling of a dream in which he saw that "the Missourians had got their heads knocked off.") The whole scene ended with Joseph introducing his friends to the people from out of town, who were astonished at the enthusiasm of the greeting, and the crowd dispersed only after he promised to address them at the temple at 4 P.M.[28]

There was another element in this story that only Clayton and a very few other confidants of Joseph Smith were privy to. As he became

deeply involved in the life of the prophet, William had frequent opportunity to observe and reflect upon the personal relations between
Joseph and Emma. It was no easy thing for Emma to be the wife of
a man who was so constantly in demand, by both friends and enemies,
and who was also teaching things she did not like. On occasion the
strain became obvious. The introduction of plural marriage was her
most difficult trial, and it was undoubtedly this issue that caused Joseph
Smith to discuss some "delicate matters" with William during that
eventful trip to Dixon. Clayton had taken his own first plural wife
less than two months earlier, had recently performed the plural marriage between Joseph Smith and Lucy Walker, and was even then allowing another of Joseph's plural wives, Desdemona Fullmer, to board
at his home.[29] It is understandable that Emma resented Clayton at this
point, and this seems to be the only explanation for Joseph confiding
in his friend not only that Emma wanted somehow to "lay a snare"
for Clayton, but also that she had treated Joseph himself coldly since
William arrived at Dixon.[30] Thus it was a particular pleasure, seven
days later, for Clayton to see the tender evidence of reconciliation as
Joseph and Emma embraced each other upon Joseph's triumphal return
to Nauvoo. "Such a feeling I never before witnessed when the Prest.
took hold of the hand of his partner in sorrow & persecution. Surely
it would have moved anything but the heart of an adamantine."

Joseph went in the house to have dinner and, ironically, among the
guests were Sheriff Reynolds and Constable Wilson. William Clayton
could not resist a comment, worth noting here because it shows so
well his disgust for anyone who abused his idol. He seemed seldom
to miss an opportunity, either in Nauvoo or later, to use whatever
descriptive talent he had to both sing the prophet's praises and damn
his enemies. "Wilson & the Sheriff were very kindly invited to sit at
table with the family & friends," he wrote in his journal, "& partook
of the kind hospitality of him whom they had so lately insulted and
abused in the most shameful manner. What a contrast between the
treatment they met with & that which they had used toward J[oseph]
while he was there prisoner. It was very evident that they were in some
measure conscious of the magnitude of their baseness & maltreat-
ment."

Reynolds and Wilson left Nauvoo, but they did not abandon efforts
to capture the prophet and return him to Missouri. In the meantime
Joseph entered his own suit against them, for illegal imprisonment and

abuse, and in May 1844 it was the ever-present William Clayton, along with Stephen Markham, who went to Dixon to see the matter through the courts. It proved to be an interesting two-week trip, and one that illustrates the diversity that could fill a short period in the life of a friend and employee of Joseph Smith.

On Thursday, May 2, Clayton spent the morning preparing to board the *Maid of Iowa*, but he was interrupted by the need to take care of several business items for the prophet. He had to rush to be at the dock by twelve minutes to ten, when the little river boat departed upstream. Joseph and Emma were there to say goodbye.

By Friday night the *Maid* was steaming up the Rock River, but on Saturday night it was stopped by rapids about twelve miles below Dixon. The next morning Clayton and Markham decided to finish the trip on foot—the wisdom of which was confirmed by their discovery that another steamer was stuck in the rapids a little ways above them. They arrived in Dixon about mid-morning and, to their surprise, found that the people of Dixon were not as friendly as expected. The reason, Clayton speculated, was that the Mormons were supporting Joseph Smith rather than Martin Van Buren for the presidency of the United States.

A second purpose of the trip to Dixon was to buy corn, and on Monday, after determining that the court would not bring up Joseph Smith's case that day, Clayton bought nearly 300 bushels and helped load it on a flatboat they had rented for $2.

Clayton spent the next two days waiting impatiently in the Dixon courtroom. "I want to be away from this place," he wrote on May 8, "for I do not like their spirit, and I feel very uneasy about my family." When the case was finally called up and a jury impanelled on May 9, Clayton expressed dismay, for he believed that about half the prospective jurors had to be dismissed because of their prejudices. "Even some that did sit acknowledged that they were much prejudiced," he wrote. "What a disgrace to a town to think that men will let their prejudice run so high against a man from rumor and report that they cannot do him justice." Clearly William's own prejudices tinted his view of the Dixonites, and one can imagine the fervor with which he defended both Joseph and the faith in a discussion that took place that evening. "We had a very interesting debate with two gentlemen on our religion," he said, "wherein truth appeared doubly beautiful and error equally ridiculous."[31]

Witnesses were examined all afternoon, and by 6 P.M. the trial was over and the jury given its charge. The next morning the verdict came, and, much to Clayton's delight, the jury had decided in favor of Joseph Smith. The prophet was awarded $40 damages, and court costs were assessed against Reynolds and Wilson. But Clayton was still unimpressed with the people of Dixon. "We were credibly informed," he recorded, "that the jury quarrelled very hard almost to a fight and did not agree on their verdict until after sunrise this morning. We were glad to see truth and virtue again triumph over tyranny and oppression & equally disgusted to witness the effects of prejudice in the jury Box. We filed our bills of costs hired a team to take us to the boat and at 10 we left Dixon, and felt truly glad to be released from such superstitious prejudice and corrupt hypocrisy."[32]

About eighteen miles downstream they boarded the *Maid of Iowa*. The next day, Saturday, they took on 280 sacks of wheat. About midafternoon the boat became hung up on the rapids. Sunday morning they were still stuck and sent for a flatboat onto which they began to unload their cargo. Finally, about 3 P.M., the steamer floated, but only at the cost of a near-tragedy. Three men in a small skiff were attempting to help them weigh anchor, and as the boat began to float the skiff capsized. Fortunately the rocks prevented it from sinking completely, and two of the men were eventually able to row it to shore. The other clung to the anchor cable and got himself aboard the steamer. They finally got the anchor up and floated downriver to a place where they could reload the cargo and continued on their way. The rest of the trip was uneventful, and at 5:30 in the afternoon of May 13 Clayton arrived in Nauvoo and reported his success to the president of the church.[33]

As important as Joseph Smith's legal affairs were, Clayton had much more to do, and sometimes found himself both overloaded and overwhelmed. He spent much of Christmas Day, 1842, for example, working with Willard Richards on Joseph Smith's history and then went home that night and continued working. All the next morning was spent on the same task, interrupted only by the need to make preparations to go to Springfield with the prophet. He was constantly writing letters for Joseph, sometimes wrote articles for the *Nauvoo Neighbor*, and was frequently appointed to take minutes at conference and other church meetings. He also, at times, assisted other church leaders with their writing, and helped Heber C. Kimball arrange his history.[34]

Generally uncomplaining at the mountainous burden he always carried, on occasion he could not help but display at least a note of dismay in his diary. On July 7, 1843, he had arranged to give a supper for the band, but suddenly Hyrum Smith had work for him to do. "Hyrum wants me to write," he wrote, "& seems to care nothing for any disappointment." Loyal workhorse that he was, Clayton took the assignment and simply asked the band to see that his share of the meal was taken to his home where he was working. His feelings about such demands would not be made public—he was much too concerned about his image as a loyal disciple for that. But he would be less than human if he had not harbored at least some note of resentment when such demands were made of him. In this case he had a slight reprieve for in the evening the band came to his home anyway, and they enjoyed themselves until midnight. Clayton then stayed up until 2 A.M. writing for Hyrum, and spent all the next day, until 7 P.M., finishing the job. It is not surprising that he was "considerable unwell" that day.

Joseph Smith was not so aloof from the world that he did not appreciate the role of practical politics in promoting the interests of the Kingdom. He was deeply involved in political affairs, though he usually made it clear that his political views were not to be considered principles of the faith or binding on his followers. But he also made it clear that he would use whatever political influence he could muster if it would further the interests of his cause. As he told a group of temple workers in February 1843: "It is our duty to concentrate all our influence to make popular that which is sound and good, and unpopular that which is unsound. 'Tis right, politically, for a man who has influence to use it as well as for a man who has no influence to use his. From henceforth I will maintain all the influence I can get."[35] His influence in western Illinois, of course, was sometimes pivotal, for the Mormons were generally willing to follow his political lead and their block voting could swing important elections. He used that influence to help formulate and promote the important city charter that made Nauvoo practically independent of the state.[36] He was not reluctant to let people know where he stood on issues or with respect to candidates, he openly threw his support to candidates friendly to his causes, and he had much to say about national issues. He was elected to the first Nauvoo City Council, and in 1843 he was elected mayor. His was

the major policymaking voice in the political life of the Mormon community in Illinois.[37]

One of the most interesting examples of Joseph Smith's political
influence occurred during the Congressional election of 1843. The Mormons generally voted Democratic, but Cyrus Walker, the Whig, and
Joseph P. Hoge, the Democrat, both found encouraging support among
influential people in Nauvoo. Hyrum Smith, Joseph's brother as well
as his "assistant president" and also patriarch to the church, was in
Hoge's camp, while William Law, a counselor to Joseph Smith, was
in Walker's. Walker was especially encouraged, for it was soon made
public that Joseph Smith had also promised him his vote.

Did the prophet's example mean that all the Saints were supposed
to vote for the Whig, even though most of them still felt the Democrats
more deserving of their support? "I never tell any man how to vote
or who to vote for,"[38] Joseph had said during an Independence Day
address, but just five days before the August election he found a unique
way to throw the election to Hoge while still keeping his promise to
Walker. Hyrum was campaigning publicly for Hoge and even declared
that it was the will of Heaven that the Saints should vote for him.
William Law angrily challenged Hyrum's right to make such a statement, saying that Joseph Smith would never sanction it. The next day,
Sunday, the prophet got out of a sickbed to preach to the Saints on
politics, though he told them, "The Lord has not given me a revelation
concerning politics. I have not asked him for one." He spoke glowingly
of Cyrus Walker, affirming his promise to vote for him in return for
Walker's past friendship and legal favors. But, he told his listeners,
this was "not for electioneering purposes." Some may have considered
this a classic tongue-in-cheek statement, however, when they heard
him also say that Walker had withdrawn "all claim to your vote and
influence if it would be detrimental to your interests as a people," then
followed with what amounted to a political bombshell: "Brother Hyrum tells me this morning that he has had a testimony to the effect it
would be better for the people to vote for Hoge; and I never knew
Hyrum to say he ever had a revelation and it failed. Let God speak
and all men hold their peace."[39] Did this mean that God really wanted
Hoge to win? William Clayton apparently thought so, for he wrote in
his diary that Joseph "stated that Hyrum had had a manifestation that
it was for our interest to vote for Hoge."[40] Clayton and, apparently,
most other Illinois Mormons were reading the obvious into what the

prophet said: he was going to keep his promise to Walker, but it was in their interests as a people to vote the other way. The Mormons swung to Hoge, and their vote decided the election in his favor.

Joseph Smith's decision to run for president grew, at least in part, from his disillusionment with the national government for its lack of action in behalf of the Mormons. His visit to Washington in 1840, in an attempt to get President Van Buren or Congress to intercede in Missouri in behalf of the Mormons, ended in total failure. On the way home, his history records, "I did not fail to proclaim the iniquity and insolence of Martin Van Buren toward myself and an injured people which will have its effect upon the public mind; and may he never be elected again to any office of trust or power, by which he may abuse the innocent and let the guilty go free."[41]

Joseph Smith continued to denounce Van Buren, becoming especially critical in his presidential campaign statement four years later. William Clayton and other disciples followed his lead—Van Buren and those like him were, in their minds, violating every principle of political and human decency by not using federal power to intervene in Missouri, protect the Mormons against mobs, and force redress for their losses. In December 1843 Joseph Smith went so far as to prophesy, "In the name of the Lord Jesus Christ, that, if Congress will not hear our petition and grant us protection they shall be broken up as a government."[42] Joseph probably had reference to whoever was in power (which was actually the Whig party in the Senate and the Democratic party in the House) rather than the national government as an institution, but statements like this affected disciples like Clayton deeply. Clayton never had a good word to say for the government of the United States as a whole—he always saw it as corrupt, an enemy of the Kingdom, and about to be overthrown because of its failure to help the Saints.

Actually, Joseph Smith and his followers were probably too hard on Martin Van Buren and other government officials who were there when Joseph was lobbying in Washington. Practically all of them, including such leading figures as John C. Calhoun and Henry Clay, treated him with courtesy, expressed sympathy for the Mormons in their time of tragedy, but, like the president, declared that it was not within the power of the national government to act. The issue was states' rights—and whether the government had the Constitutional authority to intervene within the boundaries of the states. It was generally agreed that the government could not, and the volatile slavery issue made it foolhardy for any politician with national aspirations to suggest that the federal government could for any reason violate state boundaries. It had caused a near civil war in 1832 when Andrew Jackson declared South Carolina in rebellion and threatened to send troops into the state because of its nullification of a federal tariff law. But not even this excuse could be used in the 1840s, for Missouri was hardly in a state of rebellion against the nation. The Constitution, furthermore, nowhere authorized either the president or Congress to intervene for any reason. On the contrary, it specified that the national government was to act against domestic violence only on the application of the legislature or governor of the affected state (Article IV, Section 4). It was both politically and constitutionally impossible at the time to do what the Mormons were asking.

Joseph Smith, however, had different ideas and was, in some respects, anticipating the Fourteenth Amendment. In modern times that amendment has been used to justify exactly what he was calling for—federal intervention in the states to protect the civil rights of citizens. States' rights, Joseph bitterly declared in November 1843, fed mobs. Such doctrines, he fumed, "are a dead carcass—a stink, and they shall ascend up as a stink offering in the nose of the Almighty."[43] Six weeks earlier he had made it clear what he really wanted in the Constitution. This great document had only one fault—it was not "broad enough to cover the whole ground." It did not contain the means for punishing governmental officers who refused to "protect the people in their religious rights, or punish those mobs, states, or communities who interfere with the rights of the people on account of their religion." The answer was to provide that "every officer of the Government who should neglect or refuse to extend the protection guaranteed in the Constitution should be subject to capital punishment; and then the president of the United States would not say, 'Your cause is just but I can do nothing for you.' "[44] He wanted nothing less than a powerful anti-states'-rights amendment, and in his 1844 presidential platform statement he called upon the people "to repeal and impugn that relic of folly, which makes it necessary for the governor of a state to make the demand of the president for troops, in cases of invasion or rebellion. The governor himself may be a mobber."[45] Clearly the Missouri difficulties and their political aftermath were at the heart of Joseph Smith's views on the power of the national government.

There is no evidence that William Clayton involved himself in these issues of practical political philosophy. After all, he could not even vote, for he was not yet a citizen of the United States, and it does not appear that he took the time to study such Constitutional questions for himself. Nevertheless, Joseph Smith's frequent rehearsals of the failures of the national government planted seeds of mistrust in his malleable mind, and every refusal in Washington to support the Mormons nurtured the antipathy that had been sown there by his most trusted mentor. Clayton was convinced that the American government's days were numbered, but in the meantime it seemed only right that God's prophet should put himself up as a candidate for the American presidency. Who else, after all, could the Mormons themselves support?

By late 1843 Joseph and his closest associates were seriously considering whom they would support for president in the 1844 campaign. On November 2 William Clayton was in a meeting attended also by Joseph and Hyrum Smith, Brigham Young, Heber Kimball, Willard Richards, John Taylor, and William Law—all prominent church leaders. They agreed that letters should be written to five of the leading candidates, inquiring what their course of action would be toward the Mormons and their problems if any of them were elected. Two days later the letters were written, signed by Joseph in behalf of the church, and sent to John C. Calhoun, Henry Clay, Lewis Cass, Richard M. Johnson, and Martin Van Buren. Only two replied: Calhoun and Clay, and their letters were so unsatisfactory that Joseph Smith responded with long, angry replies to each of them.[46]

On January 12, 1844, the Quorum of the Twelve decided to press Joseph Smith's candidacy, and on the same day he began working with William W. Phelps on his political statement. He may not have seriously believed he could win a national election, but he was serious about putting his views before the nation as positively as possible. The document was broad in its application, hardly mentioning the Mormons but paying specific attention to many of the national issues that were sure to find their place in election year politics: particularly reform, slavery, and expansionism. As the campaign got underway hundreds of Mormon elders, including most of the top church leaders, were sent throughout the United States not only to spread the gospel but also to spread Joseph Smith's political platform.

William Clayton was delighted and was even told by Joseph Smith on January 29 that he would be sent on a political mission. A little over a week earlier the non-Mormon sheriff, Jacob Backenstos, had agreed to support the prophet's candidacy, and Clayton apparently thought this was a hopeful sign. Four months later, however, he found the non-Mormons in Dixon ridiculing the Saints for their support of Joseph rather than Van Buren. Clayton was eager to see his leader go all the way to the White House, but the ambitious campaign would come to a tragic and sudden halt on June 27 with the prophet's murder at Carthage.

Meantime, Clayton also had his personal temporal concerns, one of which was building a home for his family. He obtained a lot in the first tract of land Joseph Smith had purchased, the Hugh White farm, thus settling in the lowlands of Nauvoo rather than on the hill. He followed to the letter the prophet's admonitions as to where the Saints should buy land.[47] Clayton's property was on the southwest corner of the block, where Durphy and Hotchkiss streets intersected. Each block was four acres square, and looking about four blocks to the north Clayton could watch the imposing Nauvoo temple slowly rising. To get to Joseph Smith's home or store he must walk five blocks south to Water Street, then three blocks west.

Clayton began erecting a fine brick home—the only brick home, in fact, on the block. Early in November 1842 he hired masons to begin laying the brick, and on April 28, 1843, they finished. It took another month for the carpenters to complete their work, and on May 28 Clayton could write in his journal, "We are occupying our new house for which I feel very thankful." He still had to haul water until the well was finished in September. The house apparently cost Clayton about $500 cash to build. Little did he imagine that the family would remain in the home for less than three years.[48]

Clayton did not keep himself so busy that he could not enjoy the social and cultural life of Nauvoo. For one thing he was, like Joseph Smith, a member of the Nauvoo Masonic Lodge, and this organization provided fraternal association as well as some important social outlets. He also enjoyed pleasure cruises aboard the *Maid of Iowa*, which could carry up to 200 noncabin passengers on its deck. But Clayton's interests were broader than that. It would be unthinkable for him to give up playing his beloved violin, and he frequently played with a small band for both public and private performances. He promoted the arts as much as he could and found himself acting as a trustee of the Nauvoo Music Association, as a member of the committee responsible for building a music hall in the city, and as a member of the choir committee. He took the choir seriously and in the early months of 1843 was a regular attender at singing school. He also went to hear visiting lecturers and attended theater performances in Nauvoo as well as in Springfield when he was there on business. When he went to St. Louis in September 1843, he even attended the circus. It would never be said that this single-minded Mormon disciple could not enjoy the finer things of the world in the same way that his exemplar, Joseph Smith, also enjoyed them. Maybe he enjoyed them even more, for there is no record that Joseph Smith ever played a musical instrument, took singing lessons, or joined a choir. On the other hand, William Clayton was never a wrestler or a stick-puller as was his athletic leader. The clerk from Penwortham preferred cultural activities that were slightly more passive. Both men, however, enjoyed dancing, dinner parties, and good visiting, all of which helped make up the social side of William Clayton's Nauvoo.

These, then, were some of William Clayton's secular concerns as he found himself building the Kingdom of God alongside Joseph the prophet. The clerk from Penwortham may have functioned in more public and semipublic capacities than almost any other person in Nauvoo. The spiritual Kingdom was very much in, if not of, the secular world, and Clayton found most of his time taken up with worldly affairs.

NOTES

1. The bond, dated 26 Sept. 1842, is in the Clayton Papers. Clayton's salary amounted to 2 percent of all he collected (see William Clayton, "An Interesting Journal," *Juvenile Instructor* 21 [1886], 86; and Dahl, *William Clayton,* 44, citing *The Wasp,* 20 Jan. 1843).

2. *History of the Church,* 5:49, 52, 58.

3. On Saturday, 21 Jan. 1843, for example, Clayton went with the prophet to sell a lot to E. J. Sabin, and a week later Joseph escorted a land agent from New York around the city and then took him into the office to continue discussing land with Clayton. See William Clayton Journals, 3 vols., Nov. 1842 to Jan. 1846, 21, 28 Jan. 1843 (in private custody and used here with special permission), hereafter cited as Clayton, Nauvoo Journal; *History of the Church,* 5:260. Evidently the land agent, a Mr. Taylor, was clerk of a New York–based

agency called the Illinois Land Agency. Clayton's diary gives the name of the agency while the *History of the Church* says he was from New York. It is interesting that on 21 January Joseph Smith did not mention that Clayton was riding around looking at property with him but did observe that Orson Hyde, an apostle, was looking at lots in the city with him.

4. Clayton, Nauvoo Journal, 9, 12-15 Feb. 1843; *History of the Church,* 5:273.

5. The work became so heavy that on occasion he attempted to have himself relieved officially from his work as land agent but without success. See Flanders, *Nauvoo,* chap. 5, for an in-depth discussion of the land business in Nauvoo.

6. *Nauvoo Neighbor,* 20 Dec. 1843, as quoted in ibid., 124.

7. Flanders, *Nauvoo,* 126.

8. See also *History of the Church,* 5:523, 525. Comparing the entries in Clayton's journal with the *History of the Church* provides an interesting insight into the way the *History* was compiled. It is obvious that Clayton was the source for this part. But in the *History of the Church* Clayton is not mentioned at all—on either date—and Joseph Smith is portrayed as the one selling the property and receiving the money. Clayton, of course, was always acting as Joseph's agent, and it appears as if whoever compiled this portion of the *History of the Church* was simply trying to give the prophet credit for doing as much as possible. This is also an example of the way Clayton was frequently subordinated—his activities overshadowed or ignored. But the fact that he was one of those who worked on compiling the *History of the Church* may be evidence that he willingly took the subordination without complaint. (See Chapter 5 herein for a short discussion of the nature of the *History of the Church* and Clayton's role in it.)

9. Ibid., 354–57.

10. Mormon historian B. H. Roberts made some interesting comments on the limitations of Joseph Smith, which included "a disposition to be over persuaded by men . . .; the dangerous weakness of too readily accepting men at their own valuation; a too implicit trust in their protestations of repentance when overtaken in their sins; a too great tenacity in friendship for men he had once taken into his confidence after they had been proven unworthy of the friendship . . .; and, perhaps, a too fierce disposition to give way to reckless denunciation when once he really broke the ties of friendship—his anger was terrible, all agree upon that." B. H. Roberts, *A Comprehensive History of The Church of Jesus Christ of Latter-day Saints* (Salt Lake City: Deseret News Press, 1930), 6:358.

11. Clayton, Nauvoo Journal, 20 May 1843; *History of the Church,* 5:394, 400. This is another place where the account in the *History of the Church* is apparently based on Clayton.

12. Clayton, Nauvoo Journal, 23 May 1843; *History of the Church,* 6:149, 272, 278–80, and other indexed entries regarding Jackson.

13. See Joseph H. Jackson, *The Adventures and Experiences of Joseph H. Jackson: Disclosing the Depths of Mormon Villainy Practiced in Nauvoo* (Warsaw, Ill.: Printed for the publisher, 1846), introduction. Note that there

are some discrepancies between the Jackson account and the Smith account of what happened between the two of them. Jackson says he presented himself to Joseph as a fugitive from Macon, Ga., and offered to be of great service to him by freeing Porter Rockwell from jail in Missouri.

14. Clayton, Nauvoo Journal, 10 Oct., 23 Nov. 1843.

15. Actually the *Maid of Iowa* was owned half by Joseph Smith and half by Dan Jones, its captain. Jones and another man built her before Jones became a Mormon. After joining the church, Jones sold half interest in the boat to Joseph, and in early 1844 Joseph purchased the remaining interest, likely in anticipation of sending Jones on a mission to his native Wales. It appears, however, that Joseph considered this to be one of the ventures he entered into in behalf of the church, for Clayton notes in May 1844 that he was preparing the papers for the transfer of the boat to the trustee-in-trust. Ibid., 1 May 1844. See also Donald L. Enders, "The Steamboat *Maid of Iowa*: Mormon Mistress of the Mississippi," *BYU Studies* 19 (Spring 1979):321–35.

16. *History of the Church*, 5:108–9; Dean C. Jessee, ed., *The Personal Writings of Joseph Smith* (Salt Lake City: Deseret Book Co., 1984), 530-37. Joseph Smith began the long dictation on 16 August and continued it on 23 August, though he never did finish all he intended to say.

17. *History of the Church*, 5:104.

18. George Miller to Clayton, 4 Sept. 1841, and D. S. Hollister to Clayton, 1 Sept. 1841, Clayton Papers; *History of the Church*, 5:145–46. The *History of the Church* does not specifically state that the account quoted here is by William Clayton, but it does indicate that it was written by "the Prophet's secretary." The evidence that leads me to conclude that this was Clayton is that (1) the first part of the account reflects specifically the idea Clayton received in the Hollister letter; (2) Clayton was, at this point, Joseph Smith's scribe; and (3) the language of the account, especially where it denounces the Missourians, is much like what Clayton uses in other places. The same heated tone is evident in many of his statements about the prophet's detractors.

19. *History of the Church*, 5:145.

20. Ibid., 164.

21. Ibid., 4:80; Clayton, Nauvoo Journal, 17 Dec. 1842. The underlining is in the original.

22. Clayton, Nauvoo Journal, 6 Jan. 1843. Clayton summarized the Springfield trip in his "History of the Nauvoo Temple," 24-29. This history is in the Church Archives under the title "Wm Clayton's Journal, etc." It is not really a journal, but actually Clayton's handwritten history of the temple. In order to avoid confusion, it is cited hereafter as "History of the Nauvoo Temple." It was later edited and serially published as "An Interesting Journal" in the *Juvenile Instructor* 21(1866). The information above was not included in the published version.

23. Clayton, Nauvoo Journal, 19 Dec. 1842. For a full account of Joseph Smith's bankruptcy proceedings, see Dallin H. Oaks and Joseph I. Bentley, "Joseph Smith and the Legal Process: In the Wake of the Steamboat Nauvoo,"

Brigham Young University Law Review (1976):735–82, revised and reprinted in *BYU Studies* 19 (Winter 1979):167–99.

24. Clayton, Nauvoo Journal, 1 Jan. 1843; compare *History of the Church,* 5:215. Clearly, the compilers of the *History of the Church* used Clayton's journal as the source for this quotation from Joseph Smith.

25. Clayton, Nauvoo Journal, 18 Jan. 1843.

26. The assumption that Clayton was on Joe Duncan comes from the comment in the *History of the Church* a few days later that this horse was "somewhat jaded, with being ridden so hastily by Brother Clayton" (*History of the Church,* 5:443). Undoubtedly, Clayton got a certain good-natured pleasure from whipping Joe Duncan up to speed if he remembered that when Joseph Smith purchased the horse on July 14, he named him after the former Illinois governor, whom he disliked. Obviously, when he whipped the horse and yelled, "Giddap, Joe Duncan," the former governor was not out of mind.

27. There is an interesting difference in the sources as to the reason Joseph gave for not preaching. In his official history Joseph says, "I kept myself quiet all day, telling my friends that if I started for home I might be kidnapped into Missouri, and thought it best to tarry at Inlet and see the result." Clayton reports, however, that Joseph thought it best not to be seen but to put out the idea that he had received a message from Springfield and had important business to attend to there. Perhaps both stories were told. Ibid., 439; Clayton, Nauvoo Journal, 11 June 1843.

28. Clayton, Nauvoo Journal, 30 June 1843. Compare *History of the Church,* 5:458–60. It is clear that Clayton's journal was the major source for the account in the *History.*

29. Clayton, Nauvoo Journal, 27 Apr., 1, 13 May 1843.

30. Ibid., 23 June 1843. Joseph Smith told Clayton of other problems that day, even suggesting that some close associates had transgressed their covenants. He then told Clayton that if Clayton would do right and abide his counsel, Joseph could save his life. "I feel desirous to do right & would rather die than to lose my interest in the celestial kingdom," Clayton responded.

31. Ibid., 9 May 1844.

32. Ibid., 10 May 1844. See Clayton's letter to the *Times and Seasons,* in *History of the Church,* 6:380–84.

33. Clayton, Nauvoo Journal, 13 May 1844.

34. Ibid., 23 Apr. 1843.

35. *History of the Church,* 5:286.

36. See James M. Kimball, "A Wall to Defend Zion: The Nauvoo Charter," *BYU Studies* 15 (Summer 1975):491–97.

37. For general treatments on the political life of Nauvoo, as well as Joseph Smith's candidacy for the presidency of the United States, see Flanders, *Nauvoo,* chaps. 4, 10; Allen and Leonard, *Story of the Latter-day Saints,* 151-54; Miller and Miller, *Nauvoo,* 41-63, 137-40; Klaus J. Hansen, *Quest for Empire: The Political Kingdom of God and the Council of Fifty in Mormon History* (East Lansing: Michigan State University Press, 1967); George R. Gaylor, "The

Mormons and Politics in Illinois," *Journal of the Illinois State Historical Society* 49 (Spring 1956):48–66.

38. *History of the Church*, 5:490.

39. Ibid., 526.

40. Clayton, Nauvoo Journal, 6 Aug. 1843. For more discussion of this election, see Flanders, *Nauvoo*, 234–39.

41. *History of the Church*, 4:89.

42. Ibid., 6:116.

43. Ibid., 95.

44. Ibid., 56–57.

45. Joseph Smith's *Views on the Powers and Policy of the Government of the United States* is reproduced in several places but is most readily accessible in *History of the Church*, 6:197–209.

46. The letter to Calhoun is reproduced in *History of the Church*, 6:155–60. The reply to Clay is found in a pamphlet printed by John Taylor in Nauvoo, 1845, and entitled *The Voice of Truth: Containing the Public Writings, Portrait, and Last Sermon of President Joseph Smith*, 52–59.

47. For a discussion of church land purchases, see Miller and Miller, *Nauvoo*, 27–40. In Salt Lake City, Nauvoo Restoration has maps, compiled by Rowena Miller and her staff, showing the location of homes, businesses, etc., and even indicating the kind of homes on certain lots and showing commercial as well as residential districts.

48. Clayton, Nauvoo Journal, 28 Apr., 26, 28 May, 10 June, 4 Sept. 1843.

CHAPTER 5

The Sacred, the Secret, and the Solemn

Economics, politics, and social life made up only part of the Nauvoo story. Equally if not more important to William Clayton was the Nauvoo he felt, deep inside: the spirit of thousands of disciples whose dedication to a cause provided the building blocks for the architects of whatever was done. "Thou has done more for me than I have deserved," he prayed in gratitude at the end of Nauvoo's most distressing year, 1844, and then continued: "And now O God I will praise thee. I will speak good of thy name for all thy mercies and I here record my gratitude to thee and my confidence in thy work and my determination to endure to the end."[1] The full meaning of the Nauvoo experience, at least for William Clayton, can hardly be understood without an appreciation for this kind of devotion, in addition to the secular controversies and excitement of the city's history.

The Nauvoo Temple became at once the most important landmark and most important symbol of the City of the Saints. At the zenith of Nauvoo's glory, this majestic hilltop edifice dominated the landscape like a citadel commanding its dependent city. Outwardly it symbolized not only the success of the church as an institution but also the sacrifice, toil, and faith of the ordinary Saints who, like William Clayton, worked so hard for its completion. More fundamentally, it said to the Saints that the veil between heaven and earth was very thin indeed, for the sacred ceremonies that would take place within its walls would win for them their final exaltation. Like the Tabernacle of Moses or the Temple of Solomon, it was the place where God would dwell—a modern Sinai where, he had promised, "I deign to reveal unto my church things which have been kept hid from before the foundation of the world, things that pertain to the dispensation of the fullness of times."[2]

From the time he went to work for Joseph Smith until he left Nauvoo four years later, Clayton's life was bound to the temple as much as to the church itself. He kept its records, wrote its history, and participated in the final exhilaration of its most sacred ceremonies. At first, however, he was hardly aware of all it would mean. All he knew was that in a revelation received by Joseph Smith in January 1841 the Saints were commanded to build the temple with the finest materials and workmanship available and were told that it would become the only place where baptisms for the dead and other ordinances "for the salvation of the living and the dead" could be performed. It would be sacred space—probably the most sacred space on earth—and the revelation spoke of "your anointings, and your washings, and your baptisms for the dead, and your solemn assemblies, and your memorials for your sacrifices by the sons of Levi, and for your oracles in your most holy places wherein ye receive conversations, and your statutes and judgements."[3] But what all this meant only God and his prophet, Joseph, seemed to know for sure.

The temple's construction was well along its way by the time Clayton became involved. The cornerstones were laid, and the limestone walls were a few feet up in the air. The basement was finished, and the beautifully carved wooden baptismal font was in use for baptisms for the dead. True to his tendencies, Clayton took every opportunity to record evidence of the divine hand in whatever happened. A miraculous healing on the day the font was dedicated, for example, impressed him deeply. Samuel Rolfe had a serious infection on one hand, and Joseph Smith instructed him to wash in the font and it would be healed. Rolfe did so, and, in spite of the fact that doctors said it would not heal until spring, "in one week afterwards his hand was perfectly healed. After this time baptisms was continued in the font and many realized great blessings both spiritually and bodily."[4]

But if the hand of God was there, so, inevitably, was the hand of man, and this brought Clayton no end of distress. The temple committee consisted of Alpheus Cutler, Elias Higbee, and Reynolds Cahoon, and in November 1842 the stonecutters brought serious charges of "oppressive and unchristian conduct" against Higbee and Cahoon. They were accused of distributing provisions unevenly and giving more iron and steel tools to Cahoon's sons than to other workers. After a ten-hour hearing before Joseph Smith the committee was fully exonerated,[5] but a month later the stonecutters were complaining again.

Joseph Smith exonerated the committee a second time and wrote a
pointed letter to the workers reminding them of its high standing and
the need to pay it "proper deference." He further instructed the la-
borers that the committee's policy in distributing pork, beef, and other
provisions was ultimately for furthering the temple and advised them
"to submit patiently to their economy and instructions; and that we,
with one accord with united feelings, submit patiently to the yoke
that is laid upon us, and thereby secure the best interest, to the Temple
of the most High God, that our limited circumstances can possible
admit of: and then having done all on our part, that great Eloheem,
who has commanded us to build a house shall abundantly bless us
and reward us for all our pains."[6] Ever the middle man, Clayton was
sent to the stone shop to read the letter to the workers. Some, he said,
were satisfied, but three "seemed not exactly so."

The squabbling broke out again, and on April 7 it was William
Clayton who brought charges against the committee before the general
conference of the church. He accused its members of partiality in
distributing goods, money, and "store pay" (i.e., credit at Joseph Smith's
store). He also noted that the son of one committee member had
received all of the above but that none of his labor had been placed
on the tithing account. This was a serious breach of religious duty,
for one day in ten was supposed to be donated as tithing labor. Committee members, furthermore, were charged with taking "store pay"
for themselves but being too tightfisted in what they would allow to
others. Hyrum Smith, however, rose to the committee's defense, and
in the end the conference sustained it in its work, thus exonerating it
for a third time. That evening Cahoon complained angrily to Clayton
about the accusations, but when the beleaguered scribe explained why
he made them (apparently to clear the air, as much as anything else),
Cahoon appeared satisfied, at least for the time being.[7] By the end of
the year, however, Cahoon was angry again and even attempted, Clayton believed, to turn the stonecutters against him.[8] Such tension among
brothers dismayed Clayton deeply, though he probably saw it also as
another test of his discipleship.

The temple rose steadily, and by the end of October 1842 a temporary
floor was laid so that preaching meetings could be held. A year later
the Twelve Apostles were given the responsibility for collecting money
for the temple wherever they traveled, and one of Clayton's jobs was
to receive and account for it. The money was also sometimes used to

sustain those who worked on the temple, and William Clayton was not above requesting a little for himself. On November 30, 1843, for example, he asked the Twelve, in behalf of the Temple Committee, to provide help for the family of William Player, the chief stone setter, promising that he would then give tithing credit to those who had furnished the means. Then he added, almost with a touch of disgruntlement at the meager pay he was receiving for all the time he was putting in, "If they will send the remainder to my family I will also work it out like a good fellow (ie) to the best of my ability."[9]

Clayton was so sure that future generations would want to know of certain unique efforts in behalf of the temple that he duly recorded some of them. Early in 1844, for example, Hyrum Smith asked the women of the church to pledge one cent per week for glass and nails, promising them first choice of seats in the main floor assembly hall when the temple was complete. When Clayton prepared his temple history a year later, he observed that many women paid a year in advance, and that already $2,000 had been raised. In July 1844 the women from La Harpe and Macedonia branches made an unusual consecration. Convinced that a new crane was needed to speed the work along, they offered the means to build it. Clayton and the temple committee decided to accept the offer, and Raymond Clark's wife collected the contributions. By the end of August the crane was complete and in operation.

For William Clayton, however, the meaning of the temple could hardly be separated from the pervasive powers of Joseph Smith over his willing heart and mind. So complete was his will to believe that like potter's clay, the young scribe from Penwortham was molded and shaped by the prophet's influence into an avid, self-confident, and even stubborn disciple. One of the finishing touches was applied on April 21, 1843, when the two were riding together on the prairie. Wrote Clayton, "He swore to me he would forever defend & protect me and divide earthly things with me if I would be faithful to him which I cheerfully promised."[10] That promise could only strengthen the loyalty that was already there.

Such experiences were sacred to Clayton, and he repaid in kind by becoming one of the prophet's most tireless and uncompromising defenders. Quick to speak up whenever he felt an injustice was in the making, he became irate at even the hint of slander. In March 1842 he wrote to William Hardman in England, taking special pains to defend the character of the prophet. Notwithstanding the disappointments of 1841, he declared, "My faith in this doctrine, and in the prophet and officers is firm, unshaken, and unmoved, nay, rather, it is strengthened and settled firmer than ever." There had been charges of business fraud that, Clayton declared, "I, MYSELF, KNOW POSITIVELY TO BE FALSE." Then, responding to rumors of intemperance, he categorically asserted:

> With regard to J. Smith getting drunk, I will say that I am now acting as clerk for him and at his office daily, and have been since February 10th, and I know that he is as much opposed to the use of intoxicating drinks as any man need be.—I have never seen him drunk, nor have I ever heard any man who has seen him drunk since we came here. I believe he does not take intoxicating drink of any kind: our city is conducted wholly upon temperance principles. As to his using snuff and tobacco, I KNOW he does no such thing. To conclude, I will add that, the more I am with him, the more I love him, the more I know of him, and the more confidence I have in him; and I am sorry that people should give heed to evil reports concerning him, when we all know the great service *he has rendered the church*.[11]

When he wrote to the *Times and Seasons* about Joseph Smith's trial at Dixon in May 1844, he was vehement against those who dared to debase the prophet. The mere fact that they criticized him was, in Clayton's mind, enough evidence to convict them. "When I hear men speak reproachfully of him," he declared, "I never ask for a second evidence of their corruptness or baseness. . . . Shame on the man or set of men who show themselves so degraded and miserably corrupt."[12] If Joseph himself sometimes used a sharp tongue against his detractors, Clayton only enjoyed what he heard. When a certain man from Quincy, for example, began to tantalize the prophet in January 1844, Clayton was delighted to hear the church leader tell the offender, "In the name of the Lord" that not many years would pass away before he was in the hands of the devil himself.[13]

Clayton saw the prophet in every mood and seemingly loved him the more for each one. On occasion he found him weeping,[14] while at other times he observed his anger. On August 1, 1843, Joseph rode in his buggy up to the temple where he began to discuss with Clayton and others the fact that some of his property was being sold for taxes. Suddenly Walter Bagby, the county assessor and collector, appeared and when Joseph confronted him with the issue, he denied all knowledge of it. As the discussion heated up, Joseph told Bagby that he was always abusing the citizens in the area, and Bagby angrily called Joseph a liar. Obviously irritated, the church leader stepped down from his buggy, whereupon Bagby picked up a stone to throw at him. Enraged, Joseph went after him and struck him two or three times, and it took Daniel H. Wells to separate the two.[15] It may have seemed out of character for the prophet to engage in fisticuffs, but the fact that on occasion he demonstrated such strictly human qualities probably made him all the more believable to William Clayton.

Joseph Smith was creating sacred history—at least that is how his followers, including William Clayton, felt. Everything he did, whether secular or religious, was important to the Kingdom, and a memory of it would be essential to preserving his place in the hearts and minds of future generations. Just as the memory of what Jesus did and said was written and compiled to become the sacred histories of the founding of Christianity, so the events in the life of the Mormon prophet, as recorded by himself as well as his disciples, would soon constitute the sacred history of the restoration.

As early as 1830, Joseph himself developed an avid concern about recording his history,[16] though in the long run he wrote very little in his own hand. Instead, during the fourteen years he led the church he either dictated his ideas to scribes or relied on clerks and other associates to record his actions as well as his sermons and other pronouncements. When, under his direction, various clerks and church historians began to compile his official history, most of it came from the notes and journals of those who had been close to him. This included the Nauvoo Journal of William Clayton.

The history was only partially complete when Joseph died, and it was finally finished in 1858. It was a monumental work, at least for the Mormons, and its place as sacred history was epitomized in a statement issued by church historians Wilford Woodruff and George A. Smith. Emphasizing their painstaking efforts to make it absolutely correct, they also explained that in its final form, the history had been revised under the "strict inspection" of Brigham Young and approved by him. "We, therefore, hereby bear our testimony," they solemnly wrote, "unto whom these words shall come, that the History of Joseph Smith is true, and it is one of the most authentic histories ever written."[17] A half-century later it was edited by B. H. Roberts and pub-

lished by the church in six volumes. Roberts reemphasized the aura
that Mormon readers would feel surrounding it. "In publishing the
History of The Church of Jesus Christ of Latter-day Saints," he wrote,
"it is felt that a solemn duty is being performed to the Saints and to
the world. The events which make up the history of the church in this
age are the most important that history can chronicle."[18]

One problem with Joseph Smith's published *History of the Church*,
however, is that it does not reflect Joseph himself as much as it reflects
the image of Joseph as he was seen by scribes and journalists.[19] The
History is written in the first person, as if Joseph were doing the
writing, though usually the first person account of an event is really
a paraphrase or adaptation of someone else's account. At times the
only essential difference is that "Joseph," "he," or "President Smith"
is changed to "I." The fact that what the compilers were doing was
well known at the time indicates that there was no intent to deceive.
They simply were using the best sources available to help them re-
construct Joseph Smith's activities and conversations. William Clayton's journal provided many such entries, which suggests that much
of the "first person" Joseph Smith portrayed in the *History* is, in reality,
only the Joseph Smith that William Clayton or someone else saw and
heard. Even with that qualification, however, the work is invaluable,
but there is a continuing concern with whether the history as reported
is always the way Joseph saw it or would have written it himself.

The famous story of the Kinderhook plates, and William Clayton's
role in it, suggests the nature of the problem. Sometime in April 1843
six small, thin, bell-shaped metal plates were "discovered" in a mound
near the town of Kinderhook, about fifty-five miles south of Nauvoo.
Each measured about 2-7/8" high and 2-1/4" wide at the bottom, and
each contained strange markings that seemed to resemble Egyptian
hieroglyphics. Quickly the news spread to Nauvoo, and by the first
of May the plates themselves had arrived. During the next few weeks
it became a common belief that Joseph Smith would soon translate
them. Even the church periodical, the *Times and Seasons*, as well as
a broadside put out by the *Nauvoo Neighbor*, told readers that a translation would be forthcoming. The latter reproduced facsimiles of all
twelve sides of the plates. Nothing more was heard about it, however,
and a later confession of one of the "discoverers" as well as a recent
electronic and chemical analysis of one surviving plate has eliminated
any doubt that the whole thing was a hoax, intended to lure Joseph

Smith into the trap of publishing a translation and then embarrassing him.

Not surprisingly, even those close to Joseph Smith gave somewhat differing accounts of the discovery, and what might be expected from it, but there is nothing directly from Joseph on the matter. Therein lies one example of the difficulty with the way Joseph Smith's *History* was compiled. In this case William Clayton's diary was the source for the only thing recorded there about the Kinderhook plates. What the prophet really said or would have written is conjectural, but the account from Clayton's diary, May 1, 1843, is as follows:

> I have seen 6 brass plates which were found in Adams County by some persons who were digging in a mound. They found a skeleton about 6 feet from the surface of the earth which was 9 foot high. [At this point there is a tracing of a plate in the journal.] The plates were on the breast of the skeleton. This diagram shows the size of the plates being drawn on the edge of one of them. They are covered with ancient characters of language containing from 30 to 40 on each side of the plates. Prest J. has translated a portion and says they contain the history of the person with whom they were found and he was a descendant of Ham through the loins of Pharoah king of Egypt, and that he received his kingdom from the ruler of heaven and earth.

For comparison's sake, the account as edited for Joseph Smith's *History* for the same date reads:

> I insert fac-similies of the six brass plates found near Kinderhook, in Pike county, Illinois, on April 23, by Mr. Robert Wiley and others, while excavating a large mound. They found a skeleton about six feet from the surface of the earth, which must have stood nine feet high. The plates were found on the breast of the skeleton and were covered on both sides with ancient characters.
>
> I have translated a portion of them, and find they contain the history of the person with whom they were found. He was a descendant of Ham, through the loins of Pharoah, king of Egypt, and that he received his kingdom from the Ruler of heaven and earth.[20]

In 1981 Stanley B. Kimball provided readers of the official church periodical, the *Ensign*, with clear evidence that the plates were a hoax, and he argued convincingly that Joseph Smith was not, in fact, ever really taken in by it.[21] In the diary Clayton was not quoting the prophet

directly, but it is evident that he *believed* Joseph had read and translated "a portion" of the plates and knew something about the person
with whose skeletal remains they were "found." It was William Clayton's understanding of what Joseph Smith believed that was transposed
into a first person account and became church history. Fortunately,
Mormon scholar Dean Jessee is in the process of clarifying the sources
for Joseph Smith's history and separating the prophet's own writings
from those of others.[22]

The Kinderhook episode was only a sidelight, and nothing came of
it, but William Clayton made other, much more important, contributions to what became Joseph Smith's official history. Several entries
in Clayton's Nauvoo Journal were the direct sources for entries in the
history, some of which are noted elsewhere in this work. In addition,
Clayton was one of several scribes who kept the "Book of the Law of
the Lord." For the most part, this large, leather-bound record contains
notations of consecrations and tithing for the building of the temple,
and 370 pages, covering the period from September 12, 1842, to May
4, 1844, is in William Clayton's handwriting. But it also contains some
manuscript sources used in compiling the *History*, and about sixty-
one pages of this material were written by Clayton, mostly in the third
person, and then later transposed to the first person for the sake of
the published history. Some of this, however, is also direct dictation
from Joseph Smith. A letter to Emma Smith, for example, is there,
though presumably Emma received the original and Clayton merely
made a copy of it before it was sent. In addition, certain tender reflections by Joseph Smith on the value of his friends, on August 16
and 23, 1842, were dictated directly to Clayton, who recorded them in
the sacred record book and later made them available for the published
History.[23] Beyond that, the original manuscripts of some revelations
that became part of the *History* as well as part of the Doctrine and
Covenants are in the handwriting of William Clayton. Section 127 of
the Doctrine and Covenants, which is a letter dealing with baptism
for the dead, is one example.

Clayton was also the source for at least one famous prophecy of
Joseph Smith, though the manuscript source of the prophecy, as it now
stands in the official *History*, is conjectural. On May 18, 1843, Joseph
and William were in Carthage, where they dined with Judge Stephen
A. Douglas at the home of Sheriff Jacob Backenstos. After dinner,
according to Clayton's journal, the prophet and the judge engaged in

conversation over "sundry matters," though the nature of the discussion was not described. It probably concerned the Missouri persecutions and the failure of the federal government to assist the Mormons, but Clayton simply reported that "the Prest. said 'I prophecy in the name of the Lord God that in a few years this government will be utterly overthrown and wasted so that there will not be a potsherd left' for their wickedness in conniving at the Missouri mobocracy. The judge appears very friendly and acknowledged the propriety of the prests. remarks."[24] Sixteen years later, however, when that part of Joseph Smith's *History* was first published in the *Deseret News*, the report of the conversation was greatly expanded, and in a curiously uncharacteristic manner. Instead of following their usual editorial practice of putting in whatever they could gather that Joseph Smith said, without identifying the sources, the compilers introduced this conversation by stating that "the following brief account is from the journal of William Clayton, who was present." Then followed a 450-word report of the conversation in which, it said, Joseph spent about three hours telling Douglas of the Missouri persecutions, in "a very minute manner." He also told of his trip to Washington in 1840, emphasizing the cool reception he received in his effort to obtain federal redress and President Martin Van Buren's "pusillanimous reply, 'Gentlemen, your cause is just, but I can do nothing for you.' " It was in this context that he prophesied that "unless the United States redress the wrongs committed upon the Saints" and punish the perpetrators, the government would be overthrown because of "their wickedness" in permitting the crimes against the Mormons. Then he added the prediction that became famous in Mormon history: "Judge you will aspire to the Presidency of the United States, and if ever you turn your hand against me or the Latter Day Saints, you will feel the weight of the hand of the Almighty upon you; and you will live to see and know that I have testified the truth to you, for the conversation of this day will stick to you through life."[25] When the *History* was published in book form, B. H. Roberts added an editorial note commenting on the fact that in 1857 Douglas gave a speech in Springfield, Illinois, that was critical of the Mormons, and observing that he did, indeed, lose his bid for the presidency in 1860 and died a year later.[26]

The question, however, is, where did this expanded version of the original entry in William Clayton's journal come from? If, as the editors of the *History* reported, Clayton was the source, then there can be only two possibilities. One is that Clayton wrote in more than one journal, perhaps another volume of the "Book of the Law of the Lord," that simply has not come to light. This is by no means impossible, for it is known that Clayton kept other books and that on occasion the things recorded in one journal were either duplicated or, in some cases, expanded upon in another.[27] The other possibility is that Clayton, who was still working with the church historians and clerks when the *History* was being completed, was asked about the prophecy and, drawing on a vivid memory of the occasion, provided the expanded account. This version is certainly not inconsistent with the original journal entry, and, given the profound impact Joseph's words always had on Clayton, it is not unlikely that he would remember clearly at least the gist of that dramatic conversation, even after many years. In any case, this is one more example of the various ways in which William Clayton helped write what he considered sacred history.

Clayton literally thrived on the teachings of Joseph Smith, no matter how new or different they were. The Nauvoo period saw more significant new ideas and practices take their place in the church than at any time in its history, and William Clayton was there when the prophet introduced many of them. Some of the ideas advanced by Joseph may have been considered, even by close associates, to be matters of personal interpretation rather than official doctrine, but not so for William Clayton: if they came from the prophet, he believed them all.[28]

The examples of new and different doctrines Clayton learned from Joseph Smith are too numerous to detail here, but some that impressed him most will illustrate the important religious metamorphosis he experienced in Nauvoo. He was intrigued, for example, with the prophet's frequent reference to the Kingdom of God, including the political implications of that Kingdom. He made special note, therefore, of a definition of the Kingdom given by the prophet. It exists, Clayton heard him say, "wherever the oracles of God are & subjects to obey those oracles. What constitutes the kingdom of God? An administrator who has the power of calling down the oracles of God, and subjects to receive those oracles no matter if there are but three, four, or six there is the kingdom of God."[29] The "oracles" were the commandments, the "administrator" was Joseph Smith, and Clayton was one of the "subjects." This was another way of saying that the church was, in fact, the earthly Kingdom of God and that Joseph Smith was God's only true prophet.

Sometimes instructions from God are delivered by heavenly messengers, and on at least two occasions Clayton heard Joseph Smith instruct certain leading church members on how to tell the difference between such a messenger and an evil spirit. The idea had been presented to the Quorum of the Twelve as early as 1839, but Clayton heard it in December 1840 and again when he was at the prophet's home on February 9, 1843. There are really two kinds of beings in heaven, Joseph said on the last occasion. "Angels, who are resurrected personages, having bodies of flesh and bones . . . [and] the spirits of just men made perfect who are not resurrected." Presumably the latter will also be resurrected in due time, but even without bodies of flesh and bones they can deliver messages to mortals. The key, then, is to ask anyone who claims to be a messenger from God to shake hands with you. If he is an angel, he will do so and you will feel it. If he is the "spirit of a just man made perfect," he will not move, for he will not deceive. But "if it be the devil as an angel of light, when you ask him to shake hands he will offer you his hand, and you will not feel anything; you may therefore detect him."[30] So confident was Clayton and other Nauvoo Mormons in the close relationship between themselves and heaven, that it would have surprised none of them to have an "angel," a "spirit of a just man," or a devil appear and talk to them. The statement was later made scripture and became Section 129 of the book of Doctrine and Covenants, and Clayton provided the source: the published version is practically verbatim from his diary.

Clayton's diary is the source for other statements of the prophet that eventually became part of Mormonism's sacred scriptures.[31] In addition, Clayton was among the scribes who recorded many doctrinal sermons, including what has been termed "Joseph Smith's greatest sermon": the famous "King Follett Discourse." Here, at the height of his career and only two months before his death, the prophet dramatically brought together several of his most important and progressive doctrinal innovations. Clayton's record of that all-important sermon was one of four from which the published text was finally amalgamated.[32]

Perhaps the most fundamental doctrines taught publicly by Joseph Smith in Nauvoo related to the nature of God and the relationship of God to men and women. It is impossible to tell how Clayton perceived God prior to his association with Joseph Smith, but before the Nauvoo period it was not necessarily a fundamental of the faith for all Mormons to believe that God the Father was a tangible being of flesh and bones. They understood that there was a clear distinction between the persons of the Father and the Son, so they were not trinitarian in the traditional Christian sense. But in the 1830s, according to the "Lectures on Faith," they were taught that the Father was a "personage of spirit, glory and power," while the Son was a "personage of tabernacle, made, or fashioned like unto man . . . possessing the same mind with the Father, which mind is the Holy Spirit."[33] Only in 1838, the year the Mormons were driven into Illinois, did a description of a more anthropomorphic God the Father begin to find its way into the Mormon press (although the idea was probably being preached before it got into print). That year Parley P. Pratt wrote that "we worship a God who has both body and parts: who has eyes, mouth and ears, and who speaks when he pleases, to whom he pleases."[34] That same year Joseph Smith began preparing the account of his first vision for publication— a narrative that clearly distinguished between the Father and the Son and implied the material nature of both. Two years later the first vision was published in missionary literature, and before the end of his life Joseph Smith made an understanding of the Godhead a fundamental of the Mormon faith.

William Clayton was present on April 2, 1843, when Joseph announced to a select group that the Father and the Son both have bodies of flesh and bones, but that the Holy Ghost is a "personage of Spirit." If this were not so, he said, the Holy Ghost could not dwell in us. "A Man may receive the Holy Ghost, and it may descend upon him and not tarry with him."[35] By this time, then, it was a fundamental Mormon doctrine that the Godhead consists of three separate, identifiable heavenly beings, that the Father and the Son are tangible beings, and that the Holy Ghost, or Holy Spirit, is a spiritual personage. A more elaborate theology of the Holy Ghost, however, was worked out more fully only many years after the death of Joseph Smith.[36]

As different as it was, this new concept of God might not have seemed quite so profound to the Mormons if it had not been coupled with another doctrine relating to man and his potential. This, in part, was the significance of the King Follett Discourse. Man, Joseph Smith revealed to his disciples, is actually a god in embryo! If we understand the true nature of God, and our relationship to him, then we also understand that it is part of his plan that we progress eternally until we become like him—gods and goddesses! "God himself was once as we are now," he said, "and is an exalted man, and sits enthroned in yonder heavens!"

It is significant that the King Follett sermon was a funeral sermon, for in discoursing on the dead Joseph could tell his listeners of the potential they all had. It was clearly related to their understanding of God and their relationship to him. "It is the first principle of the gospel," he continued, "to know for a certainty the character of God, and to know that we may converse with Him as one man converses with another, and that He was once a man like us; yea, that God himself, the Father of us all, dwelt on an earth." At the same time, he taught that all people existed, as individual spirits, prior to their being born on earth. God, the Father of these spirits, "finding he was in the midst of spirits and glory, because he was more intelligent, saw proper to institute laws whereby the rest could have a privilege to advance like himself." This was the basis for the Mormon doctrine of "eternal progression," as well as the concept of a plurality of gods, which holds that mortals can, through obeying the principles of the gospel, prepare themselves to become gods.

All this had even more implications in terms of tying together several other doctrines previously advanced. The Mormon concept of the three degrees of glory, first spelled out in 1832,[37] took on new meaning when it was realized by the Saints in Nauvoo that only those who attained the highest or "celestial" degree would have the godly exaltation they now believed possible. In 1843 Joseph went even further by indicating to Clayton and a group of close friends that if a man and his wife entered into the covenant of marriage under the authority of the priesthood (i.e., the Mormon priesthood), they would "continue to increase and have children in the celestial glory,"[38] which was another way of saying that they would become like God. This, as Clayton saw it, was part of the "new and everlasting covenant," and Joseph told his little group of disciples that to gain the highest heaven, or degree, "a man must enter into this order of the priesthood and if he dont he cant obtain it. He may enter into the other but that is the end of his kingdom he cannot have an increase."[39] This is the way Clayton recorded it in his journal, and this entry became the basis for one of the most oft-quoted statements in the Doctrine and Covenants.

The King Follett Discourse enhanced still more previous teachings and practices, including baptism for the dead. "The greatest responsibility in this world that God has laid upon us," Joseph said in his sermon, "is to seek after our dead," for, as Paul had said, "They without us cannot be made perfect." The impact of these words was that later not only baptism but also other priesthood ordinances would be performed in behalf of the dead in the temple, so that the dead, too, could continue on the road toward eternal exaltation. This doctrine symbolized the Mormon emphasis on the family and tied the generations together. Little wonder that Clayton was especially impressed with that part of the King Follett funeral sermon. Already he had lost members of his family, and even though he recorded the sermon separately, he also recorded in his diary the prophet's emphasis on the importance of being buried with one's relatives. In the resurrection, he said, "we shall want to see our relatives first & shall rejoice to strike hands with our parents, children, &c when rising from the tomb."[40]

As many more new things were taught in Nauvoo, it all must have seemed somewhat overwhelming to William Clayton. Here he was, a former English factory clerk sitting at the feet of the prophet while he received revelation, expounded upon doctrine, and planned the building of the Kingdom of God on earth. The effect on the disciple from Penwortham is seen in his journal entry for May 17, 1843. This was the second day of instruction from Joseph Smith in Ramus, Illinois, and Clayton duly recorded the most important new ideas he heard. Some of them were in the form of definitions. "Salvation," for example, meant "a mans being placed beyond the powers of all his enemies." The phrase "more sure word of prophecy" meant "a mans knowing that he was sealed up unto eternal life by revelation & the spirit of prophecy through the power of the Holy priesthood." With reference to "matter," Joseph said that "there is no such thing as immaterial matter. All spirit is matter but it is more fine or pure and can only be discerned by purer eyes. We cant see it but when our bodies are purified we shall see that it is all matter." But Joseph also told an anecdote concerning a man who had pressed him too hard to perform a marriage ordinance before the Lord was willing to have it performed.[41] "I learned from this," wrote Clayton, "never to press the prophet but wait with patience & God will bring all things right." Clayton's discipleship was maturing, as he was developing a patient hopefulness and expectation that all he wanted eventually would come. That led him to pour out another of his frequent prayers: "I feel to pray that God will let me live so that I may come to the full knowledge of truth and salvation & be prepared for the enjoyment of a fulness of the third heavens."

The impact went even further. Sitting at the feet of Joseph Smith was an honor, but Clayton saw his association with other leading men of the church as an almost equal privilege. On the evening of January 23, 1844, for example, he went to a party at which Joseph Smith was also in attendance. His poignant reflections on the evening reveal his sentimentalism as well as his tendency toward self-effacement: "Whilst hearing bro. Hancock sing a song I was led to reflect upon the feelings I had 3 years ago whilst listening to him when singing. I then felt it a privilege to associate with such men, and when I reflect upon the privileges I now enjoy I am led to conclude, truly the mercy of God has been great and I am not worthy of such great blessings."[42]

Most of these things were public, but there was another side to Clayton's spiritual Nauvoo. Like the unseen supporting structures that give stability to a house, it was the private teachings of Joseph Smith, confided in a relatively few faithful disciples, that had the most permanent effect on Clayton's life and became the most sustaining elements of his broadening religious faith. Because of his closeness to the prophet, Clayton became a member of two highly confidential groups: the Council of Fifty and Joseph Smith's private prayer circle. Each group had an impact on the church and each held great spiritual significance for the impressionable William.

The Council of Fifty (sometimes referred to as the General Council) was not an ecclesiastical organization, though it was organized and dominated by the priesthood. Joseph Smith saw it as a secular body that would handle secular and political affairs and anticipate the establishment of the political Kingdom of God on earth. It consisted wholly of men the prophet felt he could trust, for like Clayton their loyalty had already been tested and they could take without dismay the new and sometimes startling concepts he would advance. The council planned and directed Joseph Smith's political campaign for the presidency, directed the industrial development of Nauvoo after his death, and exercised important political influence in the Territory of Utah. In essence, it was seen as the political arm of the priesthood, responsible for preparing for the Second Coming of Christ and the establishment of his millennial reign.[43]

The philosophical roots for the organization of the Council of Fifty reached back many years and were directly related to the millennial expectations of the church. The immediate impetus, however, came from two letters signed by Lyman Wight and four others who were working in the church's lumber camps in Black River Falls, Wisconsin Territory. These were read at a special meeting attended by the Twelve, Bishop George Miller, and the temple committee on the evening of March 10, 1844. The letters proposed a grandiose scheme for Mormon colonization in the Southwest and led to an important discussion where, according to Clayton, "many great and glorious ideas were advanced."[44]

The next day they met again and this time organized a council to consider not only the proposal from Wisconsin but also "the best policy for this people to adopt to obtain their rights from the nation and insure protection for themselves and children; and to secure a resting place in the mountains, or some uninhabited region, where we can enjoy the liberty of conscience guaranteed to us by the Constitution." This was the official organization of the Council of Fifty, or the government of the Kingdom of God, and when the group met the following day William Clayton was appointed "Clerk of the Kingdom." What a change in status, he must have thought, for a former factory clerk from Penwortham![45]

As a member of such a prestigious body Clayton could hardly contain his exuberance. There, he wrote, "the principles of eternal truths rolled forth to the hearers without reserve and the hearts of the servants of God [were] made to rejoice exceedingly." They even voted on April 11 to make Joseph Smith their "Prophet, Priest and King," confirming him with "loud Hosannas." The deliberations of the council were confidential, and Clayton kept the confidence well, not even recording the details in his diary. He apparently kept careful notes during the meetings, then spent long hours recording them in the official minute books.[46]

The council met frequently during the last four months of Joseph Smith's life. During the first month it gradually added to its numbers until by April 18 it actually consisted of fifty-two members, including William Clayton as clerk and his friend Willard Richards as recorder. The grand significance of the council, so far as Clayton was concerned, was that it was "making laws and sanctioning principles which will in part govern the saints after the resurrection." He did not see it as an immediate replacement for civil government, but he firmly believed that whatever principles it established would govern during the millennium. "Is there not a similarity," he asked himself, "between this grand council & the council which sat previous to the organization of the world?" No wonder he felt so honored to be a part of it.[47]

Clearly the Council of Fifty had important religious significance for Clayton, but of even greater spiritual importance was his invitation to become a member of Joseph Smith's private prayer circle. In a way, this represented the culmination of his evolution from factory clerk to confidant of the prophet.

Variously called the "Holy Order," the "Quorum of the Anointed," the "First Quorum," or just the "Quorum," the prayer circle may have had its origin as early as 1842. It was not fully established with the inclusion of women, however, until September 28, 1843. From then until the death of Joseph Smith this select group met at least weekly. The members were instructed by Joseph in the ceremonies that would subsequently be administered in the Nauvoo Temple. They were initiated into the Quorum through a "washing and anointing" that symbolized the spiritual cleanliness and progress they sought to attain. At the meetings, dressed in special priesthood robes, they went through the endowment ordinances that consisted of religious instruction, learning certain symbolic "signs and tokens," and taking upon themselves sacred covenants pertaining to their personal lives and conduct. All this was held to be a most sacred part of the restoration of the "ancient order of things." They also participated in fervent prayer concerning the problems of the day. Membership was restricted—only sixty-five persons had been admitted before the death of Joseph Smith—but as soon as the temple was usable, in December 1845, this exclusiveness ended, as originally intended by the prophet. The Anointed Quorum was a preliminary training group, preparing to help introduce the endowment ceremony to the membership of the church as a whole.

It is easy to see how important it was to Clayton that he become a member of the Quorum. As a close friend of the prophet it seemed almost as if he had been deprived of a spiritual right when, by December 1843, he had not been invited to participate. He even suspected that two members of the Quorum, in particular, were keeping him out: Reynolds Cahoon, with whom he had previously disagreed because of the actions of the temple committee, and Emma Smith. All this, he lamented on December 2, "sink[s] my mind and fills me with agony." That day he even went so far as to write a long letter on the subject to the prophet. Three days later Joseph Smith personally returned the

letter, assured him that he had no need to be troubled, and explained
that it had just not been convenient as yet to admit him. He also
assured Clayton that his paranoia concerning Cahoon was ill-founded,
for Cahoon considered him to be "true blue."

On January 22, 1844, Clayton's hopes were realized when Reynolds
Cahoon himself came to his home and informed him that he had been
voted into the Quorum. "This filled my heart with joy and gratitude,"
he wrote, "for truly the mercy of the Lord and the kindness of my
brethren have been great to me." Immediately one of the women in
Nauvoo began making his priesthood robe and garment, which were
necessary for the endowment ceremony, and on February 3 he received
the washing and anointing ordinances and was admitted to the Quorum. He could not refrain from recording the depths of his feelings:
"This is one of the greatest favors ever conferred on me and for which
I feel grateful. May the God of Joseph preserve me & mine house to
walk in the paths of righteousness all the days of my life & oh that I
may never sin against him or displease him. For thou oh God knowest
my desire to do right that I may have eternal life."[48] Ruth Clayton
also became a member of the Quorum, on December 22, 1844, and
thus shared with her husband the right to introduce the endowment
to the rest of the Nauvoo Saints. For Clayton, and for all the other
Mormons who shared his experience, this *was* the meaning of Nauvoo—the steppingstone to eternal life.

True to his commitment to keep sacred things secret, Clayton noted
several meetings in his diary but never gave the most confidential
details. These meetings continued after the death of Joseph Smith, and
one of Clayton's most extensive notations, wherein he provided some
interesting insight into the nature of some of the meetings, came on
Sunday, December 7, 1845. Several members of the Quorum were meeting in the temple, clothed in their ceremonial robes, and Joseph Fielding
(Clayton's former mission president from England) gave the opening
prayer. It became a kind of testimony meeting (most appropriate for
the Sabbath) as several expressed their feelings about the privilege of
being there "in spite of the combined opposition of men and devils."
During the speaking the sacrament of the Lord's supper, consisting of
broken bread and wine, was distributed, after which Brigham Young
addressed the group. "He gave much good instruction," Clayton noted,
"and the spirit of God rested upon him." One interesting comment

provides some important insight into the attitudes toward the Quorum of this new church leader:

> He stated "that a few of the quorum had met twice a week ever since Joseph and Hyrum were killed and during the last excitement, every day and in the hotest part of it twice a day to offer up the signs and pray to our heavenly father to deliver his people and this is the cord which has bound this people together. If this quorum and those who shall be admitted into it will be as dillegent in prayer as a few has been I promise you in the name of Israels God that we shall accomplish the will of God and go out in due time from the gentiles with power and plenty and no power shall stay us."[49]

After the death of Joseph Smith, Clayton became especially anxious to see the temple completed, but giving the endowment to the Saints at large was even more important. If they could not complete the temple fully before they had to quit Nauvoo, at least they would complete and dedicate enough of it to administer these sacred ordinances to as many Saints as possible. On November 29, 1845, carpet was laid on the main floor of the attic as well as in several of the smaller rooms that surrounded it. On the next day, Sunday, the attic floor was dedicated in impressive ceremonies, with Clayton keeping the minutes, and the Anointed Quorum rehearsed parts of the temple ordinances "in order to perfect them."[50]

December 10 was the day set aside for the first official endowments to be given in the temple, but that day also saw a strange series of events that demonstrates the almost ironic circumstances in which the Saints of Nauvoo found themselves. At 11:45 A.M. a Catholic priest and his associate were admitted to the temple for the purpose of negotiating the purchase of church property, possibly including the temple itself. Paradoxically, the Saints were sacrificing to complete the temple so they could offer to everyone the ceremonies already received by the Quorum, while at the same time they were painfully aware that they soon must leave and were actually contemplating the sale of the temple. After some discussion Brigham Young proposed that the Catholics lease it for a period of five to thirty-five years and that the profits go toward finishing it and keeping it in repair. The visitors agreed to consider the proposal and left about 12:30 P.M. A few hours later Clayton and others consecrated (i.e., blessed) sixteen bottles of oil in preparation for the coming ceremonies, and at 3 P.M. the first "washings and anointings" to be performed in the temple commenced. Later that evening the full endowment ceremony was conducted for the first time in the temple. At 9:30 it was complete, and Brigham Young then called everyone into a room known as the "Celestial room" where they all knelt while Amasa Lyman offered prayers.

Clayton's main task that day was keeping records, and though it must have been a marvelous day for him it was also a long one, partially dulled by illness. "At this time," he wrote, "I went home being very unwell having been writing and keeping minutes all day." The others remained until 3:30 the next morning.[51] From that day until they finally left Nauvoo the Saints flocked to the temple, and the exclusive nature of the Quorum of the Anointed came to an end.

As important and revolutionary as these things were, it was Joseph Smith's teachings on marriage that had a more visible and far-reaching effect on William Clayton's life than anything else he learned in Nauvoo. Two doctrines, "eternal marriage" and "plural marriage," went hand-in-hand, and Clayton learned of them during the last two years of his association with the prophet.[52]

Why would the straitlaced, idealistic William Clayton, who was almost overly concerned with what people thought of him, seriously consider the practice of plural marriage when it so clearly violated all his earlier values as well as the morality and sensibilities of the society in which he lived? He had a good marriage with Ruth Moon, which had endured considerable adversity. He was also close to her family. By the time the doctrine of polygamy was presented to him Ruth had borne three children and on February 17, 1843, just two months before his second marriage, she presented him with his first son. It was no lack of love or compatibility that led him to take additional wives. The most compelling factor was his single-minded conviction that whatever Joseph Smith told him to do was right and that he must spare no pains to accomplish it. At the same time, it is clear that his affection for Sarah Crooks of Manchester was still there, and once he was convinced that the principle was true, it was only natural that he should think of her as a possible second wife.[53]

The doctrines of eternal marriage and plural marriage were both spelled out in a revelation that William Clayton recorded for Joseph Smith on July 12, 1843. The prophet had been teaching both for some time, but plural marriage, at least, remained a private doctrine and the revelation itself was not made public until 1852. It nevertheless formed the basis for all future explanations of the doctrines.

Now known as Section 132 of the book of Doctrine and Covenants, the revelation was actually concerned with something much more basic to Mormon thought than simply whether a man should have more than one wife. It began with an explanation of the eternal nature of priesthood authority and the relationship of that authority to the marriage ceremony. To the Mormons, this was fundamental, for the priesthood (the authority specifically given to man to act in the name of God) could reside only in one church on the earth. Through that authority, and through it alone, they believed God would transmit whatever information or instructions that were essential to man's eternal salvation. In this case the revelation dealt with covenants or contracts and what it was that made them eternally binding. The ordinances performed by the priesthood are eternal, it explained, and, unlike other contracts, the covenants made under that authority are everlasting. With regard to marriage, then, the Saints were told that *any* marriage not performed by one holding God's authority is binding so long as both parties live, but is invalid when they "are out of the world." This had important overtones for people like Clayton who loved their families and longed to be with them after death.

Long before 1843, Joseph Smith had begun to unfold to the Saints the concept of the eternal nature of the family. Baptism for the dead, for example, which Clayton accepted enthusiastically, implied the hope for continuing family relationships. But even baptism must be performed by proper authority. How logical it would seem to be told that the most important of all earthly covenants, marriage, would last beyond the grave only *if* it were validated by the priesthood.

The revelation informed the Saints, then, that if a marriage were performed by proper authority it would be binding for eternity. This was the doctrine of eternal marriage, and to this day faithful Mormons insist that they marry in the temple where, instead of saying "until death do you part," the authorized official says "for time and all eternity."[54]

Only after explaining the eternal nature of the priesthood and of marriage did the revelation deal with Joseph Smith's original inquiry. He had asked, it said, "wherein I, the Lord, justified my servants Abraham, Isaac, and Jacob, and also Moses, David and Solomon, my servants, as touching the principle and doctrine of their having many wives and concubines." The answer was that they had been given to the ancient prophets by the Lord himself, and that since these men "did none other things than that which they were commanded, they have entered into their exaltation . . . and sit upon thrones, and are not angels but gods." The overpowering thought that they, too, might become gods helped disciples such as Clayton understand why God would authorize the same practice in modern times. Even though a Book of Mormon prophet condemned the practice among his own people, he had also reminded them that "if I will, saith the Lord of Hosts, raise up seed unto me, I will command my people."[55]It was choice "seed"—eternal families and eternal progression—that the new revelation was about, so far as Clayton was concerned. It authorized Joseph Smith to be like the prophets of old and to instruct others in the same doctrine. The only requirement was that plural marriages be authorized and performed by proper priesthood leaders. Anything less than this was adultery. Joseph Smith taught that plural marriage was one more step in the "restoration of all things." William Clayton accepted it as such and eventually became one of the most married men in the church.

It seems probable that Clayton at least had heard of plural marriage before he was formally instructed to practice it. For several years Joseph Smith had been teaching it to a few highly trusted friends and church leaders. Their instructions, however, were to keep it secret; otherwise there would be a public outcry, both in and out of the church, and in the midst of already troubled times the Saints could hardly afford that. Selected stalwarts must be instructed first, then it would be preached to the rest.[56]

For many of those to whom it was introduced, the new doctrine was almost impossible to accept, and for some who heard it the thought was downright revolting. Joseph once said that for years even he refused to accept it, "until the angel of the Lord threatened to slay him if he did not reveal and establish this celestial principle."[57] If it was that difficult for him, it was as much or more so for his disciples. Brigham Young, John Taylor, the Pratt brothers—all felt nothing but dismay when he broached the subject to them.

William Clayton's closest friend among the apostles, Heber C. Kimball, was given a particularly difficult two-part test before he was fully convinced. Evidently Joseph wanted not only to teach him the doctrine but also to try his loyalty with a test as severe as that of Abraham.

Sometime in the summer of 1841 the prophet told Heber that he wanted his wife, Vilate. Stunned and crushed, Heber fasted and prayed in anguish for three days, but in the end he took his beloved Vilate to the prophet and told him she was his. The proffered sacrifice turned Joseph Smith to tears, and then and there he "sealed" the marriage of Heber and Vilate for time and eternity. There, in practice, Heber was taught the principle of eternal marriage. But the test was not completely over. Later the prophet told Heber that he must now secretly take a plural wife—even keeping the secret from Vilate. Again the hapless apostle anguished, though eventually he did as he was commanded. But Vilate, meanwhile, sensing her husband's misery, engaged in a long and fervent prayer of her own. The answer was a personal revelation as to what her husband had done and the truth of the principle. Again a test was passed, with the result that Vilate was as converted as anyone and fully supported her husband in what they believed were his new, eternal, priesthood responsibilities.[58]

It is unlikely that Clayton was totally surprised when it came his turn to adopt "the principle," as it was called. He was well acquainted with all the leading people in town and could easily have had at least some inkling of what was going on. At the same time, given his personal integrity as well as his obvious devotion to his wife and children, it seems equally unlikely that he seriously broached the subject for himself until he was instructed by the prophet. But, unlike others, Clayton did not question the prophet once the instruction came, and he entered this challenging new order of things almost immediately.

It may have been his continuing friendship with Sarah Crooks, in particular, that made him a willing listener when the instructions came. The record is confusing as to whether it was in February or March 1843 that he was finally taught the doctrine, but it is clear that his affection for Sarah had something to do with the way the prophet chose to tell him about it. Over thirty years later he wrote a reminiscent account of the event and had it notarized. Here he stated that the prophet discussed the subject with him sometime in February. In his daily journal, however, he made an entry on March 9 that seems to be the same incident described in his reminiscence. Allowing for the obvious possibility that his memory was not perfect, and that he did not have his diary at hand when he made the notarized statement, it seems most accurate to rely on the chronology suggested in the diary. But that raises another interesting question. Sarah Crooks was the subject of the conversation on March 9, but Clayton had already written her a letter on February 12. Was he jumping the gun, so to speak, and inviting Sarah to come even before he was sure of the prophet's authorization? This is an interesting speculation but nothing more.

Clayton's diary suggests that he had been thinking about "the principle," and had even received some preliminary instructions from Brigham Young before he heard officially from Joseph Smith. In what seems to be a cryptic reference to it, Clayton noted on March 7, 1843, that Brigham Young called him to one side and wanted, at the first opportunity, to give him some instructions on the priesthood. "He said the prophet had told him to do so & to give me a favor which I have long desired. For this again I feel grateful to God & his servant, and the desire of my heart is to do right and be saved." Two days later William and Joseph were taking a private walk when the prophet "told me it was lawful for me to send for Sarah & said he would furnish the money." Could this be the favor he had so long desired? If his later reminiscence actually reflects that conversation of March 9, then there were some other interesting and important things said:

> One day in the month of February, date not remembered [probably, in fact, March], the prophet invited me to walk with him. During our walk he said he had learned that there was a sister back in England to whom I was very much attached. I replied there was, but nothing farther than an attachment such as a brother and sister in the church might rightfully entertain for each other. He then said, "Why don't you send for her?" I replied, "In the first place I have no authority to send for her, and if I had, I have not the means to pay expenses." To this he answered, "I give you authority to send for her, and I will furnish you the means," which he did. This was the first time the prophet Joseph talked with me on the subject of plural marriage. He informed me that the doctrine and principle was right in the sight of our Heavenly Father, and that it was a doctrine which pertained to celestial order & glory. After giving me lengthy instructions and information concerning the doctrine of celestial or plural marriage he concluded his remarks by the words, "It is your privilege to have all the wives you want." After this introduction our conversations on the subject of plural marriage were very frequent, and he appeared to take particular pains to inform and instruct me in respect to the principle. He also informed me that he had other wives *living*, besides his first wife Emma, and in particular gave me to under-

stand that Eliza R. Snow, Louisa Berman, Desdemona Fullmer, and others were his lawful wives in the sight of Heaven.[59]

During the last year of Joseph's life the two were seldom together alone when the prophet did not say something about the subject. The result was that Clayton was convinced "that the doctrine of plural and celestial marriage is the most holy and important doctrine ever revealed to man on this earth, and that without obedience to that principle no man can ever attain to the fullness of exaltation in celestial glory."[60]

The stepped-up course of instruction resulted not only in new vistas of knowledge for the prophet's clerk but also in a growing sense of spiritual exhilaration. On May 16 he was with Joseph Smith and others in Ramus, Illinois. That evening, at the home of Benjamin F. Johnson, the prophet instructed the group in the matter of eternal marriage. The impact on Clayton was immediate. "I feel desirous to be united in an everlasting covenant to my wife," he wrote in his journal, "and pray that it soon may be." On July 22 that "sealing" ordinance, as it was called, took place as he and Ruth were joined together for eternity. But Clayton received an even more powerful spiritual boost, if such were possible, in the Johnson home that night of May 16. As the instruction proceeded, Joseph suddenly put his hand on William's knee and said to him, "Your life is hid with Christ in God," and then explained to Johnson that "nothing but the unpardonable sin can prevent him [i.e., Clayton] from inheriting eternal glory for he is sealed up by the power of the priesthood unto eternal life having taken the step which is necessary for that purpose."[61] Clayton was already the husband of a second wife, and he was beginning to comprehend the sealing power of the priesthood as it applied to his eternal salvation as well as to his marriages.

Incredible as it may seem, Ruth not only accepted the principle but also welcomed each new wife into the fold and treated her warmly and with affection. This was especially true, of course, with her sister Margaret, who lived in the same house with them. The prophet, on the other hand, was not so fortunate, and it caused William no end of distress to observe the problems of his leader.

The relationship between Joseph and Emma was paradoxical, to say the least. On the one hand, the evidence clearly suggests that they were deeply in love and maintained the tenderest of feelings toward each other until the day Joseph died.[62] With the obvious exception of plural marriage, Emma openly supported him in nearly all his policies. She was appointed by her husband as the first president of the Female Relief Society, and she was a central figure in the sacred Anointed Quorum. On the other hand, understandably, she simply could not accept polygamy, and it was this that caused whatever strains came into their marriage. Curiously, it never seemed to threaten the marriage itself, but the tensions it caused were sometimes almost unbearable to both. Unfortunately for William Clayton, he became privy to some of those tensions.[63] Not only that, but Joseph's brother, Hyrum, also refused to accept either eternal or plural marriage. The two people closest to the prophet, his wife and his counselor-brother, were also the source of his greatest burden as he tried to unfold these principles to them. He did not want to open the temple and perform sealings, eternal marriages, and plural marriages for everyone else, he felt, until these two accepted the doctrines and could teach them side by side with him.

Before the end of May 1843, however, Hyrum finally accepted both the principle of eternal marriage and the principle of plural marriage. Emma, too, accepted eternal marriage, and on May 28 she was sealed to her husband for eternity.[64] Meanwhile she at least nominally, though temporarily, consented to plural marriage and reluctantly agreed to Joseph's marriage to Emily and Eliza Partridge. On May 23 she watched Judge James Adams, a high priest, perform the ceremonies. Later, it appears, she also consented to Joseph's marriage to Maria and Sarah Lawrence.[65] Marriage for eternity and the sacred temple ceremonies were all now part of Emma's fundamental faith. The thought of polygamy, however, continued to plague and dismay her, in spite of her nominal consent to some marriages, and she was never really converted to the principle.

So it was that in the midst of some of his own difficulties William Clayton was called upon by Joseph Smith to record the revelation that, the prophet hoped, would help convert his wife. As Clayton reported in his journal on July 12, 1843: "This A.M. I wrote a Revelation consisting of 10 pages on the order of the priesthood, showing the designs in Moses, Abraham, David and Solomon having many wives & concubines. After it was wrote Prests. Joseph and Hyrum presented it and read it to E. who said she did not believe a word of it and appeared very rebellious."

As Clayton recounted the story in more detail later, he was working in the office of Joseph Smith's store when the two brothers came in discussing plural marriage. The recently converted Hyrum said to Joseph, "If you will write the revelation on celestial marriage, I will take and read it to Emma, and I believe I can convince her of its truth and you will hereafter have peace." Joseph simply smiled and replied, "You do not know Emma as well as I do," but Hyrum continued to press by saying that he could convince any reasonable man or woman of its truth. Still doubtful, Joseph nevertheless consented and indicated that "he knew the revelation perfectly from beginning to end."

Joseph began to dictate, and Clayton wrote it sentence by sentence as it came from the prophet. Joseph read it over, pronounced it correct, and then let Hyrum take it to Emma. Hyrum returned a wiser man, never, he reported, having been subject to a more severe "talking to."[66]

But at least the revelation was in writing, and sometime during the day it was read to several church authorities. The next day, with Joseph's permission, Joseph C. Kingsbury made an exact copy of it. A few days later Joseph Smith told Clayton and a few friends that Emma had destroyed the original copy. Continually, he said, she had teased him about it and finally "to get rid of her annoyance" and to pacify her he allowed her to destroy it. He could dictate it again if necessary but a copy had already been preserved.[67]

Clayton watched and prayed as Joseph continued his seemingly hopeless efforts to persuade his wife. The day after the revelation was recorded Joseph called William into a private room where he and Emma had been having a serious discussion. They told William of an agreement they had entered into, and, though the details are not recorded, it must have had something to do with the principle. Both Joseph and Emma stated their feelings on many subjects and "wept considerably." Deeply affected, Clayton wrote in his journal on July 13, "O may the Lord soften her heart that she may be willing to keep and abide by his Holy Law."

The sacred, the secret, and the solemn: these gave Nauvoo the most meaning for William Clayton. Of all such experiences, however, one of the most solemn was the murder of Joseph Smith. As a nasty wound eventually heals and even strengthens some member of the body, the death of the prophet left a void in Clayton's life that in the healing only strengthened his internalization of and commitment to all Joseph Smith had done.

Though Clayton, and perhaps most of the faithful Saints, did not perceive it that way, Joseph Smith's death was in some respects a political assassination. It was clear to the residents of western Illinois that the Mormons were a growing political force and that neither the Whigs nor the Democrats could count on their consistent support at the polls. At least by 1843 both parties had stopped courting their favor, and much of the populace seemed willing to believe almost any story about them. Rumors of polygamy were rampant, which was enough to raise the righteous indignation of even moderate citizens. Misperceptions of Joseph Smith's teachings about the political Kingdom of God only added to the fearful accusations that the Mormons were attempting to gain the kind of political influence that might even lead to a religious state. John C. Bennett, who had earlier maneuvered his way into the confidence of Joseph Smith and was even elected mayor of Nauvoo, became so enraged when certain of his chicaneries were discovered that he published a series of newspaper exposés denouncing Mormon leaders for allegedly threatening his life, swindling local citizens, immorality, and plotting the conquest of certain Midwest states. And after Thomas Sharp, editor of the *Warsaw Signal*, was defeated by William Smith in the 1842 election for the state House of Representatives, he bitterly stepped up his already vehement newspaper attacks on the Mormons, calling for their extermination or expulsion.[68] It did not help matters in Illinois when Joseph Smith announced his candidacy for the presidency of the United States.

The story of the deaths of Joseph and Hyrum Smith is well known, but to follow the events through the eyes of William Clayton helps one sense more deeply the mounting tenseness and apprehension felt in the preceding weeks by those closest to the prophet. The Twelve were away on missions (promoting, at least part of the time, the prophet's presidential platform), and Joseph therefore had none of the top church leaders to rely on during the final difficulties. He naturally turned to his closest friends, including William Clayton.

The final events were precipitated on June 7, when a group of bitter seceders from the church and other non-Mormons published the first and only number of the *Nauvoo Expositor*. All the charges were there, including so-called political dictatorship and polygamy, and William Clayton was incensed. He knew the prophet well enough to know he was no dictator and that his personal morality was of the highest order. "Truly," he wrote of the *Expositor* in what was almost an understatement, "it seems to be a source of falsehood and bitter misrepresentation."[69] After the city council declared the offending newspaper a public nuisance and had its press destroyed, a groundswell of outrage raced through the area and all the old hatreds seemed to focus on Joseph Smith.[70] Clayton heard rumors of mob action, heard Joseph Smith telling the Saints in Nauvoo to stand firm and protect themselves, and saw Joseph writing the Twelve, requesting them to come home without delay. It was a time of foreboding, and William Clayton sensed it deeply. Threats on the prophet's life were openly made, and the governor of the state, Thomas Ford, traveled to Carthage in a personal attempt to keep the peace.

On the evening of June 22 William Clayton called on Joseph Smith to discuss the best measures to be taken in case of mob attack. He then went home, but suddenly, at 1 A.M., he was roused with the message that Joseph wanted him. Fully aware of the plot afoot to take their lives, Joseph and Hyrum had decided that the best thing for them as well as for the church was to flee across the Mississippi and perhaps find refuge in the Rocky Mountains. Joseph, Hyrum, and Willard Richards were preparing to leave, and Joseph told William W. Phelps, another close friend and scribe, to inform their wives and get their feelings on the subject. When Clayton arrived at the river, Joseph whispered his assignment to him: he was to give the records of the Kingdom of God (i.e., the Council of Fifty) to a faithful man who would take them away to safety, or he should burn or bury them. Clayton certainly could not bear to part with or destroy the sacred and important records he had so faithfully kept, so he hurried home and early that Sunday morning gathered up not only the private records but also the public records and buried them.

That afternoon Joseph and Hyrum changed their minds, partly because Emma Smith sent a message to her husband urging them to return. They finally decided to submit themselves to arrest, go to Carthage, and try again to be released through the legal process. Late that afternoon as Joseph arrived back in Nauvoo, Clayton was there to greet him.

The next morning Joseph, Hyrum, and several others whose names appeared on a writ started for Carthage. On the way they encountered a Captain Dunn with a contingent of militia, who had orders from the governor that the state arms in possession of the citizens of Nauvoo (i.e., the Nauvoo Legion) should be turned over to him. Joseph returned to Nauvoo, countersigned the order, and instructed his followers to obey it. But Clayton caught the true feelings of the citizens of Nauvoo when he wrote: "Many of the brethren looked upon this as another preparation for a Missouri massacre nevertheless as Joseph requested they very unwillingly gave up the arms."[71] Later in the day Joseph left Nauvoo the second time, and Clayton sadly observed: "Prest Jos. rode down home to bid his family farewell. He appeared to feel solemn & though[t]ful and from expressions made to several individuals, he expects nothing but to be massacred. This he expressed before he returned from over the river but their appearing no alternative but he must either give himself up or the City be massacred by a lawless mob under the sanction of the Governor."[72]

By the next day Clayton and others were fully persuaded that mobsters were ready to attack the city. One piece of convincing evidence appeared when Joseph Smith's colorful and impetuous bodyguard, Orrin Porter Rockwell, got into a fight with one of the dissenters, Francis M. Higbee. A letter fell out of Higbee's hat, and whoever recovered it read that seventy mobsters were gathered on the Iowa side of the river planning to descend upon Nauvoo that night.[73]

On Wednesday, June 26, Clayton had his last chance to perform a service for Joseph Smith. In Carthage jail, about noon, the prophet wrote a letter to Jesse B. Thomas, presiding judge of the circuit court. Thomas was friendly to the Mormons and Joseph thought of him as "a great man and a gentleman."[74] Ten days earlier Thomas had advised Joseph with regard to the *Expositor* affair, telling him that he should go before some justice in the county and have an examination of the charges specified in the writ against him. Joseph had followed that advice and was dismissed from custody in a *habeas corpus* hearing in Nauvoo. In his letter Joseph briefly explained his circumstances and asked the judge to go to Nauvoo, make himself comfortable at the Smith home, and be ready to hear another *habeas corpus* case. Joseph, who expected to go to Nauvoo with the governor the next day, sent the letter to William Clayton with instructions that he should get a messenger to take it to Judge Thomas. Clayton received the message that afternoon, did as he was instructed, then sat down and wrote his final letter to Joseph Smith. It contained several short messages. One was that a Mr. Marsh, with whom Joseph had done business, was ready to put up bail for him in any amount. He also reported that he had sent the message to Judge Thomas and ended his letter with these words: "All is peace in Nauvoo. Many threats keep coming that the mob are determined to attack the city in your absence, but we have no fears. With fervency and true friendship, I remain yours eternally, William Clayton." The letter arrived at Carthage jail at 6:15.[75]

The next day, June 27, Clayton saw the governor arrive in Nauvoo, listened to him talk, and was outraged at what he thought was an unfair and intemperate speech. Little did he realize that late that afternoon his prophet was murdered by a mob.

Clayton went to bed on that evening, oblivious of the tragic affair taking place in Carthage. Early the next morning Orrin P. Rockwell woke him up with the stunning news that Joseph and Hyrum had been shot to death. His diary entry for that day is one of the longest he ever wrote, and it contains within it all the sorrow, solemnity, and dismay that any disciple could feel. "I went out & met brother Cutler & several others," he wrote, "and the news soon became general. Sorrow & gloom was pictured in every countenance and one universal scene of lamentation pervaded the city. The agony of the widows & orphan children [i.e., the wives and children of Joseph and Hyrum] was inexpressible and utterly beyond description." He went on with a lengthy description of what had happened at Carthage, as he understood it (which turned out to be a fairly accurate account), emphasizing what he considered to be the culpability of the governor for not providing better protection for the prophet. He then wrote a prayer that, though vengeful in its tone, is a perfect reflection of the anger and frustration felt by many at the sudden tragedy:

And now O God wilt thou not come out of thy hiding place and avenge the blood of thy servants.—that blood which thou hast so long watched over with a fatherly care—that blood so noble—so generous—so dignified, so heavenly you O Lord will thou not avenge it speedily and bring down vengeance upon the murderers of thy servants that they may be rid from off the earth and that the earth may be cleansed from these scenes, even so O Lord thy will be done. We look to thee for justice. Hear thy people O God of Jacob even so Amen.

Clayton saw the bodies of Joseph and Hyrum arrive in Nauvoo about 2 P.M. and was part of the large procession of mourners that collected on the hill and followed them to the Mansion House. There they heard exhortations to be peaceful and calm and not to utter threats. He concluded his diary entry for the day:

Few expressions were heard save the mourns for the loss of our friends. All seem to hang on the mercy of God and wait further events. Some few can scarce refrain from expressing aloud their indignation at the Governor and a few words would raise the City in arms & massacre the Cities of Carthage & Warsaw & lay them in ashes but it is wisdom to be quiet. After the bodies were laid out I went in to see them. Joseph looks very natural except being pale through loss of blood. Hyrum does not look so natural. Their aged mother is distracted with grief & it will be almost more than she can bear.

Thus ended the life of the man for whom William Clayton came to Nauvoo in the first place, the man who gave Nauvoo its ultimate meaning for him. But what *was* that meaning, both for Clayton and the Mormon people? It was different for different people, of course, but perhaps for William Clayton it can be summed up in the aftermath of the martyrdom of the prophet.

Joseph was Clayton's ideal, and his death on June 27 was a profound and indelible shock. "The blood of those men," he wrote in that long entry of June 28, "and the prayers of the widows and orphans and a suffering community will rise up to the Lord of Sabaoth for vengeance upon those murderers." Not that Clayton himself would take vengeance—violence was no part of his personality—but he fully expected that somehow, some time, the perpetrators of the crime as well as the people that allowed it to happen would be duly punished. He was shocked when those accused of the assassination, including Thomas Sharp, were tried but not convicted. "Thus the whole State of Illinois have made themselves guilty of shedding the blood of the prophets by acquitting those who committed the horrid deed," he wrote later in his history of the temple, "and it is now left to God and his saints to take vengeance in his own way and in his own time."[76]

In the confusing times that followed, Clayton observed the various claimants to church leadership and was himself in the thick of the debate over who should take Joseph's place as trustee-in-trust. He resented Emma's efforts to draw Joseph's property to herself and to influence the selection of the trustees.[77] For a short time Clayton himself was appointed as the temporary trustee. As he observed the debates on what should happen he could not help but comment that "the greatest danger that no[w] threatens us is dissensions and strifes amongst the church. There are already 4 or 5 men pointed out as successors to the Trustee & President & there is danger of feelings being manifest. All the brethren who stand at the head seem to feel the delicacy of the business."[78]

There were several seemingly viable alternatives so far as leadership was concerned. The decision one made depended in part, at least, on his personal experience in Nauvoo as well as deep emotional considerations. This was especially true of Clayton. Of all the options available, what Nauvoo meant to him could only be fulfilled in the course taken by Brigham Young and the Twelve. For him Nauvoo was Joseph Smith, but it was also the most sacred, trying, and emotional experiences to which Joseph Smith had introduced him. Only through the Twelve would the Council of Fifty, the Anointed Quorum, the endowment, the eternity of marriage, and the practice of plural marriage be maintained as he understood them. Clayton was never as intimate with Brigham Young as he was with Joseph Smith—there was, in fact, a seeming coolness at times. But because of his personal involvement with so many private activities and concerns of the prophet, it was easy for him to transfer his loyalty to the man who seemed most likely to carry on those same activities.

In a way William Clayton's Nauvoo was the secret Nauvoo, for all the things that had the most long-lasting effect on him were secrets he shared with the prophet and a limited number of faithful disciples. Thousands of other westering Mormons were introduced to the temple ceremonies before they left Nauvoo and to the concept of eternal marriage, but comparatively few were aware of polygamy and its implications. Other Mormons who may or may not have known of these things followed either Brigham Young or some other claimant to leadership for various emotional or rational reasons. But the church Clayton knew and loved in 1845 was something different from the church he knew in 1840, and Joseph Smith had been responsible for all that was new. William was absolutely committed to the change, and he would stay with it.

Clayton's Nauvoo, then, was really the Joseph Smith he knew, and in later years he kept the memory of that Joseph Smith alive. He constantly reminded the Utah Saints of what Joseph had said and done, and on one occasion was even criticized for not being able to bend enough to preach one aspect of the gospel "according to Brigham" instead of the way he remembered Joseph putting it.[79] On another occasion one of his sons found him weeping as he listened to some brethren singing, and he explained that this singing reminded him of the prophet. It was a natural opportunity for the boy to ask, "Father, did the Prophet Joseph really see an angel?" Clayton forcefully replied, "My son, he did see an angel, and don't you ever doubt it."[80] At the same time William recognized the subjective, emotional nature of his commitment to the prophet of Nauvoo, and he admitted it. As he wrote to Joseph C. Rich in 1869, "I could not hear the 'old settlers' talk coolley about the murder of the prophet and Patriarch without getting terribly mad and showing it. You did not feel it as I did, hence you can act wisely and with prudence. I could not."[81]

NOTES

1. Clayton, Nauvoo Journal, "Reflections," 1 Jan. 1845.

2. Doctrine and Covenants 124:41.

3. Ibid., 39.

4. Clayton, "History of the Nauvoo Temple," 21. For a short general account of the building of the temple, see Miller and Miller, Nauvoo, 107–21. For a description of the font, see History of the Church, 4:446–47. See also Lisle G. Brown, "The Sacred Departments for Temple Work in Nauvoo: The Assembly Room and the Council Chamber," BYU Studies 19 (Spring 1979):361–74; Stanley B. Kimball, "The Nauvoo Temple," Improvement Era 66 (Nov. 1963):974–78, 980, 982, 984; Don F. Colvin, "A Historical Study of the Mormon Temple at Nauvoo, Illinois" (Master's thesis, Brigham Young University, 1962).

5. Clayton, Nauvoo Journal, 28 Nov. 1841; History of the Church, 5:196–97.

6. Clayton, Nauvoo Journal, 21 Dec. 1842.

7. Ibid., 7 Apr. 1843; History of the Church, 5:337–38.

8. Clayton, Nauvoo Journal, 2 Dec. 1843.

9. Clayton to Brigham Young, 30 May 1843, Brigham Young Papers.

10. Clayton, Nauvoo Journal, 21 Apr. 1843.

11. Clayton to William Hardman, as printed in Millennial Star 3 (Aug. 1842):74–76, reprinted in BYU Studies 12 (Autumn 1971):120–23.

12. History of the Church, 6:383.

13. Clayton, Nauvoo Journal, 30 Jan. 1844.

14. Ibid., 9 Mar. 1844.

15. Ibid., 1 Aug. 1843. Compare History of the Church, 5:523–24. See also ibid., 531. This is Willard Richards's report of a speech given by Joseph Smith on 13 Aug. 1843, in which the prophet commented on the same incident. The report is slightly different from Clayton's account: "He then complained of the treatment he had received from Walter Bagby, the county assessor and collector, who has exercised more despotic power over the inhabitants of the city than any despot of the eastern country over his serfs. I met him, and he

gave me some abusive language, taking up a stone to throw at me: I seized him by the throat to choke him off."

16. See Doctrine and Covenants 21:1; 47:1, 3, 4; 69:3–8; 85:1, for various early revelations to Joseph Smith emphasizing the importance of historical records. Joseph Smith first began writing and dictating his own history in 1832.

17. *Deseret News*, 20 Jan. 1858, as quoted in Dean C. Jessee, "The Writing of Joseph Smith's History," *BYU Studies* 11 (Summer 1971):473.

18. In preface by B. H. Roberts to *History of the Church*, iii.

19. This concept is well developed by Dean C. Jessee in his preface to *Personal Writings of Joseph Smith*. See also Jessee, "The Reliability of Joseph Smith's History," *Journal of Mormon History* 3 (1976):23–47, for a very important critical evaluation of that work. For further details on the writing and reliability of Joseph Smith's *History*, see Jessee, *Has Mormon History Been Deliberately Falsified?* (Sandy, Utah: Mormon Miscellaneous, 1982); Howard C. Searle, "Authorship of the History of Joseph Smith, a Review Essay," *BYU Studies* 21 (Winter 1981):101–22; Searle, "Early Mormon Historiography: Writing the History of the Mormons, 1830–1858" (Ph.D. diss., University of California, Los Angeles, 1979).

20. *History of the Church*, 5:372.

21. Stanley B. Kimball, "Kinderhook Plates Brought to Joseph Smith Appear to be a Nineteenth-Century Hoax," *Ensign* 11 (Aug. 1981):66–74.

22. Jessee's *Personal Writings of Joseph Smith* is a pathbreaking publication in this effort, for here he reproduced only those items that were written in Joseph Smith's own hand or were clearly taken down verbatim as dictated by the Mormon prophet. For years Jessee has been working on the *History of the Church*, attempting to determine all the manuscript sources for it.

23. Jessee, ed., *Personal Writings of Joseph Smith*, 525–37, 690–91. Additional information on the "Book of the Law of the Lord" was graciously provided by Dean C. Jessee.

24. Clayton, Nauvoo Journal, 18 May 1843.

25. *Deseret News*, 24 Sept. 1856. Compare *History of the Church*, 5:393–94.

26. *History of the Church*, 5:395–98.

27. In 1852, for example, Clayton kept two journals while he was crossing the plains on his way to England on a mission. One was his personal journal, and the other was the official camp journal. The entries largely duplicate each other, but there are some variations.

28. A case in point is seen in some of Joseph Smith's comments on the resurrection of little children. At least as early as March 1842, he was teaching that little children would be resurrected not as full-grown individuals but with the same stature as when they died and that they would not grow further. Their intelligence, however, would be equal to that of anyone. (See Joseph Smith's sermon of 20 Mar. 1842, as reported in the *History of the Church*, 4:553–56; Woodruff Journal, 20 Mar. 1842, as reproduced in Andrew F. Ehat and Lyndon W. Cook, eds., *The Words of Joseph Smith* [Provo, Utah: BYU Religious Studies Center, 1980], 106–9.) On 18 May 1843, Clayton asked Joseph whether children who die in infancy would grow. "He answered 'no, we shall

receive them precisely in the same state as they died in no larger. They will have as much intelligence as we shall but shall always remain separate and single. They will have no increase. Children who are born dead will have full grown bodies being made up by the resurrection'" (Clayton, Nauvoo Journal, 18 May 1843). The same doctrine was also taught in the famous King Follett Discourse by Joseph Smith on 7 Apr. 1844. This doctrine never "caught on," however, in the mainstream of Mormon thought. Some have tried to explain it simply by suggesting that it may have been reported inaccurately (see, for example, B. H. Roberts's editorial comment on the March 1842 sermon in *History of the Church*, 4:556, note, and his bracketed insertions, with editorial comment, in the King Follett Discourse in ibid., 6:316). An equally reasonable explanation for Mormons, however, is that even the prophet was not above doctrinal speculation at times and that this may have been one of those occasions. Clayton's reporting of the idea in his diary adds strength to the evidence that Joseph taught the doctrine, but this should not be disturbing to Mormons who recognize that not everything the prophet ever said carried a "thus saith the Lord" stamp.

29. Clayton, Nauvoo Journal, 22 Jan. 1843. Compare *History of the Church*, 5:256–59. The sermon as recorded in the *History of the Church* dealt with much more than Clayton suggests in his journal, but he was evidently most impressed with the statement given above (compare also Doctrine and Covenants 90:4–5; 124:39, 124–26).

30. The first recorded presentation by Joseph Smith of this idea was to members of the Quorum of the Twelve on 27 June 1839, as they were preparing for their important mission to England. (See *Wilford Woodruff's Journal*, and Ehat and Cook, eds., *Words of Joseph Smith*, 6.) Apparently Joseph taught it somewhat regularly after that, however, before it was received by the church as a revelation and finally put in the Doctrine and Covenants, where it now stands as Section 129. References to his teaching it are found on 8 Aug. 1839, in December 1840, and on 21 Mar. 1841 (ibid., 12, 44, 66). The December 1840 reference is reproduced by Ehat and Cook from a reference cited as "William Clayton's Private Book." If the original of this source exists, its whereabouts is not known. L. John Nuttall and Joseph F. Smith, however, each made excerpts from it, and Ehat and Cook apparently got their quotation from the Nuttall excerpts. The excerpts constitute a relatively few pages of doctrinal teachings attributed to Joseph Smith. The Nuttall Papers are housed in the library of Brigham Young University, Provo, Utah.

31. The whole of Section 131 of the Doctrine and Covenants, for example, is excerpted from his entries for 16 and 17 May 1843.

32. See Donald Q. Cannon, "The King Follett Discourse: Joseph Smith's Greatest Sermon in Historical Perspective," *BYU Studies* 18 (Winter 1978):179–92; Stan Larson, "The King Follett Discourse: A Newly Amalgamated Text," ibid., 193–208; Van Hale, "The Doctrinal Impact of the King Follett Discourse," ibid., 209–25.

33. "Lectures on Faith," bound with the 1835 edition of the Doctrine and Covenants 52–53.

34. Parley P. Pratt, *Mormonism Unveiled: Zion's Watchman Unmasked, and Its Editor, Mr. L. R. Sunderland, Exposed: Truth Vindicated: The Devil and Priestcraft in Danger!* (New York: Parley P. Pratt, 1838), 29.

35. In Clayton's Nauvoo Journal, 2 Apr. 1843, he simply makes reference to the latter part of the statement, indicating that "the Holy Ghost is a personage, and a person cannot have the personage of the H. G. in his heart. A man may receive the gifts of the H. G., and the H. G. may descend upon a man but not tarry with him." (Compare Doctrine and Covenants 130:22–23; *History of the Church,* 5:325. See commentary in Ehat and Cook, eds., *Words of Joseph Smith,* 268, note 5.)

36. For further treatment of the development of some church doctrines, see James B. Allen, "Line Upon Line," *Ensign* 9 (July 1979):32–39; Allen, "Emergence of a Fundamental: The Expanding Role of Joseph Smith's First Vision in Mormon Religious Thought," *Journal of Mormon History* 7 (1980):43–62; Thomas G. Alexander, "The Reconstruction of Mormon Doctrine: From Joseph Smith to Progressive Theology," *Sunstone* 5 (July-Aug. 1980):24–33.

37. Doctrine and Covenants 76.

38. Clayton, Nauvoo Journal, 16 May 1843. The full quotation from Clayton is interesting: "He said that except a man and his wife enter into an everlasting covenant and be married for eternity while in this probation by the power and authority of the Holy priesthood they will cease to increase when they die (i.e., they will not have any children in the resurrection), but those who are married by the power & authority of the priesthood in this life & continue without committing the sin against the Holy Ghost will continue to increase & have children in the celestial glory."

39. Ibid.; compare Doctrine and Covenants 131:1–4.

40. Clayton, Nauvoo Journal, 16 Apr. 1843. For a more complete version of the funeral sermon, compare *History of the Church,* 5:360–63.

41. Clayton, Nauvoo Journal, 17 May 1843.

42. Ibid., 23 Jan. 1844.

43. For studies of the Council of Fifty see Hansen, *Quest for Empire;* James R. Clark, "The Kingdom of God, the Council of Fifty, and the State of Deseret," *Utah Historical Quarterly* 26 (Apr. 1958):130–48; Marvin S. Hill, "Quest for Refuge: An Hypothesis as to the Social Origins and Nature of the Mormon Political Kingdom," *Journal of Mormon History* 2 (1975):3–20; D. Michael Quinn, "The Council of Fifty and Its Members, 1844 to 1945," *BYU Studies* 20 (Winter 1980):163–97; Andrew F. Ehat, "It Seems Like Heaven Began on Earth: Joseph Smith and the Constitution of the Kingdom of God," *BYU Studies* 20 (Spring 1980):253–80.

44. *History of the Church,* 6:254–60; Flanders, *Nauvoo,* 290–92; Clayton, Nauvoo Journal, 10–11 Mar. 1844.

45. *History of the Church,* 6:260–63; Clayton, Nauvoo Journal, 13 Mar. 1844. At the beginning of 1845 Clayton reminisced about the importance of the new organization: "This organization was called the council of fifty or kingdom of God and was titled by revelation as follows, 'Verily thus saith the Lord, this is the name by which you shall be called, the kingdom of God and his

law with the keys and power thereof and judgments in the hands of his servants
Ahman Christ.' In this council was the plan arranged for supporting president
Joseph Smith as a candidate for the presidency of the U.S. Prest. Joseph was
the standing chairman of the council and myself the clerk. In this council was
also devised the plan of establishing an immigration to Texas and plans laid
for the exaltation of a standard and ensign of truths for the nations of the
earth. In this council was the plan devised to restore the Ancients to the
knowledge of the truth and the restoration of union and peace amongst ourselves. In this council was Prest. Joseph chosen as our prophet, Priest, & King
by Hosannas. In this council was the principles of eternal truths rolled forth
to the hearers without reserve and the hearts of the servants of God made to
rejoice exceedingly" (Clayton, Nauvoo Journal, 1 Jan. 1845).

46. Clayton, Nauvoo Journal, 11 Apr. 1844, records the vote: "Prest. J. was
voted our P. P. & King with loud Hosannas." This is a very important entry
so far as the history of the Council of Fifty is concerned, but the question as
to whether Joseph Smith was actually ordained a king is still debatable. Evidence presented in Hansen, *Quest for Empire*, is open to some question. Clayton, Nauvoo Journal, 18 Aug. 1844, provides one indication that Clayton spent
a lot of time copying the records of the Kingdom.

47. Clayton, Nauvoo Journal, 10 Mar. 1845. The grand council in heaven
refers to the Mormon belief that the "plan of salvation" was presented to all
God's spirit children (i.e., all mankind in their premortal state), and those who
accepted it were those who would have the privilege of coming to earth for a
probationary period. See Abraham 3:22–28 in the Pearl of Great Price. For more
on Joseph Smith's prayer circle, see D. Michael Quinn, "Latter-day Saint Prayer
Circles," *BYU Studies* 19 (Fall 1978):79–105.

48. Clayton, Nauvoo Journal, 3 Feb. 1844. With reference to the apparent
stress between William Clayton and Emma Smith, it might be noted that even
a week or so before Clayton wrote to Joseph Smith, he lamented in his journal
that Emma had power to prevent him from being admitted to Joseph's "Lodge."
The term "Lodge" seems almost certainly to refer to the Anointed Quorum
(ibid., 21 Nov. 1843).

49. Ibid., 7 Dec. 1845.

50. Ibid., 30 Nov. 1845; B. H. Roberts, ed., *History of The Church of Jesus
Christ of Latter-day Saints: Period II, from the Manuscript History of Brigham
Young and Other Original Documents* (Salt Lake City: Deseret News, 1930),
7:534-35. (This volume, hereafter cited as Roberts, ed., *History of the Church*,
is a continuation of the *History of the Church* [6 vols.].) The latter entry is
based almost verbatim on the Clayton journal, except that a few items in the
journal are omitted, such as the fact that the participants were dressed in their
temple clothing and that they rehearsed the ceremonies.

51. Clayton, Nauvoo Journal, 10-11 Dec. 1845.

52. A fine and very important paper on the origin of the concept of "eternal
marriage" and its relationship to "plural marriage" is Andrew F. Ehat's "An
Overview of the Introduction of Eternal Marriage in The Church of Jesus
Christ of Latter-day Saints: 1840–43" (unpublished manuscript in possession

of the author, 1980). This material is also incorporated in Ehat's "Joseph Smith's Introduction of Temple Ordinances and the 1844 Mormon Succession Question" (Master's thesis, Brigham Young University, 1982). Ehat marshals a great deal of evidence relating to the introduction of the eternal marriage concept. He has also done some excellent sleuthing in order to arrive at the date of Emma Smith's "sealing" to Joseph.

53. It seems sigificant to note here that, as detailed in Chapter 7 herein, Clayton's first three plural wives were women he had known in England, and that he also proposed to Sarah Crooks the moment he could get permission from the prophet. For a statistical analysis of polygamous marriages, see Stanley S. Ivins, "Notes on Mormon Polygamy," *Western Humanities Review* 10 (Summer 1956):229–30. Clayton was among the very small minority that took more than one additional wife.

54. In the modern church this is also sometimes referred to as the doctrine of "celestial marriage." There was a distinction in the days of Joseph Smith, however, as the term *celestial marriage* seemed to be used as a synonym for *plural marriage*. It is also a Mormon doctrine that living people may be "sealed" by proxy in behalf of the dead who had no chance to have the ordinance performed properly on the earth, just as they may perform proxy baptisms.

55. Jacob 2:30, in Book of Mormon.

56. For the best discussion on plural marriage in Nauvoo, and particularly with reference to the evidence dealing with Joseph Smith's wives, see Daniel W. Bachman, "A Study of the Mormon Practice of Plural Marriage before the Death of Joseph Smith" (Master's thesis, Purdue University, 1975). See also Richard S. Van Wagoner, "Mormon Polyandry in Nauvoo," *Dialogue: A Journal of Mormon Thought* 18 (Fall 1985):67–83. For an insightful discussion into the way plural marriage was generally accepted by the women of the church, see Kahlile Mehr, "Women's Response to Plural Marriage," ibid., 84–98.

57. Helen Mar Whitney, *Why We Practice Plural Marriage* (Salt Lake City: Juvenile Instructor Office, 1884), 53, as cited in Kimball, *Heber C. Kimball*, 87.

58. Kimball, *Heber C. Kimball*, 93-96.

59. William Clayton, "Another Testimony—Statement of William Clayton," 16 Feb. 1874, a statement notarized by John T. Caine, MS, Clayton Papers, 3-5. Here Clayton misspelled the name of Louisa Beaman.

60. Ibid., 12.

61. Quotations above are from Clayton, Nauvoo Journal, for the dates indicated. See also *History of the Church*, 5:391. On that occasion Joseph Smith said that the "unpardonable sin is to shed innocent blood, or be an accessory thereto." Elsewhere, denying the Holy Spirit or, in other words, denying Christ after having received the testimony of the Holy Spirit concerning the divinity of Christ, is called unforgivable. Doctrine and Covenants 76:34-35. Some Mormon authorities join these two ideas by observing that to deny Christ is the same as joining in shedding his blood. Bruce R. McConkie, *A New Witness for the Articles of Faith* (Salt Lake City: Deseret Book Company, 1985), 232-33.

62. Richard L. Anderson is currently preparing for publication the letters of Joseph and Emma. These letters clearly demonstrate this fact. In addition, a recent biography of Emma Smith, *Mormon Enigma: Emma Hale Smith* (Garden City, N.Y.: Doubleday, 1984), by Linda King Newell and Valarie Tippets Avery, has shed much new light on the relationship between Joseph and Emma.

63. Clayton provides important evidence for the fact that Emma recognized the existence of the doctrine of plural marriage, that it caused some strain between her and Joseph, and that she came near, at times, to accepting it. See James B. Allen, "One Man's Nauvoo: William Clayton's Experience in Mormon Illinois," *Journal of Mormon History* 6 (1979):44, note 17. Newell and Avery's *Mormon Enigma* provides more evidence of this.

64. Ehat, "Joseph Smith's Introduction of Temple Ordinances," 61–63. On 26 May 1843, Clayton made a special note in his Nauvoo journal that this was the day "Hyrum received the doctrine of the priesthood." This clearly meant plural marriage.

65. Newell and Avery, *Mormon Enigma*, 142–44.

66. Clayton, "Another Testimony."

67. Ibid. For a full and perceptive discussion of the authenticity of Clayton's claims concerning the revelation, see Bachman, "Plural Marriage," 204–16. For a comment on Joseph Kingsbury's involvement in copying the revelation, see Lyndon W. Cook, *Joseph C. Kingsbury: A Biography* (Provo, Utah: Grandin Book Company, 1985), 78–79.

68. For more details and references on some political issues, and on the martyrdom, see Chapter 8 herein.

69. Clayton, Nauvoo Journal, 7 Apr. 1844.

70. For a thorough study of the *Expositor* affair and its legal ramifications, see Dallin H. Oaks, "The Suppression of the *Nauvoo Expositor*," *Utah Law Review* 9 (Winter 1965):862–903.

71. Clayton, Nauvoo Journal, 24 June 1844.

72. Ibid.

73. Ibid., 25 June 1844. As Clayton described the fight: "O. P. Rockwell has been whipping F. M. Higbee."

74. *History of the Church*, 6:413.

75. Clayton, Nauvoo Journal, 26 June 1844; *History of the Church*, 6:598–99.

76. Clayton, "History of the Nauvoo Temple," 80–81.

77. Clayton's discomfort with Emma probably began during Joseph Smith's lifetime, partly because of the strains he saw over the problem of polygamy, and therefore some of his reporting may have been distorted. On 21 May 1844, for example, Clayton reported that when Joseph had ridden outside of Nauvoo to keep away from an officer with a subpoena, he sent Clayton to find out how Emma felt about Joseph's returning home. "I found her crying with rage and fury because he had gone away," Clayton wrote. "She wanted him to go home. I came and told him & he returned home at 9 o'clock." What Clayton did not report was that Emma was very ill at the time and Joseph was evidently worried about her (see *History of the Church*, 6:398–99).

78. Clayton, Nauvoo Journal, 6 July 1844.

79. Minutes of the School of the Prophets, Salt Lake City, 10 Feb. 1873, Church Archives.

80. Louis Clayton, "William Clayton," Instructor 82 (May 1947):205.

81. Clayton to Jos. C. Rich, 19 Dec. 1869, William Clayton Letterbooks, Bancroft Collection, University of California, Berkeley (microfilm in Church Archives). Hereafter, all William Clayton letters are from the Bancroft Collection unless otherwise noted.

CHAPTER 6

Tragedy's Aftermath

A few weeks after the murder of Joseph Smith, William Clayton turned thirty. He was still a young man, but his permanent attitudes toward the world around him were formed and certain idiosyncracies were indelibly stamped on his personality. One was a kind of pensiveness, almost melancholy, as he often brooded privately over his concerns. Financial difficulties, family stresses, the unsaintly actions of a few Saints, his own perceptions of his personal weaknesses, overwork, and the problems confronting the church: all these and more gave him cause to reflect deeply and sometimes darkly about both the past and the future. But his ruminations also reflected another well-formed trait: his unwavering conviction that eventually God would overrule all evil, that even the most serious problems were part of a grand scheme that must inevitably result in good, and that the Saints would one day see the fulfillment of everything Joseph Smith had taught and stood for. The triumph of the Kingdom was on the horizon, and this hope made life tolerable.

Joseph Smith was so much a part of Clayton's affairs in life, that even in death the prophet touched his every waking hour. On July 4, 1844, for example, his American Independence Day thoughts were mainly of the martyrdom. "Liberty is fled," he moaned, and the flag stained with innocent blood, for the nation had rejected the gospel and the prophets. There was no public celebration in Nauvoo: "Instead of celebrating with splendor with joy we celebrate her [the nation's] down-fall with grief and mourn for the loss of our prophet & Patriarch & pray to God to avenge their blood speedily." While in St. Louis four months later, Clayton walked down Front Street and stopped to watch a man working on a stone marker. He was astonished to find the words "high water June 27th 1844" already inscribed. "This was the day when this generation rejected the prophet of God," he was reminded. It was also the day floodwaters had overflowed the Mississippi and covered Front Street. In Clayton's mind the high water marker was a sign of the providence of God. "I suppose they never considered that this monument pointed directly to the day when they murdered the men of God," he mused. "But I thought of it and could not help but wonder at the circumstances. I feel to hope that the monument will stand to put future generations in remembrance of the circumstances and time of the murder."[1]

All Joseph's friends were affected deeply, but some took their sorrow to extremes. Orrin Porter Rockwell, the dead prophet's rough-and-ready bodyguard, even threatened violence, much to Clayton's dismay. On July 7 Robert D. Foster, an apostate presumably implicated in the murder, unwisely came to Nauvoo on business. Rockwell went into a rage, threatening to kill him if he stayed. The city council even had to appoint a bodyguard for Foster. Clayton had no sympathy for the man, but believed that public sentiment would turn in favor of the Mormons if only they would stay calm. He pleaded with Rockwell to desist for, he said, if anyone were assassinated the governor would hold the whole city responsible. The day was saved by a self-appointed committee of nine women, including Mary Fielding Smith, wife of the martyred Hyrum Smith, and Leonora Taylor, wife of the wounded John Taylor. On the tenth they paid an unexpected visit to Foster, told him they would bear his insults no longer, and threatened that if he did not leave the city forthwith he would be visited by a stronger force the next day. "The Dr was much frightened," recorded Clayton in a somewhat roguish tone, "and looked every way for fear some one would be upon him. He is gone away and there are hopes that he will never return." The next day the same sisters were ready to wait upon still more apostates and persuade them to leave in the same manner.[2]

At year-end Clayton was still engrossed in bitter thoughts of the evil world that had so brutally taken his beloved leader. He was temperamentally prepared to divorce himself from that world, and in his lengthy "Reflections" of New Year's Day 1845, he poured out all his feelings. Covering several pages in his diary, this private soliloquy was no doubt an unspoken reflection of the sentiments harbored by many disciples of Nauvoo in the aftermath of Carthage. "The year 1844 has passed away with all its sorrow, joys and extraordinary scenes," he began, and then described some of those scenes in colorful language that literally oozed bitterness and disgust. Not only was the world corrupt and full of "hellish traditions," but it was "sustained by a sectarian priesthood, whose officers are the legitimate sons and daughters of the great whore of all the earth." This "ungodly generation" was slumbering in the arms of Satan, "under whose caresses they feel perfectly safe and at ease." The Saints were thus engaged in a holy war, for, said Clayton, "These characters with mobocratic governments at their right hand, and Satin at their head run this little world and their united efforts are to destroy the few who seek to serve God according to his ordinances." God, however, was with the Saints, "their rear guard & their leader," and the important events of that year seemed to prove it. One such event had been the organization of the Kingdom of God or the Council of Fifty. Another was the period of heavy floods, while a third was the martyrdom itself. Tragic as it was, Clayton saw the murder as at least fulfilling some purpose, for it would permanently stain wicked Illinois with the "innocent blood of the two best men who ever lived on the earth," and it would indelibly write in the hearts of the Saints the memory of that awful day. In this, at least, Clayton was prophetic, for, next only to the First Vision and the Book of Mormon, the martyrdom has become a sacred story of Mormon piety.

But Clayton's year-end reflections were not all negative. He had received two new "companions" (i.e., wives: Margaret Moon and Alice Hardman) and had a "good prospect of adding another crown to my family [i.e., Diantha Farr] which is a source of great consolation to me." The Saints were united in sustaining the Twelve, and on the whole the year closed "with the blessing of Almighty God in the midst of his Saints and their never seemed to be a better feeling than at the present."

Like a clear mountain pool, Clayton's cogitations of that day both reflected and enhanced his deepest feelings. The mere act of writing undoubtedly sharpened and clarified them. He ended his introspection with a long prayer of thanksgiving, supplication, and commitment. He appealed for blessings on his family, his future wife Diantha, and his mother-in-law. But he also prayed for himself, and in words that reflected the kind of discipleship that did not seek power but, at least, craved both the recognition and the confidence of his leaders. It was this that helped bring meaning to his discipleship:

Thou hast bestowed many blessings upon me. Thou hast preserved my life. Thou hast given me favor in the eyes of thy serv-

ants. Thou hast preserved me from following in the tracts of apostates and thou has done more for me than I have deserved. . . .
And now O God I ask thee in the name of Jesus Christ thy Son
to take charge of me this year also. . . . Will thou O Lord preserve
me this year from sinning against thee . . . . Will thou save me
from having hard feelings against my brethren and will thou O
Lord continue to give me favor in their eyes. May my conduct
continually be such as to secure their good feelings and entire
confidence. . . . May I grow in wisdom, humility, virtue, patience
and gratitude to thee, yea O Lord and may my heart be purified
so that it will be fit for the principles of eternal truth to abide
there forever.

With such soul searching, Clayton and a city of disciples looked forward to 1845.

Meantime, the events of 1844 had several important effects. One was
the emergence of a new literary genre among the Mormons, occasioned
by the death of Joseph Smith. In some ways what happened to the
Mormon prophet is reminiscent of what Merrill D. Peterson has characterized as the apotheosis of Thomas Jefferson and John Adams. It
appeared to be a miracle to Americans that they both died on July 4,
1826—the fiftieth anniversary of the Declaration of Independence.
Somehow, this seemed to place the awesome stamp of divine approval
on what they had achieved and one patriotic proclamation declared
that "in this most singular coincidence the finger of Providence is
plainly visible! It hallows the Declaration of Independence as the Word
of God, and is the bow in the Heavens, that promises its principles
shall be eternal."[3] In like manner, the massacre of Joseph and Hyrum
Smith became a sacred moment that would never be forgotten by the
Mormons and would only enhance the glory of the founding prophet.

The process began almost immediately as the martyrdom spawned
a flurry of hymns, poems, songs, and essays all celebrating the mission
and greatness of Joseph Smith. The message was epitomized by John
Taylor in a statement that soon found its way into Mormon scripture.
"Joseph Smith," it boldly declared, "the Prophet and Seer of the Lord,
has done more, save Jesus only, for the salvation of men in this world,
than any other man that ever lived in it" (Doctrine and Covenants
135:3). In due time came such hymns as "Oh, Give Me Back My Prophet
Dear" and "The Seer, Joseph, the Seer," by John Taylor; "Praise to
the Man Who Communed with Jehovah," by W. W. Phelps; "We

Thank Thee, O God, for a Prophet," by William Fowler. Joseph's
significance in the process of restoring the ancient gospel was immor-
talized for the Saints in such nineteenth-century hymns as "Oh How
Lovely Was the Morning" (i.e., the morning of the prophet's first
vision), by George Manwaring, and "I Saw a Mighty Angel Fly" (i.e.,
the Angel Moroni with the Book of Mormon), by George Careless.

Much of this new Joseph Smith literature celebrated and culturally
enshrined the martyrdom. Eliza R. Snow's poem on "The Assassination
of Generals Joseph and Hyrum Smith," for example, was filled with
the emotion of a devout believer who fully expected to see God's
vengeance visited upon the perpetrators:

> Ye heavens, attend! Let all the earth give ear.
> Let Gods and seraphs, men and angels hear:
> The world on high—the Universe shall know
> What awful scenes are acted here below.
>
> Had nature's self a heart, her heart would bleed
> At the recital of so foul a deed;
> For never, since the Son of God was slain,
> Has blood so noble flow'd from human vein,
> As that which now on God for vengeance calls
> From "freedom's" ground—from Carthage prison walls.
>
> Oh, Illinois! Thy soil has drunk the blood
> Of Prophets, martyr'd for the truth of God.
> Once lov'd America! What can atone
> For the pure blood of innocence thou's sown?[4]

Clayton was eager to become a partner in creating the literature of
the martyrdom, though what he wrote was not destined to become
well known to anyone. His temple history contained a long section
on the tragedy at Carthage plus a bitter denunciation of the Illinois
judicial system that allowed the prophet's accused murderers to be
acquitted. His charge that "the whole state of Illinois have made themselves guilty of shedding the blood of the prophets by acquiting those
who committed the horrid deed" was only a reflection of the way
many Mormons felt and would feel for generations to come. And his
solemn reflection that "it is now left to God and his saints to take
vengeance in his own way and in his own time"[5] was little different
in spirit from Eliza Snow's poetic declaration that Joseph's blood "now
on God for vengeance calls." Clayton even wrote a poem in this genre—

or at least a poem entitled "The Death of the Prophets" has been attributed to him. The first three stanzas make the point:

Oh, Columbia's sons of freedom,
What is that we hear of you;
Have you slain two men of wisdom?
Yes! The story is too true.
    Holy Spirit!
Shew the wicked what they do.

Hark: the voice of justice echoes,
O'er the wide extended plain;
That the Lord will come with vengeance,
And the wicked shall be slain.
    While his servants,
Range in peace the blissful plain.

In the west there's boasted freedom,
But her sons have stained the ground,
With the blood of prophets martyr'd,
For the truth which they had found.
    But their teaching,
Shall through all the world resound.[6]

Clayton was appalled by the fact that Joseph Smith's murderers, though tried, were not convicted, and this convinced him even more that justice was at a premium in Illinois. Several of the accused assassins were tried in Carthage in May 1845, but a jury of local citizens acquitted them. In the final chapter of their book on the trial, Dallin H. Oaks and Marvin S. Hill make an important observation on the reason for the acquittal. Thomas Sharp, one of the accused, justified the killings on the grounds that this represented the will of the community. The jury agreed with Sharp's appeal to a secular "higher law," and its verdict was a kind of "ceremonial cleansing" whereby Sharp could return to society in good conscience. "The democratic version of the higher law—popular sovereignty—had been applied to his case; its spokesman, the jury, had fully exonerated him of any sense of guilt."[7] Conversely, the trial epitomized for the Mormons the deficiencies of popular sovereignty. They realized more fully than ever that they could not enjoy its benefits in Hancock County (where they were actually an electoral majority). William Clayton's reaction to the Carthage trial is a perfect example of this Mormon response. As he bitterly wrote the day after the acquittal:

From the testimony of brother Watt it appears the Judge Young is favorable to the mobocrats and manifests a disposition to acquit the murderers rather than bring them to justice. Calvin A. Warren also said if the prisoners were guilty of murder he himself was guilty, alleging that it was the public opinion that the Smiths ought to be killed, and public opinions made laws, and consequently it was not murder to kill the Smiths. Esqr. Browning also railed hard against the saints. In fact the whole proceedings of the court is nothing more than a farce, and it is evident there is no disposition on the part of the people to avenge the blood of the servants of God and it will yet be left for God himself to do it, in his own time and in his own way.[8]

Given Clayton's temperament, he probably felt a kind of ironic satisfaction when it appeared that he himself was not immune from prosecution. On May 1, 1845, Brigham Young told him that the "Rigdonites" were about to have him arrested and tried for polygamy. Ten days later Young said that the apostates were about to track him down and advised him to "keep closed up" for a week or so. He spent the next few days inside his office with the doors closed. On the fourteenth he learned that he was the object of both a writ of arrest and a subpoena. Nothing happened immediately, but late in September he went on trial for treason.

The trial, held at Carthage, proved to be little more than a pro forma hearing, and it was only a side trip to the jail that had any important significance for Clayton. On the morning of September 24 he left Nauvoo with a group of about fifty men. Several, including Clayton, were planning to surrender to the sheriff, expecting their trial to be perfunctory. When they arrived in Carthage the court was not ready, so the group went to the jail where the murder took place. An examination of the ball holes in the walls convinced Clayton that the Carthage Greys, ostensibly standing guard outside, had actually shot at the prisoners inside the jail. The two survivors of the massacre, John Taylor and Willard Richards, told the story of what happened and pointed to the positions the prisoners took to defend themselves. "It filled me with melancholy feelings," Clayton wrote, and indeed it must have been dramatic for him as he seemed to relive the moments of Joseph's death.

After returning to the courthouse, Clayton and eleven others were placed under arrest and went on trial. In a kind of comic-opera proceeding, the sole witness against them confessed that his affidavit was sworn out on the basis of rumor. They were quickly discharged and returned home by 6:30 in the evening. Clayton had little to complain of so far as his own confrontation with the law was concerned.

In a way this one-day pilgrimage to Carthage anticipated another Mormon tradition. Early in the twentieth century the church purchased the Carthage jail. Later it was restored, and now it is one of many places of pilgrimage visited each year by thousands of traveling Saints as they attempt to relive the days of their founding heroes. Tears often flow freely as they visit the jail and are shown the solemn spots where Joseph and Hyrum died. As William Clayton must have felt, many a modern Mormon also feels he is walking on holy ground.

But all was not permanently somber in the aftermath of Carthage, for the church had to go on and the Saints had to be about their work. There were at least two immediate problems relating to church organization and administration, each of which directly affected William Clayton. One was the matter of church leadership and who, if anyone, should take the place of Joseph Smith. The other was the question of who should replace Joseph as trustee-in-trust and therefore assume the responsibility of dealing with a variety of knotty issues concerning church property.

So far as Clayton was concerned the most pressing matter was the appointment of a trustee-in-trust. Immediately after the Carthage tragedy, Clayton continued to handle all Joseph Smith's property, and the complications involved in trying to identify what was church property and what was to remain with or go to Emma led to some unfortunate ill feelings between the two. It seemed impossible to handle things properly until a new trustee was appointed, and Emma wanted this taken care of immediately. Clayton seemed content to bide his time until the Twelve returned to Nauvoo.

The discussion began at least as early as July 2, 1844, when Clayton went to see Emma. He found her upset because Lucy Smith was complaining about something related to Joseph's property and was urging Samuel, her youngest son, to come to Nauvoo and take over the office of patriarch. How this would have affected Emma's claim to the property is not clear, but Clayton became alarmed at the prospect of the family quarreling over it. There was danger, he felt, that a dispute of this sort would cause Joseph's creditors to "come forward and use up all the property there is." But, he noted pragmatically, "If they will keep still there is property enough to pay the debts and plenty left for other uses." The matter of Joseph's debts and their relationship to this property was not settled by the courts until 1852, but at this point two interchurch factions seemed to be shaping up: Clayton and the apostles versus Emma Smith.

Clayton talked with Emma at length, but she was not content to wait very long before forcing the issue. She brought a lawyer, "Esquire" James W. Wood, into the matter, and on July 4 Clayton and Wood examined the prophet's affairs at Emma's home. Clayton concluded that the situation looked gloomy indeed so far as clearing Joseph's debts was concerned. The property was all in the name of the trustee while debts were considered personal. Wood advised Emma to have all the deeds recorded at Carthage, for he considered the Nauvoo records office to be illegal, but Clayton was sure this would only cause more trouble. At the same time, Emma was anxious to have William Marks, president of the Nauvoo Stake, made trustee and in a meeting at the Marks home that afternoon it seemed that this was about to happen.

The Twelve, meanwhile, had not returned to Nauvoo, and there was apparently confusion as to who was running things even temporarily. The two members of the Twelve who had been with Joseph Smith in Carthage, John Taylor and Willard Richards, were there, but Taylor was seriously wounded and could hardly function. It seemed to Clayton that Richards and William W. Phelps were acting in some things on their own responsibility, and he was not sure this was right.[9] Should the two apostles lead out in appointing a trustee, or should it be William Marks, a conference of priesthood leaders, or someone else? It did not seem clear, but on Sunday, July 7, Clayton went to a meeting of the "Quorum" (i.e., probably Joseph Smith's prayer circle and endowment group) called specifically to discuss the matter. He arrived late and found that he had been appointed an acting trustee until the Twelve returned and that he was to take care of property matters until a trustee was appointed. This group, at least, seemed to feel that only the Twelve as a Quorum were authorized to make a permanent decision.

As might be expected, Emma felt differently, and the next day she expressed her objections to Clayton. There must be a trustee appointed that week, she insisted. On July 12 Marks went up to the temple where Clayton was measuring lumber in order to counsel with him as to the best course to follow. They decided to call a meeting of the leaders of the various priesthood quorums that afternoon and there decide who should be appointed. A little later Clayton met Bishop Newell K. Whitney, who expressed some fear at the possibility that Marks would receive the appointment. Marks seemed to be in sympathy with Emma Smith in her opposition to the Quorum (and, as Clayton put it, to Joseph), and Clayton and Whitney both felt that if Marks were appointed their spiritual blessings were in jeopardy. Marks did not support "the most important matters" (i.e., eternal marriage and plural marriage). In Clayton's opinion, the trustee must be the president of the church, and he remembered that Joseph Smith had said that if he and Hyrum were both taken, their younger brother, Samuel, would be Joseph's successor. Little did he realize that on July 30 Samuel, too, would suddenly die.

The priesthood leadership meeting was held that afternoon, and Emma Smith herself was present. She urged the men to appoint a trustee immediately, but they concluded that they had no authority to do so. Emma was adamant, and in talking with Clayton the following day she even threatened to injure the church all she could by keeping the property that was in her name if they did not choose a man she approved of.

Then came a curious, though temporary, reconciliation between Clayton and Emma. Parley P. Pratt of the Quorum of the Twelve had arrived on July 10 and evidently began meeting with Richards and Phelps. On July 14 the three of them announced that they had decided to appoint four trustees when the majority of the Twelve returned. Emma was still dissatisfied and complained to Clayton. He evidently shared at least some of her concerns at this point and the next day told Richards and Phelps about it. They replied by telling him the names of those they hoped to appoint as permanent trustees, and Clayton was among them. For some unexplained reason this seemed to make Emma feel better. The détente lasted for a few weeks, at least, for at the end of the month William Clayton and Emma took a three-day business trip together to Quincy.[10]

By August 7 most of the Twelve were back in Nauvoo, and the next day the problem of leadership was settled, at least for them. Sidney Rigdon, Joseph Smith's first counselor, was there to make his claim but at a special afternoon conference the church voted to sustain the Twelve to act in the office of the First Presidency.

The next day the problem of the trustee-in-trust was taken care of, as Heber C. Kimball, Newell K. Whitney, and George Miller were named trustees.[11] Clayton was appointed to assist them.

Emma, meanwhile, obtained an appointment as administratrix of Joseph Smith's estate, and her continuing efforts to get control of certain properties created more tension with Clayton. On August 15, for example, they got into a heated discussion concerning the way Esquire Wood wanted the estate settled. Wood wanted lists of all lands and titles conveyed to Joseph either as trustee or in his own name as well as all Joseph's notes and accounts. He further wanted a list of all real or personal property belonging to the heirs and the papers pertaining to the *Maid of Iowa*. Clayton was incensed, for he considered these to be private church matters and felt that Wood was simply laying a snare against the church. He immediately went to Brigham Young, who advised him not to give any trustee accounts to Wood. The two of them went to see Bishop Newell K. Whitney, who gave the same advice. They all believed Wood was trying to interfere with the affairs of the church. When Clayton went back to Emma with his opinion, she "became warm," as he put it in his diary, and insisted that everything must be made public. She criticized Clayton for spending so much time in secret with the Twelve, even arguing that it was such secret meetings that cost Joseph and Hyrum their lives. Clayton insisted that some things must remain secret, and, he wrote, "I told her that I would rather die than do anything to ruin the church." He tried to convince her that he was really her friend, but failed. Two days later Emma found some money missing, and by the following day Clayton was convinced that she had engineered the loss simply to accuse him and get him into trouble. On August 19 he was further disturbed when Emma refused to turn over to the church a writing desk that he considered church property. Clearly, he was estranged from Emma, but even so on October 1 and 11, 1844, he participated with the Twelve in prayers for her. Not long after that Emma lost her appointment as administratrix by failing to post an additional bond, and it appears that Clayton had little to do with her after that time. Officially he was still an assistant to the trustees, but before long he would be preoccupied with other matters.

Intertwined, meanwhile with all these problems was the problem of church leadership. At one time or another Joseph Smith had identified several possible successors, but he had also bestowed the "keys of the kingdom" upon the Quorum of the Twelve. No new president of the church was chosen at the August 8 meeting, but the powers of the presidency were vested in the Twelve, and Brigham Young had been president of that Quorum since 1840. Though this settled the issue for most church members, including Clayton, various groups and individuals continued to make other claims and organize splinter groups. The largest and most prominent was the Reorganized Church of Jesus Christ of Latter-Day Saints, formally established in 1860 on the basis of the claim that Joseph Smith had ordained his son, Joseph III, to be his successor. Emma Smith adhered to that group.[12]

Clayton had little patience with those who refused to follow the Twelve. Early in September, for example, Sidney Rigdon and several of his followers were excommunicated. Clayton wryly observed that Rigdon's disciples were soon ordained prophets and "immediately receive the same spirit as E[lde]r Rigdon is of." After hearing a fiery anti-Rigdon speech from Apostle Orson Hyde, he became convinced that Rigdon was not only trying to break up the church but also conspiring with apostates to bring a mob upon the Saints.[13]

There was also disagreement between William Smith, still a member of the Quorum of the Twelve, and his colleagues. Like most of the Twelve, Smith was doing missionary work in the East when his brothers were murdered, and Brigham Young characterized him as "a great man in his calling." Elder Smith's wife was with him on the mission, but because she was seriously ill the two returned to Nauvoo much later than the rest. In the meantime, the apostles began to hear uncomfortable reports that Elder Smith, along with Samuel Brannan and George J. Adams, was pursuing an "injudicious course," though after his return he expressed satisfaction with the way the apostles had organized the church and things seemed, for a time, to progress amicably.[14] By mid-May, however, William Smith was openly discussing the special role of his family in the founding of the church and was asking for community support.[15]

The subtleties of William Smith's activities were not lost on Clayton, who deplored anything that seemed to undermine the position of the Twelve. He was irate when he heard that Adams had organized a rival church in Iowa Territory calling for young Joseph Smith III to become president and for William Smith to be the patriarch. "Wm. Smith is coming out in opposition to the Twelve and in favor of Adams," he lamented on May 23. It angered Clayton to think that William Smith claimed to have "sealed some women to men" (i.e., performed the ordinance of eternal marriage, which Clayton believed he was not authorized to do) and that "he considers he is not accountable to Brigham nor the Twelve nor any one else." If he feared any claimant to church leadership it was, ironically, the prophet's own brother, for, he wrote, "There is more danger from William than from any other source, and I fear his course will bring us much trouble."[16] That evening the Quorum of the Twelve discussed at length the "improper course" of William Smith. "It appears he is determined to rule the church and monopolize the whole to himself," grumbled the anxious scribe as he wrote that night in his diary.[17]

Despite all this, the next afternoon the Twelve ordained William, the last of the Smith brothers, patriarch to the church, thus filling the position held first by his father and then by his older brother, Hyrum. "There was a warm interchange of good feeling between William Smith and the quorum," the official record states.

The temporary reconciliation was undoubtedly genuine, but it was likely affected also by the intensely solemn tone that hung over Nauvoo on that wet and chilly Saturday. That was the day the capstone was laid on the temple at 6:22 A.M., after which funeral services were held for William Smith's thirty-year-old wife, Caroline, who had died just two days earlier. She was buried at 10 A.M. in the tomb originally occupied by Joseph. What compelling, though sad, thoughts must have raced through the new patriarch's mind as he thought of his three brothers who had died within the year (as well, perhaps, of a fourth brother, Alvin, who died before the church was organized), remembered all he had been taught to believe about the special heritage of the Smith family, saw the temple begun by Joseph nearing completion, mourned his wife, saw her buried in Joseph's tomb, and was then ordained to the high office of patriarch. Interestingly enough, William Clayton noted in his journal all the important events of the day except Smith's ordination.[18]

As patriarch, William Smith could give sacred blessings to any member of the church, but Brigham Young and the other apostles asserted that this responsibility must always be exercised under the direction of the Twelve. Smith, on the other hand, believed that his office was independent of the Twelve. He claimed to be patriarch *over* the church, not just patriarch *to* the church, as the rest of the Twelve maintained. He also began to claim that Joseph Smith III was, by right of lineage, the true successor to the presidency but that he, William, was to be a guardian and president *pro tem* until young Joseph came of age.[19] It was clear to Clayton that the apostles could not allow such contention to go on. Smith, after all, still carried the family aura, and his views would not go unheeded. But how could they stop him? On the evening of May 29 eight apostles, along with a few other church leaders and William Clayton, met in Willard Richards's home to seek the help of heaven. They prayed for many things, wrote Clayton, but especially "that the Lord would over-rule the movements of Wm. Smith who is endeavoring to ride the Twelve down."[20]

About a month later the Twelve had a direct confrontation with Smith who, in a fit of anger, had assaulted a police officer who had refused to follow some of his instructions. According to the record, he reeled off a list of wrongs sustained by the Smith brothers, then claimed that "we are all dependent upon his family for the priesthood." Brigham Young lashed back with a sermon to Smith, telling him he had no more rights than anyone in town and that they all got their priesthood from God, through Joseph, and not through William Smith. Smith seemed subdued, but only for the moment.[21]

Lucy Mack Smith, revered in Nauvoo as the prophet's mother, was sympathetic with some of William Smith's ideas. Toward the end of June 1845, she received a vision in which, she said, she saw him as "president over the patriarchs to *guide and council the church*." She even wrote the revelation down, but William Clayton was convinced that in written form it had been "corrected and altered by William Smith so as to suit his wishes by representing him as the legal successor of Joseph Smith in the presidency." On June 30 Clayton went with Brigham Young and others to visit Lucy Smith at her home, and they held a long conversation about the vision. Clayton wanted to copy it, but she would not allow it. William Smith refused to attend the gathering, though he sent a long letter spelling out his position on the patriarchal office. Brigham Young dictated, and Clayton wrote, a reply affirming the authority of the Twelve. They, after all, were acting as a body in the position of the presidency, and, said Young, "the president of the church stands at the head of all the officers in the church." As patriarch, William could officiate in all the world and perform any ordinance, but he was still subject to the direction of the presiding body. Young and the others discussed this at length with Lucy Smith, and evidently she was persuaded. They informed her son of this, but he persisted in his opposition and finally, in October, was dropped from the Quorum and excommunicated from the church.[22]

William Clayton was never busier than during the last year-and-a-half in Nauvoo. Almost immediately after the death of the prophet he was back to work, seemingly with greater zealousness than ever. Ten days after he buried the records he was responsible for, he dug them up and commenced working on them again. Unfortunately, in his haste to bury the records he had not waterproofed them and moisture had seeped in and damaged them.[23] He kept up all his regular activities, going to the office almost daily, and frequently wrote letters for Brigham Young and other church leaders. When the temple was finished he became official recorder for all the sacred ceremonies performed there. He was involved in almost every important matter in Nauvoo, to the extent that his overwork and worry may have contributed to his ill health. "I feel quite sick," he wrote in April 1845, "and feel that my severe confinement to the books and business is hurting my health and constitution."[24]

The month of March was particularly difficult, and at the end he seemed resigned that the "vast press of business" weighing on his mind probably would not grow any better. "I have labored diligently and faithfully but seem to get worse behind," he sighed through his pen. "My health seems to be impairing and sinking, and it seems impossible to get rest enough to recruit my strength." But most important, it all had a spiritual meaning for him, whether he got credit for his work or not, as Joseph Smith still dominated his thoughts and ambitions. "I still feel determined to do all I can and be as faithful as I know how," he wrote, "but my greatest desire is to so live that I may secure for myself and mine the highest degree of exaltation and glory which is possible for me to obtain, and to be with my friend Joseph in the eternal world."[25]

One irony in all this is that Clayton's name would never become prominent in the pages of Mormon history. One reason is obvious: history tends to be elitist, while Clayton's work, attitudes, and ambitions were those of a follower. As important as they were, his contributions were all supportive in nature. They were the kind that tend to be forgotten when compared with the dramatic impact of dynamic leaders or the natural reverence the writers of sacred history show for top ecclesiastical authorities. Even when he was involved in important council meetings Clayton's name was often left out of the official

histories that chronicled those meetings. Brigham Young's history for
April 28, 1845, for example, tells of a council attended by himself, Heber
C. Kimball, John Taylor, and Newell K. Whitney where "we read
letters from Parley P. Pratt" pertaining to his activities in the East. But
Clayton was also at that meeting, and it was he who actually read
Pratt's letters to the council.[26] Such examples of official nonrecognition
abound.

Even the most faithful disciples have their breaking point, and Clayton was no exception. Sometimes he felt put upon, even used, by the
men he was working so hard to support, and on occasion he could
not refrain from pouring out his disappointments in his diary. He
longed for sympathy and recognition, and his mettle as a disciple was
tried when he did not receive as much as he thought he deserved.
Complaints did not come frequently, but those that did provide a brief
glimpse at some of the personal tensions that existed within the Mormon community.

During the hectic month of March, when the Council of Fifty met
often and when Clayton was under tremendous pressures in connection with the temple, he even developed a touch of paranoia. It seemed
to him that some of his brethren were not as supportive of him as
they should be (though he probably was not giving due consideration
to their own pressures and preoccupations), and he even began to
suspect that they might be trying to discredit him in the eyes of some
of his wives and draw them away from him. This led to one of his
rare commentaries on how much work he did with little or no recognition:

> I am a perfect slave to them all the while. I have as much work
> to receive the tithings for the Temple as an ordinary penman could
> keep up with, but more than this I spend about 3 and 4 days a
> week in council and recording records of the kingdom. I have also
> spent day after day writing brother Kimball's journal for the press,
> besides writing letters and attending to a multitude of contingent
> business. I have two dollars a day for six days in the week and
> spend near every sabbath for no compensation. Other men who
> don't do half the work have a great deal more money and good
> property for their comfort than I have and they seem to be extolled
> to the skies. The church has given me a poor lot for an inheritance
> but they have also given other men better lots who work no harder
> than I do and have more money to sport in.[27]

One series of complaints, late in 1845, reveals even more dramatically the tensions building up within the loyal and apparently overburdened William Clayton. He still had charge of all the tithing accounts related to the temple, and on October 19 he was stunned to hear, from two gossiping friends, that Bishop Newell K. Whitney was dissatisfied with the way he was handling Joseph C. Kingsbury's account. This brought down a tirade, at least on paper, for Clayton was already angry at the apparent favoritism being given by Whitney to Kingsbury who had married Whitney's younger sister.[28] Kingsbury, Clayton complained, was earning $2 a day at the temple, paid no rent, obtained feed for his horse from temple goods, got extra money when he asked for it, got first pick of all the goods that came in for tithing, and usually got twice as much sugar and honey as anyone else. By contrast, he observed, Clayton had been at his job for nearly four years yet he was earning no more per day than Kingsbury, he had a family of ten to support (as compared with Kingsbury's household of four), he paid for everything himself instead of taking anything extra from temple goods, he worked at the job on Sundays and counted this labor as tithing, which in his mind meant he was paying one-seventh of his means instead of the required one-tenth. To top it off, when he asked the bishop for some flannel in order to make some winter undergarments, the bishop denied the request. Apparently feeling that some future historian might read his account, he added a telling defense of his long complaint: "I could not help being grieved and angry and I make this record that if ever the question should arise in my absence as to the cause of my present feelings here it is."

But he was not finished yet, for he had something to say about the families of Bishop Whitney and Bishop George Miller. Their boys, he sullenly complained, had free access to everything in the tithing store, and whenever sugar arrived they would "eat and waste it fluently." They took penknifes and pencils from the desk and were "unrestrained, and meanly impudent." "These are the things that have caused me sorrow," he lamented, for even though the bishops generally treated him as well as anyone else, at this point he felt that they treated him "more like a servant than a brother." Then, apparently attempting to explain to himself as well as to his readers such a surprisingly long and bitter indictment of prominent people, he wrote the following: "I have endeavored under all circumstances to take as little notice as possible of all these things but they sometimes force themselves on me and gall my feelings. . . . I respect Bishop Whitney as I do my own father but this does not make me insensible of feeling to see so much of what I consider to be unjust partiallity and especially when I reflect that there has been so much complaints of others for doing precisely the same things."[29]

Obviously Clayton's lament revealed only one side of the story, and it was not long before he felt chagrined at what he had said—and probably should have. Just two days later Bishop Whitney approved the flannel Clayton wanted, and the next evening Clayton finally confronted him with what he had been told about the bishop's criticism. He learned, to his embarrassment, that he had been misinformed and that Whitney had said none of the things reported. The bishop even told Clayton that he was going to raise his wages by a half dollar a day. Good feelings were restored, though a little over a month later Clayton and Whitney had another misunderstanding. Whitney complained that he was unable to get into the office on a Saturday night for Clayton had the key, and he asked that the clerks begin working nights. Clayton's temper flared again, and that time he told the bishop outright that he considered this oppressive, since they were already working every day, including Sundays, and had done so for twelve months. "We had some pretty cutting retorts back and forth and talked about 2 hours," he reported, "and finally concluded to part without feelings."[30]

Clayton also got caught in the middle of a controversy between Bishops Whitney and Miller. According to Clayton, the two could not agree at all on how to manage their financial operations (though he did not clarify specific issues), and they had "placed me as a mark for both to shoot at." Clayton generally supported Whitney's view, but he also provided a commentary on church protocol when he explained that Whitney was the senior bishop and therefore deserved his support. Besides, he opined, Whitney was a far more careful manager.[31]

Pressure is a catalyst for tension, and Clayton's tensions undoubtedly reflected a variety of hidden pressures that affected many citizens of Nauvoo. That these tensions existed is not surprising, but that disciples such as Clayton endured in spite of them suggests the real dynamics of Mormonism. At the same time, Clayton seemed ready to forgive those whom he felt had wronged him and was as ready to record reconciliation and forgiveness in his diary as he was fears and accusations. When one man called on him in April seeking forgiveness for the "hard feelings and speeches" he had used against him while Joseph was alive, Clayton quickly forgave him. "I am glad for his sake he has taken the course he has to make the matter right & shall cherish no unkind feeling against him," he wrote in his journal.[32]

As in Joseph's day, the busy life of Nauvoo was not without its social side. Clayton got a great deal of relaxation and enjoyment from playing with the band—whether it was on his violin, his drum, or the new French horn he got from bandleader William Pitt in November 1845. He continued attending plays and concerts, and he was a member of the board of trustees responsible for erecting the concert hall in Nauvoo. Nor did he forget his ever-expanding family as part of his public social life. On March 28, 1845, for example, he played with the band at a party at the mansion house, and he was accompanied by three wives. Margaret Moon and Diantha Farr were not publicly known to be his wives, but since they were all friends anyway this did not look peculiar and it was Clayton's way of making sure all his wives had as good a social life as possible. He loved such times and as a member of the band was frequently part of the entertainment. On July 29, 1845, after a hard day at the office, he went to the home of John Kays where, he said, "we played till near 1 o'clock chiefly with the violin. There was a first rate supper provided with plenty of wine and good things." On November 29 the band spent the evening at the home of Brigham Young, where everyone must have been delighted to see their host and Heber C. Kimball of the Twelve and Joseph Young and Levi W. Hancock of the Seventies dance "a french four" together. Clayton and the Nauvoo Saints were anything but sad-faced recluses.

Next to settling Joseph Smith's business affairs, the most pressing matter for Clayton was completing the temple. He kept track of its progress in his diary, and one can sense not only his anxiety for the work to be finished but also his exhilaration as he saw his (and Joseph's) dream nearing fulfillment. Monday, April 21, seemed to be a landmark. Clayton spent the morning at his office, but he knew that across the street William Player, chief stonecutter, was preparing to put in place the first of thirty "star stones" that would grace the temple some fifty-five feet above the ground. At 2:30, Player was ready, and as Clayton headed out to observe he met his old friend, Heber Kimball. The two sat on Alpheus Cutler's fence, talked about religious matters, and watched a huge crane lift the stone into place. At exactly 3:00 it was set, when suddenly two workers sprang for the top of the star in a contest to see who could be the first to stand on it. Edward Miller, "being a little the smartest," won.

Clayton watched the little scuffle with amusement, but there were weightier things on his mind. This was one of those events that provided renewed hope that the temple actually would be finished. He thought of that, but also thought of the economic problems of the Saints, especially those whose only livelihood came from the goods they received for working there. More men were seeking employment than Clayton and the temple committee could possibly take care of, and more, in fact, than were needed for the work at hand. That day the committee gave the "steady hands" (those who had worked regularly) with large families a full barrel of flour each, and those who had small families a half barrel. To others they dealt out flour in small quantities. "The Lord blesses the labors of his servants," Clayton wrote that night, "and the higher the Temple rises the more means we have to build it with."[33]

He grew more optimistic as the work went on. "The works of the Temple progress very rapidly and there is a better feeling amongst the brethren than I ever saw," he wrote on May 7, 1845. "Everything moves beautifully and harmoniously and the prayers of the saints ascend up daily that we may be sustained until the Temple and Nauvoo House are finished and the saints receive their endowment." The next day he was delighted to report the visit of some people from Kentucky who were "astonished" at the industry of the Mormons and the beauty of the temple.

On May 24, 1845, the final capstone was placed and the exterior, at least, was complete. The occasion was dramatically celebrated by appropriate ceremonies before a large crowd of Saints, beginning at 6 A.M. The band played two numbers, and then, in the reverent silence of the crowd, William Player began spreading the mortar on the southeast corner of the temple. Brigham Young and Heber C. Kimball stood near him on the wall of the temple and as Player and his helpers placed the final stone President Young took a large beetle (a wooden beating or ramming instrument) and began hammering it into place. At exactly 6:22 the job was finished, and the band struck up the "Capstone March." Brigham Young spoke to the congregation from atop the temple wall, telling them how to conduct the sacred "Hosannah" shout, and uttered a prayer that the Almighty would "defend us in this place and sustain us until the temple is finished and we have all got our endowment."

Immediately the congregation shouted in unison, "Hosannah, hosannah, hosannah, to God and the Lamb! Amen, amen and amen!"
Brigham Young made a few more remarks, gave the temple workers
a well-deserved day off for rest and prayer, dismissed the assembly,
and retired with the Twelve to a place of safety. The ceremony was
held that early in the morning to escape the notice of officers from
Carthage who were "prowling around" the city in hopes of arresting
Brigham Young. Later that day, it will be remembered, Caroline Smith
was buried and her husband, William, was ordained patriarch. The
activities of this day made up a fitting representation of the mixture
of euphoria, sadness, and tenseness that characterized Nauvoo in those
final days as a Mormon stronghold.[34]

The day before the laying of the capstone, Clayton proposed to the
Twelve that he should write a history of the temple and that this
document, along with other things, should be placed in the cornerstone. The council agreed, and for a week the anxious scribe worked
on the project. On June 1 he read part of his work to a group of church
leaders, and Brigham Young decided that it was not as complete as he
wanted. It was not deposited, therefore, and instead a full set of the
Times and Seasons was placed in the cornerstone. Clayton did not
carry his history beyond the end of May. Indeed, he may have been
too preoccupied with other things even to think of it. But his manuscript remained with his papers, and seven years after his death an
edited version was published serially in Utah in the *Juvenile Instructor.*

It would be another year before the temple was fully complete and
dedicated, though, as observed earlier, temple endowments and other
ceremonies were performed in certain rooms even before then. It was
a sad irony for Clayton that he was not there when, on May 1, 1846,
the edifice he had devoted so much of his life to was finally, officially
dedicated. Instead, he was slogging his way across the Iowa prairie
with the vanguard pioneer company bent on finding a new place to
build another City of the Saints, and church leaders were trying unsuccessfully to sell the temple. That thought was almost sacrilege to
Clayton, even though he knew there was little choice. On May 27 he
was at a council meeting when a decision was made to accept a $200,000
offer received through Orson Hyde. Clayton was told to write Elder
Hyde saying that if the sale went through $25,000 must be sent for
the benefit of the pioneer camp and the rest would be appropriated to

help those who had worked on the temple, along with the "faithful poor." That night he rationalized the potential sale as best he could in his journal: "It is as lawful to sell it to help the poor saints as to sell our inheritance. We do it because we are compelled to do it."[35]

It seemed surprising to Mormonism's antagonists that after the death of Joseph Smith the church did not shrivel up and die. Instead, the founding prophet's program seemed revitalized, and Nauvoo appeared to be rising even faster. Priesthood quorums were strengthened, missionary work was continued, and branches of the church outside Nauvoo were revitalized. Within the city a short era of prosperity set in, visibly symbolized by the construction of more new homes, the erection of several public buildings, the beginning of a stone dike across the Mississippi, and, of course, the feverish completion of the temple. Indeed, even though the Saints were planning to leave, outward appearances would suggest they were planning to stay. As late as August 28, 1845, for example, William Clayton began building a barn. Three weeks later Clayton heard Brigham Young declare that they would finish the temple and the Nauvoo House (a boardinghouse begun by Joseph Smith) if they had to "hold the sword in the one hand and the Trowel in the other."[36]

Politically, the Saints seemed in just as much difficulty as ever. On January 24, 1845, the Illinois legislature repealed the powerful Nauvoo Charter, thus disincorporating the city as well as the Nauvoo Legion. The vote was nearly two to one, making it clear that the Mormons had little political support in the state.

William Clayton's reaction was one of disgust more than alarm. He knew the Kingdom could survive in the face of all odds, but he was convinced that this new political setback was another evidence of the power of the anti-Mormon mob. To him, in fact, the Saints were involved in nothing less than civil war. Perhaps he went to extremes, but his view of the relationship between the Mormons and the state of Illinois was not unlike the position the famous southern statesman John C. Calhoun took five years later as he tried to characterize the relationship between the South and the rest of the union if the Compromise of 1850 should pass. Calhoun went on at length about the gradual breaking of the ties that bound the two sections, threatening that if the compromise should pass the final cord would be severed. Clayton practically declared Mormon political independence in his tirade against the legislature. "The State of Illinois has severed from us every tie that could possibly bind us to them as a government," he protested in his journal on February 28, "and as a last mark of their vengeance they have taken away our charter and left us open to the enemy without the least shield of law to protect us." The Masonic lodge, too, had taken away its charter from Nauvoo, thus breaking another bond with the people of the state, "so that every tie is gone, and we can now rely on the arm of Jehovah alone for protection and safety from our enemies." His next statement was an even more extreme assessment of their relationship with the world around them, but it nevertheless reflected the feelings of many Mormons that they were no longer able to support a government that had seemingly allowed so much wrong to come upon them. "We are an independent people claiming no aliance with any of the kingdoms of the earth. We are hunted and oppressed something like the Lamanites were on the first settlement of the United States by the whites. The mobs are continually getting out writs for the best of our men and seem determined to blot us out from the face of the earth." His hope, however, lay in the belief that "the kingdom is the Lords and he will do as seemeth him good though all the world boil over."

Such sentiment may have reflected something Clayton heard just two days earlier from Brigham Young. While returning from a visit to some outlying Mormon settlements, the new church leader preached about the problems of the Saints. "The nation has severed us from them in every respect," he told his listeners, "and made us a distinct nation just as much as the Lamanites, and it is my prayer that we may soon find a place where we can have a home and live in peace according to the Law of God." As such thoughts worked in his mind Clayton could easily exaggerate their meaning and apply them literally to the situation he saw developing. His private declaration of independence may not have been shared by all the citizens of Nauvoo, but Clayton at least reflected the unity of the Saints as he wrote of their "determination to let no more men be dragged out of our midst to be massacred, but if we cannot have protection from the laws of the land we will seek it from the great God and his people."[37]

The disincorporation of Nauvoo did not mean the end of government in the Mormon community but only the elimination of the broad, sweeping powers that made Nauvoo practically independent from the state. Indeed, contrary to Clayton's assessment, the city's relationship with the state was actually more in line with that of other

Illinois communities, for in April the Mormons reincorporated under existing state legislation for towns. Only a one-mile-square section could be incorporated, but all the elements of effective city government were soon established.

Nevertheless a sense of anxiety pervaded the Mormon capital as various forms of harassment began again and continued sporadically until the final expulsion in 1846. As early as September 1844, a so-called wolf hunt turned out to be a marauding campaign against outlying Mormon settlements, though it was thwarted when Governor Ford ordered the state militia to intervene. Various antagonists came to Nauvoo from time to time, setting themselves at odds with the Mormons and creating new tensions. Clayton's diary is laced with comments on the activities of "the mob": whether they were legal threats against church members, the machinations of a few individuals, or organized bands of marauders and troublemakers, all were the work of mobsters to him.

Security against outside agitators and ruffians was provided not only by a police force, captained by Hosea Stout, but also by several informal and extralegal (though not illegal) methods. The church organization itself provided some protection, as priesthood quorums were held in readiness to respond to threats. The disincorporated Nauvoo Legion did not disband but continued under the direction of the priesthood to act as an emergency force. Citizens armed themselves, and on September 24, 1844, even the mild-mannered William Clayton borrowed a gun from Brigham Young with which to protect his family. Perhaps, if necessary, he would have used it also to protect his beloved temple, for two days later he was irate when he learned that Ira Miles and others were in town with the apparent intent of burning the lumber around the sacred building and tearing down the capitals. Four watchmen were placed at the temple every night and, commented Clayton, "It seems that all hell is let loose at once but we feel calm for we know that God is with us."[38]

The newly armed scribe was ready to defend himself and the Kingdom and was not unwilling to ride with armed groups as he went about church and community business. On February 24, for example, he was with a group of ten men, including Brigham Young, who went to the outlying settlement of Macedonia on church business. Among them they carried forty-six loaded pistols.[39] On April 26 Clayton participated in a band concert across the river from Nauvoo, but as he

was returning home late at night the group he was with found itself
harassed by antagonists. "If the mobsters had not seen that we were
all armed," he later recorded, "no doubt we would have had to borne
abuse, but we were well prepared and did not fear them."[40]

There were other, more subtle, ways of discouraging potential troublemakers. One was simply to send those with writs against them on
missions, and on March 11, 1845, Clayton attended a meeting of the
Council of Fifty where such a decision was made.[41] Another was the
formation of groups such as the "whistling and whittling brigade":
young men and boys armed with knives and sticks who, like flies,
would swarm around an unwanted visitor and annoy him until he left
town. Still more discouragement came from the angry, sometimes im-
pish, spur-of-the-moment responses of individuals. Clayton reported
with a certain degree of roguish satisfaction the treatment received by
Washington Peck, whom he characterized as "one of those mean traitors who lurks about continually in our midst communicating with
our enemies & seeking to have the twelve destroyed." One night someone waylaid Peck and "bedaubed him all over with privy dirt. He
screamed murder as loud as he could till the police came to his assistance."[42]

It was clear all along, however, that the Mormons must find another
home. Joseph Smith had anticipated the move, and the Twelve continued making definite plans by gathering all the information they
could about the West.[43] As early as March 1, 1845, the Council of Fifty
decided to send out Lewis Dana, an Indian convert, at the head of a
small exploring party seeking for a possible site to settle. In some new
gathering place, Clayton believed, the Saints could "erect the ensign
& standard of liberty for the nations, and live by the laws of God
without being oppressed and mobbed under a tyrannical government
without protection from the laws."[44] His separatist tendencies were
still evident.

The only question was, where would they finally settle? California,
Oregon, Texas: all were within the realms of possibility, but most of
the talk seemed to center on California. Even though this region still
belonged to Mexico, Mormon leaders were well aware of that country's
lack of effective control and of the colonization possibilities in the
area. Loosely defined, especially in popular perception, "upper California" could refer to almost anyplace in the Far West, including the
Great Basin. During a meeting of the Council of Fifty on April 11

Apostle John Taylor composed a song that clearly portrayed the Mormon determination to flee from the bondage of their present circumstances to a place of independence in California. It also reflected the separatist impulse Clayton felt so strongly, and that may be one reason he recorded it in his diary:

1

The upper California, O thats the land for me
It lies between the mountains & the great Pacific sea,
The saints can be supported there
And taste the sweets of liberty;
With flocks & herds abounding, O thats the land for me
O that's the land for me, O that's the land for me

2

We'll go and lift our standard, we'll go there & be free
We'll go to California and have our Jubilee
A land that blooms with endless spring
A land of joy and liberty,
In upper California,
O thats the land for me. &c

3

We'll burst off all our fetters & break the gentile yoke
For long it has beset us, but now it shall be broke
No more shall Jacob bow his neck,
Henceforth he shall be great and free,
In upper California, O that's the land for me &c.

4

We'll reign, we'll rule, and triumph & God shall be our King
The plains, the hills & vallies, shall with Hosannas ring,
Our towers & Temples there shall rise
Along the great Pacific Sea,
In upper California, O that's the land for me, &c.

5

We'll ask our cousin Lemuel, to join us heart & hand
And spread abroad our curtains throughout fair Zions land
Till this is done we'll pitch our tents

Beside the great Pacific Sea,
In upper California, O that's the land for me.

6

Then join with me my brethren, & let us hasten there
And lift our glorious standard & raise our house of prayer
We'll call on all the nations round
To join our standard and be free
In upper California, O thats the land for me. &c.[45]

Plans for the exodus from Nauvoo were discussed continually throughout the summer, and by the end of August the Twelve had decided that they should be with the vanguard company that selected the final place for settlement.[46] It was not until mid-September, however, that they made their plans public. Many Saints were surprised, and some objected seriously to leaving. Church officials spent considerable time in the October conference assuring them that the move was necessary and that it would be well planned and orderly. The stepped-up violence of the past few weeks made it abundantly clear that the apostles were right: Nauvoo must be abandoned. Brigham Young, meanwhile, selected certain members of the Council of Fifty to go west early, and William Clayton was on the list. He was also on a committee designated to help bring Saints from outlying settlements into Nauvoo, in preparation for the big move planned for spring. Mobbings, home burnings, destruction of mills and farm buildings, and various other brutalities were making it impossible for Mormons in these areas to survive. "It is very evident," Clayton wrote in repetition of attitudes expressed earlier, "that the time is come for this people to separate themselves from all gentile governments and go to a place where they can erect the standard and live according to the law of God."[47]

If such separatist tendencies seem harsh to modern readers, to the Mormons of Clayton's day they seemed the only resort. Brigham Young and his followers were not by nature rebels, nor, under normal conditions, would they want anything but unity with America and its government. In their view, after all, the Constitution of the United States was inspired of God, and they were not only willing but also anxious to live under its protection. But they had reached a point where they could no longer see how they could find peace for themselves within any populated area of the nation. "I find no fault with the

Constitution or the laws of our country," Brigham Young declared in January, "they are good enough. It is the abuse of those laws which I despise, and which God, good men and angels abhor."[48] Everything they were experiencing in Illinois demonstrated that no peace was to be had there, and whatever they could learn from Washington seemed to say that not even the national government would stretch out its arm to protect them. Some messages, in fact, suggested that even certain federal officials were planning their overthrow as a people. Whether or not these impressions were true was difficult, if not impossible, to determine, but as long as they continued to hear such things the Mormons could only feel that their best refuge was in some unsettled area where they could be free to govern themselves as they pleased.

In December Brigham Young received a distressing letter from Samuel Brannan, the Mormon leader in New York City. He had been to Washington, Brannan reported, and learned that Postmaster General Cave Johnson as well as Secretary of War William Marcy and other officials were making preparations to stop the Mormons from going west. It was against the law, the federal officers were allegedly saying, for an "armed body of men" to go into foreign territory. Technically, of course, this was not improbable, for if the Mormons went west they would be marching into Mexican Territory. Perhaps the Saints could understand that much, but the rest of the message was beyond comprehension.

The setting for the message was particularly touching. The endowment rooms of the temple had just been completed, and December 11 was the second day in which the full ceremony was administered in that building. William Clayton spent the morning writing the history of the sacred proceedings in Heber C. Kimball's journal, and in the afternoon he and several others participated in the impressive temple rituals. At about 7:30 P.M. the ceremonies ended and a special prayer circle was held. But then Brigham Young called the apostles, the two bishops (Newell K. Whitney and George Miller), and William Clayton into the special room set aside for Heber C. Kimball. There he announced that he had received Brannan's letter. Not only did it seem that some government officers did not want them to go into foreign territory—neither did they want them to remain in the states. As Clayton understood the message, "They say the Mormons must not be suffered to remain in the States and neither will it do to let us go to

California and there is no other way but to exterminate them and obliterate them from the face of the earth."[49]

Whether Brannan's report was accurate or not is highly conjectural, but to the little group of church leaders meeting in the attic room of the Nauvoo temple it was only additional evidence of the need to flee the United States as quickly as possible. But they did not panic. Instead, they simply offered up again the sacred signs connected with the temple ceremony and prayed to God that he would "overrule them and inasmuch as the heads of this government are plotting the utter destruction of this people that he will curse them and let all the evil which they design to bring upon us come upon themselves." Brigham Young then prophesied that the Saints would leave Nauvoo in spite of the new threat, and, said Clayton, "all the brethren felt agreed that God will deliver us from the grasp of this ungodly and mobocratic nation." Then, demonstrating the marvelous contrasts of the day, Clayton wrote in his diary: "At 9 o'clock me and my wife went home thankful for the blessings and privileges of the day."[50]

As pressures against the Mormons mounted, Brigham Young and the apostles finally promised they would leave in the spring. In return they were promised a respite from mob activity, though it was clear that the citizenry wanted total evacuation as soon as possible.

Planning for the exodus was an awesome task. It was not just a matter of moving thousands of people, but doing it soon. The decision to leave in the spring meant that the Saints had about six months to prepare. Emigrant companies were organized into groups of 100, with captains over each, and subgroups of fifty and ten, with captains over each of those. Each company set about building wagons and gathering provisions. By Thanksgiving over 1,500 wagons were ready, and nearly 1,900 more were under construction. The Saints were also trying to sell their homes, farms, shops, and other property; for a few of them, such as some members of the Knight family, this was the fifth time they had taken such a course for the sake of the Mormon gospel.

The apostles and the Council of Fifty, meanwhile, were making preparations for a vanguard company to lead out and locate the actual spot. The general location was pretty well determined by the end of December, and many church leaders as well as William Clayton were to be among the first company to go there. In January some of the Saints expressed dissatisfaction, seeing only that the Twelve and some others were going west without taking the whole church. It was, of course, unrealistic even to think of taking the whole church at once: the members were hardly prepared even to set up temporary camps, and certainly a vanguard company must take time to find the best routes to the new location, determine its feasibility, and make a multitude of preparations before a whole population could arrive. The Saints had no cause to complain, Clayton thought to himself, for those going ahead could help pave the way for the others to follow comfortably. Besides, he observed, "The Twelve & some others have to go to save their lives for there are plans laid for their destruction."[51]

Church leaders soon made another hard decision. Instead of waiting until April, the Saints who were ready would depart immediately—in the dead of winter. In December they heard not only Brannan's report that federal officers would attempt to stop them from leaving but also of an indictment that was issued in Springfield against Brigham Young and eight of the apostles. They were charged with complicity in counterfeiting, and state officers were ready to arrest them. On December 23 Brigham Young escaped arrest when a friend, William Miller, disguised himself as the church leader and was arrested by a marshal while leaving the temple. With such incidents making it apparent that they could not wait until grass grew and water ran, they decided on February 2 to leave immediately. Some 2,000 Saints were willing (though not all were really prepared) to go, and two days later they began to cross the Mississippi on skiffs and flatboats. The cold and bitter exodus continued daily, helped somewhat by the fact that the mighty Mississippi froze over on February 24, and the Saints were able, for a few days at least, to cross on ice.

The exodus continued through most of the year, but in spite of what was happening the temple was pushed to completion and dedicated in April. In September more blood was shed in Nauvoo as the mobs became impatient and fighting broke out. Though a few stragglers remained, most of the Mormons who would follow Brigham Young were gone from Nauvoo by the end of the year. The mighty city of the Saints or, as they called it, the City of Joseph, had fallen.[52]

The multitude of activities, problems, and concerns facing various members of the Mormon community as they prepared for their now-legendary departure is well illustrated in the story of William Clayton's last two months in the city. Everyone had his own difficulties, but, like the rays of the sun focused through a lens, all the possible problems growing out of Joseph Smith's legacy seemed to center on the disciple from Penwortham. It was no longer a test of faith—he had long since passed that hurdle. It had become a test of patience and endurance.

During the last week of December, including Christmas Day, Clayton spent every day at the office, settling tithing affairs, working on land records, and handling other bookkeeping matters. By the end of the week he was ill, but there was no time to confine himself to bed. There were his wives and children to think about, and he felt especially compelled to spend time with his young, pregnant wife, Diantha. She was also ill and would soon become the only member of his family that he must leave behind. He spent several evenings visiting her and on December 29 conducted her through the temple ceremonies. Thinking not only of her but also of the rest of his family, he recorded in his journal what was probably the typical prayer of the Mormon temple-goer in those tense days: "I feel thankful for the privileges my family have enjoyed and hope to be able to magnify my calling and receive all my dear friends into the Celestial kingdom. O. God grant me this blessing and thy name shall have praise for ever, Amen."[53] Such feelings recorded that night stood in sharp contrast to the resentment he must have felt that afternoon when, during the ceremonies, state troops attempted unsuccessfully to get into the temple.

Amazingly, Clayton also spent two nights that week playing with the brass band and two other nights with the quadrille band. In spite of the impending downfall of their city, he and his friends were trying to live life as normally as possible.

New Year's Day was nothing more than a work day, and an evening of music-making at the home of Horace Burgess. The week continued in the same pattern. Even Sunday was a work day, as it had been all year for William Clayton. That week he heard more evidence to support his belief that federal troops would soon be in Nauvoo to arrest the Twelve and restrain the Saints in their move, and he also heard that even though the Catholics would purchase the temple they could not insure its safety against fire and mobs. "So we may now conclude," he opined, "that our only help is from God and each other all human influence and means being shut out from us."[54]

Clayton was plagued by poor health, but on Sunday, January 11, he spent all morning with the Council of Fifty planning for their early departure. By Thursday he was suffering with a violent headache, as well as a toothache, and the next day he finally stayed home trying to recover. On Saturday afternoon he was back to work, in the evening he attended a concert, and the next day he met again with the Council of Fifty.

During all this trying time, Clayton and thousands of Mormons like him had one fundamental objective clearly in mind: that of providing the sacred temple ordinances for as many Saints as possible before they left Nauvoo. From December 10 until the exodus began, Brigham Young, Heber C. Kimball and many other men and women already initiated worked long days and nights at the temple so that by February 7 they had administered over 5,600 ordinances to others. On a few occasions those who remained at the end of the day enjoyed some welcome relaxation consisting of music and even a little dancing in the attic assembly hall. On the night of Friday, January 2, for example, some forty priesthood leaders were entertained by the quadrille band, consisting of William Pitt, William Clayton, J. F. Hutchinson, and James Smithies. Clayton and Hutchinson also sang an appropriate new song composed by Clayton, "Come Go With Me."[55]

Daily work at the office, the temple, frequent visits to the ailing Diantha, playing with the quadrille band: these were the activities that seemed to dominate the month of January for William Clayton. But they were interspersed with both the spiritual highlights and the depths of personal dismay that the doctrines of Mormonism could produce. The spiritual highlight came on Monday, January 26, when he took three wives, Ruth, Margaret, and Diantha, to the temple where they were all "sealed" in the "everlasting covenant" of marriage. The dismay was expressed in his journal entry of two days earlier. Lydia Moon, the youngest sister of Ruth and Margaret, was now "in the way of apostacy." For disciples such as the Claytons and the Moons, to have a loved one leave the church was to lose that person forever: the eternal "sealing" power of the priesthood simply did not apply to those who rejected it.

An eight-day gap in William Clayton's journal for this period speaks loudly of what he was doing. On January 30 he was working in the office all day, but nothing more was recorded until February 8. By that time the announcement of immediate departure had been made, and many of the Saints were on their way. Most likely the new plans put such pressure on the harried clerk that he simply had no time to write. When he finally wrote again, it was only to record an uncharacteristically short, terse comment that on Sunday, February 8, he was in the

office all day packing public goods and at the Farr home in the evening
writing a letter of instruction to the trustees for Joseph's estate.[56]
Having the responsibility of nearly all the official records of the
church, Clayton must pack them safely for the journey west in addition
to getting all his wives, children, and in-laws ready to go. He spent all
day Monday, Tuesday, and Wednesday packing office records, and
only on Thursday did he spend the full day at home preparing to
move. The next day he sent four wagonloads of goods across the
Mississippi, and for the next few days he continued packing, sending
goods across, and riding around town hunting for teams of horses. By
February 18 he was nearly ready to go himself, but the next several
days were so windy, cold, and snowy that he simply could not go.
The delay seemed interminable, though much of the time was spent
"running after things, fixing wagons and chopping fire wood."[57]

Finally, on Friday, February 27, he decided to go. Early in the morning he began to send wagons and teams over on the ice, and about
noon he took his family across. That night they pitched tents and
camped on the freezing plains of Iowa, about seven and a half miles
from Nauvoo, having joined the company of the Nauvoo band. The
camp consisted of nearly 400 heavily loaded wagons, and prospects
were less than hopeful. There were only about half enough teams of
horses to make a rapid trip, and many of the exiles had provisions for
only a few days. Others were destitute, in spite of the months of
counsel they had received about getting prepared. The temperature at
6 P.M. was 21 degrees.[58] But the Saints were determined to make the
best of it. The next afternoon the members of the band were asked to
go back along the trail to meet Bishop Newell K. Whitney. This they
did, accompanied by apostles Brigham Young, Heber C. Kimball, Parley P. Pratt, and Orson Pratt. They met the bishop about five miles
back and greeted him with band music, playing "quite some time"
before they returned to camp. That night the band entertained the
camp. What better way for William Clayton and his friends to begin
the most difficult months of their lives?

NOTES

1. Clayton, Nauvoo Journal, 4 July, 10 Nov. 1844.
2. Ibid., 7, 10, 11 July 1844; Roberts, ed., *History of the Church*, 7:176.

3. Merrill D. Peterson, *The Jefferson Image in the American Mind* (New York: Oxford University Press, 1960), 5–6. Peterson provides an excellent treatise on this point, and on the way Jefferson became a cultural hero after his death.

4. This poem was first printed in the *Times and Seasons* 5 (1 July 1844):575.

5. Clayton, "History of the Nauvoo Temple," 89.

6. A folder in the Church Archives marked "Clayton, the Death of the Prophets," contains a single printed sheet, n.d., n.p., that includes on it this poem, "The Death of the Prophets," as well as another entitled "Written While Crossing the Atlantic." The latter is identified as by William Clayton, while the former has no specific author's name. It may have been an assumption on the part of the cataloger that Clayton wrote this, but the general tone is enough like Clayton that we have felt justified in including it here.

7. Dallin H. Oaks and Marvin S. Hill, *Carthage Conspiracy* (Urbana: University of Illinois Press, 1975), 214.

8. Clayton, Nauvoo Journal, 31 May 1845. Calvin A. Warren and Orville H. Browning were both Quincy attorneys, and both became defense lawyers for those accused of murdering Joseph Smith. See Oaks and Hill, *Carthage Conspiracy*, various indexed references.

9. Ibid., 6 July 1844.

10. William and Emma went to Quincy on 30 July and returned on August 1. Clayton went at Emma's request to settle what he called "the Lawrence business." This had reference to the inheritance of Maria and Sarah Lawrence, sisters who went to live with Joseph and Emma after they came from Canada without their parents in 1840. Maria was about eighteen and Sarah about fifteen at the time. Later Joseph married them, with Emma's knowledge and apparent consent, as plural wives. He also became their legal guardian. The girls, in the meantime, had inherited $8,000, and Joseph spent a great deal of time trying to settle the estate for them. The purpose of this trip to Quincy was to attempt to settle the matter, and Emma obviously took Clayton because he was so much involved in the effort to settle Joseph's business affairs. Clayton visited a Judge Miller and was told that the matter could not be settled until another legal guardian was appointed for the girls. Details on the Lawrence sisters are included in King and Avery, *Mormon Enigma*. Clayton's Nauvoo Journal, 30 July–1 Aug. 1844, gives only sketchy details of his involvement.

11. The Clayton Nauvoo Journal mentions only Whitney and Miller, but Roberts, ed., *History of the Church*, 7:247, gives all three names.

12. D. Michael Quinn, "Joseph Smith III's Blessing and the Mormons of Utah," *John Whitmer Historical Association Journal* 1 (1981):12–27; Ronald K. Esplin, "Joseph, Brigham and the Twelve: A Succession of Continuity," *BYU Studies* 21 (Summer 1981):301–41.

13. Clayton, Nauvoo Journal, 4, 5 Sept. 1844. This, Clayton believed, "is now reduced to a certainty." But Clayton was probably wrong in his extreme views, for there seems to be little evidence that Sidney Rigdon would stoop to mobocracy in his efforts to take over the church or to embarrass Brigham Young and the Twelve.

14. Roberts, ed., *History of the Church*, 7:209, 294, 312, 406, passim.

15. *Times and Seasons* 6 (15 May 1845):904–5, as cited in Irene M. Bates, "William Smith, 1811–1893: Problematic Patriarch," *Dialogue: A Journal of Mormon Thought* 16 (Summer 1983):21.

16. Clayton, Nauvoo Journal, 22 May 1845.

17. Ibid.

18. Roberts, ed., *History of the Church*, 7:417–18; Clayton, Nauvoo Journal, 24 May 1845. Clayton was not at the ordination, for he went home ill after the capstone ceremony and did little else the rest of the day. He did, however, comment on Caroline's burial.

19. Clayton, Nauvoo Journal, 23 May 1845.

20. Ibid., 29 May 1845. Compare Roberts, ed., *History of the Church*, 7:420. Here is another of the numerous places where the official history ignores Clayton. Clayton's journal clearly puts him, as well as Apostle George A. Smith, in the meeting, yet the official history mentions neither of them. The subject of the prayer as worded in the official history is verbatim from Clayton's journal, and continues, also verbatim, "also that the Lord would overrule the proceedings of the mob so that we may dwell in peace until the Temple is finished." Clearly, Clayton is the source for the official history, yet, as in so many other instances, his attendance at the meeting was ignored by whoever pieced the history together.

21. Roberts, ed., *History of the Church*, 7:428–29.

22. Clayton made only passing note in his diary of each of these events, though he did comment on the fact that Smith had published a pamphlet against the Twelve (Clayton, Nauvoo Journal, 28, 30 June, 4 July, 6, 19 Oct. 1845). Clayton recorded the letter of William Smith in his diary on 30 June, but did not record Brigham Young's reply until 4 July.

23. Ibid., 3 July 1844.

24. Ibid., 9 Apr. 1845.

25. Ibid., 31 Mar. 1845.

26. Ibid., 28 Apr. 1845; Roberts, ed., *History of the Church*, 7:405.

27. Clayton, Nauvoo Journal, 26 Mar. 1845.

28. There is an interesting discussion on whether Kingsbury's wife Caroline was Bishop Whitney's daughter or sister in Cook, *Joseph C. Kingsbury*, 40, 50, note 17. Clayton's journal implies that she was a daughter, but Cook makes a good case that she was actually a younger sister who had been "adopted" into Bishop Whitney's "gospel family," though the records are not consistent.

29. Clayton, Nauvoo Journal, 19 Oct. 1845.

30. Ibid., 20, 21 Oct., 24 Nov. 1845.

31. Ibid., 17 Nov. 1845.

32. Ibid., 15 Apr. 1845.

33. Ibid., 21 Apr. 1845; Clayton, "History of the Nauvoo Temple," 68–69.

34. Clayton, Nauvoo Journal, 24 May 1845; Roberts, ed., *History of the Church*, 7:417–18; Clayton, "History of the Nauvoo Temple," 72–77.

35. William Clayton, *William Clayton's Journal* (Salt Lake City: Published by the Clayton Family Association, 1921), 25–26. To distinguish clearly between

this and the Clayton Nauvoo journal, this publication will hereafter be cited as *William Clayton's Journal*. This journal begins on 8 Feb. 1846 and goes to 21 Oct. 1847 and is readily available.

36. Clayton, Nauvoo Journal, 19 Sept. 1845.

37. The Brigham Young quotation is from ibid., 26 Feb. 1845 (compare Roberts, ed., *History of the Church*, 7:37); the Clayton quotations are from some "Reflections" in his journal, 28 Feb. 1845. For the Calhoun speech, see *Congressional Globe*, 31st Congress, 1st session, 451–55.

38. Clayton, Nauvoo Journal, 26 Sept. 1844; Roberts, ed., *History of the Church*, 7:275.

39. Clayton, Nauvoo Journal, 24, 26 Feb. 1845; compare Roberts, ed., *History of the Church*, 7:375–77.

40. Clayton, Nauvoo Journal, 26 Apr. 1845.

41. Ibid., 11 Mar. 1845; compare Roberts, ed., *History of the Church*, 7:380.

42. Clayton, Nauvoo Journal, 28 Feb. 1845.

43. The information they had at hand included John C. Frémont's report of his explorations in California and Oregon, as well as Lansford Hasting's *Emigrant Guide to Oregon and California*. They were also familiar with other expeditions to the West.

44. Clayton, Nauvoo Journal, 1 Mar. 1845.

45. Ibid., 17 Apr. 1845.

46. Ibid., 31 Aug. 1845. Three days earlier the council had decided to send 3,000 men to California, with their families, in the spring. Ibid., 28 Aug. 1845.

47. Ibid., 11, 24 Sept. 1845.

48. Roberts, ed., *History of the Church*, 7:573.

49. Clayton, Nauvoo Journal, 11 Dec. 1845. Compare Roberts, ed., *History of the Church*, 7:544.

50. Clayton, Nauvoo Journal, 11 Dec. 1845.

51. Ibid., 23 Jan. 1846.

52. For an account of the last days of Nauvoo, see Flanders, *Nauvoo*, Chap. 11, "The Fall of the Kingdom."

53. Clayton, Nauvoo Journal, 29 Dec. 1845.

54. Ibid., 6, 7 Jan. 1845; compare Roberts, ed., *History of the Church*, 7:565.

55. Heber C. Kimball Journal, 2 Jan. 1846, Church Archives. Clayton also composed another song about this time, "O Hide Ye My People." Clayton, Nauvoo Journal, 6 Jan. 1846.

56. *William Clayton's Journal*, 8 Feb. 1846. The third volume of what we have been citing as Clayton's Nauvoo Journal ended on Jan. 30, 1846, and he began a new volume on Feb. 8.

57. Ibid., 20 Feb. 1846.

58. Roberts, ed., *History of the Church*, 7:600.

CHAPTER 7

One Man's Families

Among all the doctrines and practices of nineteenth-century Mormonism, none was more controversial than plural marriage. Even the most faithful Saints found it difficult to accept, and in the long run it was practiced only by a minority. Most men who accepted "the principle" took only one additional wife and rarely did anyone take more than two.[1] William Clayton was the husband of ten women and the father of forty-two children. The story of his marriages is not, therefore, the typical Mormon story, though it provides an ideal case study of the possible consequences of "the principle," as well as the kind of faith and determination that could make it surprisingly successful. Nauvoo was especially significant, for there the practice was kept secret even from most members of the church, and there Clayton semisecretly courted, married, and lived with four young women besides Ruth.

Ruth Moon was nineteen years old when she married the twenty-two-year-old William Clayton in 1836. Spiritually they were atune, for she was a stalwart disciple in her own right and had endured much even before the advent of plural marriage. The lengthy separation while her husband did missionary work, crossing the Atlantic, the cruel hardships of that year on the Iowa prairie as they struggled against the elements to eke out a new kind of living in a strange new world, and the loss of her infant daughter all made Ruth's tests of discipleship as severe as those of her husband. Together, the two of them were firmly committed to whatever seemed necessary for building the Kingdom.

By the time her discipleship was challenged by polygamy, Ruth was the mother of three children and a fourth was on the way. Then came the test. Though her specific feelings are not recorded, it seems likely that her reaction to the doctrine was the same as that of many other Mormon wives: emotional agony at first, but then, after a time of prayer, a spiritual confirmation that this, too, was the will of God. She seems never to have complained, and she even went so far, it appears, as to help select at least some of her husband's additional partners. She and others like her were passing their own extreme tests of discipleship but in a quiet way that has often gone unheralded in Mormon history. Her relationship with William remained harmonious throughout their lives, and between 1837 and 1857 she bore him ten children.

To be convinced of a principle is quite different from putting it into practice, and therein lay a great human drama for William Clayton. When Joseph Smith first told him that it was "lawful" to send for Sarah Crooks, Clayton was delighted with the possibility that she would become one of his first plural wives. All the memories of Manchester undoubtedly came flooding back, and that Ruth and Sarah got along so well was a blessing indeed. When Sarah received the letter Clayton wrote on February 12, 1844, she immediately started for America. She arrived in Nauvoo on May 31.

Clayton, meanwhile, saw no reason to wait for Sarah before putting the principle into practice, and by the time she came on the scene he had already taken his first plural wife. In the process he helped establish a pattern that became fairly common among the Mormons. The principle required, ideally, the consent of the first wife before a second marriage could take place, and this often meant that she also helped make the choice of who her sister wife would be. Oftimes it was a real sister, and in Clayton's case it was Ruth's younger sister Margaret. Interestingly enough, Clayton's mother-in-law and some of her children, including Margaret, already were living in his home, and the day after the marriage they all moved into his new brick house. It would not seem strange to most people for William often to be seen with Margaret.

Margaret, however, had a difficult choice to make. She was already engaged to marry Aaron Farr, but he was away on a mission and the prophet himself encouraged her to marry William Clayton. Painfully aware of the tension a polygamous marriage could bring, Joseph Smith may have been attempting to ease the burden for Ruth and William by keeping their first one in the family. But it placed Margaret on the horns of a cruel dilemma as Clayton courted her, instructed her in the principle, and expressed a deep affection for her. "She is a lovely woman and desires to do right in all things and will submit to council with all her heart," he confided in his diary.[2] Margaret finally consented and on Thursday, April 27, 1843, the ceremony took place. But what a contrast from traditional marriages, with public ceremonies and celebrations. Since the people of Nauvoo were still not supposed to know of plural marriage, it was impossible for William and his new bride even to hint at what was happening. Everything must be done in secret. Clayton spent part of the morning at the temple, then went to see Joseph Smith who rode with him to the home of Heber C. Kimball. There, waiting, was Margaret and, as Clayton put it in his diary, she was "sealed up by the priesthood" and married to him by Joseph Smith. No friends, no relatives, not even her mother, were there to see her take the most important step of her life! Nor could there be a celebration of any sort, so the new bride merely went home while her husband went back to his routine duties at the office.

There was a final incident on this strange wedding day that seems incredible if the implications we read in Clayton's brief journal entry are correct. "Evening told Motherinlaw concerning the priesthood," the diary reads. In the context of all that was happening in the inner circles of Nauvoo, that language could only mean that Clayton finally told Lydia Moon about the priesthood principles of eternal and plural marriage only after he had married her second daughter as a plural wife. He does not tell us why he waited so long, but we can imagine that he was more than slightly intimidated by the fear that his strong-willed mother-in-law would take the news even less kindly than Emma Smith. Neither does he tell us how she reacted or whether he told her the whole story by informing her of his marriage to Margaret. It is apparent from what occurred later, however, that she did not like what she knew and that the full realization of what was happening in her own household did not immediately dawn upon her. When the light did come it almost resulted in tragedy.

It is not difficult to imagine the anguish experienced by William, Ruth, and Margaret, but especially Margaret. She was married by the power of the priesthood, yet not in the eyes of the law. She could tell no one about it—not even, at first, her mother—and she had to meet her husband furtively. To make matters worse, she still had feelings for the absent Aaron, and she could not hide them. This worried Clayton and finally, a little over two weeks after their marriage, they took a private walk where they discussed the situation and she promised faithfully that she would be true to him. But she could not get Aaron out of her mind, especially after she received a letter from him on June 11. Two days later William and Margaret talked about the possibility that when Aaron returned she still might want to marry him, but she promised that if such thoughts ever seriously crossed her mind she would immediately tell her husband and seek his counsel. She was going through a terrible time of testing—more trying, no doubt, than anything William had ever faced—yet she had the stubborn determination not to turn back once she had entered into a covenant that she considered sacred. On July 8 she finally wrote a letter to Aaron, which Clayton dictated, informing the still unsuspecting missionary that she would not marry him.

On July 21 Aaron returned to Nauvoo, still blissfully unaware of the doctrine of plurality of wives. The next day Margaret had a long talk with him. "She stood true to her covenant," Clayton happily observed, and then the two men also had a talk. Just who told the hapless Aaron about the marriage is not clear, but, said Clayton, "although the shock is severe he endures it patiently."

At the same time Clayton, too, was in anguish, his heart aching for both Margaret and Aaron and almost wishing he had never known her. He even began to pray that either his affections be weaned entirely from Margaret or that hers be given fully to him for, he said, "to live in this state of feeling I cannot." To add to the tender irony of it all, that same day William was "sealed" in the "everlasting" marriage covenant to his first wife, Ruth.

The next day, July 23, Clayton talked further with Margaret. She was still miserable, he said, "which makes me doubly so." He even offered to ask Joseph Smith if their marriage covenant could be released but Margaret, though most unhappy, refused to allow it. Clayton may not have known it, but by that time Margaret was about two months pregnant, and this probably contributed to her resolute determination. Her distress, however, was more than Clayton could bear. "What shall I do?" he cried to himself on July 24. "How shall I recompense? And how long must I thus suffer worse than death for that which I have always regarded as being the will of the Lord." With Margaret determined to stay with him yet seeming almost to hate him, not even wanting to come near him, he poured out his soul to heaven for her affections and for "things to be pleasant and happy between us." "Wilt thou not grant me this blessing," he pleaded, "and relieve my aching heart from this worst of all troubles which ever befell me in the course of my life?"

His prayer was not answered quickly, for Margaret's feelings remained bitter. One can easily empathize with her as she realized more fully the long-range impact of the strange marriage to which she had consented. At this point she may have felt that she had been rushed into it by her sister's husband and by the prophet, and that at least she should have waited for Aaron's return before making up her mind. Nevertheless, she had made her commitment and was determined to stick with it—especially, no doubt, since a child was on the way. Though bitter at the moment, when her distraught husband showed signs of wavering she appeared even more resolute than he. If it were possible for the covenant to be broken, he asked her again on July 26, and if Aaron were willing to take her "under all circumstances," would she consent? She emphatically rejected the idea—not for her own sake, she said, but for the peace of William's family.

Strangely, Margaret's response made William even more determined to pursue the matter and, against her wishes, he went to see the prophet. On the way he talked with Aaron and satisfied himself that he actually would be willing to take Margaret under any circumstances. He also tried to persuade Aaron that in marrying Margaret he had done the right thing, so far as he knew what was right, but it is understandable that the newly returned missionary was not quite convinced. Clayton then called on Joseph and asked if the covenant could be revoked, but the prophet merely shook his head and answered, "No."

When William returned home he found Margaret and Aaron together in the garden, reported on his visit with the prophet, and advised them simply to make all things right between themselves. At this point Clayton had mixed feelings. Distraught over the anguish he saw in Margaret and Aaron, he had made an honest attempt to have the marriage annulled, but when he failed he felt great relief for he believed he had done all he could and he really did not want the covenant broken anyway. "I feel that I have done right in the sight of God and that he has abundantly blessed me for which I thank him," he confided in his diary, "and something tells me that the time will come when M[argaret] will love those whom she ought and when she will feel perfectly satisfied with her situation and rejoice that things remain as they are."

Margaret still avoided William as much as possible, but within a few days the situation seemed to improve. On July 30 Margaret was ill, and Clayton spent the whole morning at home talking with her. But then another blow struck the unfortunate disciple. His mother-in-law, obviously distraught at what she was only beginning to understand and clearly upset over the fact that William and Margaret had spent the morning together, threatened suicide. "Truly my heart aches with trouble," lamented Clayton. A week later Mother Moon threatened to move out. It would take time for this tragic human drama to reach a happy conclusion.[3]

Lydia Moon was mortified not just by what she saw happening at home but also by ugly rumors that began circulating in the community. No matter how hard they tried to keep it secret, Mormons involved in plural marriage could not avoid becoming the objects of suspicion and criticism, even from those who knew what was happening. So it was that someone went to Joseph Smith and accused Clayton of wrongfully stealing Margaret away from Aaron. Emma Smith was also displeased with Clayton, though, Joseph assured him, "she will soon get over it." At that point all his agony caught up with him again, and Clayton told his leader that he was sorry he had ever done it. William was not to say such things, Joseph replied, trying to assure him that he had done no wrong.[4]

Aaron Farr apparently took a long time to realize that the marriage between William and Margaret actually had been consummated. He may have believed that she was simply a "spiritual wife," though it seems incredible that he would not have guessed more than that. Sometime near the middle of August Margaret finally explained all the facts to him, and he seems then to have convinced himself that Clayton was guilty of seduction. By that time there were several people who with Aaron were ready to charge Clayton with immorality. Joseph had already promised William that if such a thing should happen he would defend him to the utmost, but it is difficult to imagine what kind of defense would be effective, especially as Margaret's pregnancy became apparent, if the new doctrine could not be made public. One can understand what Clayton meant as he lamented on one occasion, "I feel as though I was in some measure a child of sorrow but am determined to do right in all things."[5]

If there is anything to the adage that "absence makes the heart grow fonder," it was demonstrated by the fact that it took a short separation to hasten the reconciliation between William and Margaret. Margaret, after all, never really disliked her husband. She only resented what had happened to her so suddenly, and he was the natural target for that resentment. The strain on Clayton, meanwhile, became so strong that once he even resolved to try to change his feelings for her,[6] but this proved impossible. At the end of September, however, Joseph Smith told Clayton that he must spend a month aboard the *Maid of Iowa* regulating the books. Accordingly, he boarded the little steamboat on September 23 for a trip to St. Louis, arriving there on October 5. On the way the boat stopped overnight at Peru, to take on passengers, and the next morning Clayton climbed a hill above the town and sat there on the summit meditating about home. It must have suddenly struck him that family was much more important than this errand for Joseph Smith. "Never did M[argaret] and my little family appear more lovely and endearing," he reflected, and the very day he arrived in St. Louis he booked passage on another boat and began his return to Nauvoo. It took the *Swifture* less than two days to make the trip.

Margaret, meanwhile, also thought and dreamed about William. When he arrived home at 10:45 A.M. on October 7, all the family except Margaret had gone to a general conference meeting. It was a tender reunion between the two, especially in contrast to the tensions of the previous months. "We had a joyful meeting," he wrote, "and she gave me a warm evidence of her love, and never did my affections glow more warmly than during our meeting embrace."[7]

The reconciliation was complete, and there is no further evidence of serious strain between them. But there was still the problem of what to do as Margaret's pregnancy became apparent. By the middle of October she was five months along, and it was Emma Smith, curiously, who advised them on the matter. Apparently Emma had become somewhat more tolerant or, at least, recognized the pragmatic problems that must be dealt with. Her advice, relayed through Joseph Smith, was simply that Margaret should not be sent away but, rather, should be kept at home until the child was born. Joseph agreed with this counsel, even though tongues would wag more intently and some well-meaning Saints might even call for church discipline against Clayton. In what was obviously a bit of tongue-in-cheek commentary on the potential of the situation, Joseph remarked, "Just keep her home and brook it and if they raise trouble about it and bring you before me I will give you an awful scourging and probably cut you off from the church and then I will baptise you and set you ahead as good as ever."[8]

On February 18, 1844, Margaret's child was born—a baby boy whom they named Daniel, and her mother acted as midwife.[9] Six months later, on August 27, little Daniel died. The tragic entry in Clayton's diary reveals all the possible pathos connected with the problem of having children that one loved but could not publicly recognize and of the gossip that inevitably flowed even in the community of the Saints. "Thus," wrote the grief-stricken father, "has ended the earthly career of an innocent sufferer who has known no comfort in this life. . . . The tongue of slander has swung freely against him." Clayton could only console himself with the gospel he had learned from Joseph Smith, that the babe "is gone to rest with the just and will come forth again to inherit kingdoms, dominions, principalities and powers in the mansions of his father."[10]

Even after all that, Aaron Farr did not give up in his efforts to win Margaret away from Clayton. For a brief time in January 1845, he talked with both William and Margaret about it, and Clayton found himself fearful that he might succeed. Apparently Aaron had finally accepted plural marriage in principle, for by this time he was married and yet still talking of trying to win Margaret. Clayton and Margaret talked about their marriage covenant, and she assured him again that she would never break it if he did not give her up. Heber C. Kimball promised he would talk to Farr about the danger of what he was doing, and after that nothing more came of the matter. William and Margaret stayed together and eventually became the parents of five more children.[11]

The results were just the opposite in Clayton's efforts to win the young woman he hoped would be his third wife: Sarah Crooks. In spite of the affection and goodwill she shared with the Claytons in England, Sarah simply could not become reconciled to the doctrine of plural marriage. "She seems willing to comply with her privilege," Clayton observed hopefully after her arrival in Nauvoo, and the next day he took Sarah, along with his two wives, on a pleasure cruise aboard the *Maid of Iowa*. But Sarah's initial willingness faded fast,[12] and by mid-April 1844 she was showing open hostility toward Joseph Smith. Clayton sadly interpreted this as a "wicked spirit." Sarah eventually married a man named William Cook, also from Manchester, and it must have been difficult indeed for Clayton when he wrote their names on a list of people who had aided and abetted in the activities that led to the martyrdom of the prophet.[13] Even after all that, however, and even after Clayton had entertained a paranoid conviction that Sarah was "laying a snare" for him, he continued at times to think of her and as late as September 20 was told by Heber Kimball that he would yet marry her. Old fondnesses die hard, and Clayton's feelings for the working girl from Manchester died especially hard.[14]

Clayton was more successful in courting Alice Hardman, whom he had also known in Manchester. Her family ran the boardinghouse on Maria Street where he stayed while serving as branch president, and even then he seemed to take a special interest in her. He noted in his diary when she was ill, took her to meetings with him, wrote to her when he was away from Manchester visiting his own home in Penwortham, and listened patiently as she confided family problems to him.[15] In Nauvoo she seemed to accept the plurality doctrine with little hesitation, and on September 13, 1844, the two were married by Heber C. Kimball. Unlike Margaret, Alice did not live in the Clayton home, but William frequently visited her at her own home, and Ruth and Margaret seemed to accept her readily. There is no evidence of strain while in Nauvoo, and she eventually bore him four children.

Just as we assume that Ruth helped select Margaret as Clayton's second wife, it is also possible that Alice helped select his fourth: her cousin, Jane Hardman. Jane had also lived in Manchester while Clayton was there, and it was he who baptized her on May 31, 1840. Later she was among those who provided money to assist him as a missionary, and when he emigrated to America she gave him a watch guard to remember her by. He indeed remembered, and after he had accepted the principle of plural marriage he visited her frequently in Nauvoo. "She prefers me for a Savior to any one else, so she says," Clayton once recorded in an obvious reference to the concepts of eternal and plural marriage (it was common understanding that a woman was saved, in part, through the priesthood of her husband).[16] Finally, on November 20, 1844, Clayton took Brigham Young with him to see Jane and there "Prest. Young blessed her with the blessings of the ever lasting covenant and she was sealed up to eternal life and to W[illiam] C[layton] for time and for all eternity." What happened after that is not clear, except that for some reason the marriage quickly failed. When or why we simply do not know, but she was not with him when he left Nauvoo in 1846. She apparently later married a man whose name was Thomas Richardson.[17]

So it was that William Clayton involved himself in a strange new marriage system that created a maze of challenges, difficulties, and unusual circumstances. Nothing could be more frustrating, for example, than trying to convince a reluctant mother-in-law that it was all right not only to marry another of her daughters but also to court and marry still more wives. Clayton had been so close to the Moon family that the heartbreak was particularly difficult for him when Mother Moon almost lost her mind over the situation. "I also ask thee to bless my wife's mother," he cried out to his God as the new year of 1845 dawned, "that she may delight in the principles of eternal truth and may be a comfort and a blessing to her children." At the same time he believed he must take still more wives, and his diary is sprinkled with comments indicating his thoughts of marrying at least four other young ladies. But it is also clear that he made no effort to keep his thoughts from Ruth or the other wives. Some of the young women, in fact, were very friendly with his family, visiting with Ruth and William often. Once *the* principle had been accepted *in* principle, the practicing Mormon quickly learned several new principles of human relations.

One of Clayton's most interesting unsuccessful courtships was his quest to marry the youngest Moon sister, Lydia. One can imagine the feelings of "Old Lydia" if she ever had heard of that. But Mother Moon had no cause to worry this time, for Lydia was not about to let anything, not even the prophet, persuade her to enter the new marriage system, and she evidently had a healthy streak of her mother's stubbornness.

Even before Lydia had a chance to refuse, however, Joseph Smith put a surprising wrinkle in William Clayton's agenda. A man could marry only two women from the same family, the prophet told Clayton, for to have more than two from one family "was apt to cause wrangles and trouble."[18] Then came a surprising request. Joseph Smith hoped to marry Lydia himself, and asked William to speak to her in his behalf. Two days later the faithful disciple became a Mormon John Alden. Lydia was not offended and even received the suggestion kindly, but nevertheless she turned the prophet down. She had promised her mother, she explained, that she would not marry while her mother

still lived. A few days later Joseph spoke for himself, but still the
resolute Lydia refused.[19]

What happened after Joseph's death is significant, especially in view
of the new doctrines Clayton had learned in Nauvoo. He still wanted
to marry Lydia, and in August Heber C. Kimball advised him to do
so, but only "for time."[20] Evidently Kimball believed that Lydia still
should be "sealed" to Joseph, by proxy, for eternity—a common practice at the time. Clayton could marry her for this life, but in the
eternities she would be part of the family of Joseph Smith. The next
day Clayton discussed the matter with Lydia and again she turned him
down. But he would not give up and finally, some time in 1845, she
consented to marry him for "time and eternity," though she moved
away to Burlington before a marriage could take place. When she
returned she became infatuated with Clayton's younger brother, James,
whom she eventually married. It appeared to the disappointed William,
however, that she had lost her faith.[21]

Perhaps one of the most tender stories in the annals of plural marriage is that of William Clayton and Diantha Farr. A beautiful young
woman, Diantha was only fourteen years old when her brother, Aaron,
lost Margaret Moon to Clayton. As members of the Farr family displayed some natural hostility toward Clayton, young Diantha was
distressed, wanting to stay as close as possible to both Margaret and
William. The family strain was real, so much so that the Farrs even
neglected to invite the Claytons to a wedding party in honor of another
daughter, Olive.[22] Within a year, however, William was actively courting Diantha and on December 5, 1844, Brigham Young consented to
the marriage and instructed Heber C. Kimball to perform it. Diantha
herself was not fully convinced, though Clayton was confident he
could soon persuade her.

The irony of the whole plural marriage system is seen partly in what
was happening at the same time. Even while William was courting
Diantha, with Ruth's apparent knowledge, Ruth presented him with
another baby daughter, on December 8, 1844. The next day Diantha
along with Helen Mar Kimball (another young lady in whom Clayton
had some interest) called at the Clayton home, and the proud father
good-naturedly said he would give these two the privilege of naming
his new child. They called her "Helen Diantha Clayton," but for some
reason the rest of the family resisted the name and she was finally
christened Vilate Ruth. That same day Clayton had more conversation

about marriage with Diantha and, he said, she seemed to "feel right" about it.

Diantha, however, was not about to make up her mind lightly and exercised her right to change it frequently. Clayton continued the strange courtship anyway and also sought the consent of Diantha's father, Winslow Farr. On December 27 that consent was given, but in the meantime Diantha had developed an interest in a young man by the name of Franklin Cutler. Clayton, nevertheless, had not offended her with his proposals, and as he looked forward to 1845 he could say with hope, "I have a good prospect of adding another crown to my family."[23]

There were differences between William and Diantha—more than those between him and his other wives—and such differences could make any marriage difficult, let alone a plural marriage. Diantha was the first American girl he had courted—all his other wives came from England and had known him there. More serious, Clayton was thirty years old and Diantha was only sixteen. In a sense, they were living in different generations. Involved as he was with all the cares of the Kingdom as well as his own personal problems, Clayton was not only more mature but also a little too solemn and straitlaced for the relatively carefree teenage girl he wanted to marry. He probably judged too harshly when he considered some of her activities too "gay and trifling," and when he became disturbed with some of the youthful company she kept. Nevertheless there was a seemingly magnetic attraction between the two: Clayton thought of her, prayed often about her, and kept up his visits, and Diantha did nothing to discourage him.

Finally, on the night of January 9, 1845, an unusual assembly convened in the home of Winslow Farr. Clayton and Heber C. Kimball arrived shortly after 7:30 and found Diantha, her parents, her brother Lorin and his wife Nancy, and her sister Olive with her husband William Walker. Aaron was notably absent. Two important marriages were about to take place. First, Kimball "sealed" Winslow Farr and his wife, Olive Huntington, for time and eternity after which, as Clayton worded it, the "seal of the covenant" was put upon Diantha. Kimball then asked the Farrs if they freely gave up Diantha, and they all responded affirmatively. So William and Diantha were finally married, but at what a sacrifice to the romantic young bride. She could not make it public or even be with her husband on their wedding night. Her husband and Heber Kimball left the Farr home about 8:30, and Diantha was left only with her thoughts. Clayton could only go home and write in his journal a poignant prayer: "May she never violate her covenant, but may she with her companion realize to the full all the blessings promised. And may there never [be] the first jar or unkind feeling toward each other exist to all eternity." Three days later Diantha went to the Clayton home and stayed with the family all night. Such was the curious nature of a polygamous honeymoon.

Diantha continued to live with her parents, though her husband visited her often and on occasion she spent the night at the Clayton home. There are hints that even though Ruth and Margaret welcomed her into the family, the new situation was not without its strains. Very early in the marriage Diantha began to develop either a streak of jealousy or a mild paranoia about her sister wives, wondering if they really trusted her. The strain is understandable when one imagines the feelings of the mature sisters trying their best to welcome into the fold a beautiful young girl who was not even out of school. They would be less than human if some streak of jealousy or pride did not pierce their faithful souls, as it did Diantha's. At the same time Clayton was accepted warmly in the Farr household. One evening Mrs. Farr sent for him, worried because Diantha was not yet home from school. While he waited with her the two had a long talk about all that had happened in the past several weeks, and Clayton was assured of his new mother-in-law's affection for him. Finally, about 7:30, Diantha arrived. "She grows more and more indearing," he wrote of his young bride after he got home that night.[24]

The endearment grew, and sometime late in the summer Diantha became pregnant. Undoubtedly Clayton felt a particular concern for one so young, and it provided some kind of special satisfaction for him to conduct her through the endowment ceremony in the temple on December 29. Then, on January 26, his venture into the principles of both eternal and plural marriage reached a fitting zenith when he took Ruth, Margaret, and Diantha all to the temple at the same time. Even though they had been "sealed" before, here, clothed in robes of white, they were all sealed to each other again by Brigham Young. In Clayton's mind, nothing could provide a more appropriate conclusion for his career in Joseph Smith's Nauvoo.

The seventeen-year-old Diantha was only a month away from delivering her first child when, in February 1846, William Clayton was forced to leave his home. The Mormons were on their way west, and

Clayton was one of those required to go first. But Diantha, frail and pregnant, was in no condition to face the hardships of a wintry trek. Besides, her husband had three other wives and four children to care for, and no certain place to live except on the frigid Iowa prairie in a wagon or tent. On February 27 he took all of them, except Diantha, across the frozen Mississippi. The youngest Clayton wife remained where she had been all her married life—with her parents.

The Claytons and their friends marched westward in weather that was cold and rainy. The roads were muddy, the ground was often frozen, cold winds toppled their tents, and no one escaped the hell of winter chill and wetness. Understandably there were times when William was less than happy. Nerves wore thin, some of the pioneers lost their tempers, and the loyal disciple even hinted at dissatisfaction with the fact that Brigham Young was able to get wood for a wagon box, but he, William, could not. And all the time he was wondering about Diantha, writing to her frequently, and preparing for her to join the family after the baby was born.

Diantha, meantime, was lonely for her husband, and her letter of March 16 undoubtedly intensified William's own longing for her. It also expressed the most tender feelings a marriage can evoke, even under such a system as polygamy. "My beloved but absent William," she began,

It rejoised my heart to heare a word from you but it would have given me more joy to have had a line from you but I am thankful for a little you know that is the way to get more.

To tell you I want to see you is useless yet true you are constantly in my mind by day and I dream about you almost every night, as to my helth it is about the same as when you left onley a little more so I often wish you had taken your house a long for it looks so lonesome it seems a long time sinse I saw you but how much longer it will be before I can have the priviledge of conversing with you face to face it is yet unknown to me father is [   ] as fast as he can he wants to get away soon after conference if possible Mother sends her best respects to you, and often says how lonesome it seems dont you think Wm will come to night I expect it would cheer her heart as well as mine to hear your voice once more, dear Wm as often as you can send for one line from you would do my heart good.

I must draw to a close for I am in haste

I will try to compose myself as well as I can. I never shall consent
to have you leave again.
Farewell, Farewell[25]

Clayton was not in a particularly pleasant mood on the morning of
April 15. He had spent the night on watch, frustrated because cattle
and horses were breaking into tents and wagons. He needed something
to lift his spirits, and suddenly it came. Helen Kimball[26] found him
and told him that Brother Pond had just received a letter that said that
Diantha had given birth to a son! He hurried to Pond's wagon to read
the letter for himself. "She had a fine fat boy on the 30th," he wrote
that night, "but she was sick with ague and the mumps. Truly I feel
to rejoice at this intelligence but feel sorry to hear of her sickness."
That evening the proud father invited a group of friends to his tent
for a "social christening." It was a happy celebration with music, singing, and rejoicing until midnight. They "drank health to my son," he
said, and in this long-distance christening they called him Adriel Be-
noni Clayton. It was only for the moment, however, for his real name
became Moroni. That night Clayton also got permission from Brigham
Young to send for Diantha as soon as they reached the Grand River.

It was in this atmosphere of hardship, tenseness, and sudden rejoicing that William Clayton unknowingly performed a special service
for posterity. That same morning, almost as soon as he heard the news,
he sat down and wrote a song that not only had special meaning for
him, but would also bring tears and inspiration to Mormons for generations to come. He called it "All is Well," but it is known today as
"Come, Come Ye Saints." The combination of tribulation and exhilaration that came rushing over him is obvious in the words:

> Come, come, ye Saints, no toil nor labor fear
>   But with joy wend your way
> Tho' hard to you this journey may appear
>   Grace shall be as your day.
>
> 'Tis better far for us to strive
>   Our useless cares from us to drive;
> Do this, and joy your hearts will swell—
>   All is well! All is well!
>
> And should we die before our journey's through
>   Happy day! All is well!
> We then are free from toil and sorrow too;
>   With the just we shall dwell.

> But if our lives are spared again
> To see the Saints their rest obtain,
> O how we'll make this chorus swell
> All is well! All is well![27]

The pioneers continued westward, William continued to think of and write to Diantha, and his anxiety only increased on the night of May 3 when he dreamed of the absent mother and baby, and that the baby was seemingly dead. He had not heard from her by the end of May, but he assumed that by then she had left Nauvoo and was on her way to join the family. He was doing all he could to prepare and spent the full day of June 4 fixing a wagon for her.

On June 22 Clayton learned that Diantha was with her brother, Lorin, about twenty miles east of the temporary settlement of Mt. Pisgah. Clayton was several miles beyond Pisgah, but he made up his mind to go after her the next day. As usual, a new problem arose the next morning when Ruth's eighteen-month-old daughter, Vilate Ruth, became ill, and William had to stay with the family. That day, however, he received two letters from Diantha telling him where she was and how anxious she was that he should come to her or send for her. He could wait no longer, and the next day he started. Four days later, on a Sunday morning, he arrived at Mt. Pisgah and learned that Diantha was only four miles away. He hurried on and at five in the afternoon found his bride of less than a year and her little son. The touching scene is recorded in his pioneer journal:

> Diantha was very glad to see me and burst into tears. My little boy is far beyond all my expectations. He is very fat and well formed and has a noble countenance. They are both well and I feel to thank my heavenly Father for his mercies to them and Father Chase and his family and may the Lord bless them for it, and oh Lord, bless my family and preserve them forever. Bless my Diantha and my boy and preserve their lives on the earth to bring honor to Thy name and give us a prosperous journey back again is the prayer of thy servant William. Amen.[28]

Clayton's family was together again, and it consisted of himself, four wives, five children, and two mothers-in-law: Mother Moon and Mother Farr. But they would not be together for long. On April 14, 1847, Brigham Young suddenly called Clayton to leave the rest behind and join the company heading out from Winter Quarters to select the final place of refuge in the West. He did not see them again until late

that fall, when he returned to Winter Quarters from the Great Basin.
Would such tests of his discipleship never end?

He went, of course, and in reality he was not so different from the
others in the vanguard company. Nearly all of them had to leave their
families behind. Clayton missed his wives and children terribly and
almost immediately wrote a letter urging them to have family prayer
in his absence, something he had neglected since leaving Nauvoo. On
April 19 he heard from Diantha, Ruth, and Margaret. Margaret's letter
caused him to feel chagrined and proved, he said, that "Ruth and
Margaret's virtue and integrity have for the last year been far superior
to mine." They, of all people, needed no reminder about family prayer:
"They informed me that they had done that when I was at home but
unknown to me, and they had then, and still continue to bear me up
before their Heavenly Father. Oh, what integrity, what faithfulness. I
feel unworthy to possess two such treasures, but still feel to try to
reward them for it, and may my Father in heaven bless them, and all
my family."[29]

The story of William and Diantha ended suddenly when the frail
young wife died on September 11, 1850, less than a month after the
birth of their third child. Sadly Clayton took pen in hand and tried to
compose a fitting poem. The result was a verse that at least caught the
pent-up love he had for Diantha as well as his recognition of her
persistent weakness, that unfortunate strain of jealousy:

Sweet in life, beautiful in death. Aged twenty-one years, ten months
and 29 days.

> Diantha has gone to the regions of rest,
> To commune with her friends in the realms of the blest,
> Her sufferings are o'er, her deep sorrows past.
> And the long sighed-for-peace is her portion at last.
> No more shall the poison of jealousy fill
> That bosom so pure, so free from all ill.
> Henceforth thou art free from all sorrow and pain.
> Our deeply felt loss is thy infinite gain.[30]

Clayton married five more wives after the Saints arrived in the Great
Basin. His sixth wife was Augusta Braddock, a native of Bedfordshire,
England, whom he married on October 5, 1850. Between 1853 and 1870,
Augusta bore him eight children.

Sarah Ann Walters, from Sheffield, England, became his seventh wife. It was Clayton himself who brought the Mormon gospel to her family during his 1852-53 mission, when Sarah Ann was just fourteen years old. In 1856 her parents, Archer and Harriet Walters, and their five children emigrated. They crossed the plains to Utah with a handcart company, arriving in Salt Lake Valley in mid-October.[31] On November 30, Sarah Ann was married to William by Brigham Young. She bore her husband eleven children, the last one being born in December 1879, about three weeks after Clayton's death.

By this time the disciple from Penwortham was taking wives much younger than himself, but these new marriages reflected a well-recognized and accepted practice among much-married Mormons. One purpose of polygamy was to raise up children in the Kingdom of God and to insure oneself a large eternal posterity. New wives, then, must be of childbearing age, and in every case but one Clayton conformed to this pattern. When he married Diantha he was thirty, and she was sixteen. Augusta Braddock was not quite seventeen when he married her in 1850, and he was thirty-six. Sarah Ann Walters had just turned eighteen when she married Clayton, who was forty-two, in 1856.

It was another ten years before William took his eighth wife. This time, at age fifty-two, he chose the seventeen-year-old Maria Louisa Lyman, daughter of Amasa Lyman of the Council of the Twelve. Apostle Lyman and Clayton were close friends, and this may have had something to do with Maria's willingness to marry him. She gave him only one child. Four years later, in 1870, Clayton married Anna Elizabeth Higgs. She was seventeen and he was fifty-six, and in the next eight years she bore four children. Clayton lived the law of celestial marriage to the fullest.[32]

There was sometimes another consideration involved in plural marriage, and Clayton's tenth marriage may have been an example of this. It was not uncommon for Mormon men to marry the widows of their friends, even if they had no intention of having children by them, in order to assure that they would be properly cared for. One of Brigham Young's plural wives, for example, Eliza R. Snow, had been a plural wife of Joseph Smith. In 1868 Clayton furnished money to assist in the emigration from England of Elizabeth Ainsworth. Elizabeth, a widow with four children, was a cousin of Ruth and Margaret Moon. Her deceased husband had not been a member of the church. Two of Elizabeth's sons were grown and willing to support her, but the other children still needed to be taken care of. Upon her arrival in Salt Lake City in June, she went to live with the Clayton family, and the following March William wrote to Brigham Young asking permission to marry her. "She is a good Latter-day Saint," he told the church leader, "and her children are the same. She has not had her endowments. She desires to be married to me under the new and Everlasting covenant for time and eternity, and this also the family desires. If you consent she will desire to go through the ordinances as soon as convenient, and I will wait upon her if you say yes." On December 19 they were married in the Endowment House in Salt Lake City. Clayton was fifty-six and Elizabeth forty-eight, and there is no indication that she had any children by him. She died in 1877.[33]

Still another aspect of the Mormon marriage system was illustrated in William Clayton. It was a common practice for "worthy" Mormon priesthood holders to have women who had died "sealed" to them, by proxy, for eternity. This presumed, of course, that these women had not been "sealed" to anyone else. On December 19, 1869 (the same day he was married to Elizabeth), Clayton was "sealed" to Ellen Melling, who was dead, with Ruth standing in as proxy.[34] Such events were sacred experiences for the Mormons and emphasize how thin, for them, the veil was that separated the realities of this life from the realities of the next.

If the experience of William Clayton demonstrates that genuine love and tenderness were possible within polygamous marriages, it also suggests some of the problems that could, and did, arise. Internal relations within the extended family had many potential rough spots. Though there is little information on the relationships among Clayton's wives in Utah, one episode suggests that a relative, Matthew Clayton, did not always use discretion in dealing with William's wives and children. In 1860 Matthew was boarding at William's house but his host became disturbed when, without asking permission, Matthew began to take some of his wives and daughters to various social functions. "No man has a right to take a wife or daughter of mine to a ball or party or anywhere else without my knowledge and consent," the irate husband complained in a formal letter, "and as it has become time to put a stop to such disgraceful conduct I commence at home." Matthew was asked to find another boarding place within a month and was bluntly told that "if you pay attention to this, all right, the past shall be forgiven; if not, I shall take other steps to bring about that which I consider necessary and imperative."[35]

Sometimes there were more serious problems, and divorce in polygamous families was not uncommon. Financial difficulties, lack of attention or affection, dissatisfaction from the church, unfulfilled expectations in marriage, incompatibility, personal tensions, and jealousies were all among the reasons that helped account for breakups, suggesting that in some ways polygamous marriages were not all that different from normal marriages. One study has demonstrated that during his thirty years as church president, Brigham Young authorized over 1,600 divorces, many of them in polygamous families. Another study shows that polygamous men experienced more divorces than monogamists with a rate of 9 percent as compared to 0.9 percent. Looking at that data another way reveals that less than 3 percent of the polygamous wives experienced divorce. By comparison with other polygamous men, however, Clayton's 30 percent was a high divorce rate.[36]

In William Clayton's case at least four of his marriages ran into difficulty. As indicated earlier, the first wife to leave him was Jane Hardman. The next was her cousin, Alice Hardman. Again we have no hint as to the specific problem, but there still exists an original divorce document signed on December 13, 1858, by both William and Alice. That this procedure was not an uncommon way to end a plural marriage is suggested by the fact that the document is in printed form: all they had to do was fill in the appropriate names and dates.[37]

The reason for Clayton's third marriage failure is well documented. It involved the problem of apostasy, and in the process Clayton demonstrated all the anguish anyone can have as he sees a marriage he wants very much tumbling to ruins about him and finds he can do nothing about it.

Clayton once wrote Amasa Lyman that his daughter Maria, who was in charge of a school Clayton had established for his children, was "a good girl, and a wife with whom I have much enjoyment. I wish there were more such."[38] It was a rude shock for him, then, not only when Lyman joined the apostate Godbeite faction, but also when Maria supported him. When Lyman first told William and Maria of his decision, Clayton bitterly denounced him, and, as Lyman put it, "all the charity he extended to me was his silence and permission to visit our *Maria*." Maria could only weep, but she reassured her father that she would always love and honor him and would "do all I can to smooth off the rough edges of the trials he has to pass through in this life."[39] By July she had left her husband and taken their only son, Marion, to the Lyman family home in Fillmore. A year later Clayton sadly reported to Maria's brother that she had "entirely left" his premises and had taken with her everything she could. "She is entirely gone over to the apostates," he lamented, "and what her end will be I know not, but I fear the worst." He predicted only sorrow and heartache for her, then, suggesting the wound to his pride as well as his emotions, added, "It will be long before she finds as good a house as she has deserted, but she has chosen her course."[40]

In October 1871, Maria instituted divorce proceedings in a Utah federal district court.[41] This was strange indeed, for the district court could hardly grant a divorce when it did not recognize the legality of a plural marriage in the first place. Clayton was disgusted, to say the least, when non-Mormon Judge James B. McKean tried to solve the problem by not allowing the case to come up for a final hearing yet at the same time ordering him to pay $200 in alimony. Little wonder that he was among those pressing for McKean's removal from the Utah bench, declaring bitterly to Utah's congressional delegate, "I would like to see an honest judge on the bench."[42]

It is not clear how the case was disposed of legally, but Maria never returned to Clayton. At the same time, even though he accused her of stealing his property and had a hard time forgiving her apostasy, he longed for her return and for their child. "If she feels any more mellow I would like to learn it," he wrote her brother in 1872, "for I dreamed that she came back again feeling right. I would like to have that boy with me, but while she feels as bitter as she did here it would be no comfort to see or hear from her."[43] A year later he was still anxious. "Have you heard anything about Maria L. and my boy lately," he inquired of her brother. "For several days . . . I have been filled with most terrible anxiety on her account. I don't know what the reason is, but my anxiety is terrible. She is my wife, the mother of my child. This I can never forget. Would to God she would make up her mind to do right and come home, but alas!" But Maria was gone for good, and about six weeks later she married John Smith Tredder in southern Utah.[44] By him she had two children, and she died in Beaver, Utah, in 1877.

Clayton's final marriage problem was apparently nothing more than an estrangement brought about by an unfortunate misunderstanding. On January 3, 1873, his ninth wife, Anna E. Higgs, left home. They had been married just over two years and had one child. Clayton was told, and at first believed, that a non-Mormon posing as a federal officer had wooed her away from him. Since Anna was only nineteen at the time, and apparently an attractive girl, it would not be difficult to believe that a "gentile fiend," as Clayton called him, should attempt such a thing. How much substance there was to the story is not clear but for some reason Anna started south and, like Maria before her, took her furniture and other possessions that Clayton considered his own and began to sell them "in every direction." She got as far as Payson, Utah, and tried to stay at the home of a Mrs. Crandall, offering also to sell her a sewing machine. Mrs. Crandall was indignant and, refusing either to harbor a runaway wife or purchase the sewing machine, immediately wrote all the details to Clayton. The letter must have exaggerated, for even though Clayton believed it at the time, he later wrote that "many busy tongues have misrepresented things very much."[45]

Clayton immediately wrote to Abraham O. Smoot in Provo, asking him to intercept the sewing machine at the railroad station and hold it for him. Within twenty-four hours he had a long talk with his wife, which brought about "a complete reconciliation and determination to bury the past in oblivion." The couple remained together and had three more children—the last only a year before Clayton's death.[46]

In Nauvoo Clayton could hardly defend polygamy publicly, since the church itself was denying that it existed. In Utah, however, his whole-hearted acceptance of "the principle" made him one of its most vigorous public defenders. Some of his statements tell us some interesting things about the Mormon mind (or, at least, about some Mormon minds) of the nineteenth century. They seem representative of the general attitudes of the most-married Mormons, although in some cases Clayton also went to extremes.

A most interesting defense of the principle is found in an 1864 letter to John F. Kinney, former chief justice of the Territory of Utah who was considered a friend of the Mormons. Bitterly complaining about the actions of Kinney's successor, John Titus, Clayton launched into a defense of polygamy as well as an indictment of the society that had recently outlawed it. If the polygamous Bible prophets, he wrote,

had lived in this day, and should take a notion to cross the Med-
iteranean and Atlantic and seek a residence under the broad folds
of the "Flag of our Union," and should appear before his Honor
Judge Titus, they very likely could not be admitted to citizenship
for the reason that they were polygamists of the first class. Happy
they who lived in an age when a man need not be outlawed because
he believed and obeyed the law of God. Happy they who lived in
an age when virtue was not considered vice and vice virtue. Happy
they who lived in an age when the most holy, the most exalted,
the most important principle ever revealed to man could be obeyed
and honored without exposing those who obeyed and honored it
to all kinds of persecution.[47]

The notion that plural marriage was "the most important principle
ever revealed to man" was constant with Clayton from the time he
first began commenting on it until his death. In his mind it was the
keystone to exaltation in the Celestial Kingdom, and in this sense he
may well have exaggerated the actual importance of the doctrine. But
since it was so pivotal to him, he and some other Mormons may have
created for themselves a distorted image of those who opposed the
principle: those who were not with them were not only against them
but were also enemies of God. The rejection of polygamy, then, became
another element in Clayton's indignant contempt for the people of the
world. Never very diplomatic, he had harsh words for the people of
the United States who were sinking ever more deeply into degradation
and yet "are constantly howling abolish the great crime of polygamy
in Utah. Poor fools!"[48] If only the world would read the Bible, he
reasoned, it would discover that God created more than one woman
for Adam, and therefore polygamy was instituted from the beginning:

> Cain after being banished from the presence of the Lord, fled to
> the land of Nod and there took a wife. If Adam had only one
> wife where did the woman come from who became Cain's wife?
> Eternity will reveal the fact that Adam had many wives, but the
> Bible only gives the history of that line who held the Priesthood.
> These pious hypocrites call polygamy wicked and are ready to
> persecute to the death those who believe and practice it, yet they
> will admit that Abraham and Jacob were polygamists, and of these
> the Savior says "Many shall come from the East and West and
> North and South and sit down with Abraham, Isaac and Jacob in
> the Kingdom of Heaven." . . . In my humble opinion it is not

polygamy they care about but they see in the Mormon plurality a constant living reproof to their adulterous practices.[49]

The author of such fulminations could hardly accept the idea that some opponents of polygamy were really people of great integrity and commendable values. Judge James B. McKean, for instance, was a moral, high-minded Methodist who was revolted by the idea of polygamy. That revulsion led him to excesses on the Utah territorial bench, and such excesses only fed the fire in the souls of true believers like William Clayton.[50]

Clayton's defense of polygamy was not confined to such attacks upon the enemies of the Kingdom. In a more positive way he considered it his calling to witness publicly that he, indeed, was the one who wrote the revelation as it came from the lips of Joseph Smith and that he knew for a certainty of its accuracy. One such affirmation came in a letter to Madison M. Scott, dated November 11, 1871. Scott had asked about the claim of Joseph Smith III that his father never introduced the doctrine. "Mere bosh!" Clayton replied, and with all the power he could inject into his pen declared himself ready to testify to all the world that he wrote the revelation as it was given through the prophet. Brigham Young and his associates, he said, were doing all they could to carry out the plans of Joseph Smith, and "any one who says to the contrary does not know Joseph nor the mission the Lord gave him to fulfill."[51] Finally, on August 17, 1874, Clayton appeared before notary public John T. Caine and swore out an affidavit giving in greater detail than any other document the circumstances surrounding the origin of the written revelation.

In his zeal for the doctrine Clayton, like other disciples, was probably guilty of preaching ideas that did not strictly conform with those of his church leaders in Utah—maybe not even with what Joseph Smith would have said. He said a few things that came under official scrutiny and question. He was absolutely convinced that whatever he said he had received from Joseph Smith, but after nearly thirty years memory of things unwritten becomes a mixture of fact and personal interpretation. Whatever the case, on February 10, 1873, it was reported to the influential School of the Prophets in Salt Lake City that Clayton had preached in the Seventeenth Ward that no man could ever enter the Celestial Kingdom unless he had more than one wife. This would indeed be harsh doctrine, for it would leave out over 75 percent of the

men of the church. No wonder it attracted the attention of the school
and touched off a lengthy discussion.

Interestingly enough, there was little sympathy in the school for
what Clayton was supposed to have said. Wilford Woodruff said he
did not believe it, commenting especially on those who died before
they had a chance to obtain additional wives. Certainly, he thought,
they would still be entitled to a celestial glory. Bishop Samuel A. Wool-
ley recalled a speech of Brigham Young in which the church leader
said that whether some men had one wife and others had ten, each
would be entitled to a celestial glory, "though varied in capacity."
Several others agreed, including such leading apostles and polygamists
as John Taylor, Orson Pratt, and Joseph F. Smith. Pratt suggested a
modification of the prevailing view by saying that anyone who was
"personally commanded to take more wives by the Almighty through
his servants, and should refuse—they should be damned."

Toward the end, the discussion turned on one of the most fundamental aspects of Mormon discipleship: the necessity of following
living prophets, even if their policies seemed to differ from those of
past prophets. The Mormon doctrine of "continuing revelation" implies that changes in policy and understanding will come, but that they
must come through the appointed living leader. With William Clayton
obviously in mind, Bishop A. H. Raleigh observed that many "who
had been favoured with a close and intimate acquaintance with Joseph
. . . stood in great danger of being tripped up" unless they "continued
to walk in the spirit" beside the living leaders. And the good bishop
was probably right—Clayton had been so caught up with Joseph and
so affected by his death that he was unable to accept the refinements
that were coming through the founder's living successors. Not that he
opposed the refinements—he was incapable of opposing his leaders—
he just did not understand them. And maybe Clayton remembered
more than Joseph actually taught anyway—letting his own view of
what *should* be taught become superimposed on his memory of what
Joseph Smith *actually* taught. Daniel H. Wells, a counselor to Brigham
Young, commented that Clayton "had enjoyed extraordinary privileges
with Brother Joseph" and that even though most of his ideas were
correct, he may have erred on the present issue. When elders preached
publicly, he said, it would be a good thing if they "would preach the
Gospel according to Brigham."[52]

There is no evidence that Clayton was reprimanded or publicly corrected, but it is clear that he was carrying the doctrinal implications of polygamy further than some of his living leaders and therefore was not in lock step with them as he was with Joseph. But he was not unique, for others shared his views. It was such disciples who found it difficult when President Wilford Woodruff issued his Manifesto ending polygamy in 1890, and some refused to go along. President John Taylor, they believed, had announced a position that required them to continue. We presume that Clayton would have acquiesced—he was that kind of follower—but it would have been difficult.

If, as we have suggested, people went into plural marriages largely because church leaders persuaded them that the gospel required it, the social question remains as to how satisfying and fulfilling such relationships could be. Did the love of a polygamous wife compare in any way with that of a monogamous wife? Was it possible for a man to share his affection equally with all his wives and feel as deeply about one as about another? Could a father with a family as huge as Clayton's give all his children the same individual attention and personal affection as a father with a smaller kingdom? Such questions will never be answered with finality, nor are they fully within the scope of this study, but Clayton's experience at least suggests some possibilities.

Part of the answer, obviously, is that any answer could be true—it will vary with individual personalities and circumstances, and one can probably find as many "yes" as "no" answers to any such question, as well as several answers in between. In Clayton's case, he had a huge capacity for love, affection, and concern, and, at least so far as his papers reveal, he could share it fully with any who would accept it. His diary and personal letters are the only contemporary evidence of this, but family traditions speak of it loudly. A granddaughter of Sarah Walters later wrote: "No man was loved and honored more. . . . Grandmother Clayton never got over his death. She could never talk about it. . . . But we did know that she worshipped William Clayton."[53]

William could also keep his affection in bounds, and even though his thoughts turned to women whom he hoped to marry, he scrupulously avoided the temptations that could have ruined his relationship with his wives and church, to say nothing of the salvation of his soul. If ever suspected of slipping, or even of seeking additional wives improperly, he responded with firm and convincing assurances of his fidelity. While on his mission to England, for example, he was accused of attempting to obtain new wives secretly, but he wrote with calm assurance to a friend: "As to trying to make covenants with women I have no fears of that, for God knows I love my family too well to seek any others while absent from them. I have seen none yet that has begun to tempt me. In fact that is a thing that troubles my mind less than anything else for which I am thankful."[54]

Clayton also displayed the same concerns for his children as fathers of normal families—living a "higher law" hardly exempted him from the day-to-day troubles of fatherhood. Being an earthly god in embryo with twenty to thirty children around could be a bed of thorns.

Nevertheless, Clayton sometimes came up with bits of sound advice to his children that were models of fatherly love and wisdom. To Moroni, who at age sixteen was cultivating his own land and had planted an acre of wheat, he wrote: "My great anxiety is, as I have often told you, to have you do well for yourself, and to do this you, with all the rest of us, will have to work and work hard, for there are but few men who can live without hard work of one kind or another. Idleness begets mischief, and a long train of other evils, while the hard working, industrious man is generally virtuous, honest and respected. . . . As I have said previously, I want you to listen to uncle Winslow's counsel, and not follow, too much, your own opinions. You are young yet in experience, and if you will listen to your uncle he will do you good."[55]

Clayton could also be stern, at times to his own regret, yet this sternness reflected his single-minded devotion to what he thought were correct feelings. One sad experience suggests that sometimes he was too rigid—that he went too far in demanding strict compliance with his own views. To the degree that a father of scores of children can have special feelings for one, William's feelings for Rachel Amelia, Diantha's last child, must have been especially tender as he watched her grow up motherless. He also paid close attention, and with considerable less favor, to the many admirers who came to call on the beautiful young woman. Like most fathers, he was determined that his children would marry within the faith—so determined, in fact, that when young gentile suitors came to call he firmly turned them away. But nothing he could do prevented Rachel and Jimmy Day, an especially determined non-Mormon, from falling in love, and the young couple soon eloped. Clayton, in both sorrow and dismay, went to the extreme: he disowned his twenty-year-old daughter.

Less than a year later the story came to a tragic yet bittersweet conclusion. On her twenty-first birthday Rachel gave birth to a child, but complications set in and it became clear that Rachel would die. Word was sent to her father, and he was asked to come to her. Still full of love, in spite of his previous precipitous action, the fifty-seven-year-old Clayton hurried to his daughter's bedside, and on her deathbed the two were reconciled. Both Rachel and the baby died, but somehow Jimmy Day had a change of heart so far as the church was concerned. He joined it, and before long he had arranged for himself and Rachel to be sealed for eternity according to its ordinances.[56]

Whenever he could, Clayton enjoyed being with and working with his family. In 1870, for example, he was using a "magic lantern" and glass slides to provide family evening entertainment.[57] He tried to train his boys to work with him and sent them on expeditions to buy goods for the entire family.[58] While his son, Newell, was on a mission to England, he mildly chastised him for not taking advantage of the money deposited for his use. There was no need to suffer exposure from lack of good shoes, he had earlier assured Newel, for his London agent had plenty of money on deposit. When Newel still did not show up at the agent's office but instead wrote other family members for money, Clayton was chagrined. Newel simply may have been trying to keep his father solvent, knowing that behind the generous front there were financial difficulties, but, wrote Clayton to him, "I consider this very disrespectful in you, when you know that there is always money laying in Mr. Starrs's hands, which you can freely use. . . . After you have had twenty or thirty years more experience, you will look upon this matter with regret, and wish you had taken a different course."[59]

If Clayton found cause to reprimand Newel for not taking his money, he found even more cause for at least some disappointment in other actions of his sons. Like most fathers, he often felt that they did not respect his experience-based wisdom. "Could I get the boys to work in unison with me and do all I want them to," he lamented in typical fatherly fashion in 1872, "I could soon make the farm pay handsomely, but it seems impossible to get them to understand that I know anything about my own business."[60]

When William Clayton died he left four living widows: Ruth, age sixty-three; Augusta, age forty-six; Sarah Ann, age forty-one; and Anna Elizabeth, age twenty-six. He also had thirty-three living children, ranging in ages from ten to forty-three. As a family man he was again a representative disciple, and his experiences provide important insight into the complexities of polygamy and the attitudes of those who practiced it. Marriage itself was sacred, and plural marriage was even more sacred, for it was a divine principle that must be lived in order to gain the highest possible salvation (so Clayton believed). William found satisfaction in his wives and families, even though he experienced some problems, including divorce. He also produced a large posterity for whom he demonstrated great love and personal concern. On balance, if plural marriage was another test of his discipleship, then Clayton probably passed that test as well as most who went into it.

NOTES

1. See Ivins, "Notes on Mormon Polygamy," and Phillip R. Kunz, "One Wife or Several? A Comparative Study of Late Nineteenth-Century Marriage in Utah," in Thomas G. Alexander, ed., *The Mormon People: Their Character and Traditions* (Provo: Brigham Young University Press, 1980), 53-71. According to Kunz, only 27.2 percent of the men in early Utah took polygamous wives (see Table 1, 59). Of these, 70.24 percent took two wives and 20.75 percent took three wives. Those who took ten or more wives amounted to only 0.24 percent of the polygamous men or 0.06 percent of all the men in Utah. The average number of children born to Utah monogamous wives in the nineteenth century was 7.82, while polygamous wives had a slightly lower 7.46 offspring. (See James E. Smith and Phillip R. Kunz, "Polygyny and Fertility in Nineteenth-century America," *Population Studies* 30 [1976]:471.) Two wives bore Clayton no children, but the other eight gave him an average of 5.25 each.

2. Clayton, Nauvoo Journal, 22 Mar., 24 Apr. 1843. On 22 March Clayton wrote that he conversed with Margaret on the priesthood. In context, this could only mean that he was talking about plural marriage, which was regularly referred to as an order of the priesthood.

3. Ibid., 30 July, 5 Aug. 1843. The journal entry for 30 July simply refers to "mother," but it is clear in context that Clayton is referring to his mother-in-law, who was living in his home. Mother Moon threatened to go live with her son, John Moon.

4. Ibid., 11 Aug. 1843. In answer to Clayton's question as to whether he had done wrong, Joseph replied no—that Clayton had a right to all the wives he could obtain.

5. Ibid., 27 July, 13, 18 Aug. 1843.

6. Ibid., 23 Aug. 1843.

7. Clayton expressed the same feelings for the rest of his family that day. He was alone with Margaret until 3 P.M. when, he said, "the rest of my dear family returned home. My bosom heaved with joy to find them all well al-

though my Sarah & Margaret [his daughters] had both been sick. I felt to return thanks to my heavenly father for his kindness in thus sparing our lives and preserving us for this privilege" (ibid., 7 Oct. 1843).

8. Ibid., 19 Oct. 1843. When this conversation took place Joseph and Clayton were on a trip together. Joseph told Clayton that Emma had turned quite friendly and kind and also that she had recently been anointed—an obvious reference to her admittance to the Quorum of the Anointed. It may have been this deeply spiritual experience that mellowed Emma, at least for the time being.

9. Again, this is based on the assumption that when Clayton said "mother" in his journal he was referring to his mother-in-law.

10. Ibid., 27 Aug. 1844.

11. Ibid., 25–28 Jan. 1845.

12. On 13 June, for example, she "went away abruptly" (she was staying at the Clayton home), though she returned the next day. Clayton says little more about her in his diary, though it is interesting to note that as late as 20 Sept. 1844 he still had some hopes of reconciliation.

13. Ibid., 18 Apr., 17 June 1844; compare Roberts, ed., History of the Church, 7:146. As Clayton made the list in his journal entry of 27 June he simply listed names with, for the most part, no commentary. But when he came to these two, he extended the entry: "Wm Cook & Sarah his wife formerly Sarah Crooks of Manchester England." The fact that he would do this suggests the pain he felt.

14. Clayton, Nauvoo Journal, 5, 20 Sept. 1844.

15. See Allen and Alexander, eds., Manchester Mormons 93, 114, 126, 147, and other entries listed in the index.

16. Clayton, Nauvoo Journal, 8 Nov. 1844.

17. At the Genealogical Department of the LDS Church there is a family group sheet on file for William Clayton and Jane Hardman. It lists their wedding date as above and also indicates another husband by the name of Thomas Richardson.

18. Clayton, Nauvoo Journal, 15 Sept. 1843.

19. Ibid., 21 Sept. 1843.

20. Ibid., 29 Aug. 1844.

21. Ibid., 23 Jan. 1846; Clayton family group sheets, Genealogical Society of the Church.

22. Ibid., 10 Aug., 1 Nov. 1843. Diantha was under so much stress at this point that she even threatened to "tell all she knew" and then commit suicide.

23. Ibid., 31 Dec. 1844, 1 Jan. 1845.

24. Ibid., 10 Feb. 1845.

25. Diantha Clayton to William Clayton, 16 Mar. 1846, Clayton Papers.

26. Clayton says in his journal that it was Ellen Kimball, the wife of Heber C. Kimball. See, however, the account by Kimball's daughter, Helen Mar Whitney, "Our Travels Beyond the Mississippi," Woman's Exponent 12 (15 Jan. 1884):126–27. The evidence here indicates that it was Helen who told the story to Clayton. It is possible that Clayton simply misspelled her name in his diary

or in his excitement simply wrote hurriedly and did not realize what he was writing.

27. For further commentary on the hymn, see J. Spencer Cornwall, *A Century of Singing: The Salt Lake Mormon Tabernacle Choir* (Salt Lake City: Deseret Book Company, 1958), 300–327. It is traditionally held that the hymn was set to "an old English tune." Recent scholarship suggests, however, that no published version of such an old English tune can be found. The earliest known source for the tune is a pamphlet entitled *Revival Melodies*, or *Songs of Zion*, published in Boston in 1842. The pamphlet contained hymns sung at revival meetings by Jacob Knapp, a famous Baptist evangelist. (See David W. Music, "A New Source for the Tune 'All is Well,' " *The Hymn* 29 [Apr. 1978]:78–82.)

28. *William Clayton's Journal*, 51.

29. Ibid., 82.

30. The poem is recorded on the back of William Clayton and Diantha Farr's family group sheet, Genealogical Society of the Church, and was provided by June M. McDonnel. It is also reproduced in Dahl, *William Clayton*, 215–16.

31. "Biographical Sketch of Sarah Walters Clayton (Handcart Pioneer of 1856)" (n.a., n.p., n.d.), typescript in author's possession, provided by S. L. Ferris; "Journal of Archer Walters Enroute from England to Utah, U.S.A., March 18, 1856 to September 5th, 1856," typescript prepared by Irene Clayton, copy in possession of the author. This journal ends before the arrival of the Walterses in the valley.

32. The number of children is based on Dahl, *William Clayton*, Appendix III, and confirmed by the Clayton family group sheets in the Genealogical Society of the Church. The birthdate of each wife is also recorded in the back of William Clayton, "Missionary Journal, 1852–53," Church Archives.

33. Clayton to Brigham Young, 9 Mar. 1869. Dahl does not list Elizabeth as a wife, but the list in the back of Clayton's 1852–53 missionary journal includes her name as number ten. Whoever made this list may have put her in the last position simply because they did not know the exact marriage date. The Computer Files Index in the Genealogical Society of the Church gives a record of Clayton's marriage to Elizabeth Mort in the Endowment House. It seems to be a safe assumption that Mort was Elizabeth Ainsworth's maiden name, and that assumption provides the basis for some of the dates given in the text.

34. Sealing Records, Genealogical Society of the Church. We are not sure who Ellen Melling was, but she may have been related to Peter Melling, the first church patriarch in England.

35. William Clayton to Matthew Clayton, 3 Mar. 1860.

36. Eugene E. Campbell and Bruce L. Campbell, "Divorce among Mormon Polygamists: Extent and Explanations," *Utah Historical Quarterly* 46 (Winter 1978):5; Kunz, "One Wife or Several?" 69.

37. A copy of the document is found in the Brigham Young Papers. Church records in the Genealogical Society of the Church show that on the same day, 13 Dec. 1858, Alice Hardman's "sealing" to William Clayton was officially cancelled. In addition, one of the Clayton family group sheets in the Geneal-

ogical Society Library indicates that in 1955 Alice Hardman was sealed by proxy to William Clayton, thus reuniting for eternity the family that had been broken by divorce. It appears that Alice remarried, but Mormon doctrine would not prohibit the "sealing" to Clayton if her other marriage was not a marriage for eternity. The doctrine suggests that the efficacy of such ordinances is ultimately determined not just by the authority of the priesthood (though that is essential), but also by the individual worthiness and willingness of the people involved. The family group sheet for William Clayton and Alice Hardman in the Genealogical Society simply lists a "Mr. Suzzey" as her second husband. We have been unable to find any information on him.

The divorce document reads: "Know all persons by these Presents:—That we the undersigned *Wm Clayton* and *Alice Clayton* his Wife, (before her marriage to him *Alice Hardman*) do hereby mutually Covenant, Promise and Agree to DISSOLVE all the relations which have hitherto existed between us as HUSBAND AND WIFE, and to keep ourselves SEPARATE and APART from each other, from this time forth.

"IN WITNESS WHEREOF, We hereunto set our hands at *Great Salt Lake City* this 13th day of Decr A.D. 1858." The document was signed by William and Alice as well as two witnesses.

38. Clayton to Amasa Lyman, 3 Dec. 1868, Amasa Lyman Papers, Church Archives.

39. Maria Louisa Lyman Clayton to Amasa Lyman, 15 July 1870, Amasa Lyman Papers.

40. Clayton to Francis M. Lyman, 24 July 1871.

41. See Melvin A. Lyman, *Amasa Lyman Family History* (Delta, Utah, 1969), 124–26. On 30 Oct. 1871 the *Deseret News* carried an account of a preliminary hearing in a divorce proceeding against William Clayton, but curiously the wife was listed as having the name Emilie. As reported in the paper, "The complainant in the case was Emilie, wife of Mr. William Clayton, of this city, and as the parties are very old residents here, and well known, far more than ordinary interest is manifested in the proceedings." That this is really the case of Maria Lyman seems evident from the dates, as well as the fact that there was no other William Clayton so prominent in Salt Lake City as to warrant this kind of comment. Why the newspaper reported a different name is a mystery.

42. Clayton to William H. Hooper, 2 Mar. 1872.

43. Clayton to Francis M. Lyman, 16 July 1872.

44. Clayton to Francis M. Lyman, 29 Apr. 1873; Lyman, *Amasa Lyman Family History*, 124–26.

45. Clayton to Abraham O. Smoot, 24 Jan. 1873. See also Clayton to Smoot, 23 Jan. 1873.

46. Clayton to Smoot, 24 Jan. 1873. Church records in the Genealogical Society of the Church show that on 11 Apr. 1873 Anna Higgs's sealing to William Clayton was cancelled, but they were sealed again in the Endowment House on 2 June 1873. This implies that there may have been another temporary

setback in their relationship, causing an actual divorce, but that again the reconciliation was quick and this time complete.

47. Clayton to John F. Kinney, 25 Mar. 1864.

48. Clayton to "Brother East," 13 Feb. 1870.

49. Ibid.

50. See Thomas G. Alexander, "Federal Authority versus Polygamic Theocracy: James B. McKean and the Mormons, 1870–1875," *Dialogue: A Journal of Mormon Thought* 1 (Autumn 1966):85–100.

51. Clayton to Madison M. Scott, 11 Nov. 1871. The letter is reproduced in *Blood Atonement and the Origin of Plural Marriage. A Discussion—Correspondence between Elders Joseph Fielding Smith, Jr., and Mr. Richard G. Evans* (Salt Lake City: Deseret News Press, n.d.).

52. Minutes of the School of the Prophets, Salt Lake City, 10 Feb. 1873.

53. "Biographical Sketch of Sarah Walters Clayton," 4–5.

54. Clayton to Thomas Bullock, 5 Feb. 1853, Thomas Bullock Papers, Church Archives.

55. William Clayton to Moroni Clayton, 18 July 1862.

56. This story was provided by June M. McDonnel on the back of a William Clayton and Diantha Farr Clayton family group sheet, Genealogical Society of the Church.

57. Clayton to Charles G. Ewing, 24 Apr. 1870.

58. See William Clayton letters of 25 Apr., 18 May, 4, 8, 18 June 1864, all addressed to "Dear Boys," and discussing a buying trip some of his boys were on.

59. William Clayton to Newell Clayton, 25 Nov. 1872, 7 Feb. 1873.

60. William Clayton to Newell Clayton, 25 Nov. 1872.

William Clayton

Eight of William Clayton's Ten Wives

Ruth Moon

Margaret Moon

Alice Hardman

Diantha Farr

Augusta Braddock

Sarah Ann Walters

Maria Louisa Lyman

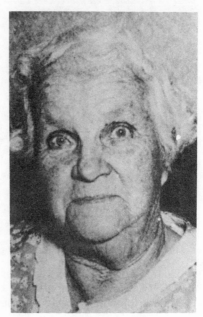

Anna Elizabeth Higgs

William Clayton and one of his wives, Maria Louisa Lyman, daughter of
Amasa Lyman. Maria eventually left Clayton in connection with the
problems surrounding her father's apostasy from the church.

Salt Lake City, around 1860, showing the old tabernacle and the bowery, where public meetings were often held.

Pioneer home of William Clayton and Sarah Ann Walters Clayton. Sarah is on the right, with two daughters, Vickie and Lucy.

William Clayton

CHAPTER 8

The Pioneer

Leaving home for the sake of the gospel was no new experience for William Clayton or any of the other followers of the prophet. In 1840 he had left his native land with pleasure, looking forward to a new home among the Saints in Nauvoo. But to be *driven* from home early in 1846 was something new.

The epic journey Clayton was about to undertake was no challenge to his faith, for he was already convinced that the Lord's chosen Saints could expect severe trials in their quest to establish the Kingdom of God. At the same time, the pioneer trek would provide the vehicle for him to make his most memorable contributions to the Mormon community. Out of this experience came that most poignant of all distinctly Mormon hymns, "Come, Come Ye Saints"; the most important pioneer guide for later Mormon immigrants, *The Latter-day Saints' Emigrants' Guide;* and one of the finest firsthand accounts of that memorable crossing, later to be published as *William Clayton's Journal.* In addition, his experiences provide important insight into many elements of that vanguard pioneer trek by letting us see it through the eyes of one who was not a leader but a representative disciple.

It was the lot of the pioneers of 1846 to spend that year preparing for the final push west. They built temporary settlements and planted crops at strategic points in Iowa, not only to house and feed themselves, but also to aid the Saints who would follow them the next year. Farthest west, at what is now Florence, Nebraska, was the largest encampment, Winter Quarters, which reached a population of some 3,500 by the end of the year. There William Clayton spent the winter. There also Brigham Young and the bulk of the Council of Fifty spent the winter laying plans for 1847 and beyond.

It is not our purpose here to recount the full story of the epic crossing of the plains, for it has been well told elsewhere[1] and Clayton's personal account is published and readily available. Rather, we will focus on Clayton's personal reactions to some of the events of the westward migration in an effort to better understand the concerns and achievements of this representative disciple.

Clayton had a role to play in the organization and activity of the 1846 emigration. Always valued for his services as a scribe, on February 17 he was designated general clerk of the "Camp of Israel."[2] In March, when the main camp was organized into companies of fifty, Clayton was placed in the company that included all the members of the brass band. He presided over the band itself and, in the absence of Peter Haws, over the whole company of fifty.[3] Clayton was frequently called upon to write letters regarding church business, and he was responsible for making up the reporting forms used by the clerks of the various companies as well as for instructing the clerks in their recordkeeping responsibilities.[4] His skills were well used on this historic adventure.

At the same time Clayton had to organize his own affairs. He had his personal goods to care for as well as certain church properties, and therefore he was responsible for several teams and wagons. He had three wives and four children with him when he left Nauvoo; they could hardly be expected to manage alone. Much of his time, however, was spent writing letters for Brigham Young. Clayton had teamsters working for him, but he worried about keeping enough of them employed and having enough wagons in good repair. One bit of help came on April 1 when Brigham Young sent him two yoke of oxen, a wagon, and a Brother James, owner of the equipment, to help out. Nevertheless Clayton was unable to provide riding space for all his family, and one comment in his journal on April 22 was probably typical of many pioneer experiences: "We are all comfortable but very tired," he wrote, "having travelled about ten miles. My wife Ruth walked all the way and myself also. The rest walked by turns."

To be a Mormon pioneer in 1846 required sacrifice, but only infrequently did Clayton complain in his journal. He often wondered where future meals might come from, however, and how he would pay for them. That some sacrifice was simply a way of life is suggested in his entry for April 17. In company with a few members of the band, he went to Keosugua, Iowa, to play. At the same time, in an amazing display of self-restraint, he wrote, "I took my music box and china to try and sell them." One can imagine the unexpressed agony of this young English musician when he realized that he must sell these prized personal or family possessions, yet no complaint was recorded. To him, it was only one of those things that the pioneers of 1846 should expect.

Some members of the Camp of Israel were required to share their goods with their brothers and sisters who were less fortunate. Some families were well prepared, having put away food and provisions to last for many months, while others left Nauvoo with very little. Clayton was among those who were moderately well prepared, and therefore, naturally, one of those to whom others came for aid. Clayton shared, though sometimes with a touch of disgruntlement toward those whom he felt had not done their part.

On April 3 Clayton found himself saddened at the distress of two members of the camp guard who reported themselves destitute. Hosea Stout, captain of the guard, had "used them very hard," Clayton reported, and they had lived on nothing but cornmeal gruel for a week. "I dealt out some of my own flour and bacon to them," he wrote, "determined to comfort them some if I could and not being willing to see anyone in our company suffer while I have anything left."[5] A month later, however, he heard from his wife, Margaret, that some of the band members were complaining that he was not generous enough. With a note of distress he observed that he had loaned "Miss Kay" a pair of shoes and divided a bag of biscuits among the needy. "I have all the time let them have flour, sugar, bacon and other things as I had them and to hear of dissatisfaction because I will not let them have the last I have grieves me. I have given to the band as near as I can estimate, twelve hundred pounds of flour, about four or five hundred pounds of bacon besides much of the other things."[6] William Clayton could share when he felt it was needed, but he was learning the hard truth that other human beings could see him quite differently than he saw himself.

The realities of human nature made it impossible even for the Camp of Israel to proceed without some disagreement and personality conflicts. Clayton's reports were certainly not unbiased, but at least his journal suggests the problems that could occur on such a trip. On May 17 he expressed disappointment with Bishop Miller, who had passed by without leaving him any cattle, though the bishop himself had plenty.[7] A month later, as he rationed out bread to his company, he noted that the men seemed "very much dissatisfied and growl to each other very much."[8] Such grumbling was not uncommon, but perhaps

more serious was the personal animosity between Clayton and at least
one other member of the camp. Hosea Stout seemed to dislike the
camp clerk with a passion, and the feeling was returned. The reason
for the conflict escapes the historian, but, as Clayton saw it, Stout even
threatened to kill him.[9] Some potential problems were avoided when,
after William Clayton was instructed to go west with the pioneers of
1847, Brigham Young unexpectedly told Stout to remain as the captain
of the guard at Winter Quarters.

As if the problems connected with moving his own family and goods
were not enough, Clayton's assignment as camp clerk and the additional duties that came to him because of his skill as a scribe added
an extra burden that he did not always appreciate. Sometimes his meticulous concern for detail even got him into difficulty. On May 4, for
example, he learned that some of the clerks had complained to Brigham
Young that he had ordered them to include in their reports the name
of each wife a man had. Apparently the clerks saw no need for this.
Clayton denied that he had gone that far and said that his only request
was that each name recorded should be listed in full, according to a
previous council order. Brigham Young responded that it did not matter whether the names were in full or not, but Clayton confided in
his diary, "I think after days it will prove it does." Present-day historians will appreciate Clayton's perspective, but Brigham Young, said
the scribe, appeared quite angry about it.[10]

Sometimes the duties imposed on him became, in Clayton's mind,
excessive. When Apostle Willard Richards wrote two official letters on
May 12, for example, he instructed Clayton to copy them, in spite of
the fact that he had three men waiting to weigh and load his wagons.
At that point, as a multitude of concerns seemed to rush together into
a near-impossible situation, he complained in frustration:

> The fact is I can scarcely ever go to council but Dr. Richards wants
> me to do his writing, although I have more writing to do as clerk
> of the camp than I can possibly do. Moreover I have to unpack
> the chest and wait on all of them with the public goods in my
> charge which keeps me busy all the time. President Young, Heber,
> Dr. Richards and Bishop Whitney have all made out to get lumber
> sawed to make their wagons comfortable but I can't get enough
> to make a hind board for one of my wagons, which has none.
> They are tolerably well prepared with wagons and teams but I am
> here with about five tons of stuff and only six wagons and five

yoke of oxen to take it. I have dealt out nearly all of my provisions and have to get more before I can go on. It looks as if I had to be a slave and take slave's fare all the journey for it has worked that way so far.[11]

Clayton needed both time and money to do his family justice, and his clerking and writing activities were keeping him from both. Two months later he was still upset that Brigham Young and Heber C. Kimball could purchase a pony, cloth, and other things, "and seem to have money enough but there is none to buy me flour."[12] Not until September, apparently, did he hit upon a plan that would help him make a profit from the tasks he seemed destined to perform anyway. On September 8 he made a formal, written proposal to Brigham Young. He was willing, he said, to engage in "any kind of common clerking" for a dollar per day, though, he added, "if it is to be copying letters or other documents I would rather have a dollar and a quarter for this is very tedious business." Alternatively, he would work for three cents a word. He then poured out his problems to his church leader, whom he had addressed as "Dr. Friend." "I . . . do not feel ever to undertake again to do two men's work for one man's wages which has often been my unfortunate lot," he said. He was willing to "be advised" if his terms were too high, but, "I have got to make some desperate effort to get something this winter or I can go no further next spring for I lack every kind of provisions and necessaries for my family as well as considerable clothing." Making his case as impressive as possible, he alluded to the illness that had plagued him for days. He asked to start work as soon as possible, "for I believe if I can get a little nourishment and victual that I can eat, I shall soon be healthy again, but I find it slow work on bread made of sour flour and nothing to improve it with." He closed his letter with an obvious plea for sympathy by asking the church leader to act as he saw best, but if he obtained a job for him "be assured you will have the blessing of our grateful heart even if it be only yours in sickness W. C."[13] His strategy must have worked, for the following day Brigham Young and Willard Richards replied, authorizing him to charge a dollar per day or three cents per word for his services and assuring him of their friendship.[14] Three days later Brigham Young gave Clayton $8 and Richards gave him some letters to copy, which he did without complaint.[15]

Of all the Mormon pioneers, the exiles of 1846 probably suffered the most acute hardships. William Clayton was not spared the difficulties. On April 9 his group planned to travel eight miles, but about noon a heavy rainstorm hit and the road turned to mud. "Several of my teams stuck," he wrote, "and we had to work till dark to get part of them to camp and two wagons we were compelled to leave overnight." They traveled only five miles that day, and since their provisions wagon was stuck behind they had very little for supper. The next day was worse. A cold wind struck as the teams were sent back to recover some of the wagons. "It rains and blows very badly and is very severe on our women and teams. Margaret and Lidia are out all the time and continually wetting both feet and all over. . . . Our teams fare hard with wet and cold, having very little corn."[16]

On top of such regular mishaps, sickness plagued Clayton and his family. By June 21 he was so desperate that he seriously considered the possibility of not continuing to Winter Quarters. "I asked the President what I should do but could get no answer. I have not been able to get any satisfaction from any of the council as to what I should do and am totally at a loss to know whether to tarry here or go on. My provisions are nearly out and my teamsters all gone and nearly all the cattle strayed away and no one to hunt them except James and Corbitt and they are sick."[17] But he went on anyway, only to encounter such days as July 26, when nearly every tent in camp was blown down and considerable damage was done to many wagons and provisions.[18]

But Clayton's hardships were, in his mind, small compared to those of the vastly outnumbered Saints who remained in Nauvoo and after fierce but short-lived resistance were brutally driven out by mobs in October. He recorded all he heard about it, commenting especially on the way the Saints fought back. "The brethren did not fire so much in proportion," he observed, "but did much more execution. Truly, the Lord fights the battles of his saints." It was with the assurance that the Lord really did care for the Saints that Clayton continued to Winter Quarters where he spent the winter of 1846–47.

Life was not all rain, mud, wind, and illness during the 1846 migration. Clayton played the violin well, and as a member of the band he was responsible for arranging concerts in some of the Iowa settlements in order to raise money. On March 4, for example, the band played in the afternoon at the principal hotel in Farmington, then spent the early evening playing at the schoolhouse. For their efforts the band members were given a fine dinner and $5 in cash. Two days later they were at Keosaugua, where they worked especially hard for what they got. Arriving in town about 3 P.M., they first played for a grocer, who paid them by letting them each take "a little" of his goods. Next a tavern owner insisted that they come to his place so "we played him a tune," said Clayton, "and then took some of his cake and beer." In the evening after supper they played and sang at the hotel for a large audience and by the end of that day they had cleared a profit of $25.[19] Such concerts were frequent, as Clayton and his friends were trying to make ends meet. They also played on occasion for the pioneers themselves, providing much-needed diversion from the rigors of the difficult days.

Sometimes the band was disappointed in its pay, but on one occasion Clayton reported with apparent satisfaction what was done about a recalcitrant debtor. A farmer had requested them to play for his family, promising them some honey in return. They played, but no honey was forthcoming. "Very slyly," however, after the rest had left, one member of the band filled a pail with honey and hid it under his cloak.[20] Clayton did not seem to mind a little trickery in such a case.

All this was only preparatory for the big push to the Rocky Mountains the following spring. Clayton spent his time in Winter Quarters preparing his supplies, working as a bookkeeper in the store, and frequently in bed with illness. Then, on April 14, came the call for him to leave with the vanguard group. That morning he was in severe pain with what he described as rheumatism in his face, but at 11 A.M. Brigham Young and Willard Richards appeared at his house, and Young told him "to rise up and start with the pioneers in half an hour's notice."[21] Immediately he set his family to work getting his clothes ready, and by 2 o'clock he was on his way in Heber C. Kimball's carriage. They traveled nineteen miles that day and the following day joined the main pioneer camp, some forty-seven miles from Winter Quarters.

The next day the first pioneer company started out. Clayton, having no wagons, horses, or carriage of his own, had no place for his trunk or clothing, so he put them in Appleton Harmon's wagon. Soon he began rotating from one wagon or carriage to another for riding and sleeping.

As Clayton recorded the events of those first few days, he was seized by a kind of historic sense that told him of the natural curiosity future Saints would have about this company. He dutifully recorded the now-famous tally of 143 men and boys, three women, two children, and "72 wagons, 93 horses, 52 mules, 66 oxen, 19 cows, and 17 dogs, and chickens." Then, as if awed by the little pioneer party's prophetic destiny, he described it as constituting "a total of 148 souls who have started to go west of the mountains as pioneers to find a home where the saints can live in peace and enjoy the fruits of their labors, and where we shall not be under the dominion of gentile governments, subject to the wrath of mobs and where the standards of peace can be raised, the Ensign to the nations reared and the kingdom of God flourish until truth shall prevail, and the saints enjoy the fulness of the gospel."[22]

Thomas Bullock was the *official* camp scribe on the trek from Winter Quarters to the Great Salt Lake, but William Clayton was appointed to assist Bullock in keeping minutes. He was also assigned by Heber C. Kimball to keep that church leader's personal journal. That alone was a time consuming task, as he suggested in his own diary on May 21. Already Clayton was behind on the job, so Kimball suggested that he leave several pages blank to catch up on later, and start from the present to keep it up as a diary. "He furnished me a candle," the scribe reported, "and I wrote the journal of this day's travel by candle light in his journal, leaving fifty-six pages blank."[23]

The pioneer company of 1847 was not truly an exploring or trail-blazing expedition. The route to the Great Basin was already well known, and at times the pioneers even saw sign boards telling them how far they were from Fort Laramie. At other times they left their own sign boards for the benefit of following companies. They frequently met other travelers, such as freight wagoners returning from Fort Laramie, and they had with them a map of the western region published by John C. Frémont, as well as Lansford Hasting's *Emigrant Guide to Oregon and California*. It was not a tragic journey, nor a particularly difficult one. Its significance lay simply in that this vanguard company, under the leadership of Brigham Young, selected the site for the Saints' new refuge in the West and began the first permanent settlement in the valley of the Great Salt Lake.

William Clayton dutifully recorded, though sometimes rather sketchily, each day's travels, the buffalo hunts, camp problems, discipline, conversations with travelers, and many other items of interest. But as a journalist he was interested in more than simply the daily happenings. Attracted, like many of his contemporaries, to the grandly "picturesque" and observing for the first time the varied, fantastic beauty of the great American West, this romantic English disciple was

compelled to record his impressions. Though he was no Francis Park-
man, he nevertheless left some intriguing, well-written descriptions of
what he saw.

[April 23, after leaving the Pawnee mission station] The country
here is indeed beautiful and appears rich, but there is very little
timber. . . . We are now camped about a quarter of a mile from
the old Pawnee village on a splendid table of land, pleasant as
heart could desire. It is not much over three quarters of a mile
wide and shielded on the north by beautiful rolling bluffs and on
the south by the Loop Fork of the Platte. From this bank can be
seen the timber on the banks of the main Platte, the bottom from
here to it appears very level. There is something romantic in the
scenery around here, and the prospect cannot well be exaggerated.[24]

[May 6] We have never been out of sight of herds of buffalo today,
and from where we are camped, I am satisfied we can see over
five thousand with the glass. The largest herd, we have yet seen
is still ahead of us. The prairie looks black with them, both on
this and the other side of the river. . . . It is truly a sight wonderful
to behold, and can scarcely be credited by those who have not
actually seen them.[25]

[May 22, on nearing Chimney Rock, one of the major landmarks
for westering travelers] The scenery after this [storm] was indeed
sublime, the sun peering out from under the heavy clouds reflecting long rays upwards which were imitated in the east. The romantic bluffs on the north and the lightning playing in the southeast all tended to fill my mind with pleasant reflections, on the
goodness and majesty of the Creator and Governor of the universe,
and the beauty of the works of his hands.[26]

[May 27] We have seen a number of romantic spots on our journey,
but I consider our view this morning more sublime than any other.
Chimney Rock lies southeast, opposite detached bluffs of various
shapes and sizes. To the southwest, Scott's Bluffs look majestic
and sublime. The prairie over which our route lies is very level
and green as far as we can see. The bluffs on the north low, and
about three miles distant. The scenery is truly delightful beyond
imagination.[27]

Clayton thought often of his family, and when on May 4 the pioneers passed a group of wagons on the other side of the river going
eastward, he and many of his companions hurriedly wrote letters for
the travelers to deliver to their families.[28] The following Sunday Clayton bathed in the Platte River, put on clean clothes, then sat down,
and "gave way to a long train of solemn reflections respecting many
things, especially in regard to my family and their welfare for time
and eternity." Always introspective, he refrained from putting all his
tender thoughts in his journal, for he knew it would one day pass
through hands other than those of his family. He was determined,
rather, to write to them privately, so that each member of his family
would get his share, "whether before my death or after, it matters
not."[29]

As usual, William Clayton also worried about the imperfections of
the Saints (including himself). They were, after all, on God's errand,
and this vanguard company supposedly represented the best of mod-
ern-day Israel. It is significant, then, that one of the longest entries in
his journal came on Saturday, May 29, when Brigham Young severely
reprimanded the Camp of Israel for too much levity, frivolity, general
laxness in keeping all the commandments, and wasting time. They
were beyond the power of the gentiles, he said, but the devil could
still work on their minds and spirits, and he was disgusted with how
some of them had succumbed. "Give me the man of prayers, give me
the man of faith, give me the man of meditation, a sober-minded man,"
he scolded, "and I would far rather go amongst the savages with six
or eight such men than to trust myself with the whole of this camp
with the spirit they possess."

Already Brigham Young's colorful, direct, and hard-hitting prose was
well known, and the tongue-lashing he gave his followers that day
met every expectation. One of the most persistent problems, he warned,
was "a mean, low, groveling, covetous, quarrelsome spirit." Another
was too much dancing. "The brethren say they want a little exercise
to pass away time in the evenings, but if you can't tire yourselves bad
enough with a day's journey without dancing every night, carry your
guns on your shoulders and walk, carry your wood to camp instead
of lounging and lying asleep in your wagons." But card playing was
the worst time-waster, and on this the pioneer leader's displeasure
waxed especially warm. "I would rather see in your hand the dirtiest
thing you could find on earth," he fumed, "than a pack of cards. You

never read of gambling, playing cards, checkers, dominoes, etc., in the scriptures, but you do read of men praising the Lord in the dance, but who ever read of praising the Lord in a game of cards?" If they had sense enough to dance and play cards with moderation it might be fine, but, he scolded, "you want to keep up till midnight and every night, and all the time. You don't know how to control your senses." He went on to other things, such as "joking, nonsense, profane language, trifling conversation and laughter," all of which, he declared, had no place in that camp. For Brigham Young to decry joking was seemingly out of character, for the twinkle in his eye and his general sense of humor became legendary, but this solemn expedition was an exception to him, and it called for exceptional behavior. "I have not given a joke to any man on this journey nor felt like it; neither have I insulted any man's feelings but I have hollowed pretty loud and spoken sharply to the brethren when I have seen their awkwardness at coming to camp." Then, as he neared the end of his reprimand he called upon every man to "repent of his weakness, of his follies, of his meanness, and every kind of wickedness, and stop your swearing and profane language. . . . I have said nothing about it, but I now tell you, if you don't stop it you shall be cursed by the Almighty and shall dwindle away and be damned. Such things shall not be suffered in this camp. You shall honor God, and confess His name or else you shall suffer the penalty."

The chastising itself was not enough. Brigham called for a prayer meeting the next day, where they would all come fasting, ready "to humble ourselves and turn to the Lord and he will forgive us." He then lined them all up according to their priesthood: apostles, high priests, seventies, elders, and, lastly, all the others. He put each group, in turn, under a solemn covenant "to turn to the Lord with all their hearts, to repent of all their follies, to cease from all their evils and serve God according to His laws." Everyone accepted the covenant by raising his hand, after which the church leader blessed them and prayed that God would help them fulfill their covenants.

After such an experience the Camp of Israel was, to say the least, subdued. The next morning a prayer meeting was held, and in the afternoon the members of the Council of Fifty found a quiet, secluded spot, surrounded by bluffs and therefore out of sight, and held a private prayer circle. Albert Carrington and Orrin Porter Rockwell stood guard a little distance away in order to prevent interruption, while the rest donned their "priestly garments" (temple clothing) and offered prayer for themselves, the rest of the camp, their brethren who had joined the army to help fight the war with Mexico, their families, and all the Saints. At the end of the day Clayton made a poignant comment in his diary that reflected the impact of two days of preaching and praying. "I never noticed the brethren so still and sober on a Sunday since we started as today. There is no jesting nor laughing, nor nonsense. All appear to be sober and feel to remember their covenant which makes things look far more pleasant than they have done heretofore."[30]

For Clayton, the pioneer trek was a spiritual odyssey as much as anything else, and standing in sacred prayer circles with Brigham Young and other church leaders was one of his continuing links with Joseph Smith and Nauvoo. The first such occasion had come exactly a year before, while the Saints were still on the plains of Iowa. Traveling some three miles away from the main camp, thirteen men met together and pitched two tents, "fixed up" for the sacred ceremony. Clayton had borrowed a temple robe from his brother-in-law, Aaron Farr. With two men standing guard outside the makeshift temple, the men inside donned their robes, went through a portion of the temple ceremony, and offered prayer.[31]

As the vanguard company moved westward, all other concerns were increasingly overshadowed by the anticipation of the end of the journey. "The idea of dwelling with my family in a land of peace," wrote Clayton on June 1, "in the midst of the Saints of God is better felt than described, but the mild, still scenery of this morning puts me in mind of it." He was eager to learn more about the Great Basin, where he knew they were heading, and he recorded various descriptions of the region provided by people they met along the way. The descriptions conflicted, however, and nothing could fully satisfy the company until they saw the region for themselves.[32]

So it was that as they neared journey's end, Clayton's descriptions reflected an increasing concern for the kind of environment that would sustain life. "There is not much grass here," he wrote on July 19 as they were struggling down what is now Emigration Canyon, "but is said to be more plentiful a little farther." The next day he made note of rose and gooseberry bushes, as well as poplar and birch trees, but also observed that the area around them was swampy and dangerous for cattle. The soil looked sandy, except in low moist places where it was "black and good," and though pine was seen occasionally timber was scarce. "A few house logs might be cut, but this is truly a wild looking place,"[33] he wrote. One can sense an element of apprehension that must have hovered over all the disciples, including Clayton, who were sure they were being led to a promised land, but were not yet satisfied that it was choice above all other promised lands.

The next day he seemed to grow a little more optimistic. He saw a great many serviceberries that were "good and rich when ripe," though he also noted that there was little grass at their camping spot and therefore "a poor chance for cattle." At the same time he observed a grove of sugar maple, much timber along the creek, and beds of green rushes in several places. Water and growing plants were cause for hope. Then, on July 22, he caught his first dramatic view of his future home. While some of his brethren were cutting a road, Clayton climbed to the top of a hill. There, he said, he "was much cheered by a handsome view of the Great Salt Lake." He sat down to "contemplate and view the surrounding scenery" and wrote a vivid description of the huge valley in his journal. He noted especially that the valley seemed to be "well supplied with streams, creeks, and lakes, some of the latter are evidently salt." His only objection to the valley was that he could see little timber, though "we have not expected to find a timbered country." Reflecting one of the chief concerns of the future homebuilders, he speculated on the probability of timber in the surrounding canyons but observed that to build log houses would take a great deal of time and labor. But "we can make Spanish brick [i.e., adobe] and dry them in the sun; or we can build lodges as the Pawnee Indians do in their villages." (Actually the pioneers used both timber and adobe for building their first homes.) "For my own part," he declared, "I am happily disappointed in the appearance of the valley of the Salt Lake, but if the land be as rich as it has the appearance of being, I have no fears but the Saints can live here and do well while we will do right."

As the group struggled down the canyon, Clayton continued to observe the elements that would affect and sustain life. Grass, birds, and signs of game animals were all observed, but so was the fact that the ground seemed "literally alive with the very large black crickets crawling around up grass and bushes." They appeared loathsome to Clayton, but he took comfort in the saying that they were excellent for fattening hogs. The bears, they had been told, lived mostly on these crickets during the summer. Little did he realize that a year later those same black crickets would sweep down upon the crops in the valley and that only the "miracle of the seagulls" would save the settlers from almost total ruin. He also noted the apparent lack of rain, but believed that irrigation could solve the problem since streams were plentiful.

On Sunday, July 25, the day after Brigham Young and the last group of the Vanguard company had arrived in the valley, a special religious service was held, and gratitude was expressed for the blessings of the trek. "Not a man, woman, or child has died on the journey," Clayton gratefully recorded, "not even a horse, mule, ox, cow or chicken has died during the journey." A full 100 percent of the original company of men, boys, women, children, wagons, horses, mules, oxen, cows, dogs, and chickens that the pioneer journalist had so carefully enumerated at the beginning had arrived at the journey's end. Together with the promise of fertile soil and plenty of water, what more comforting evidence could there be that the Lord indeed had been their guide? It had all been summed up in Clayton's thoughts three days earlier, as he thrilled with his first view of the new promised land:

> When I commune with my own heart and ask myself whether I would choose to dwell here in this wild looking country amongst the Saints surrounded by friends, though poor, enjoying the privileges and blessings of the everlasting priesthood, with God for our King and Father, or dwell amongst the gentiles with all their wealth and good things of the earth, to be eternally mobbed, harrassed, hunted, our best men murdered and every man's life continually in danger, the soft whisper echoes loud and reverberates back in tones of stern determination; give me the quiet wilderness and my family to associate with, surrounded by the Saints and adieu to the gentile world till God says return and avenge you of your enemies.[34]

The pioneer company lost no time in beginning to build the new western metropolis. The day before Brigham Young arrived in the valley, an advance party was already plowing the hard, dry ground and building a dam in what they called City Creek to get water on the land. A few days later Brigham designated the spot for the temple, declaring that the city would spread out from there in a series of square, ten-acre blocks, eight lots to each block, streets eight rods wide with twenty-foot sidewalks, and a house set twenty feet back on each lot. Four blocks were set aside for public purposes. At first the new community was given the grandiose name of Great Salt Lake City of the

Great Basin, North America, but it was quickly changed to Great Salt Lake City and, in 1868, just Salt Lake City. Here, after 1848, William Clayton would spend practically all the rest of his life.

On August 2 Orson Pratt began the official survey of the city, and five days later the leaders of the church, soon to return to Winter Quarters, became the first to select their own lots. Brigham took an entire block east of the temple site (much of which would be used for church purposes) as well as other lots in other parts of the city, and the rest of the apostles also selected choice and convenient locations. On August 16 William Clayton also got to make an early selection, since he, too, would be going back, and he chose lots 1, 7, and 8 on block 95, just west of Temple Square. As Clayton wrote in his journal, however, "Brigham Young broke into our arrangements and wanted 7 and 8 reserved, consequently I made choice of lots 1, 2 and 3."

Clayton spent a little over three weeks in the valley before returning to Winter Quarters, busily engaged in almost everything except plowing and planting. On August 26, riding a horse provided by Brigham Young, he joined the pioneer leader and several other apostles on a short exploring expedition that took them to the low hills just north of the present city, then north and west to some hot sulfur springs, later to become popular recreation spots. Elders Richards, Ezra T. Benson, and Kimball, in fact, began the process by bathing there and then.

"The more I view the country," Clayton reported, "the better I am satisfied that the Saints can live here and raise abundant crops." He observed and wrote at length in his journal about many events of this pivotal time: the progress of plowing and planting; building the bowery on Temple Square; the visits and activities of various Indians, who, he felt, sometimes took unfair trading advantage of the pioneers who were willing to pay twenty charges of powder and balls for a buck skin when the usual price was three (evidently he did not know enough about the usual history of Indian trade to see the poetic justice in this); the discovery that one could swim and not sink in the Great Salt Lake; the firm instructions from Brigham Young pertaining to what would and would not be allowed in the city; the arrival of a group of southern Saints and a detachment from the Mormon Battalion, under Captain James Brown, who had all spent the winter at Pueblo, Colorado; stirring Sunday sermons from Young, Kimball, and other apostles; and the beginning of at least seventeen cabins in the new settlement. He assisted Orson Pratt in his survey of the temple lot, worked on a

roadometer that had been and would continue to be so important to
him in recorded mileages (though William King actually performed
the major repairs and modifications on the machine), took his own
swim (or float) in the Great Salt Lake, wrote prodigiously in his diary,
and, on August 2, received instructions from Brigham Young to start
early on the return to Winter Quarters so he would have plenty of
time to record the distances traveled and other details. Little did Brigham
realize that a few Mormon Battalion boys were so anxious to get back
to their families that they would leave the valley secretly even before
Clayton and his advance group got started.

As Clayton sat spellbound at his first sight of the valley of Great Salt
Lake, not all his thoughts were pleasant. "I dread nothing so much as
the journey back again," he ruminated, "and when I think of the many
dangers from accident which families travelling this road are continually liable to and especially this last mountain road from Weber River,
it makes me almost shudder to think of it."[35] But back again he must
go, for his family was still in Winter Quarters waiting for him to return
and take them to the new Zion the following year.

The returning travelers made up two companies. Clayton's group
started out on August 17 and consisted of seventy-one men and thirty-
three wagons. This included several pioneers plus a group of men from
the Mormon Battalion who had come from California and were anxious to return to their families. Sometimes dubbed the "ox train," for
its teams were composed mainly of oxen, Clayton's company was sent
ahead on the assumption that the oxen would travel more slowly than
horses, and that the main company, which included Brigham Young,
eventually would catch up.[36] The ox train was to kill buffalo and thus
provide meat for all of them. Unfortunately, the horses traveled slower
than expected, and the two groups never did join together.

Clayton was not specific about what caused the first disagreement
in his camp, but on September 14 something made him decide to go
ahead of the others. Some of the company opposed it, he said, "not
with good grace," and there was apparently some threat to report him
to the council for disciplinary action. He believed the council would
refuse to censure him when they learned his story, but, he said, "If
they do I will bear the censure in preference to what I now bear."
Though these cryptic remarks tell us nothing about the nature of the

difficulty, the members of the advance company clearly were having some disagreements.

The next day, however, Clayton and those who went ahead with him changed their minds. They had traveled twenty-one miles by the end of the day but found that the ox teams were nearly keeping up. For some unexplained reason, they discovered, the rest of the company meant to keep up with them even if it meant killing the oxen. If the teams were thus injured in the haste, Clayton reasoned, his group would be blamed for it so they gave up their plan to go ahead in order to save the teams.[37] Perhaps it was a good thing, for the Indians along the trail at times seemed more hostile than before, and undoubtedly there was safety in numbers.

Brigham Young's company, meanwhile, was struggling along behind, experiencing difficulties. On the night of September 9 about thirty horses were stolen by Indians. Twelve days later a band of Sioux attacked the camp and got away with about ten more horses.[38] As they proceeded farther their horse teams grew weaker, and, though this helped them learn that oxen were really superior to horses for this kind of travel, they needed another kind of blessing at the moment. Food was running short, and in their effort to catch up with the ox team they had little time to hunt and kill buffalo.

On September 30 the ox team company camped at Rattlesnake Creek, exactly 678 1/2 miles from the City of the Great Salt Lake by Clayton's reckoning. Before going on the next morning Clayton wrote a letter of concern to Brigham Young. He reported that they had killed and dried a great deal of buffalo meat, though they were still short of supplies. There was considerable anxiety among them because the president and his group had not caught up. Nevertheless, Clayton explained, "Circumstances seem to urge the necessity of our moving on slowly to save the teams, and we are expecting to see you come up every day."[39]

A few members of the company wanted to stop and wait for the trailing group, but the rest felt it would be best to move on, at least beyond the Pawnee Indian village. Clayton had a special reason for wanting to hurry. He was trying to make an accurate table of distances between Salt Lake and Winter Quarters, but his calculations depended upon the pioneer roadometer. He saw signs of rain and was fearful that if it came the wagon wheels would swell and throw off the accuracy of his measurements. If that happened, he wrote, "I am defeated." If there were any who would insist on going faster than the rest, Clayton was determined to go with them.

Before they broke camp the next morning Clayton secured his letter in a post beside the road, expecting that it would be found when their trailing brethren finally came by. Sure enough, six days later a Frenchman traveling with Brigham Young's company found it and brought it to camp.[40] Now that they knew how far ahead the others were, some of them, at least, reluctantly accepted the fact that they never would catch up. When Apostle Lyman got hold of the note, he scribbled these interesting words across the bottom: "Wednesday evening 6th 1847 All well and going ahead we shall overtake them if it is at Winter quarters. Amasa Lyman."

On October 6 the men in Clayton's company again disagreed over how fast they should travel, and Clayton and the others who "felt more willing to go on than tarry" again left their comrades behind. Two days later they changed their minds again, this time with more direct incentive than before. Accosted by hostile Indians, they decided that the better part of valor was to turn around. The Indians quickly departed, though not before stealing a horse, four oxen, and some provisions. Clayton's little group found the rest of the company some six miles back.

Tempers flared as Clayton's party returned, possibly because the men who stayed behind felt that those who went ahead had made the whole company more vulnerable to danger. Besides, the group returned in such haste that they had left some oxen behind. Some "slang and insults" flew, but there was little time for argument, for they were concerned with protecting their wagons and provisions from the Indians. They loaded their guns and moved on, and when they came to where Clayton's group had encountered the Indians, they found the oxen still there. Posting an extra guard, they camped for the night.

Still all was not well as more charges and countercharges were exchanged among the discordant brethren, and those who had started ahead were accused of mutiny and ordered from then on to travel at the rear of the company. Young Lorenzo Babcock, who had stayed behind, even shook his fist in the face of his captain, Zebedee Coltrin, "damned him," and threatened to whip him. Dismayed, Clayton observed that such conduct had induced some of them to go ahead in the first place and that it would leave feelings of hatred and revenge that would require much time to heal. "For my part," he wrote, "I shall be glad when I get in more peaceable society, and I think I shall not easily be caught in such a scrape again."[41] The group probably needed another sermon from Brigham Young, but he was too far behind to know what was happening.

Meanwhile, the Saints in Winter Quarters heard that American troops were on the march in the vicinity. Not sure of the army's intentions, they became concerned for the returning pioneers and sent a company of sixteen men out to meet and help them. On October 8, the day of the Indian attack on Clayton's group, the company set out from Winter Quarters under the leadership of none other than Clayton's old nemesis, police captain Hosea Stout.[42]

We have no record of exactly what passed between the two men when they met again on October 14. Clayton only noted that they saw the company of "old police" going to meet the pioneers behind them and that they were "gladdened with the news they bring from Winter Quarters." Stout, however, put a different kind of entry in his journal for that date. He recorded the joyful meeting, though from his perspective the joy was to hear from the Salt Lake Valley. But he also became disgusted with the whole advance company. They had gone ahead, he believed, to lay up buffalo for the group behind, but instead they "were now out of Buffalo country leaving those who were to follow to shift for themselves."[43] He also accused the group of refusing to stop when their trailing comrades sent word for them to wait after they had been attacked by Indians and lost eighty horses. (Actually, only about forty horses had been stolen.) Thus the "ox train" pioneers were accused by Stout of deserting their president and other brethren in time of trouble.

The hapless William Clayton came in for special abuse, for apparently the men with whom he had haggled all along now accused him and John Pack of leading out in this presumed treachery, "with some more to back them up." "The main body of the camp," Stout wrote in his diary, "were true and faithful Saints and viewed this treacherous act in its true light. . . . You may imagine our feeling of joy, anger & surprise on meeting them and receiving this intelligence."[44]

How much substance there was to Stout's charges is impossible to determine, but the unhappy incident serves to illustrate again an important truism characteristic of any society composed of mortals. Even among the most well-meaning disciples there will always be differing perspectives on many things. It would be out of character for the sensitive, contemplative Clayton deliberately to leave behind the church leader whom he revered as a prophet and friend, on whom he so often relied for both economic and spiritual aid, and who shared his confidence as a member of the Council of Fifty. On the other hand, though apparently a rigid disciplinarian, Stout was not unfeeling, and it is unlikely that he would concoct an accusation such as this out of nothing more than his imagination. The likely answer is that these two habitual antagonists had such conflicting personalities and differing general attitudes on some things that they could never be fully compatible, and when Stout heard elements of the story, his old dislike for the quiet English scribe made it easy for him to believe the worst. Clayton, apparently, returned the sentiment, though in this instance he simply chose to ignore the man so far as his diary was concerned.

For modern idealistic Saints who might be shocked at such divergent discipleship, the Clayton-Stout dispute provides some thought-provoking insights into Mormon history. Great as they were, the Saints were not perfect, for, after all, the Lord never expected his servants to achieve perfection in this life. Indeed, he had even told their prophet, Joseph Smith, that the "fullness of the gospel" would be proclaimed, not by those who had been perfected, but by the "weak and simple unto the ends of the world."[45] Within five years both Stout and Clayton were called on missions to different parts of the world,[46] but so long as they remained Saints they also remained human, and so long as they remained human they never rose above at least some of the failings of the natural man. Both returned home in disappointment, after only a few months in their respective fields of labor, but both also remained faithful, active Saints throughout their lives.

Clayton finally arrived in Winter Quarters on October 21, 1847. "I find my family all well," he wrote with gratitude, "except Moroni, who is very sick and his mother is somewhat sick. Their circumstances are not good, but in other respects they have been prosperous for which I thank my God."[47] He soon set about publishing his *Emigrants' Guide*, and the following season he took his family to the valley of the Great Salt Lake. They arrived on September 24, 1848, and Clayton soon began the work of building homes for his family. For the third and last time he was helping to lay the foundation for a new community on the American frontier.

All this gives important perspective, through Clayton's eyes, on the Mormon pioneer experience, but it does not fully reveal his enduring contributions to the total pioneer effort. Clayton is still known not only for his important pioneer journal, but also for his role in developing the pioneer roadometer[48] and for his irreplaceable *Emigrants' Guide*.

Almost immediately after the vanguard company left Winter Quarters for the Great Basin, the meticulous Clayton recognized the need for a better system of keeping track of the distance traveled each day. Estimates would not be good enough if later companies must depend on whatever information his group provided. Accordingly, on April 19 he suggested to Apostle Orson Pratt the idea of "fixing a set of wooden cogwheels" to a wagon wheel in order to determine with exactness the distance traveled each day. He also suggested the idea to others, and several pioneers, including Elder Pratt, seemed to think the plan would work.

By May 8 nothing had been done, and Clayton was disappointed. Especially irritating was the fact that mileage estimates by different people varied each day by as much as four miles, and most camp members seemed to think that Clayton's estimates were too low. Accordingly, he decided to find out for sure. Measuring one of the wheels on Heber C. Kimball's wagon, he was astonished to find that 360 revolutions would constitute one mile, "not varying one fraction." He spent the whole day, therefore, walking beside the wagon and counting the revolutions. He found that the company had traveled, by the end of the day, eleven and a quarter miles, with twenty revolutions over, and noted with some gratification that others had estimated as much as thirteen or fourteen miles. The lesson was not lost, for several more people began to take his suggestion seriously. But for the next three days Clayton continued to walk beside the wagon, counting every revolution.

Apparently Clayton did not consider himself skilled enough to even try to undertake manufacturing his machine, so his only recourse was to nag until the leaders took him seriously. Finally, on May 10, Brigham Young assigned Orson Pratt to give the subject some attention. Pratt, a mathematician, proposed what he called a "double ended screw," which would record up to thirty miles traveled. Obviously based on Clayton's suggestions, the plan called for a large screw connected to two cog wheels that, as the wagon wheel went round, would record the miles. The plan was turned over to Appleton Harmon, who was soon at work constructing it. Clayton, meanwhile, continued to count wagon wheel revolutions each day—a tedious pioneer adventure to say the least. On May 12 the new device was installed.

As might be expected in such an enterprise, a controversy arose over who really invented the new machinery. Actually, the idea was not original with the pioneers, though how much they knew of earlier devices is only conjectural. But just two days after the machinery was installed, Harmon apparently began to take credit for its invention, and William Clayton took offense. "He is not the inventor of it by a long way," he wrote, "but he has made the machinery, after being told how to do it."[49] Another pioneer, Howard Egan, agreed with Clayton. Harmon, he said, "knew nothing about the first principles of it, neither did he know how to do the work only as Brother Clayton told him from time to time. It shows the weakness of human nature."[50]

Actually, credit probably belongs to all three major figures in the process. Clayton certainly suggested the idea in the first place, and Orson Pratt was the one who devised the original working plan. Pratt, however, gave considerable credit to Clayton when he wrote on May 12: "William Clayton, with the assistance of Appleton Harmon, a mechanic, has constructed a machine and to-day attached it to a wagon."[51] But Harmon was a skilled mechanic and was certainly justified in taking some credit. Apparently he even simplified Pratt's plan by cutting down the number of cogs on the second wheel, though the possible number of miles recorded was reduced to ten. Several months later, before Clayton headed back for Winter Quarters, the roadometer, as it was then being called, was modified by William A. King so that it could record a thousand miles of travel.

The success of the roadometer enabled William Clayton to complete his most cherished pioneer project, *The Latter-day Saints' Emigrants' Guide*. When the idea for the guide first struck him is not known, but before he left the valley to return to Winter Quarters he was assigned to make a table of distances covering the entire route. As usual, he took the assignment seriously, even though he felt that the rest of his company had no interest in what he was doing,[52] and his meticulous efforts resulted in an invaluable aid to future travelers. The day they arrived in Winter Quarters he observed that he was now prepared "to make a complete traveller's guide from here to the Great Salt Lake, having been careful in taking the distance from creek to creek, over bluffs, mountains, etc."[53] The entire distance was 1,032 miles.

Almost immediately, it seems, the Saints at Winter Quarters recognized the value of what Clayton had done and began to ask for copies. He declined, however, for he wanted Brigham Young's approval before he made any distribution. Besides, it took him two full days to make one copy and that, he said, "of course puts it out of the reach of profit if I was inclined to help myself a little by it."[54] Nevertheless he did make a copy for Brigham Young and sent it to him for his perusal and seeking his suggestions for improvement. He also wanted permission to sell a few copies.

Clayton received no word from the church leader for over two months, but nevertheless he went ahead with plans to publish his work. He hoped that by selling it to the emigrating Saints he could raise enough to buy the necessary equipment to leave again in the spring. "I dread the idea of having to be left," he told Brigham Young.[55] By early February he was ready to go to St. Louis to seek a publisher, but he wanted appropriate letters of introduction from Brigham Young as well as the church leader's approval of the project. He got both, for on February 8 Willard Richards wrote, in behalf of Brigham Young and the council, the desired letters. Addressed to Nathaniel H. Felt (apparently the presiding elder in St. Louis) and a certain Mr. William Pickert (or Picket), the letter introduced Clayton and his project. It verified the desire of the church leaders to have the guide published and asked the recipients to do all they could to help. "By his getting the same published it will be but a very trifling expence to the Emigrating Saints in comparison to the labor of handscribing same for each company."[56]

On February 10 Clayton was on his way to St. Louis with Lucius N. Scovil, and nineteen days later they arrived. In a short time he was able to arrange with the Chambers & Knapp publishing house to have 5,000 copies of the guide printed.[57] From then on the guides were sold to those who wanted them, and William Clayton's good friend, Thomas Bullock, was one of those who peddled them among the Saints in the spring of 1848.[58] A year later a Utah settler wrote a friend in Missouri what must have been a typical reaction to the value of Clayton's work:

If you could have learned the great demand there has been for the Guide . . . and could have had them on the road, they would have brought a good piece. Five dollars is what they have been sold for, but twenty-five dollars has been offered for them, and they could not be had. The emigrants say that they have realized

great advantages from them, and if they had to travel this route
again, they would gladly give twenty-five dollars, rather than be
without them. I have only got a few here, and I shall not take for
them less than $2.00 a piece. I wish I had some more, and when
you, or any of you come, I wish you to bring four or five hundred
of them.[59]

The letter writer was not exaggerating, for the little book was indeed
a marvelously detailed and helpful guide to every mile the emigrant
could expect to travel. Every major stream, hill, swamp, or other landmark was listed, and brief descriptions were given of what might be
found there. Suggestions were given as to camp sites, watering places,
and forage, and Clayton was very careful to tell his readers how and
where to cross the streams. In addition, he told the traveler how far
away he was from Winter Quarters, how far to the next landmark,
and the distance from each landmark to the City of Great Salt Lake.
Who could ask for more?

It was not only the Mormons who appreciated Clayton's guide.
When Joseph E. Ware, in 1849, published *The Emigrants' Guide to
California*, he abridged with hardly any change in wording Clayton's
description of the 500 miles between Fort Laramie and the Bear River.
"Plagiarism," commented western historian John Caughey when he
later edited Ware's work, "but from the best handbook for this section
of the trail."[60] Not just the Mormons but thousands of other pioneers
bound for Oregon or California subsequently used Clayton's guide for
the appropriate portions of their journey, and the original edition has
practically disappeared, "presumably," commented one editor, "from
the fact that the copies were read to pieces."[61] Its importance was
further recognized by the fact that several facsimile printings have been
made, even as late as 1983. The meticulous care and sense of accuracy
with which Clayton always worked resulted in a most significant contribution to the saga of the West.

We do not know how many editions of the guide were printed for
pioneer use, but Clayton reported in 1852 that a new edition had been
issued then and that it was selling for fifty cents. Apparently he had
not authorized this edition for, he said, he offered to sell the press of
Fisher and Bennett the copyright, "but they considered themselves
perfectly safe without it." He was on his way to England on a mission
and intended to republish the work there. Nearly all the European
emigrants would pass through that country and by selling it there he

would beat Fisher and Bennett to the market and "spoil their speculations."[62] His unexpectedly quick return from England, however, prevented him from completing his plans.

William Clayton, the pioneer, reflected the faith, hopes, problems,
foibles, and frustrations of many a faithful follower among the Mormons of that day. He also contributed in a very significant way, through
his *Emigrants' Guide*, to the success of the epic crossing of the plains.
But in spite of all his faithfulness and exemplary loyalty to his leaders,
he could not help but let down on a few occasions and confide his
innermost frustrations to his diary and his future readers. He seemed
well aware that one day his account of the vanguard company would
come to public attention,[63] yet shortly after he arrived in the valley
in 1847 he seemed compelled to tell it all so far as the burdens he
carried were concerned. His remarks may seem self-serving, but none
could more profoundly express the combination of faith and frustration that undoubtedly waged battle in the soul of many a Saint in that
generation:

> I have received from Elder Kimball a pair of buckskin pants, as a
> present I suppose, but as I have on similar occasions been branded
> with the idea of receiving a great many kindnesses without con-
> sideration I will for this once state a little particular on the other
> side of the question. I acknowledge that I have had the privilege
> of riding in a wagon and sleeping in it, of having my victuals
> cooked and some meat and milk, and occasionally a little tea and
> coffee furnished. My flour I furnished myself. I have no team to
> take care of. Howard Egan has done most of my washing until a
> month ago in consideration of the privilege of copying from my
> journal, using my ink, etc. The balance of my washing I have
> hired. Now what have I done for Brother Kimball? Am I justly
> indebted on this journey? Answer: I have written in his journal
> 124 pages of close matter on an average of 600 words to a page,
> which if paid at the price of recording deeds in Illinois would
> amount to over $110.00. I have collected the matter myself, besides
> writing letters, etc. This has been for his special benefit. I have
> kept an account of the distances we have travelled for over 800
> miles of the journey, attended to the measurement of the road,
> kept the distances from creek to creek and from one encampment
> to another; put up a guide board every ten miles from Fort John
> to this place with the assistance of Philo Johnson. I have mapped
> some for Dr. Richards and keeping my own journal forms the

whole benefit to be derived by my family from this mission. I have yet considerable to write in Elder Kimball's journal before I return. I am expected to keep a table of distances of the whole route returning from here to Winter Quarters and make a map when I get through, and this for public benefit. Now how much am I considered to be in debt, and how often will it be said that I was furnished by others with victuals, clothing, etc., that I might enjoy this journey as a mission of pleasure.[64]

Perhaps like many quiet followers, Clayton cried inwardly for at least a portion of the recognition he thought he deserved but might never receive. Except for two short journals, William Clayton's diaries abruptly end with his return to Winter Quarters in 1847. As camp historian for a southern exploring expedition in 1852, he kept a journal that covered less than a month, and as a missionary in 1852–53 he kept another for about five months. Beyond that we have nothing—and with no apparent reason except, perhaps, the possibility that other journals are still in someone's attic or, more likely, that new responsibilities and challenges (especially economic) left him with no time to do what he had done before.

Whatever the reasons, the basic personal manuscript sources for Clayton's life in Utah are letters rather than diaries. His letterbooks, filled mostly with day-to-day business transactions in connection with his official duties as territorial auditor and as recorder of marks and brands, are usually routine, repetitious, and dull. But tucked amid the tedium are several interesting letters that cast light on various topics of concern both to Clayton and to Mormonism during the next three decades. It is partly because of what these and other sources reveal that the balance of this work will focus on a few significant themes: economics, missionary work, Clayton's apocalyptic fervor, and his curious flirtations with pseudoscience. But first, a general overview of his life from 1848 to the time of his death will provide a framework for the chapters that follow.

NOTES

1. See Roberts, *Comprehensive History*, 3:70–91; Wallace Stegner, *The Gathering of Zion: The Story of the Mormon Trail* (New York: McGraw-Hill Book Co., 1964); Leland H. Creer, ed., "Journey to Zion: From the Journal of Erastus Snow," *Utah Humanities Review* 2 (April, July 1948):107–28, 264–84.

2. Journal History, 17 Feb. 1846.

3. *William Clayton's Journal*, 9–10.

4. Ibid., 10, 26.

5. Ibid., 12.

6. Ibid., 29.

7. "This agrees with his course," he complained, "for from about two months before we left Nauvoo to the present, he has done nothing but for himself." Ibid., 34.

8. Ibid., 46.

9. Ibid., 73–74. Juanita Brooks speculates that Hosea Stout was angry because Clayton had not satisfied Stout with his guard duty, and had even failed to stand guard when he should have. But this speculation is based on nothing more than one earlier entry in Stout's journal, an entry in which Stout refuses to name the guard he is angry with. (Juanita Brooks, ed., *On the Mormon Frontier: The Diary of Hosea Stout* [Salt Lake City: University of Utah Press, 1964], 1:232.) As early as 5 Dec. 1845, Clayton revealed some concern when he wrote in his Nauvoo journal that he had a conference with Bishop Miller and others about Stout, who was captain of the police and who "appears dishonest and oppressive to some of the police."

10. *William Clayton's Journal*, 28–29.

11. Ibid., 31–32.

12. Ibid., 57.

13. Clayton to Brigham Young, 8 Sept. 1846, Brigham Young Papers.

14. This reply, dated 9 Sept. 1846, was written on the back of the letter cited in note 13.

15. *William Clayton's Journal*, 62–63. It is not clear whether Clayton is being paid at this point for copying Richards's letters, but at least he seems to feel better about doing so.

16. Ibid., 16–17.

17. Ibid., 55–56.

18. Ibid., 56.

19. Ibid., 3, 5.

20. Ibid., 8.

21. Ibid., 74. See also Heber C. Kimball Journal, 13 Apr. 1847. According to this account, Heber C. Kimball, Brigham Young, and Bishop Whitney talked to Clayton a day earlier, urging him to go. He "cheerfully" consented if it could be arranged for his family to have some assistance. This was agreed.

22. *William Clayton's Journal*, 76–77.

23. Ibid., 169. It is presumed that Clayton wrote Kimball's journal partly on the basis of his own journal. Kimball's journal for this day reads: "Clayton remarked tonight that it was going to be difficult for him to keep up my journal on account of having to help make a map of the country for Dr. Richards. I felt anxious to have my journal kept up daily and proposed to him to leave a space sufficient for the past history, and commence from today, keep it up hereafter & fetch us the rest as fast as possible. I let him have a candle to write

at night." It is interesting to note that there are still several blank pages in Kimball's journal.

24. *William Clayton's Journal,* 93–94.

25. Ibid., 135.

26. Ibid., 173. Continuing the entry for the day, Clayton gives a beautiful description of what he saw after a group of them had climbed the nearby bluffs and could see Chimney Rock. "The whole of the scenery around is one of romantic beauty which cannot be described with either pen or tongue" (ibid., 174–75).

27. Ibid., 186.

28. Ibid., 129.

29. Ibid., 138.

30. Ibid., 203.

31. Ibid., 40.

32. Ibid., 271–72, 275–78, gives some of the descriptions that were provided for the pioneers by people who had been there.

33. Ibid., 304.

34. Ibid., 309–10. Clayton slightly exaggerated the report of no losses. One of Brigham Young's horses was accidentally shot in Wyoming.

35. Ibid., 310.

36. Ibid., 346; Roberts, *Comprehensive History,* 3:293.

37. *William Clayton's Journal,* 363.

38. Roberts, *Comprehensive History,* 3:298–99.

39. Clayton to Young and the Council, 1 Oct. 1847, Brigham Young Papers.

40. Journal History, 7 Oct. 1847.

41. *William Clayton's Journal,* 371–72. Apparently tempers were raging severely in this situation, as the camp members hurled at each other such epithets as "damned hypocrite" and "damned liars."

42. Brooks, ed., *Diary of Hosea Stout,* 1:278.

43. Ibid., 281.

44. Ibid.

45. Doctrine and Covenants 1:23.

46. In August 1852 William Clayton was called to England and Hosea Stout was called to China.

47. *William Clayton's Journal,* 376.

48. The story of the roadometer is a standard story based on Clayton's journal. For another account with slight variations in interpretation, see Guy E. Stringham, "The Pioneer Roadometer," *Utah Historical Quarterly* 42 (Summer 1974):258–72.

49. *William Clayton's Journal,* 149.

50. Howard Egan, *Pioneering the West: 1846 to 1878* (Richmond, Utah: Howard Egan Estate, 1917), 39.

51. Andrew Jenson, *The Historical Record* 9 (Mar. 1890):33, excerpt from Orson Pratt's journal.

52. *William Clayton's Journal,* 344, 376.

53. Ibid., 376.

54. Clayton to Young, 15 Nov. 1847, Brigham Young Papers.

55. Clayton to Young, 7 Feb. 1848, Brigham Young Papers.

56. A copy of this letter, with numerous crossings out and corrections, is in the Clayton Papers. Although evidently a first draft, it was, perhaps, the only draft.

57. Journal History, 29 Feb., 28 Mar. 1848.

58. Ibid., 2 June 1848.

59. Ibid., 16 July 1849, excerpt from *Missouri Republican* (St. Louis), 3 Oct. 1849.

60. Joseph E. Ware, *The Emigrants' Guide to California*, reprinted from the 1840 edition with introduction and notes by John Caughey (Princeton: Princeton University Press, 1932), 20n.

61. In 1974 a beautiful facsimile edition of the *Emigrants' Guide* was published by Ye Galleon Press, Fairfield, Wash. Three hundred copies were printed. The quotation above is on page 26. The publisher noted that only about ten copies of the original edition still exist. In 1983 Patrice Press, Gerald, Missouri, published another facsimile edition of the *Guide*, edited by Stanley B. Kimball and with an introduction by James B. Allen. Kimball's preface and notes are invaluable to anyone interested in the geographic details of the pioneer trail.

62. Clayton, "Missionary Journal, 1852–53," 26 Nov. 1852.

63. *William Clayton's Journal*, 138.

64. Ibid., 343–44.

CHAPTER 9

Remembering Joseph but Following Brigham: An Overview of the Utah Years

Shortly after William Clayton arrived in the Salt Lake Valley in 1847, he joined the rest of the vanguard pioneer company in an important symbolic act. On Friday, August 6, the members of the Council of the Twelve set the example by having themselves rebaptized in the waters of City Creek. "As we had come into a glorious valley to locate & build a temple & build up Zion we felt like renewing our Covenants before the Lord and each other," explained Wilford Woodruff, and the apostles instructed everyone else to do the same. Clayton, along with fifty-four others, was baptized the next evening by Heber Kimball, and by Sunday night all the Camp of Israel had been rebaptized for re- mission of sins, had the hands of the apostles laid on their heads for reconfirmation of churchly blessings, and rededicated themselves to building the Kingdom. All this dramatically portrayed the pioneers' vision of another new beginning for the church as well as for them- selves, and it demonstrated publicly their renewed commitment to follow the direction of their leaders. They were determined to build a new community in the West—a community that would be both a refuge from the world and a light on a hill—and they must reconsecrate their lives to the proposition that nothing would let it fail.[1]

Neither the church leaders nor William Clayton, however, spent the winter in the valley. Instead, they were back on the plains of Iowa setting in order the affairs of the church and making preparation for the next season's migration. It had been over three years since the death of Joseph Smith, and even though the Twelve were recognized by the westward-bound Saints as his rightful successors, many wondered if the First Presidency should not be reorganized. On December 27, 1847, in a small log tabernacle near Kanesville, a general conference of the church sustained Brigham Young as president, along with Heber C. Kimball and Willard Richards as his counselors. This settled the matter for the westering Saints, and the action was subsequently ratified in several meetings throughout the scattered pioneer camps as well as in the annual conference the following April. Undoubtedly Clayton attended at least one, if not more, of those meetings and raised his hand along with the others as evidence of his support for the man who now fully replaced Joseph Smith, so far as church administration was concerned.

Clayton spent the winter of 1847–48 making his own preparations for taking his family to Salt Lake Valley. With four wives and all their children, his job was difficult, to say the least. In June they were on their way, and Clayton, as might be expected, was made clerk of his pioneer company.[2] They were part of two huge "encampments," under the leadership, respectively, of Brigham Young and Heber C. Kimball, each divided into groups of hundreds, fifties, and tens—the same plan that worked so well in 1847. Brigham Young's encampment consisted of 1,229 people and 397 wagons, while Kimball's totaled 1,891 people and 623 wagons. They traveled more slowly than the vanguard company of 1847, for they had in tow not only household goods, foodstuff, and other supplies, but also the livestock needed to plant and sustain a whole new empire in the West. They could hardly gallop across the plains while driving, coaxing, herding, or otherwise carrying a huge assortment of horses, mules, oxen, cows, sheep, pigs, chickens, cats, dogs, geese, beehives, doves, and ducks. Kimball's group, according to the record, even counted one squirrel among its numbers![3] They all arrived in the valley late in September, followed three weeks later by a similar large encampment headed by Willard Richards. At the end of the summer Clayton was among some 5,000 settlers who would spend the Mormons' second winter there.

Meanwhile, the winter of 1847–48 was not easy for the 2,000 pioneers already camped in the valley. To protect themselves against possible Indian attacks, most moved into a typical frontier log and adobe fort. There was a small harvest that fall and the winter was relatively mild, but food was in short supply and by spring many were living on rose haws, sego lily, thistle roots, wild animals and birds, and anything else remotely edible. They planted early, but a frost destroyed much of the

crop and delayed the harvest. Then, in May and June, hordes of the
black, wingless crickets that Clayton had observed in the hills appeared
in the fields, adding near despair to the discouragement the settlers
already felt. Some people, in fact, became so disheartened that they
made plans to move to California. Others went out to fight the in-
vading insects with shovels, brooms, fire, and anything else they could
think of, but all to no avail—until suddenly flocks of seagulls appeared
and, instead of joining in devouring the crops, began to devour the
crickets, disgorge them in nearby streams or ditches, and come back
for more. The "miracle of the gulls," as it is still known among the
Mormons, saved enough foodstuff to assure the colony's survival the
following winter.[4]

At the same time, the settlers moved out of the fort and began
selecting, by lottery, the lots where they would build their homes and
plant their gardens. By the time Clayton arrived in September, the
huge planned community was taking shape. Within a year or so, not
only many adobe homes but also a Council House, several stores and
shops, a post office, a printing office, a church building, and several
other structures denoted the permanence of Salt Lake City. Clayton
built his own adobe home just two blocks west of Brigham Young's
estate, and for the next thirty years of his life he was inextricably
entwined with the life of Salt Lake City.[5]

Much changed for Clayton after 1847. He became one of Salt Lake
City's most prominent and well-respected citizens, but he was never
as close to the center of power as he had been in the days of Joseph.
No longer was he the prophet's official scribe and bookkeeper, though
for a time he worked in Brigham Young's office and kept some of the
financial records of the church. He also performed the duties of historian or clerk as periodically assigned. In 1852 he went on a mission,
but after that, it appears, he stood progressively further outside the
prophet's inner circle.[6] Though Clayton continued to preach in public
meetings and take care of miscellaneous tasks at the request of church
leaders, he frequently found himself looking backward, longing for his
former closeness to the seat of power and in particular the intimate
friendship with the men of power that he had once enjoyed as one of
Joseph's right-hand men.

Clayton's life took on several new elements, however. On September
23, 1851, he applied for U.S. citizenship, and on December 5, 1853, his
petition was granted by the Supreme Court of the Territory of Utah.

He broadened his cultural activities, and his personal interests became much more secular than before. Since he no longer earned his living working primarily for the church, he directed his energies into private business and public service. As breadwinner for one of Utah's largest families, he had reason to pay more attention than ever before to the necessities of seeking mammon as well as serving God.

He continued, nevertheless, to ponder the things of the Kingdom, but he sometimes let his reflections carry him to the edges of orthodoxy. His image of how things ought to be was colored by his personal reconstruction of how he thought Joseph would respond. In 1863, for example, dismayed at the unseemly manners he observed in the Salt Lake Theater, he wrote to George Q. Cannon: "I often think of the cautions we used to receive on such matters years ago in Nauvoo. Brother Joseph used to tell us that were there an assembly of Saints and the angels of God present, if one of the Saints even laughed aloud the angels would immediately take their departure."[7] Whether or not Joseph really preached such doctrine, it is doubtful that Brigham would have said it just that way. In William's mind, however, the true test of orthodoxy was in measuring whatever was said or done against the way Joseph would have responded.

In a sense, Clayton's life in Utah might be more representative of one dilemma of Mormon discipleship than was his life in Nauvoo. Being further away from the inner circles of power, and hence from the decision-making process, he was more like the rest of the Saints. Many did not always understand or agree with every word they heard from the pulpit, and it was a struggle for some to reconcile their personal views and actions with everything that came from church headquarters. Clayton was not untypical: he never doubted the prophetic calling of Brigham Young and the apostles but on a few occasions he had private doubts about the wisdom of some things they did. The dilemma had no easy solution.

One early incident suggests the biting nature of the dilemma. We have only William's side of the story, but between the lines we sense at least two aspects of human nature: the deepening paranoia that might follow a series of rebuffs that a disciple like Clayton felt were undeserved, and a very human tendency among some Saints to judge too quickly when the actions of their fellow Saints seemed out of phase with the ideal.

The episode began innocently enough on the night of Monday, February 18, 1850. To earn a little extra money Clayton had agreed to play with the band for a dancing party. He took along his youngest wife, Diantha, and during the course of the evening suggested that she dance with a certain Mr. Grist, a gentile. The band, however, played a waltz, and the sensibilities of some good Saints were suddenly shocked to see the wife of William Clayton not only waltzing, but waltzing with a gentile! Waltzing was still frowned upon in many proper Victorian circles, for it brought the couples in closer physical contact than traditional jigs and square dances. Waltzing with a gentile, in some minds, only compounded the offense.

So tongues began to wag, and the winds of gossip soon carried this and other tidbits to top authorities. Suddenly, on Wednesday morning, after Clayton had gone to work, an apostle and another elder arrived at his home and confronted Diantha. According to William, they accused her of three serious errors unbefitting a Latter-day Saint: (1) waltzing with a gentile on Monday night, (2) "harboring and encouraging" gentiles in her home during the past winter," and (3) "slandering the authorities of the church to the Gentiles." "The peace of my family is in a great degree destroyed," the distraught disciple wrote to Brigham Young that night, for the priesthood leader had given his young wife a "very severe chastisement."[8]

Few sets of charges could illustrate the social concerns of the Mormon community in 1850 better than those made against Diantha Farr Clayton. Even though the Mormons welcomed gentiles to the city and were happy to do business with them, they tried to remain apart from them—and hence from "the world"—so far as their social and religious life was concerned. The same thought was behind the charge of "harboring" gentiles—that is, allowing them to visit at length in one's home. Mingling socially could too easily bring undesirable influences into the Kingdom.

Equally serious was speaking ill of the leaders of the church. It was a cardinal virtue among the Mormons to uphold church authorities as prophets and to defend their good names before the world. Slander from within could only cause division and therefore undermine the Kingdom. "Cursed are all those that shall lift up the heel against mine anointed,"[9] the Lord had said to Joseph Smith, and Clayton was understandably upset that his wife should be so accused. He also felt the delicacy of his own position as he wrote six agonizing, legal-size pages to the prophet, knowing that his letter easily could be interpreted as improper criticism.

William was especially dismayed because no one seemed ready to defend Diantha's good name, so he set out to do it. So far as dancing with Grist was concerned, Clayton had made the suggestion to Diantha himself. With regard to "harboring" gentiles, he declared that only two had been in his home at all that winter, and in each case it was at his own invitation and while he was present. So far as the charge of maligning the authorities was concerned, Clayton was furious but frustrated, for he had no desire to criticize an apostle. "If it was from any source but from the heads of the church, I would treat it with contempt," he wrote. As it was, he could only declare, respectfully but firmly, that the charge was false and that Diantha was absolutely loyal. "I know Diantha's feelings in regard to the heads of the church, and instead of her saying anything *against them*, say nothing of *slandering them*, she has invariably spoke well of them when conversing with the gentiles." "I never was more surprised than when I heard the story," he pleaded, suggesting that the church leader "must have been very much misinformed."

Clayton did not blame the leaders for starting the rumors, but he was not above suggesting that the apostle could have found a more discreet way to confront them with the problem. If he "had asked me to be present, or told me of it before chastising her, I should have felt it more as a mark of friendship," he wrote with some constraint.

Unfortunately, Clayton's dismay only added to his intensely self-conscious paranoia and to his tendency to exaggerate. In this case he again began to believe that somewhere among the Saints there was a conspiracy against him. "I cannot help but conclude," he said, "as I have done in times past, that some person or persons make it their business to injure and crush me." As with most such charges there was no hint as to who was lurking behind the bushes, or why. Nevertheless, his deep, though momentary, depression led him to wonder if he was welcome anywhere. At the office as well as in the Legislative Council, he said, he felt in the way, as though "my room would be preferable to my company." He felt rejected even by friends among the leaders, for in all the time they had been in the valley, none had paid a social visit to his home.

In a p.s. that carried a final flourish of the dramatic, he told Brigham Young that since music was the cause of his present problem, he now intended to quit. For a man who loved his music as much as Clayton, it would take a severe emotional crisis to make him even consider such a drastic gesture. As one might suspect, that resolution was short-lived.

The tragedy is that the depression evident in Clayton's letter could have been avoided—in part if the accusing parties had been more discreet in their reporting and investigation, and in part if Clayton had not allowed himself to see conspiracy in so many corners. But Clayton eventually found a silver lining around most of his clouds, and in later years he probably opined that it took such times as these to strengthen him for even greater trials to come. Something in him—whether it was faith, credulity, optimism, or all of these combined with a stubborn will—was always in the long run stronger than his tendency toward gloom.

Certainly a high degree of optimism and willpower was necessary as Clayton began to carve a role for himself in the economic and public life of Salt Lake City. His proven clerical skills again served him well as he made another new beginning. For a brief time he worked in the church mint in Salt Lake City, making coins from the gold dust brought in from California. He continued to work, at least for a while, with the financial records of the church, and presumably he was paid for that. At least into the 1860s he was reading the financial report of the trustee-in-trust in the general conferences of the church.[10] But beyond his church employment he was also publicly and self-employed. In 1850 he set up a book shop in Salt Lake City's Council House and also opened a boardinghouse for the benefit of passing emigrants.[11] Presumably neither of these activities made him much money. In 1849 he was appointed public auditor for the State of Deseret, and in 1852, after the Territory of Utah had been organized, he was appointed territorial auditor as well as recorder of marks and brands. After returning from his 1852-53 mission to England, he was reappointed to those positions and held them until his death.

These appointments, however, hardly provided enough to sustain a family such as William Clayton's. In 1864 he received an annual salary of $400 as auditor and $300 as recorder of marks and brands, though he had to pay for his own printing of brand sheets. In 1867 his auditor's salary was $1,000, but in 1868 it was down to $600. By 1875 he was complaining that it was still only $50 per month and that this did not go far in a family of thirty.[12] In 1867 he became treasurer of the newly incorporated Deseret Telegraph Company, and from 1869-71 he served as secretary of Zion's Cooperative Mercantile Institution, the church-controlled co-op that began to dominate the economy of Utah in the 1870s. Beyond all that, he ventured into such private business efforts as collecting debts, filing land claims, acting as an attorney, lending money, merchandising, the lumber business, farming, and speculating in mining.

Though Clayton was engaged in several business ventures, much of his daily working time was taken up with his duties as territorial auditor and as recorder of marks and brands. Such work was not exciting, but it was important as well as time consuming. As auditor he was thorough and meticulous, but this meant that he spent long hours going over accounts, balancing books, preparing reports, and writing people who owed money to the territory. Not surprisingly, his religious terminology often spilled over into his official duties. When writing the Weber County assessor and collector in 1875, for instance, appealing for prompt payment of $546.75 owed to the territory, William did not hesitate to address him as "Dear Brother."[13] Such mixing of brotherhood and business was common among the Mormons.

One of the few controversial situations in which Clayton found himself as auditor came in 1870. U.S. Marshal M. T. Patrick demanded funds from Clayton to pay the expenses of the U.S. courts in Utah, but Clayton understood that such funds could be disbursed only on the order of J. D. T. McAllister, territorial marshal. The territorial attorney general confirmed his view, and Clayton refused Patrick's request. Angered, Patrick threatened to take the auditor's books and property by force. Nothing came of the threat, but a few days later a certain G. W. Bostwick appeared in Clayton's office with a commission from anti-Mormon Governor J. Wilson Shaffer appointing Bostwick as territorial auditor. Clayton rejected this affront on the grounds that only the legislature had the authority to make such an appointment. That ended the matter so far as the auditor's position was concerned, but Patrick persisted in other attacks. Governor Shaffer appointed Samuel Kahn a director of the penitentiary. Patrick joined with Kahn and R. H. Robertson in posting bonds and then demanded funds for the penitentiary from Clayton. Again Clayton refused, holding that the bonds presented were illegal, and again the marshal could do nothing. The auditor's office thus became indirectly involved in the Mormon-gentile conflict, but except for a few such incidents the life of the auditor was monotonously routine.[14]

As recorder of marks and brands, Clayton also performed an important but routine public service. He began his duties as early as 1849 and methodically recorded the nature, size, and location on the animal of each brand submitted to him. In 1855 he published the *Book of One Thousand Marks and Brands, Alphabetically Arranged*, which was expanded in later editions as new brands were recorded. The book still stands as an important source of information for anyone interested in early livestock history and, like everything else Clayton did, is exemplary in its attention to detail.

William Clayton also played a background, though minor, role in the political life of Utah Territory. His only elections to public office came in 1862 and 1864 when he was elected a city alderman.[15] Several public appointments, however, kept him close to much of what was going on. In December 1849 he was appointed to a committee to draft an ordinance for the legislature in relation to branding horses, mules, and cattle. The following December he was appointed secretary for the General Assembly of the State of Deseret, and for over a decade after that he was regularly appointed as assistant secretary or as secretary for the Legislative Council of the territory. He was also secretary *pro tem* of the Constitutional Convention held in January 1862, in one of Utah's several attempts to achieve statehood, and it was he that signed the official letter notifying Brigham Young of his "election" as governor of the hoped-for State of Deseret. That same year Clayton also acted as chief clerk in the territorial House of Representatives.

For the most part, then, Clayton's political activity was, like his other activities, that of a loyal workhorse who was willing to take the tedious, routine assignments and who had the reputation of completing such assignments well. He was never in the political forefront, though he readily participated when meetings were called to express community feelings. On March 3, 1862, for example, a mass meeting in Salt Lake City adopted a petition calling for the removal of Governor Stephen S. Harding and Associate Utah Supreme Court Justices Charles B. Waite and Thomas J. Drake. Clayton was there, and he and Thomas Williams were appointed clerks of the meeting.[16] At the end of June Clayton became chairman of a committee of three to select the names of people to fill various vacancies in county office. He reported back a slate of nominees, noting his belief that "every gentleman therein named will receive the cordial and unanimous support of the electors of Great Salt Lake County."[17] This was no doubt typical of general election procedures in Utah where in most cases a caucus selected one slate of nominees and it was generally known that that slate represented a church consensus. The nominees were nearly always elected.

Clayton also had slightly higher political ambitions—he wanted to become the federally appointed secretary of the Territory of Utah. On August 7, 1863, he wrote a former secretary, Frank Fuller, asking him to intercede with the president. In spite of the paranoid tendency noted earlier, in this case he seemed to have high confidence in his own acceptability to the people of Utah. "The people here from the highest to the lowest would appreciate the favor if you would write to President Lincoln and solicit the appointment of the writer to the office of Secretary," he wrote.[18] Whether Fuller made the effort is not known, but Clayton never received the appointment.

Salt Lake City became the religious and economic center for a vast group of settlements throughout the intermountain West. Under the direction of Brigham Young, colonists were sent to establish communities north and south along the Wasatch front, further north into Cache Valley and Idaho, further south into Nevada, Arizona, and California, west to Mormon Station (now Genoa) in Nevada, and east into eastern Utah and Colorado. By the time Brigham Young died, over 350 new communities had been settled or planned under his direction.

Among the most important sites for settlement was Iron County in southern Utah. In late November 1849 a Southern Exploring Company under the leadership of apostle Parley P. Pratt left Salt Lake City to scout out the region, traveling also into the present St. George area—eventually to be known as Utah's Dixie. The party returned on February 2, 1850, and reported, among other things, the discovery of a mountain of iron. It was not long before a call went out for volunteers to pull up stakes and join the "Iron Mission," and in mid-December a company of some 167 Saints was on its way to establish a new colony at Parowan. Later in 1851 another colony, Cedar City, was planted farther south, and these settlements eventually became the nucleus for at least a dozen more in the area. That same year Brigham Young took the first of his annual excursions to southern Utah.

When the church president made his second trip south in 1852, William Clayton was assigned to go along and was also appointed camp historian. The group had an auspicious mission: "visiting the southern settlements, exploring the country, ascertain[ing] the situation of the

Indians, making roads, building bridges, killing snakes, preaching the gospel, and doing and performing all other acts and things needed to be done, as they may be led by the Good Spirit."[19] Clayton must have felt almost as if he were back in the "good old days," and, beginning April 21, he kept a daily journal. That was the day he left Salt Lake City. Three days later his group rendezvoused with Brigham Young's at Springville. The expedition eventually traveled over 300 miles southward, a little beyond Parowan, and returned to Salt Lake City on May 21.

Kingdom building in the West was still in its early stages, and Clayton took the opportunity to record in his journal a few impressions of how that process was proceeding.[20] The weather was cold and stormy the first few days, so much so that Clayton made special note of the generous hospitality of Edward Robison when his party arrived at Robison's cabin, in the south end of Salt Lake Valley about noon on April 22. The next day was no improvement, with heavy rain and hail punctuating their progress toward Provo, some forty-five miles south of Salt Lake City. Clayton was unimpressed with the two-year-old Mormon outpost in Utah Valley. "This town looks dirty," he wrote. "The houses look miserable, and many young men idling in the streets. It seems there is not much energy here and there seems to be little spirit of accommodation or friendship among the people." The reception could not have been quite that bad, however, for that evening William Pitt's band (which was part of the expedition) went to the home of Josh. Worthen where it played while the others danced cotillions. Like the pioneer company of 1847, the members of this expedition were well prepared to enjoy themselves.

As territorial auditor, Clayton had with him the delinquent tax list for Utah County, which he delivered to Probate Judge George Bean. His group then proceeded to Springville, where they met Brigham Young and his nineteen wagons. Clayton was much more impressed with this little community than he was with Provo: "Springville is one of the most handsome locations we have seen on the route. The land is beautifully situated, plenty of water. The houses look clean and neat, and the hand of industry is clearly manifested throughout the village."

At several points along the way the company made contact with local Indians, and Clayton's extensive comments suggest several elements of the sometimes precarious relationship between the races in

Mormon Utah. On Sunday, the twenty-fifth, for example, after pitching camp in Payson, Brigham Young went to visit Chief Walker. This famous Indian leader had been baptized in 1850, though it is apparent that he really was not a converted Mormon. Such acts of friendship were among Brigham Young's efforts to establish peaceful relations between the two peoples. On this visit he gave Walker some flour and potatoes and had a long conversation with him, possibly trying to keep rising tensions at a minimum. This was not completely successful, however, for the next day one of the explorers, Elijah Ward, claimed that someone in Walker's band had stolen his horse. Three days later Brigham Young and Heber Kimball paid a visit to Walker's brother, Arapene, who was ill, and they "laid hands on him and blessed him." Two days after that Arapene was reportedly much better and tensions were again subsiding. When the explorers arrived at Fillmore the following Sunday, they met another band of Indians who, Clayton reported, "are good looking and have the character of being very peaceable." The chief, nevertheless, came into camp complaining that the Mormons took advantages of them in trading and were not feeding them enough. The next day the local bishops canvassed the camp collecting food for the Indians and, observed the camp historian, "they received enough to give them quite a feast."

On May 5 the company met a group of Indians who were anxious to trade children for guns. Albert P. Rockwood had previously traded for a child, and on this occasion James Ferguson made a similar purchase. On the return trip they met more Indians, some of whom tried to trade a little girl for a gun and two blankets. The Mormons did not seem shocked at these open invitations to participate in the slave trade. Rather, in this instance they simply were not disposed to give so much for the child! The Saints were well aware of the Indian practice of trading children into slavery and of the brutal treatment they often received as slaves. For this reason, Brigham Young actually encouraged his followers to purchase such children and then to raise them, educate them, and teach them the gospel. He even successfully urged the territorial legislature to pass an Indian slave act, thus legally authorizing the purchases and providing the Mormons with a chance to help in the process of "civilizing" the natives. This, they hoped, would virtually eliminate the Indian slave trade. On this occasion, D. B. Huntington talked to the Indians camped near Fillmore, urging them to "quit stealing from the Mormons and go to work as the Mormons

do." He told the Indians to cease killing other Indians, preached the
Mormon doctrine of baptism to them, "hinted at the resurrection and
told them that God made the law for Mormons as well as them." He
further advised them to stop trading their children to the Spaniards,
assuring them that if they would trade them to the Mormons they
would be taught to read and write as well as be "clothed like Mormons
are." Such idealism presupposed, of course, that the nomadic tribes
saw some advantage in being able to read and write or in wearing
clothes like the Mormons—something that was not necessarily true in
those days of cultural conflict. Nevertheless, according to Clayton's
report, the local chief, Canosha (or Kanosh), appeared pleased with the
discussions and promised the Indians would do everything Huntington
asked. The ironic reality of the situation, however, was subtly suggested when the chief added that "when they see the Mormons' fat
cattle and they are hungry, it is hard work to keep from killing them."
The following year, Utah's Walker War broke out, and Brigham Young
found it hard work to keep the Mormons from killing the Indians as
he tried to pursue a policy of strong defensive ability tempered by
peaceful reconciliation.[21]

The exploring party eventually visited all the Mormon settlements
between Salt Lake City and Parowan. One part of the group took a
week's side trip from Fillmore, searching for a lead mine presumably
discovered earlier by Elijah Ward. The explorers were also trying to
find silver, but they found neither. The expedition is not known for
any significant contribution to Mormon history, and it was the last
such exploring trip to be taken by Clayton. The only other time he
acted as a camp historian or scribe was on the outward leg of his 1852
missionary trip to England.

In his private life William Clayton remained an avid patron of the
arts. Despite his hasty 1850 resolution to quit music, he was equally
if not more active in the musical world. He was partly responsible for
organizing the Nauvoo Legion Band (the Nauvoo Legion was actually
the name of the Utah militia). It was in his home, on February 20,
1852, that the Deseret Musical and Dramatic Association was organized.
Clayton often participated in the productions of this group, sometimes
as a member of the orchestra and other times simply as a prompter.
Throughout the 1850s it was he who arranged the publicity for grand
concerts, which at first were held in the bowery. He was a member
and at times leader of the quadrille band, and this popular musical

group provided the backdrop for much of the social life of Salt Lake City. In the early days it even, at times, marched through the streets on wintry nights, serenading various people. At other times it provided the music for the most prestigious social affairs. During the first week of February 1861, for instance, with Clayton leading, the band played at a splendid inaugural ball where it was reported that the music, both vocal and instrumental, was excellent and the dancing superb.[22] Clayton was versatile, and even when he could hardly afford it he purchased an ophicleide (a deep-toned brass wind instrument consisting of a large tapering tube bent double), which he wanted to learn to play.[23] Whatever his role, it was clear that he enjoyed both music and drama and did everything he could to promote them in Salt Lake City.[24]

The all-pervading influence of the Mormon church is clearly seen in Clayton's musical activity. He did not write music, but he enjoyed composing lyrics to set to tunes already well known, and he took almost any occasion to do so. "Gentle Gale" was sung regularly in Nauvoo, probably because it reflected so well the spirit of the immigrants who continued to flow into the city, and "O God Save the Band" was written sometime after the death of Joseph Smith. Though most of Clayton's literary efforts have not endured, this song well represented the optimism of Mormon discipleship. To quote two stanzas:

O God save the Band, whose hearts are all one
To sound forth thy praise even with music and song,
To sound forth thy praise in marches so grand,
To play the sweet tones: of God Save the Band.

We ask that the Twelve may regard us in love
And lead us to play with the band that's above
Where Joseph and Hyrum forever will stand
And join the rich strains of God save the Band.[25]

"Come, Come Ye Saints," became his most famous piece, but another, "When First the Glorious Light of Truth," survived in the LDS hymnal until 1985. It first appeared in 1853 under the title "Resurrection Day" and was sung to the tune of "The Field of Monteray."[26] In 1851 he wrote a piece entitled "A Home for the Saints," which was sung at an assembly celebrating the fourth anniversary of the arrival of the pioneers in the Salt Lake Valley.[27]

Clayton also had wide-ranging tastes in literature. The reading material he ordered in the 1860s and 1870s, for instance, included history, such as a biography of Mary, queen of Scots; MacNalley's *Complete School Geography*; many novels, including Hugo's *Les Misérables*, Dumas's *Count of Monte Cristo*, and Cooper's *Deerslayer*; popular story magazines such as *Weekly Novellette* and *Dollar Monthly*; and a newspaper, the *Baltimore Sun*. When he ordered *Les Misérables* through the mail, he told James Linforth that he had searched the entire city for the novel and found only two copies, owned by private individuals. "I always prefer buying to borrowing," he commented.[28]

The single overriding factor in William Clayton's Utah life, however, was his Mormonism. As noted earlier, after his immigration from England he held no further leadership positions. One might expect that such a dedicated builder of the Kingdom and prominent citizen in Salt Lake City should rise at least to some kind of additional ecclesiastical authority. The explanation might be, simply, that he was thought of primarily as a clerk, and that church leaders felt this was the place he could make his best contribution. Clayton also did not seek religious office—more important to him, it appears, was recognition from his leaders for the services he performed. Too frequently he chafed inwardly at the uncomfortable suspicion that his work was not appreciated.

But Clayton was not ignored. He continued, at least in the early 1850s, to meet with Brigham Young and other leaders in private prayer groups, where those in attendance not only prayed but also discussed important matters of the Kingdom.[29] Some of these meetings had political implications. On June 27, 1852, for instance, he met and prayed with the "council" (what "council" the sources do not say) that appointed Apostles Willard Richards and Orson Hyde take the places of a federal judge and the territorial secretary, who had left Utah rather hastily after some serious disagreements with Mormon leaders.[30] Making the new appointments was actually a federal responsibility, but the council felt that someone must function in those capacities until the government in Washington could act.

Clayton was also called upon to speak before general church meetings as well as in the local ecclesiastical wards. In the early days of Salt Lake City, general preaching meetings were held every Sunday, first in a temporary bowery and then in the tabernacle. Brigham Young and William Clayton were the preachers in a bowery meeting on May 12, 1852,[31] and Clayton continued to preach in such meetings at least until the early 1860s. Most likely his reputation as a friend of the first prophet and his keen memory of the life and teachings of Joseph Smith made him a welcome speaker. Beyond clerking, it appears, his church service was to help the Saints remember and cherish their heritage. It was a service he relished. As Elder Daniel H. Wells remarked at Clayton's funeral, "It always afforded me a great deal of pleasure when opportunity occurred, to stop and talk with him on the things of the kingdom. This topic was the burden of his mind. I never knew him to converse upon anything else. When he had any leisure and also in his preaching, the prophet Joseph and the Kingdom of God were uppermost in his mind."[32]

There are only two brief accounts of what Clayton preached about when he got a chance to stand before the Saints, and both come from Salt Lake City's Seventeenth Ward, where he regularly attended church. The first account, moreover, provides an instructive glimpse into the nature of pioneer preaching meetings. On June 11, 1854, at a meeting in the schoolhouse, the bishop made a few preliminary comments, then called on Clayton to speak on anything he had on his mind. Clayton thought it best, he said, to preach on what he had heard that morning in the tabernacle, and he gave a "beautiful discourse" on the growing prosperity of the Saints, tithing, how to govern, the persecutions of the Saints, and building the temple—probably a typical sermon in pioneer Utah. But that did not end the meeting. The bishop got up again and discussed several matters that were on his mind concerning the Seventeenth Ward, then he told the congregation that Clayton would preach every Sunday evening "until he is satisfied." What that cryptic remark meant is unclear, but perhaps Clayton had made it known that he had a lot to say, and it seems that the people were as eager to listen to him as to anyone in the ward, at least for the immediate future. The bishop also told the brethren in the congregation not to forget the upcoming tithing day, reminding them that their ward was as well off as any other in the city. Finally, the clerk dutifully wrote at the end of the record, "As no body had nothing more to say, the meeting was brought to a close." So ended a typical church service day for William Clayton.[33]

The following Sunday Clayton preached again, but this time his topic, the concept of "eternal progression," might have been a bit controversial. As indicated earlier, Joseph Smith taught that every human being existed in a premortal life as an actual spirit-child of God and that mortality is only one step in an eternal process of progression.

Eventually, according to the divine plan, if one is worthy enough he might even progress to become like God.[34] The unanswered question was whether God himself (who was once like man) is still "progressing" in any way. Clayton took the position popularized by Orson Pratt. "Does our God always progress in knowledge, power and dominion?" he asked. His answer was that God had arrived to a full degree of knowledge of everything that had been and that would be. One wonders how he might have responded if he knew Brigham Young would soon take the opposite position. This and other such topics, however, are among those on which the church has never announced a firm, official doctrine, nor is it likely to. Mormon theology was never so rigid that Saints could not find room somewhere for debate and speculation. Controversial or not, the audience apparently enjoyed Clayton's sermon that day. It included at least two other topics—the resurrection and the priesthood—and, according to the clerk, it was another "beautiful, and also very interesting discourse, the congregation was very attentive."[35]

If William Clayton said anything in public that was contrary to Brigham Young's views, he probably did not know it at the time, for he was one of those who seemed to go out of their way not to offend the church leader. For some unexplained reason, early in 1856 Clayton and a group of friends even felt the need to get Brigham Young's permission before they took on a seemingly innocent new musical activity. Perhaps the consecration movement of the mid-1850s helped create a spirit of rededication and reform that really anticipated the dramatic reform movement that swept Utah beginning in the fall of 1856.[36] If so, that might account for Clayton's unusual letter to Brigham Young dated January 2, 1856. William Pitt (leader of the famous pioneer brass band), David Calder, Hugh Findlay, James Smithies, Horace K. Whitney, a Brother Barson, and William Clayton wanted to start meeting together privately to sing and play "original compositions adapted to the reformation and the spirit of the times." Their private choir would consist of four male voices accompanied by two violins, a base viol, and a flute. None of them, however, wanted to go ahead without President Young's approval, and Clayton was selected to contact him. Unable to get an appointment, he wrote the letter seeking permission. "If there is a shade of doubt on your mind in regard to it," he declared, "we drop it where it is. If it is all right, please say *yes* to brother Calder, and we will meet and go ahead, but we feel careful not to engage in any thing which would not meet with your hearty approval."[37] Such complete deference to church authority, even in Mormon Utah, seems a little extreme, but at least the letter suggests the paramount role of church considerations even in the private lives of some devoted pioneers. We have no record of Brigham Young's response.

Public service, music, drama, dancing, reading, associating with friends and family, and preaching the doctrines of the Kingdom: these were the pleasures of William Clayton's life in Utah. But they were balanced by trials and disappointments, some of which would sorely test his ability to retain the attitude of his famous pioneer hymn: "All is Well! All is Well!"

One of his problems was personal health. His eyesight gave him difficulty, and at least by the 1860s it was hard for him to work without reading glasses.[38] Aches and pains of various other sorts plagued him throughout his life, and in Utah they seemed to come more frequently than in either England or Nauvoo. For one thing, the malaria he contracted in Zarahemla seemed to recur for the rest of his life, because from that time on he frequently complained of fever as well as other persistent ailments. It was not unusual for him to comment in personal letters, as he did to J. C. Wright in 1865, that "my health is unusually poor this spring." The following year he took a three-week trip to southern Utah expressly to improve his health, and upon returning he reported to James Linforth that he had gained some fifteen pounds during the trip and was as strong and hearty as ever.[39] For the last ten years of his life, however, Clayton complained of a variety of ailments, including erysipelas (a disease characterized by fever and serious skin inflammations). "My right hand is now so bad that it is with the greatest difficulty I write," he confided to a friend in 1870. "It is through my system and keeps me sick indeed."[40] Such comments appear frequently in his letters, and during the last few months of his life he lived in almost constant suffering.

All this was undoubtedly the cause of Clayton's interest in various popular remedies. In 1872, for example, he was convinced that wormwood root was good for "purifying the blood in the spring," and when grasshoppers destroyed most of the crop in Salt Lake City, he wrote a friend asking for twenty to thirty roots, declaring that "I need some very much."[41] A year later he was praising the virtues of vapor baths as "one of the greatest boons ever offered to suffering humanity, and should be in every family."[42] They had cured him, he claimed in a letter to a friend, of a spinal disease, dyspepsia, and a palpitation of the heart, and earlier that week he had cured one of his children who was "insensible" with typhoid by administering vapor baths. If the people of Sanpete County had such baths, he said, they would have stamped out smallpox in a week. In 1875 he began taking certain powders, apparently offered through the mail by one Dr. George F. Munro. He thought they were improving his health, he wrote Munro shortly after receiving the first supply, for he was sleeping better, the pain in his head was not so intense, and "neither is the buzzing sound so bad," though his nerves were no quieter. "While writing this my hand jumps and trembles so I can scarcely write. The powders will be done two days hence, and as I cannot hear from you in that time, I shall duplicate the prescription."[43] Another popular remedy was alcohol, and it is apparent that Clayton's frequent illness was one reason why he continued to use it. It was not unusual, in Utah or elsewhere, for people to take "spiritous liquors" for medicinal purposes.[44]

One of the most difficult burdens this Mormon disciple had to bear came with his frequent self-criticism and the uncomfortable thought that he might not be living up to all the requirements of the Kingdom. His faith that Mormonism was God's only true religion carried with it a Puritan-like commitment to make the community of the Saints a light on a hill, and any action unbecoming a Saint was also an embarrassment to the Kingdom. It was in this spirit that what he perceived to be his personal imperfections often gnawed at him even more than the disappointment he sometimes felt at the actions of others.

In the bittersweet life of most early Utah Mormons, however, it was the principle of repentance and the possibility of forgiveness that often turned a suffering conscience into a rejoicing one. During the dramatic "Mormon Reformation" of 1856–57, thousands of Saints, including Clayton, went through another period of intensive soul-searching and made firm new commitments to live exemplary lives. Such efforts to overcome faults, rather than the faults themselves, were really the most significant aspects of Mormon discipleship in that remarkable year of reform.[45]

The reform movement, sparked by the fiery preaching of Jedediah M. Grant of the church's First Presidency, was just the kind of thing Clayton would think right for the Mormon community. There were backsliders among the Saints, and church leaders began to call upon all members to reexamine their lives, repent of their sins, and rededicate themselves to the service of the Kingdom. They were to clean up not only their lives but also their homes and yards, as the reform was designed to sink deep into every aspect of Mormon living.[46] It affected all levels of Mormonism—church leaders as well as ordinary members. The symbol of rededication was rebaptism, and thousands of Saints responded to the call. For many, including William Clayton, this was at least the third time they had gone through such soul-searching and been baptized: first when they initially joined the church, again as a symbolic rededication when they arrived in the Salt Lake Valley in 1847, and now as part of the reformation.[47]

All the drama of personal visions, speaking in tongues, and more accompanied the new movement, and it was even reported that the territorial legislature experienced the Pentecostal fervor. When the legislature met in Salt Lake City in December 1856, Heber C. Kimball preached a reformation sermon and demanded that all members repent of their sins and be baptized before the lawmaking began, which they did.[48] Nor did William Clayton's Seventeenth Ward escape the fires of reform, and undoubtedly Clayton was deeply affected by what went on there. He probably heard Phil Margets sing a new song, "The Reformation," in the Seventeenth Ward schoolhouse. It went, in part, as follows:

> The reformation has commenced,
>   All hail! the glorious day,
> May God his Holy Spirit send
>   To guide us on his way;
> Now, brethren, the time has come
>   For wickedness to cease;
> So live like honest Saints of God,
>   And righteousness increase
>   . . . Chorus

> Then, O, brethren, come
>   And let us all agree
> And strive to gain the blessings
>   In store for you and me.

> To gain these blessings we must try
>   And do what we are told;
> I'll tell you what we ought to do,
>   If you won't think me bold:
> We ought to put down wickedness,

We ought to watch and pray,
We ought to build the kingdom up—
Not loaf our time away.

. . . .

We ought our bishops to sustain,
Their counsels to abide
And knock down every dwelling
Where wicked folks reside:
We ought our Teachers to respect,
Not give them looks nor snubs;
And keep our ditches free from pots,
Likewise from stinking tubs.

. . . .

Now, brethren, let us study
To do the will of God;
If it's sowing, reaping, preaching,
We'll get a just reward:
Keep sacred all your covenants,
And do the best you can;
I pray that God will bless you all,
Worlds without end, Amen.[49]

Though the reform had its dramatic and exciting moments, it was certainly much more than a frenzy of fiery preaching and platitudes. It got down to fundamental Christian virtues, as seen in a catechism read by Brigham Young at a priesthood meeting in November. The questions he asked were really the cardinal principles of reform. Had anyone committed adultery, betrayed a brother, borne false witness against a neighbor, gotten drunk, stolen, lied, contracted debts they could not pay, coveted, taken the name of the Lord in vain? Had they done such positive things as working faithfully for their wages, presiding in their families as servants of God, and tithed? Soon these and other questions were being asked in Latter-day Saint homes by ward teachers, and the new questions inquired into whether or not the Saints taught their families the gospel, spoke against the brethren or the principles taught in the scriptures, kept their bodies clean, worked six days and worshipped on the seventh, attended ward meetings, or oppressed "the hireling in his wages."[50] Such catechisms reveal the genuine religious nature of the movement. The Saints were also advised to confess and make restitution to those whom they had injured, and, if necessary, to confess to proper church authorities. Church officers were warned, however, not to pry into sins that were "between a person and his or her God."[51] Every student of the reformation agrees that it had the overall effect of raising the spiritual tone of the entire Mormon community in Utah.

As William Clayton looked at himself through the eyes of the reformation, he judged himself harshly, particularly with regard to his use of alcohol. The problem was not new with him, and it is possible that by this time he had developed a tendency toward alcoholism. Today's experts disagree on precise definitions of alcoholism, but at least a few of the characteristics consistently described in the literature were shown by Clayton.[52] In any case, he interpreted his taste for alcohol as a personal failing, and the height of the reformation became the occasion for a poignant letter to Brigham Young in which Clayton did just what good Mormons were supposed to do—recognized his fault, resolved to change, and asked humbly for the church leader's forgiveness. In the Mormon mind God's forgiveness would come only after an erring soul sought also the forgiveness of those he had wronged, and Clayton felt he had offended Brigham Young. The president's forgiveness, Clayton wrote, "will give me courage to go on in the reformation, with far superior feelings . . ., for when I am called up in the ward meetings I feel as if I had no business to teach others until I have made restitution to you."[53]

For lack of more specifics, we can only surmise that Brigham Young assured Clayton of his forgiveness. The pioneer leader was plainspoken, denouncing evil in harsh and colorful language, yet beneath his rough exterior was a generous and understanding heart. If he was critical of sin, he was also critical of anyone who would unduly fault a man for one mistake when that man had many other good qualities. "When we have done good ninety-nine times and then do an evil," he once reminded the Saints, "how common it is . . . to look at that one evil all the day long and never think of the good." Before judging, he said, "we should look at the design of the heart."[54] The Saints, above all people, he believed, should be willing to forgive an erring brother who sought forgiveness.[55]

It does not appear, in any case, that the church leader faulted William Clayton too severely, for he continued to give him various church-related assignments, to recommend his professional services, and to allow him to speak in public meetings. In the long run, Clayton was probably no less successful than most other Utah saints in their striving for perfection. But the striving itself was a prime ingredient in the lives of Mormons such as he.

William Clayton's Utah years were filled with new challenges, old memories, and continuing personal struggles. Some of those struggles were the type that could come to anyone. Others represented the tests, enigmas, and paradoxes sometimes connected with Mormon discipleship in particular and provide interesting insights into several other aspects of the Mormon community in nineteenth-century Utah.

NOTES

1. *Wilford Woodruff's Journal*, 3:249; *William Clayton's Journal*, 342; Roberts, *Comprehensive History*, 3:286.

2. Journal History, 8 June 1848.

3. Roberts, *Comprehensive History*, 3:319.

4. The leading article on the seagull and cricket story is William Hartley, "Mormons, Crickets and Gulls: A New Look at an Old Story," *Utah Historical Quarterly* 38 (Summer 1970):224–39.

5. For further details on the settlement and subsequent history of Salt Lake City, see Thomas G. Alexander and James B. Allen, *Mormons and Gentiles: A History of Salt Lake City* (Boulder, Colo.: Pruett Press, 1984).

6. For example, references to his participation in Brigham Young's prayer circle or in the Council of Fifty cease after 1852.

7. Clayton to George Q. Cannon, 22 Feb. 1863.

8. Clayton to Brigham Young, 20 Feb. 1850, Brigham Young Papers.

9. Doctrine and Covenants 121:16.

10. Journal History, 7, 8 Apr. 1862. Also, various entries in the 1850s show Clayton working in Brigham Young's office on tithing and other financial records.

11. Ibid., 24 June 1850.

12. Clayton to Huldah H. Clayton, 18 Nov. 1875.

13. Clayton to Jos. A. West, Esq., 26 May 1875.

14. These incidents are recorded in a printed pamphlet entitled *Communication of Attorney-General Mr. Z. Snow to the Legislative Assembly* (Salt Lake City, 23 Jan. 1872). Most of the material in this pamphlet consists of correspondence between Clayton and Snow.

15. Edward W. Tullidge, *History of Salt Lake City* (Salt Lake City: Star Printing Company, 1886), 871.

16. Journal History, 3 Mar. 1862.

17. Ibid., 30 June 1862.

18. Clayton to Frank Fuller, 7 Aug. 1863.

19. Journal History, 22 Apr. 1852.

20. William Clayton, "Diary April 21, 1852–May 16, 1852," Clayton Papers. This small diary is actually found in the back of Edward Hunter's "Account Book 1857–1897." One must turn the account book upside down to read the journal. The Clayton Papers also have a typescript of the journal. All of the quotations in the following account are taken from this journal.

21. For somewhat conflicting treatments of Brigham Young's Indian policy, see Lawrence G. Coates, "Brigham Young and Mormon Indian Policies: The Formative Period, 1836–1851," *BYU Studies* 18 (Spring 1978):428–52; Howard A. Christy, "Open Hand and Mailed Fist: Mormon-Indian Relations in Utah, 1847–52," *Utah Historical Quarterly* 46 (Summer 1978):216–35. See also Gustive O. Larson, "Walkara's Half Century," *Western Humanities Review* 6 (Summer 1952):235–59; Howard A. Christy, "The Walker War: Defense and Conciliation as Strategy," *Utah Historical Quarterly* 47 (Fall 1979):395–420; Leonard J. Arrington and Davis Bitton, *The Mormon Experience* (New York: Alfred A. Knopf, 1979), chap. 8, "Mormons and Native Americans"; Charles S. Peterson, "Jacob Hamblin, Apostle to the Lamanites, and the Indian Mission," *Journal of Mormon History* 2 (1975):21–34. In the long run, the problems that occurred between the Mormons and the Indians were not too much different in nature from those experienced by other white settlers, and many aspects of Mormon policy were very comparable.

22. Journal History, 6 Feb. 1861.

23. Later Clayton decided to sell the ophicleide, but had problems when someone questioned whether or not he really owned it. William Clayton to Young, 10 Feb. 1854, Brigham Young Papers.

24. Dahl, *William Clayton*, 171–76.

25. MS copy on file in Clayton Papers. In the last stanza quoted above, Clayton wrote "that" instead of "that's," but it is edited here for the effect Clayton obviously intended.

26. Dahl, *William Clayton*, 173–74.

27. Journal History, 24 July 1851.

28. Clayton to James Linforth, 21 Mar. 1865. Numerous orders for books and other reading material are found in the Clayton Letterbooks.

29. On 15 Aug. 1852, for example, Clayton was there when the topic of plural marriage was discussed (Journal History, 15 Aug. 1852). This was undoubtedly a very important discussion, for it immediately preceded the public announcement of the doctrine of plural marriage to the world.

30. Ibid., 27 June 1852.

31. Ibid., 12 May 1852.

32. Clayton's funeral service is printed in *Deseret Evening News*, 9 Dec. 1879.

33. Salt Lake City Seventeenth Ward, Historical Record, 11 June 1854, Church Archives. The written record actually is 10 June, but the clerk evidently made an error, for Sunday was the 11th.

34. This idea was presented by Joseph Smith in his famous King Follett Discourse in 1844, and it has since become an intrinsic element in Mormon theology. See Chapter 6 herein for more discussion.

35. Salt Lake City Seventeenth Ward, Historical Record, 18 June 1854.

36. Gustive O. Larson suggests that the consecration movement was an important forerunner to the reformation in his "The Mormon Reformation," *Utah Historical Quarterly* 26 (Jan. 1958):45–63. For a discussion of the consecration movement, see Leonard J. Arrington, Feramorz Y. Fox, and Dean L. May, *Building the City of God* (Salt Lake City: Deseret Book Company, 1976), chap. 4.

37. Clayton to Young, 2 Jan. 1856, Brigham Young Papers.

38. Clayton to Linforth, 20 Apr. 1863.

39. Clayton to Linforth, 6 Oct. 1866.

40. Clayton to "Brother Jesse," 20 June 1870.

41. Clayton to William Douglas, 16 Apr. 1872.

42. Clayton to Henry Mills, 11 Sept. 1873.

43. Clayton to Dr. George F. Munro, 7 Nov. 1875.

44. Brigham Young, it appears, became disgusted with the too frequent use of liquor, even for medicinal purposes. In a Salt Lake City sermon on 8 Oct. 1859 (three years after the incident discussed), he lashed out furiously at drunkenness and declared: "In the name of the Lord Jesus Christ I command the Elders of Israel—those who have been in the habit of getting drunk—to ease drinking strong drink from this time hence forth, until you really need it." The last phrase may, at first, have seemed like a justification of medicinal use, but Brigham Young soon put that idea to rest. "But some may think they need it as soon as they go out of this house. Let me be your physician in the matter. So long as you are able to walk and attend to your business, it is folly to say that you need ardent spirits to keep you alive. The constitution that a person has should be nourished and cherished; and whenever we take anything into the system to force and stimulate it beyond its natural capacity, it shortens life. I am physician enough to know that. When you are tired and think you need a little spiritous liquor, take some bread-and-butter, or bread-and-milk, and lie down and rest. Do not labor so hard as to deem it requisite to get half-drunk in order to keep up your spirits. If you will follow this counsel, you will be full of life and health, and will increase your intelligence, your joy, and comfort.

"As I have already requested, I now again request the authorities of the church in their various localities to sever from this society those who will not cease getting drunk" (*Journal of Discourses*, 26 vols. [London: Latter-day Saints' Book Depot, 1854–86; reprint ed., 1967], 7:337–38).

45. The leading study on the reformation is Paul H. Peterson, "The Mormon Reformation" (Ph.D. dissertation, Brigham Young University, 1981). See also Larson, "Mormon Reformation"; and Gene A. Sessions, *Mormon Thunder: A Documentary History of Jedediah Morgan Grant* (Urbana: University of Illinois Press, 1982), 203–51.

46. "It is your duty to keep clean," Jedediah Grant proclaimed in October. "The first work of the reformation with some, should be to clear away the filth about their premises."

"I want to see the people wake up and reform," he thundered in November, "forsake all their evil habits and everything that is dark, loathsome and impure. I want to see them eschew all dirt, and filth, and degradation and cease profaning the Sabbath. . . . I want to see them become at least as moral and temperate as any people in the Gentile world" (*Journal of Discourses*, 4:188–89, 73).

47. We have no actual record of Clayton's rebaptism nor of most of those rebaptized at this time. Our assumption that Clayton was rebaptized is based on the fact that it would have been completely out of character for him not to participate, in view of all that was going on. The intensity of the reformation, the numbers of people who were baptized, all we know about the nature of Clayton's own commitment, and the fact that in March 1857 all the Salt Lake City wards were rebaptized almost en masse make it almost inevitable that Clayton was rebaptized. Significantly, no official lists of those rebaptized exist, probably because this act was not intended to replace the initial baptism necessary for entrance into the church. The initial ceremony was the one that must be recorded, while a rebaptism was merely an important symbol of personal rededication.

48. One legislator reported, on 23 Dec., that Heber C. Kimball preached "with great power being filled with the Spirit of God. Nearly all the members spoke all being filled with the spirit. . . . The power and testimony of the Elders of Israel exceeded any thing that I have seen in many a day. It was truly a pentecost" (Larson, "Mormon Reformation," 59; Brooks, ed., *Diary of Hosea Stout*, 2:611). There is some discrepancy between Stout and Isaac Haight, both of whom are cited in Larson, on the date of this experience.

49. *Deseret News*, 26 Nov. 1856, as quoted in Larson, "Mormon Reformation," 57–58. Another few lines of this poem may have affected Clayton's wives, for he took another wife on 30 Nov. 1856. The lines read:

> Now, sisters, list to what I say,
> With trials this world is rife
> You can't expect to miss them all,
> Help husband get a wife!
> Now, this advice I freely give,
> If exalted you would be,
> Remember that your husband must
> Be blessed with more than thee.

50. Autobiography of John Powell, as quoted in Larson, "Mormon Reformation," 53–54.

51. Ibid., 55.

52. Those who discuss alcoholism as a disease include Ronald J. Catanzaro in "The Disease: Alcoholism," chap. 1, in Catanzaro, ed., *Alcoholism: The Total Treatment Approach* (Springfield: Charles C. Thomas, 1968), 5–25; Ruth Fox, in her preface to *Aspects of Alcoholism*, vol. 2, a collection of articles produced by Roche Laboratories (Philadelphia: J. B. Lippincott Company, 1966). A firm rejection of applying the word "disease" is seen in D. L. Davies, "De-

fining Alcoholism," in Marcus Grant and Paul Gwinner, eds., *Alcoholism in Perspective* (Baltimore: University Park Press, 1979), 42–51. All agree, however, that alcoholism is extremely complex, that it has physiological, psychological, and, in some cases, religious overtones, and that it is treatable.

So far as the available records imply, Clayton did not show the most extreme characteristics of the alcoholic described in the literature, such as showing "marked hostility towards those closest to him." On the other hand, his frequent moodiness, his growing paranoia, and his apparently frequent but unsuccessful resolutions to abstain completely from any drinking suggest an alcoholic tendency.

53. Clayton to Young, 17 Aug. 1856, Brigham Young Papers.

54. Sermon in Salt Lake City, 29 Mar. 1868, *Journal of Discourses*, 12:173.

55. "The members of the Church . . . often commit sins that if they were to commit in the world would cut them off from the church anti-christ," Brigham Young preached, "yet we retain them as members of the Church of Christ in mercy, and in consideration of the weaknesses of poor human nature, and they pass along unscathed, receiving the fellowship of the faithful brethren and sisters with the hope that they will reform and learn to live their religion more faithfully" (sermon in Salt Lake City, 16 Feb. 1868, ibid., 12:163).

CHAPTER 10

Happy Days and Lonely Hours: Clayton's Mission to England

"I believe the happiest days any Elder ever spent in this world, are these, when he is dispensing the truths of Heaven to his fellow man,—sons and daughters of our Father in Heaven, at least, this has been my experience."[1] These deeply felt sentiments, penned by William Clayton five years before his death, express the typical feelings of devoted, missionary-minded Latter-day Saint disciples in every generation. The story of his 1852-53 mission to England demonstrates this devotion, but it also illustrates how such happy, longed-for opportunities could themselves become severe tests of discipleship.

The missionary impulse was second nature with William Clayton from the moment he joined the church. His mission to Manchester, his appointment to the British mission presidency, and his plan to remain as a missionary in England when his family emigrated all suggest how important it was to him to be active in spreading the gospel. On January 20, 1843, his heart leaped with delight at the possibility of accompanying Joseph and Hyrum Smith and the Council of the Twelve on a grand mission to Europe and Jerusalem, but that mission never came to fruition. He appreciated being in America—the land of Zion—but he had a constant longing to return to his native land and complete his interrupted missionary calling. In 1852 that opportunity finally came.

On August 28 and 29, 1852, a special conference was held in Salt Lake City. The occasion was the calling of nearly a hundred missionaries to go to the nations of the earth. They were to make an early start, before the onset of bad weather. The largest portion of the group was on its way to England, and William Clayton was among that number. "This is a privilege which I have desired for years," he confided in his journal, "inasmuch as when I left England in the year 1840

I had then a mission appointed me to Birmingham which I have never fulfilled and I have often felt a deep desire to bear my testimony once more in my native country."[2]

The encouragement and instructions given at the August conference well reflected the missionary spirit of the times. Apostle George A. Smith, for example, simply assumed that the missionaries were willing to be away from home for several years. Nevertheless, he said, it really would not be for very long: "probably from 3 to 7 years will be as long as any man will be absent from his family."[3] The present generation may look with bemusement at the idea that three to seven years away from home is not very long, and Apostle Smith may have said it partly tongue-in-cheek, but the statement was an important reflection of the reality that faced all missionaries of that day. Clayton had little or no idea of when he would return.

The missionary-disciple was committed to the importance of following explicitly the instructions of the living prophet. No matter what the program, even if one disagreed with it, true discipleship meant obedience to priesthood authority. In Clayton's case, it was not simply obedience for the sake of obedience—it was enthusiastic obedience for the sake of building the Kingdom. On this occasion some 2,000 followers of the prophet, among them William Clayton, literally trembled with enthusiasm as they heard Heber C. Kimball preach a long and dramatic sermon on doing the will of God, which by interpretation meant doing the will of Brigham Young. "You all believe that, don't you," he demanded, "without an exception? Well, if this is your faith. . . . I want you to manifest it by raising your right hands and saying AYE." The response was a forest of hands waving in the air accompanied by 2,000 voices shouting, "AYE," and Kimball saying with satisfaction, "There it is, and it cannot be any other way."

The practical result of such enthusiasm is seen in the fact that the thirty-eight-year-old Clayton, husband of four living wives and father of fifteen children as well as two children on the way, had no question about whether he should go. He could well sing with the Saints of today the traditional hymn, "I'll Go Where You Want Me to Go, Dear Lord," and mean it literally.

It was impossible, of course, for the missionaries to forget their families, but the spirit of their call demanded that they should try. At least they should not *worry* about their families, for the Lord would take care of them. "I say to those who are elected to go on missions," declared Kimball, " *go, and if you never return,* and commit what you have into the hands of God—your wives, your children, your brethren and your property." Brigham Young went even further: "When you leave, understand it, you have neither wife nor children; you have handed them all over to the Lord Jesus Christ. Let the brethren go and say, I will keep my eyes straight before me on the object of my mission, and when I have done, it is all right, I am willing to go home, if the Lord wishes me to do so."

Clayton left his family in what he considered "poor circumstances,"and even after getting away from home he wrote Brigham Young requesting, if possible, that some $800 due him for services as auditor be given to the family. Some of his children even had to borrow shoes in order to attend church meetings before he left, but his hope was that this money would clothe them until he came home.[4]

Despite such important temporal concerns, William Clayton made every effort to follow counsel and forget his family—or so his diary and correspondence would suggest—and he expected the same effort on the part of his companions. As the missionaries traveled eastward from the Great Basin, Clayton happily observed that they were all full of the spirit and that there was neither murmuring about home nor wondering about their families. "In fact," he wrote in his journal, "wives and children are rarely mentioned, only in prayer night and morning, and even then they are sometimes forgot."[5] He said the same thing in a letter to Brigham Young: "It is rare to hear families mentioned except in our prayers night and morning, and then they are frequently forgotten, knowing that they are in the hands of God, and while we are faithfully engaged in his work, we believe that both he, and his servants will not forget to bless them."[6]

The advice given to those at home was equally demanding. Apostle George A. Smith was challenging the wives as much as he was their missionary husbands when he said, "If any of the elders refuse to go, they may expect that their wives will not live with them; for there is not a Mormon sister who would live with a man a day who would refuse to go on a mission. There is no other way for a man to save his family." The wives were to support their husbands in accepting a call from the Lord, and that was it. Brigham Young stated it just as colorfully. "Don't cling to them one particle," he advised wives and children, "but let them go as cheerfully as you would give a weary traveller a cup of cold water. If you live, it is all right, and if you fall asleep before they return, it is all right; don't send your hearts after them one step, nor suffer your spirits to cling to them one moment; then you wives in very deed will be blessed and be help mates to your husbands." A woman who clung to her husband or kept him in her embrace would be dead weight, for the husband would be conscious of it and let it hinder him in his work. "The man cannot be useful in his labors while she is all the time weeping and mourning, every day of her life."

But the personal impact of a mission call for Mormon disciples went far beyond simply forgetting the cares of home and family. It was, and still is, often a time of rededication and repentance—a time to analyze one's life, make changes, and somehow use the great experience ahead to compensate for past weaknesses and mistakes. To prepare for a mission was also to resolve that nothing would interfere with making it a truly spiritual odyssey, literally the happiest time of one's life. At least that is the way it was with William Clayton.

For some reason, unexplained in the records, William Clayton had fallen out of favor with Brigham Young some months before his mission.[7] In addition, his correspondence suggests that he had made some personal, though unspecified, mistakes that he wanted deeply to overcome. The mission, then, became a most appropriate occasion for retrospection and resolution. He was well prepared to hear Brigham Young say at the August conference: "If the elders cannot go with clean hands, and pure hearts, they had better stay here and wash a little longer, don't go thinking when you arrive at the Missouri river, at the Mississippi, at the Ohio, or at the Atlantic, that then you will purify yourselves; but start from here with clean hands and pure hearts; and be pure from the crown of the head to the soles of your feet. Then live so every hour; go in the manner, and in that manner labor, and return again as clean as a piece of white paper."

Clayton, no doubt typical of Mormon disciples in all generations, approached his mission with exuberance and with a determination never again to succumb to whatever weaknesses he had. "I have not felt so well for years," he wrote a friend, "and my daily prayer is that I may magnify my calling on this mission, and return home (when sent for, for I don't intend to return until I am called back, if it be seven years) with honor and the approbation of my brethren."[8] Later he wrote the prophet, "I feel more happy and contented than I have felt for years. . . . I consider that this mission, is to me, the greatest blessing you ever put upon me. I am William Clayton again, and intend to remain so. As I told you in your office, I left my follies in the City, and by the help of God I don't intend to ever take them up again."[9] And when on November 1 the large group of missionaries broke up to find their own ways to England, Clayton reflected in his diary on their general faithfulness and desire to return home with clean hands and pure hearts. Then he wrote, "This feeling strongly possessed my heart, and having a constant fear of my own failings, I felt to pray that God will preserve me, that I may do a good work in his Kingdom."[10]

But the missionary spirit included more than the desire for self-improvement: it also meant love and concern for others, the desire to "do good" among mankind. As they traveled eastward from Salt Lake City the missionaries were instructed that they must not be critical of the people of the world when they preached to them. Rather, they were to show love and compassion toward them.[11] Clayton's own feelings were expressed to Brigham Young: "If I may judge my feelings and daily experiences I shall be blest on this mission, for I never felt more satisfied, more confidence, or a greater anxiety to do good than I have felt since I left home." Then, in a poignant summary of the whole effect of his retrospection, repentance, and rededication, he remarked, "I feel free from every earthly care, and I feel constantly satisfied that, come life or death it is all right if I may only be enabled to do good as long as I live. . . . I am striving daily, and intend to strive not only to get good to myself, but to do good to others."[12]

The 1852 missionary call had a special significance not only for Clayton but also for the church: this was the first time missionaries had ever been called upon to preach the doctrine of plural marriage in public. As Clayton recorded in his journal, his appointment to England was "to preach the gospel, and sustain the Revelation on Celestial Marriage, given to our beloved prophet July 12th 1843."[13] The practice had been kept secret from the world and never preached in public until August 29, 1852, the second day of the conference. At that time Orson Pratt of the Quorum of the Twelve Apostles was selected to give the first public sermon on the subject.[14] From that point on it was the obligation of the missionaries to preach the new doctrine boldly and openly, along with the other principles of the gospel.[15]

On Monday, September 13, the missionaries began to gather for their journey, and two days later the group met at Kanyon Creek. Clayton left his family affairs in the charge of his brother, Thomas, and another relative, Matthew Clayton, who both pledged themselves to do the best they could in his absence. That same day Clayton met Brigham Young, who was just leaving his home in a carriage. The prophet asked him what he wanted to do when he got to England, to which he replied, "If I had my own way, I would go and visit all the branches of the church and bear my testimony to them." The prophet's reply was simply, "Well, go and do it and you shall be blessed in it."[16] About six weeks later Brigham Young wrote to Samuel W. Richards, president of the British Mission, about William Clayton. Clayton did not know of the letter until the following February, but when he read it he thrilled at the prophet's acceptance of him and his desires:

> Bro. William Clayton as you will observe by the minutes of Conference is appointed on a mission to England; he is now with the rest of the missionaries on his way, and will probably arrive early in the winter. Bro. William has always been closely tied up to business; and previous to his coming from England travelled but very little outside his native country. It is therefore my wish, as it is his desire that he be permitted to visit the Conferences in England and the adjacent countries. In this capacity of a travelling Elder, he may prove a very useful auxiliary and be the means of accomplishing a great work, which his eminent qualifications and abilities so well enable him to perform, and realize the just expectations of his friends so reasonably inspired by the superior advantage which he has enjoyed to obtain intelligence, and the well known capacity and strength of mind which he unquestionably possess.[17]

On September 16 the missionary group was on its way, and the camp was organized. Clayton walked much of the way across the plains, which was particularly uncomfortable for him because on September 21 his shoes began to break open. As the official camp journalist he was kept especially busy, for he also had to take his turn at gathering wood and doing other camp chores.[18]

It would be unlike Clayton not to write a song for the occasion. He even gave, or sent, a copy to the editor of the *Deseret News*, who published it on November 27. Capturing much of the idealism of the August missionary conference, it was probably intended to remind the elders of just that. It went, in part:

> Come brethren let us sing a song of praise unto the Lord,

Who hath chosen us and sent us forth to preach his holy word,
'Mong distant nations far away, where sin and sorrows reign—
Where dire commotion fills the land with wretchedness and
    pain.

Chorus

Then brethren let us not forget to work, and watch, and pray;
Our God will never us forsake, but guard us night and day.

We go to teach eternal truth, to saints and sinners too,
To tell the world the glorious things the saints have got in
    view;
 . . . .

We leave behind us, those we hold most sacred, fond and dear;
We KNOW they're in the hands of God, and what have we to fear;
The joys of home we now forego our mission to fulfill,
And go to do what God requires—we have no other will.

Since they were on the Lord's errand, the missionaries were assured
that they would be divinely protected and cared for. At the August
conference they were told by Orson Pratt to leave any cash they had
at home for their families. "The Lord will always provide some way
to get along and the faithful servant of God has nothing to fear, only
his own weakness and his own imperfections and follies."[19] As a result,
the missionaries naturally looked for signs that they were being divinely protected. On September 18, for example, Clayton recorded a
miraculous incident. While ascending a hill, Chauncey Webb's wagon
accidentally broke away from his team. The horses ran off at a fast
gallop, carrying their full harnessing and gear with them, and were in
danger of being injured. Then, through "some unseen cause" the whippletrees became detached, and the horses were saved from injury. Considering it impossible for the whippletrees to loose themselves, the
missionaries rejoiced in what seemed to them evidence that "the angel
of the Lord" was guarding them. "If the brethren will continue to
cherish the same feelings they have hitherto done," Clayton wrote
home a few days later, "we need have no fears, for God is with us."
On September 25, summarizing the blessings of the week, Clayton
reflected on various mishaps that turned out well, commented on how
they had been blessed, and ended with the words he was already famous
for, "All is well."[20]

Orson Pratt was the highest church leader in the group that traveled eastward. He was on his way to Washington, D. C., where he would take charge of all the eastern branches of the church in America, and where he would publish an important periodical, *The Seer*. It was Elder Pratt who had formulated the basic approach to preaching plural marriage that many missionaries would follow, and in the pages of *The Seer* he dealt effectively with the subject.

As the missionaries traveled eastward, Orson Pratt had with him an article on plural marriage that he was preparing for publication, and on occasion he read it to the elders after they had camped.for the evening. "It is truly an able work," William Clayton reported after one such reading, "and invaluable to the Elders."[21] On Sunday, September 19, Elder Pratt read the original revelation on polygamy to the missionaries, clarifying for them various passages and doctrines, "all of which," felt Clayton, "will be highly beneficial to the Elders during the present mission."[22]

The missionaries also spent considerable time discussing other doctrines and ideas. On many a night they sat around the campfire listening to the expoundings of Orson Pratt and debating various religious concepts. On September 28 Orson Spencer, who had been appointed chaplain of the group, proposed that since the evenings were long and the brethren seemed disposed to sit up late, they should spend their time in "devotional exercises," including singing, preaching, and discussion. Everyone approved, and the first topic of discussion that night was the resurrection. The most interesting speculation arose over what they called the "baby resurrection." This meant, as Clayton described the strange idea, "that instead of bodies being raised out of the ground &c we shall again be born of a woman, as we were when we came into the world." There was a clear division of opinion, and Clayton himself was astonished at the doctrine. The discussion continued for the next two days and nights, sometimes growing very warm.

Clayton was no speculator on doctrine, and he was not impressed with the propriety of discussing such mysteries. Views differed widely, he said, "and there was very little light manifested by any one." When it came his turn to speak he simply gave it as his opinion that the "keys of the resurrection" were not yet given and that it was useless to pry into things not yet revealed. He told the missionaries that they were not sent out to preach the resurrection and that they could spend their time more profitably discussing subjects they understood and would soon have to defend before the world. For a while his view seemed to win out, for a majority voted to discontinue the subject, but then five elders, including Orson Spencer and Orson Pratt, took it up again. Elder Pratt declared that there was as much or more revealed on the resurrection as any other subject and that he wanted to hear the views of the elders. They continued the discussion along the road all the next day but, as Clayton saw it, "with little satisfaction to anyone."

It was difficult for Clayton to countenance these doctrinal debates when they began to warm up, for in his mind it was tremendously important that the elders all have good feelings toward each other and express a spirit of unity. "I never saw the same number of men travel together with as much union and good feeling, as has been manifested in this camp thus far," he had written a few days earlier. Even doctrinal discussions had been edifying up to that point, for, he said, "There is a general disposition manifested to store their minds with useful knowledge; and after the duties of the day are over, the time is generally spent in reading, writing, or in edifying conversation, and the spirit of peace prevails in camp."[23] The sudden division and sometimes ruffled feelings unnerved the disciple who had been so overwhelmed with love and goodwill. It was with some satisfaction, therefore, that he recorded, on September 30, a soothing statement by Orson Pratt. After delivering his own discourse on the resurrection, the apostle advised the elders never to advance an idea before the world that could not be substantiated by revelation. He then discussed the problem of difference in opinion and said something that, for Clayton at least, was undoubtedly the epitome of wisdom and saintly brotherhood: "It is reasonable to suppose that every brother entertains his opinions honestly; and if we know anyone to be in error and cannot convince him of his error by sound argument and revelation, [we are] not to ridicule him for his opinion, but treat him with respect." This sermon, Clayton observed, was not only interesting and profitable, but was also delivered meekly and kindly.[24]

The doctrinal discussions continued. On October 2 Orson Pratt read a treatise, which Clayton liked very much, on celestial marriage (i.e., plural marriage) and on the premortal existence of man. The next day, Sunday, Orson Spencer and Orson Pratt had a public debate concerning the kind of being Adam was when he first came to earth. Spencer held that Adam had been placed on the earth as a resurrected being, while Pratt forcefully maintained that his body was molded from the dust of this earth. It was the general understanding of the group that Spencer was only supporting Brigham Young's position.[25] Clayton agreed with Spencer, and in reporting the debate to Brigham Young referred to the doctrine of an earthly creation as little more than "the popular opinion of the world."

At the same time, Clayton again faced a practical problem of discipleship that would occur more than once in the years to come: What does one do when he disagrees with a superior in the church? Clayton obviously had great respect for Apostle Pratt, but in this case, he told Brigham Young, "brother Pratt and myself have rather locked horns." Clayton decided, however, that a loyal follower should not publicly argue with his priesthood-appointed leader. "There can be no difficulty between us," he wrote, "as he is my superior and I shall not argue against him; but if it were an equal I should be apt to speak any feelings in full." Even more important to the spirit of missionary work, Clayton saw some positive good come from these discussions, distressing as they were to him. They had convinced the brethren that "it will be wise to let all such subjects alone when we get amongst the benighted nations, and confine ourselves to plain principles which can easily be established from the revelations already given."[26]

The doctrinal debates continued, but in a better spirit of brotherhood.[27] Clayton observed that there were no more harsh words or jarring controversies, and such disagreements as there were all took place with good feelings. Evidently Orson Pratt's advice had taken effect,[28] though the doctrines discussed had just as great a potential for conflict. On one occasion they debated whether or not a person who had been resurrected in the two lower degrees of "glory" could advance to the celestial.[29] On another occasion Orson Pratt preached that the Saints do not worship the person of God but, rather, the "attributes" or "properties" that constitute the Godhead.[30]

But the doctrine most loaded with potential for conflict was Orson Pratt's discussion of the nature of God. With reference to the Mormon concept of "eternal progression," Pratt preached that the gods do not "eternally progress in knowledge and wisdom." Rather, at some point they arrive at a "fulness," when they have learned all there is to learn, and therefore progress no more in knowledge. Clayton and the other missionaries were aware of the seeming difference of opinion between

Pratt and President Young on this as well as other items, but he also recorded Elder Pratt's effort to minimize it. Actually, said the apostle, there was no real difference between them, only an *"apparent difference"* arising from the fact that they had not taken time to "connect" their ideas. "When Prest. Young speaks by the power of the spirit," he said, "there is frequently such a flood of revelation that he has not time to explain every particular, and unless we have the spirit of God resting upon us, it is easy to get wrong ideas." Eight years later Elder Pratt publicly recognized that he and Brigham Young did, indeed, differ, and that his personal ideas were not to be considered church doctrine.[31]

Such were the theological discussions among the missionaries of 1852. Their interest in probing mysterious, seemingly unfathomable areas was a natural impulse among a people who felt that modern prophets had been raised up partly for the purpose of revealing new information on the eternities. At the same time, Clayton's concern that their speculative doctrines not be argued before the world is significantly similar to the clear instructions given to modern missionaries: preach the simple truths of the gospel and let the mysteries alone.

On November 2 the missionaries reached the Missouri River, whereupon Clayton and his traveling companion sold their wagon for $35. After traveling further by lumber wagon and by stage, Clayton arrived in St. Louis on November 21.

Orson Pratt was already there, proclaiming the doctrine of plural marriage and reading the revelation in public. Understandably it received mixed responses, and in this case a number of church members "sent in their resignation" because of it. It was here that Clayton suffered his first abuse relating to the doctrine. He stayed at the home of his sister. His sixth wife, Augusta Braddock, also had a sister in St. Louis who called to see him but was so "mad and fiery" that they could not even carry on a conversation. Her husband later came and was so angry at Clayton that he threatened to kill him on the spot. Ordered out of the house, the husband nevertheless continued to stand across the street "foaming and threatening dreadfully."[32]

Clayton remained in St. Louis for several days then took boat passage to Cincinnati and from there to Youngstown. On December 9 he arrived at Philadelphia, having taken Pennsylvania's famous railroad that maneuvered the cars over the mountains by using stationary engines to haul them up a series of inclines. From there he went to New York, where he finally took passage for England on December 17.

On January 4, 1853, Clayton stepped ashore at Liverpool where he was welcomed by President Samuel W. Richards and some other missionaries. After dinner he quickly repaired to a public bathhouse where he took "a glorious scrubbing for about an hour." He then visited the mission president again before going to his lodgings for a welcome night's rest in a warm bed.

Clayton was soon assigned as pastor of the Sheffield and Lincolnshire conferences, and as he traveled to his place of duty he met old friends and visited scenes of his childhood, which gave him "many solemn thoughts" of days gone by.[33] On January 8 he went to Manchester where he expected to deliver letters to several Saints and to renew some old acquaintances. Tragically, it was here, where he had once presided so well as branch president, that the trouble began that ultimately shattered his hopes of a long and joyous mission in his homeland.

When the missionaries arrived in England, the introduction of the new doctrine of plural marriage became one of their most important and sensitive tasks. The first group landed in Liverpool on December 20, 1852, some two weeks before Clayton. With that first contingent was Daniel Spencer and his brother, Orson. Daniel may well have been trying to prepare the minds of the British Saints for the new doctrine when, on Christmas Day, he preached a sermon to the priesthood on the subject of obedience to authority. "If you are found obedient to council," he told them, "nothing will stumble you, neither 'Spiritual Wifeism,' nor anything else. You will swallow all good things down."[34]

The *Millennial Star* had said nothing to promote plural marriage, and, except for the missionaries and a few leaders, the British Saints in general apparently knew nothing of it. Beginning in January 1853, however, the *Star* soon gave them ample explanations and the missionaries began to preach the doctrine regularly. The first issue of the *Star* in 1853 commented on the hundred missionaries who had just left their homes "for the purpose of travelling to strange and distant nations to preach doctrines obnoxious to and universally despised by the world."[35] It also contained the 1843 revelation to Joseph Smith. The second issue carried an editorial comment on the revelation, emphasizing not just plural marriage but also the eternal nature of marriage, and declared it to be "one of the most important Revelations that have come through the prophet Joseph unto man in this last dispensation.

None seems to penetrate so deep, or be so well calculated to shake to its very centre the social structure which has been reared, and vainly nurtured by this professedly wise and Christian generation. . . . None more portray the eternity of God's purposes—and we may say, none have carried so weighty an influence, or had the power to stamp their divinity upon the mind, by absorbing every feeling of the soul to the extent the one has which appeared in our last."[36]

By the end of January the editors of the *Star* had also prepared a special supplement, which sold inexpensively, containing the minutes of the special conference of August 28 and 29, 1852. It further promoted enthusiastically Orson Pratt's new periodical, *The Seer*, which contained in its early issues expanded and powerful explanations of polygamy.[37] The supplement also promoted an important pamphlet by Orson Spencer, whose missionary assignment was in Prussia, entitled "Patriarchal Order, or Plurality of Wives!"[38] Finally, the *Star* published serially in February and March a lengthy statement entitled "Polygamy" by Elder John Jaques and commented editorially on the series: "The simplicity and perspicuity in which the doctrine is set forth, as not only being Scriptural, but one of the prominent characteristics of the Latter-day work, will, no doubt, render it most agreeably interesting to our numerous readers, who have Truth the object of their search. . . . When the institutions of God are revealed to men they are made obligatory upon them; and if used by men for other purposes than those for which they are ordained of Him, they bring cursings, wrath, and indignation. The wise will therefore take heed how they have to do with the sacred things of God."[39]

The efforts of the *Star* to promote the new doctrine were faithfully supplemented by the missionaries, who soon began to preach it regularly among the Saints. On January 23 William Clayton made note of one missionary lecturing in Sheffield on the newly published revelation and described him as "a fine man and a good speaker. His heart is in the work and he enjoys the spirit to a good degree." The next day Clayton also instructed members of the priesthood with regard to the revelation, and his companion, William Glover, discussed the same subject.[40]

It was to be expected that as in America the new doctrine would offend some of the Saints in England. On January 25, for example, Clayton preached plural marriage in Attercliffe and found a few of the Saints "very attentive." But at least one man was so vigorously opposed to the doctrine that he asked to be cut off from the church.[41] Evidently many Saints had already heard the rumors and irresponsible reports that later spread all over Europe and hindered missionary work even into the twentieth century. The Saints in Manchester had heard that in Utah a man's wife could be taken from him without consent and given to another and that young unmarried women were given to men as wives contrary to their feelings. On the evening of February 2, 1853, Clayton spent an hour and a half trying to disabuse some Manchester Mormons of such ridiculous ideas. When he finished, he reported, "They appeared to feel much better, and fully satisfied in regard to the plurality."[42] On February 23 he spent the full afternoon preaching to a group of women in the church who had heard the "wicked reports" that had been circulating. They had been told that when immigrant families arrived in Salt Lake Valley, husbands and wives were separated and daughters were taken from their parents to be given to whomever the authorities thought proper, regardless of their feelings. "I took great pleasure," Clayton said, "in correcting the reports, and taught them the true principle, which seemed to cheer them much." That night he held a meeting in the home of one of the Saints where he preached on plural marriage and other principles until nearly midnight.

Clayton was one of the most avid preachers of the doctrine of plural marriage, but ironically and inadvertently his enthusiasm contributed to the distressing events that brought his mission to a quick and disappointing end. Some details of the story are obscure, and only two sources provide much help in piecing it together. One is Clayton's own missionary journal, but here an unfortunate deletion clouds the situation. The entry of January 8, 1853, tells of his finding lodging in Manchester. "I found a place to stay," he wrote, "which I afterwards learned to my sorrow was the house of an apostate Mormon; and through him I have passed through the most unpleasant, and bitterest period of my life." But the next five pages of the journal are blank, and it appears as if a few additional pages following the blank ones have been removed. By the time of the next entry, January 23, the incidents that originated the trouble were past.

The other source is a letter written by Clayton on February 5 to his good friend in Utah, Thomas Bullock.[43] It tells the story of Clayton's mission from the time of his arrival in England until that date, and since the parts covered by the diary are reported almost precisely the same way in the letter, there is no doubt that the letter accurately reflects what should have been in the rest of the diary. The letter reveals a sad and frustrated William Clayton who had just seen a notice in the *Millennial Star* announcing that he had been released from his duties as pastor of the Sheffield conference. Realizing that the notice would shock his family and associates, he confided the whole story to his friend. He did not want the story told if it were not necessary, but for the sake of truth, he said, "I feel constrained to relate the facts of the case, so that as a friend you may be enabled to correct any false impressions that may arise from the notice referred to. If there is no public rumor in regards to it, then keep this to yourself." After relating the circumstances, Clayton sadly observed that he had explained it satisfactorily to the mission leaders but too late to keep the notice from appearing in the *Star.* Then, almost as if he were pleading for future historians to rescue his reputation from the gulf, he added, "But there stands the notice, and will stand in print as long as the church stands I suppose, without one palliating fact being given to show the reasons, or the full state of the case."

Clayton and his missionary companion, William Glover, were on their way to Sheffield when they stopped in Manchester on January 8. They had difficulty finding everyone to whom Clayton was to deliver messages, and Glover became tired. They separated, therefore, with Glover going to dinner with the local presiding elder and Clayton continuing his search for people. They were to meet at the railway station at 4:30 to continue their trip to Sheffield. On this midwinter day Clayton was wearing a heavy cloak that, as he exerted himself hurrying from place to place, caused him to become "wet through the sweating." Hot, tired, and wet, he rushed to the station but missed the train by seconds and was forced to stay in Manchester. "From this circumstance," he wrote Bullock, "I may date my ill luck, and cause of my present unfortunate position."

There was nothing to do but find a place to stay for the night, and the first place Clayton found that took in lodgers was the home of an apostate Mormon. That night Clayton came down with a severe cold, was seized with pain in his limbs, and became so hoarse he could barely speak. For a week he lay in bed coughing up phlegm, and he could consume no solid food for ten days. During all this time he was treated well by his hosts, but on Sunday, January 17, they somehow heard of the doctrine of plural marriage. Then the storm broke, or, as Clayton put it, "The scale turned sure enough, and of all the cursing and blaspheming he used, I have not often heard the equal." The former Mormon was outraged, and Clayton's efforts to reason with him met nothing but a brick wall of anger.

The distraught missionary finally persuaded his irate host, who had severely threatened him, to let him stay one more night. The next morning, scarcely able to walk, he made his way to the railroad station. It did him no good, in his weakened condition, to stand for several hours in the cold waiting for the train to Sheffield.

It was out of this event that the first serious charge was brought against Clayton. "This scoundrel," as he characterized his Manchester host, construed Clayton's scriptural arguments in favor of plural marriage to make it appear that he had admitted to having more than one wife. Evidently some missionaries, Clayton included, were not publicly acknowledging their personal involvement in the practice until the doctrine could be fully taught and generally accepted. At any rate, the angry apostate began to spread distortions throughout Manchester, even going so far as to accuse the hapless missionary of immorality.[44] It is understandable that the Saints in Manchester, some of whom were there thirteen years earlier when Clayton was their branch president, should be shocked at the sudden accusations. Perhaps the shock effect itself led some of them to believe the worst, and someone wrote the mission president, Samuel Richards, repeating the charges.

But for Clayton misfortunes seemed to come in bunches. In this case they only began with the rumor-mongering related to his plural marriages. They continued with another incident that, though understandable enough from his perspective, he might have avoided with slightly more discretion. He finally boarded the train for Sheffield but, upon his arrival, felt so "weak and poorly" from all he had gone through that he could barely stand. He was on his way to the home of a Brother Albiston but decided he must have a glass of gin "to stimulate me for the task." "Unfortunate Act," wrote Clayton. "The weakness of my body, and being so long without food, caused it to take hold of me, so that I knew it must be noticed." When he reached the home of Brother Albiston several other Saints were there, and by that time the alcohol had so affected his weakened body that he appeared to be in a state of drunkenness. "The effects of the gin almost made me crazy," he recalled, and his illness again became so severe that he had to stay in bed another few days at the Albiston home.

Even after he was able to move about, his weakness and hoarseness lingered for weeks.

As in Manchester, there were those among the Saints in Sheffield who felt it their obligation to report to the mission president and almost immediately one of the brethren left for Liverpool. At this point, as in the life of all disciples, indiscretions from the distant past seemed also to catch up with Clayton. As he told his friend: "As brother Samuel knew that I have indulged too much in times past, I suppose he naturally concluded that the report must be true. Hence the notice in the Star, before I ever knew a syllable of what was going on."

We have no authentic information about what went on in Samuel Richards's mind when he heard the two reports on William Clayton. It is clear, however, that he felt that Clayton should not function in a leadership position, at least until the charges were cleared up, for he placed the following notice in the *Millennial Star* dated February 5 (though actually distributed several days earlier): "Elder William Clayton, by late appointment Pastor of the Sheffield and Lincolnshire Conferences, is suspended from acting in any official capacity in the Church of Jesus Christ of Latter-day Saints."

Clayton, meanwhile, was not about to sit idly by while such charges were circulating. On Wednesday, January 26, he received a letter from President Richards that contained "intimations" of the accusations against him. Within fifteen minutes he was on his way to Liverpool and the next day he had an interview with Richards and his counselor, Daniel Spencer. Spencer had left Salt Lake City with Clayton only four months earlier, which doubtless made the need now to sit in judgment a special sadness for them both.

It seems apparent that by the time Clayton arrived in Liverpool Richards had already decided to place the fateful notice in the church periodical, though he did not inform Clayton of it at the time. The fact that the paper was being distributed by February 1 suggests that the copy work, typesetting, and printing were all at least in process, if not finished, when Clayton met with him on January 27. In any case Clayton came away from that interview feeling that both mission leaders believed the false reports.[45]

As Clayton left the mission office, Richards asked him to call again at 5 o'clock that evening. We can only imagine the thoughts that went through his mind as he wandered around alone, not able even to do missionary work. He spent the day simply strolling along the docks at Liverpool, looking at the shipping and, no doubt, sadly reflecting on how such happy days could suddenly become so tragic. At five he met again with Richards, who apparently had not changed his views and felt it wise for Clayton to be released from duty. By this time he at least may have begun to see Clayton's side of the story, but, as Clayton wrote to Bullock, "it was too late. The malice was in print, and could not be recalled." Richards advised Clayton not to act in any "public capacity" or even preach for a week or two and took his ministerial license as a guarantee that he would not. Clayton promised to conform. Richards gave the distraught elder some money to help pay expenses and then, Clayton wrote in his diary, "I bid him goodby with a heavy heart, seeing plainly that the devil is determined to destroy me if possible."

Alone, disgraced, and seemingly rejected by those who could control his future, Clayton brooded. But it was impossible for him to stay in his room alone, so he spent the evening wandering through a zoo in order to pass away the time. The next day he returned to Sheffield. If ever a person felt alone in a crowd, it was William Clayton as that night he went to a circus "to pass away a lonely hour." He would have many such lonely hours before his mission was complete.

At the same time, Clayton was not without sympathy among the Saints. When he returned to Sheffield he met with church officers, explained the circumstances, and in a humble spirit asked forgiveness if he had hurt the feelings of anyone. Unanimously the priesthood leaders voted to forgive him. They also wrote the mission president, recounting the facts as they saw them and asking that Clayton be restored to his leadership position. How warm with gratitude he must have felt when he wrote in his diary, "The brethren appear to feel very well towards me." He assured Bullock that "the Elders and officers here have rejoiced in my council, and have gratefully acknowledged the benefits they have received under my instructions." Such a feeling of acceptance could not completely pay for the torment he had experienced, but at least it helped.

Clayton could not perform any official pastoral duties, but he spent the next several days catching up on his journal, writing letters, sightseeing, and, when he felt it was appropriate, teaching the Saints. Even plural marriage was among the subjects he taught. Such opportunities were great therapy for him during these trying days, as one can sense in his entry of Sunday, February 6. "In the evening a number of the brethren called, and I felt well while instructing them on the principles of eternal life." But he could not be satisfied until he was back to his labors full time. "In a few weeks things will take a change and I shall be busy in the field of labor," he wrote Bullock, "but time seems to go slow when I am not preaching every day."

In due time the longed-for restoration came, and in the intervening days Clayton found himself gaining renewed hope for the success of his mission. On February 7 he received a "consoling letter" from Samuel Richards, which included not only comforting words from the mission president but also a copy of the comments Brigham Young had made about Clayton in a letter to Richards written on October 29, 1852. The confidence of the prophet was just what Clayton needed at that point. It "inspired me with fresh energy to be faithful and do the will of God," he said, "that the anticipations of my brethren in regard to me may be fully realized, and that I may be the means of doing a good work during my stay in this country. And may the Lord enable me to do it, for I have no other object and desire but to do this thing." Finally, on February 12 he received word from Richards that he had been restored to office. On February 17 he received a copy of the *Millenial Star* (dated February 26) that announced his restoration, and his companion, William Glover, returned from a trip to Liverpool bringing personal assurances that Richards and Spencer both had confidence in him.[46]

Delighted and renewed by his exoneration, Clayton resumed his conference leadership vigorously. He led out in planning a series of lectures in Sheffield and in raising the money to support it. He raised money to send elders on foreign missions, and he was able to obtain a reconciliation with some of the elders who had opposed him. He confided in his diary that "we feel now that every obstacle is removed, and the Lord has wrought every thing round to our hearts desire." Then, reflecting the exuberance that was finally his again, he wrote: "We could not have been more blest in regard to these matters, even if we had had the privilege of asking the Lord for them, face to face; and to his name be all the praise and glory forever and ever."

The last entry in Clayton's missionary journal is that of March 2, and by this time he seemed confident all would go well from then on. What happened between then and April is a mystery, but sometime during the month Samuel Richards suggested that he return home.[47] The answer may be that despite the support Clayton received in Sheffield, there were still those who were critical of him, and President Richards simply felt it wise to avoid possible conflict and division. There is nothing in the record to suggest any more specific incidents, but it is not difficult to imagine that the controversy swirling about him did not subside merely because the mission president restored him. In any case, on April 6 the ship *Camillus* cleared the port of Liverpool with the last company of Saints to emigrate that season. William Clayton was among them and undoubtedly spent many more lonely hours amid the crowd of Saints. Though he was still officially listed as a "minister" by occupation,[48] the "happiest days any Elder ever spent in this world" were, for him, at an end.

What did all this mean to the faith and discipleship of William Clayton? Nothing in the available records sheds further light on the mission, but his letter to Bullock portrays an attitude that deserves comment. In the midst of his frustration, Clayton became deeply introspective and made new and determined commitments. A lesser disciple may have let the criticism and discipline dismay him to the point of giving up—returning home and even, perhaps, deciding that church activity simply was not worth the trouble. Indeed, it is not unheard of among the Mormons for former missionaries to lose their faith over lesser things. But disciples of Clayton's stripe took a different tack.

Clayton revealed the nature of his faith to Bullock. Far from predicting that the experience would affect him negatively for life, he was already looking on the bright side and had decided that in the long run it would have a good effect. He was determined that the whole experience "will be an effectual preventative against my touching intoxicating drinks. It has weaned me from that folly, and I now feel to deprecate the practice as much as any man can do, and deeply mourn over my past follies in times that are gone." But he went even further, and in a passage that beautifully illustrates a special kind of self-denying discipleship, he told Bullock that even though this was a hard lesson, "I acknowledge that I deserve it for my conduct in past times and therefore I will acknowledge the hand of God in it for good and try to bear it with meekness." The experience gave him a greater determination than ever before to "do right" and, more important, a "deeper interest in the prosperity of the work." No better expression of this kind of discipleship could be penned than the following:

> If it is necessary that I should endure this severe penalty for the
> good of the work, so let it be, for I feel not only willing to bear

this but to lay my life down for the cause, if necessary. Before this evil occurred I had commenced to visit the branches in this Conference, and the saints seemed anxious to hear. I had just begun to feel in my element . . . but the Devil or some other agency has stopped me for a week or two. I often think of an expression brother Hunter made use of just before I left home. His remark was this: "*the Devil hates you, he will kill you if he can, be careful.*" And I think he spoke the truth. However, the whole only makes me more determined to do right, live humble, and do all the good I can.

The true disciple feels not only the need to do good, but also the burden of setting a good example. Clayton felt this deeply: "I intend to take a course that will place it beyond the reach of either saint or sinner to find fault with me, and have the last semblance of truth on their side. Brother Samuel said like this. 'Brother William; the saints and the world expect more of you than of any other man,' and indeed it seems true." Other priesthood members, he observed, had committed sins in England "compared with which my fault is trifling . . . but when an American Elder comes here, he has got to walk perfect as an angel or have his nose rubbed. Well I will try to be perfect, the Lord being my helper, and will try to set them an example which the best need not be ashamed to follow."

NOTES

1. Clayton to Francis M. Lyman, 19 July 1874.

2. Clayton, "Missionary Journal, 1852–53," 28 Aug. 1853

3. The minutes of this conference are recorded, as clipped from the *Deseret News*, in Journal History, 28 Aug. 1852. All quotations herein from the conference are from that source.

4. Clayton to Brigham Young, 4 Oct. 1852, Brigham Young Papers.

5. Clayton, "Missionary Journal, 1852–53," 18 Sept. 1852.

6. Clayton to Young, 4 Oct. 1852, Brigham Young Papers. Of course, Clayton also may have been gently reminding the church leader of his obligation to look after the families of the missionaries. See also Clayton to "Dear Doctor," 23 Sept. 1852, in *Deseret News*, 2 Oct. 1852: "Every man seems to be filled with the spirit of his mission. . . . You hear no mourning about home, or wives, or children; no wondering how their families are getting along; in fact, as far as I can learn, the brethren have left their families in the hands of God and their brethren."

7. The main indication of this is in a letter from Clayton to Young, 2 June 1852, Brigham Young Papers, in which Clayton discusses very formally some aspects of Young's accounts and says, "But if it were lawful, and I were not so far fallen beneath your confidence, I would suggest a few ideas, which to me look just and right." He closes the letter, "Yours in the depths of sorrow, Wm. Clayton." The tone of part of the letter of 4 Oct. 1852, quoted frequently here, also suggests a former falling out with Brigham.

8. Clayton to "Dear Doctor," 23 Sept. 1852, in *Deseret News*, 2 Oct. 1852.

9. Clayton to Young, 4 Oct. 1852, Brigham Young Papers.

10. Clayton, "Missionary Journal, 1852–53," 1 Nov. 1852.

11. Ibid., 26 Sept. 1852. Both Orson Spencer and Daniel Spencer apparently preached this doctrine very strongly that day.

12. Clayton to Young, 4 Oct. 1852, Brigham Young Papers.

13. Clayton, "Missionary Journal, 1852–53," 28 Aug. 1852. Further evidence that it was the intent of church leaders to have the elders preach polygamy on this mission is seen in a letter of Brigham Young to John M. Bernhisel. The day after the conference ended he wrote: "The work which you mentioned in one of your former letters on plurality is about ready and will be forthcoming when the Elders go down to the nations." Brigham Young to John M. Bernhisel, 28, 30 Aug. 1852, Journal History, 28 Aug. 1852.

14. Elder Orson Pratt's journal is recorded in the conference minutes and also in *Journal of Discourses*, 1:53–66. In the sermon he noted that this subject is "rather new ground to the inhabitants of the United States, and not only to them, but to a portion of the inhabitants of Europe; a portion of them have not been in the habit of preaching a doctrine of this description."

15. On 15 Aug. 1852 William Clayton met with Brigham Young in his prayer circle. One of the main topics of conversation that afternoon was plural marriage. This prayer meeting may have been one of the important preparatory steps for the mission (Journal History, 15 Aug. 1852). For an important essay on this special mission, and on the preaching of polygamy in some parts of the world, see David J. Whittaker, "Early Mormon Pamphleteering" (Ph.D. diss., Brigham Young University, 1982), chap. 6, "Early Mormon Polygamy Defenses."

16. Clayton, "Missionary Journal, 1852–53," 15 Sept. 1852.

17. Ibid., 7 Feb. 1853.

18. He was a particularly fine camp journalist, for he not only kept good notes on important events but also commented on how he felt about them.

19. At this same August conference, a somewhat humorous incident took place when Pratt suggested to the missionaries that when they arrived in the states they should sell their mules and horses in order to get a little cash, but a voice in the stand was heard to yell out, "Send them back."

20. Ibid., 18, 25 Sept. 1852; and Clayton to "Dear Doctor," 23 Sept. 1852, in *Deseret News*, 2 Oct. 1852.

21. Clayton, "Missionary Journal, 1852–53," 27 Sept. 1852. The Pratt material was widely circulated through *The Seer*.

22. Clayton, "Missionary Journal, 1852–53," 19 Sept. 1852.

23. Clayton to "Dear Doctor," 23 Sept. 1852, in *Deseret News*, 2 Oct. 1852.

24. Clayton, "Missionary Journal, 1852–53," 30 Sept. 1852.

25. Ibid., 2, 3 Oct. 1852.

26. Clayton to Young, 4 Oct. 1852, Brigham Young Papers.

27. On October 4 Clayton commented in his missionary journal that the discussion "has evidently taken a turn, and the most of the time has been spent in bearing testimony to the truth of the work."

28. See, for example, Clayton, "Missionary Journal, 1852–53," 4, 10, 12, 29 Oct. 1852.

29. Ibid., 13 Oct. 1852. See Doctrine and Covenants 76 for Joseph Smith's revelation on the "three degrees of glory."

30. Clayton, "Missionary Journal, 1852–53," 16 Oct. 1852. On this occasion he also got into a deep discussion of the idea that there is a substance that fills eternity called the "Holy Spirit," which is separate from the personage of the "Holy Spirit."

31. The dispute over this doctrine came, in part, as a result of Orson Pratt's attempt to systemize the gospel according to certain broad philosophical principles. In 1860 Brigham Young specifically rejected some of Pratt's ideas, saying that they were not to be considered the doctrine of the church. Among them was the concept that "the Father and the Son do not progress in glory and wisdom because they already know all things past, present, and to come. None of the Gods knows more than another and none are progressing in knowledge neither in the acquirement of any truth." (*Deseret News*, 25 July 1860, as cited and discussed in Wendell O. Rich, *Distinctive Teachings of the Restoration* [Salt Lake City: Deseret News Press, 1967], 72–73.) Earlier Jedediah Grant, a counselor in the presidency of the church, clearly hinted at the disagreement when he said that Pratt had "lariatted out the Gods in his theory; his circle is as far as the string extends. My God is not lariatted out" (*Journal of Discourses* 4:126 [sermon of 26 Oct. 1856]). On 29 Jan. 1860 Orson Pratt humbly and publicly recognized that he had taught some things in error and emphasized the importance of submitting to "living oracles" (that is, the living prophet) on all such matters (ibid., 7:371–76). Several years later, however, the debate was still going on, and Brigham Young declared flatly that certain people "appear to be bound in their capacity for acquiring knowledge, as Brother Orson Pratt, has in theory, bounded the capacity of God. According to his theory, God can progress no further in knowledge and power; but the God that I serve is progressing eternally, and so are his children: they will increase to all eternity if they are faithful" (ibid., 11:286 [sermon of 13 Jan. 1867]).

32. Clayton, "Missionary Journal, 1852–53," 21, 22 Nov. 1853. This account does not specifically state that the couple were angry because of polygamy, but the context would suggest that there was no other reason.

33. The outline for this brief sketch is taken from Clayton's missionary diary. See also William Clayton to Thomas Bullock, 5 Feb. 1853, Bullock Papers. On the point here mentioned, Clayton wrote to Bullock of a visit to Preston on 6 January. "After an early dinner we took an hack and went to Bashalls Factory on a visit. We went through the whole building, which was quite a treat to

brother Glover. When we went into the resting room, one of the old hands knew me, and she flew at me, put her arms around my neck and gave me a good hug. The hands were indeed glad to see me. From here we went to the old house where I was born and looked around."

34. *Millennial Star* 15 (5 Feb. 1853):90. The term *spiritual wifeism* was sometimes used in derision to describe the little-understood concept of marriage for eternity as well as polygamy.

35. Ibid., 15 (1 Jan. 1853):1.

36. Ibid., 15 (8 Jan. 1853):35–36.

37. See, for example, ibid., 15 (15 Jan. 1853):41; 15 (22 Jan. 1853):57, 59. These notices make it clear that a major intent was to promote the doctrine of plurality through the circulation of this periodical.

38. Ibid., 15 (22 Jan. 1853):57; 15 (26 Mar. 1853):208. The pamphlet, dated 13 Jan. 1853, was published in Liverpool by Orson Spencer. Reflecting the general Mormon explanations of polygamy, Spencer traced the practice back to Abraham and justified it with numerous biblical passages. He also emphasized the importance of plural marriage to eternal progression, which was the standard LDS way of explaining it. He ended with the bold explanation that men might even be required to leave their "rebellious" wives for the sake of the principle.

39. See John Jaques to Mr. J—— G——, 13 Jan. 1853, in *Millennial Star* 15 (1853):97, 102, 133–36, 161–66; and editorial comment, ibid., 168–69.

40. Clayton, "Missionary Journal 1852–53," 23, 24 Jan. 1853.

41. Ibid., 25 Jan. 1853. Whether the man was actually excommunicated or not is not clear. The members at the meeting voted to cut him off, but Clayton said that "mercy was exercised toward him, as the brethren wished to save him if possible."

42. Ibid., 2 Feb. 1853.

43. Clayton to Bullock, 5 Feb. 1853. So far as this writer can tell, no one who has previously written on William Clayton was aware of this tremendously important letter, even though Clayton says in his diary that he wrote it. If it had been known earlier, much unfortunate speculation could have been avoided.

44. As late as 1856 William Clayton made reference to this unfortunate accusation in a touching letter to Brigham Young. The charge of immorality, he said, was brought against him while "absent on my unfortunate mission in 1852–53. I am satisfied that you no longer believe that accusation, for there was no circumstance in my conduct while gone that could ever give the least reason to believe such a report. On that subject my heart is at rest, for the Lord knows my innocence, and there lives not the woman on the earth that I have any fear to meet on that subject, for none will accuse me. But of this I feel satisfied that you are assured of my innocence" (Clayton to Young, 17 Nov. 1856, Brigham Young Papers; see also Clayton to Bullock, 5 Feb. 1853).

45. At this point the chronology becomes slightly confused as one tries to compare the two main sources—the letter and the diary. The letter implies that Clayton saw the notice in the *Star* before he ever "knew a syllable of what was going on," and that Willard Richards wrote him the letter after the notice appeared. The notice in the *Star* appeared in the issue dated 5 February,

although it was actually printed earlier than that. In the diary Clayton records on 26 January that he received the letter from Richards on that date, went to Liverpool immediately, and returned on 29 January. On 2 February, he said in the diary, "I was astonished to see a notice in the Star of the 5th inst that I was suspended from office." The dichotomy may be accounted for in part simply by the fact that in writing the letter Clayton was pouring out his emotions to a friend and may have been guilty of a natural emotional exaggeration. Just how much earlier the *Star* appeared is not certain. In the text cited I have reconstructed what appears to be the most logical chronology.

46. The notice in the *Star* read: "Elder William Clayton is fully restored to the pastoral charge of the Sheffield and Lincolnshire Conference, and has our confidence in the discharge of all duties in his office and calling in the Church of Jesus Christ of Latter-day Saints."

47. Journal History, 22 Apr. 1853, from *Deseret News*, 10 July 1853. See also "British Mission," MS.

48. "British Mission," MS.

CHAPTER 11

Apocalyptic Discipleship: William Clayton and Mormon Millennial Expectations of the 1860s

In 1874 William Clayton held some private concerns about the timing of the recent introduction of an economic system known as the "United Order" among the Mormons in Utah. Was it too soon in the divine scheme to inaugurate the perfect economic order? This Mormon disciple thought it was, for he expected much more of God's wrath to be poured out upon the earth before it would be ready for the fullness of God's Kingdom. In a letter to a friend Clayton expressed a typical Mormon feeling about the imminence of the great apocalypse:

> Before this order is established I look for a literal fulfilment of the 5th paragraph of the "Revelation given August, 1883," D&C page 243, edition of 1854. That paragraph tells us what we may expect, before the Order of Enoch can be established or Zion redeemed. The Lord there says, "I will visit her according to all her works, with sore affliction, with pestilence, with plagues, with swords, with vengeance, with devouring fire." That we deserve this chastisement I think none will deny. That it will surely come, I firmly believe, and that it is nigh, even at our very doors, I also believe. Recklessness, apostasy, vanity, whoredoms, self-pollution, rebellion, covetousness and kindred evils, are rampant, on every hand. These will have to be purged out before the Order of Enoch can be a success, and that the day of reckoning is close upon us I am as fully satisfied, as of anything in existence.[1]

Few things were taught more forcefully among the Mormons of the nineteenth century than that the destruction of the earth, the Second Coming of Christ, and the establishment of the millennial reign were all about to happen. Despite the fact that church leaders declined to make *official* pronouncements even approximating the time, there was enough preaching from the pulpit on its imminence, enough watching the "signs of the times," and enough private speculation in both high and low places that it was an uncommon Mormon who did not have some feeling that he could witness the winding up scenes in his own lifetime.[2]

Students of Mormon history have long recognized the intense millennial expectations that characterized the church a hundred years ago,[3] but their studies have tended to be elitist in nature. Practically everything written to date is drawn from statements of prominent church leaders, and no one yet has attempted to analyze the attitudes of the ordinary Saints, the direct impact of such teachings in *their* lives, and the significance of *their* reaction (or, more often, nonreaction) if their expectations were not fulfilled. To the degree that William Clayton represents these faithful followers, his millennialist experience adds to our understanding of the Mormon community as a whole in the nineteenth century.

Millennialism,[4] in one form or another, is as old as religion itself, and no matter what era or group we study we find at least some common elements.[5] Among the ancient Jews, as well as among both early and modern Christians, many prophets proclaimed that wickedness was about to be destroyed and that the living generation would see the coming of a Messiah. When their prophecies failed, some groups, of course, faded away in disillusionment. But others survived. Whatever they had, whether it be faith or credulity, its strength gave them an impressive flexibility. They could adapt to new realities, change their prophetic interpretations, yet not lose the basic structure of their beliefs. Among the disciples of William Miller, for example, there were those whose faith in the immediate advent of the Savior could not withstand the repeated failures of Miller's dating, while others, though disappointed, were so convinced of the ultimate reality of the Parousia that they followed Ellen G. White into a vital and enduring Adventist faith. Among the Mormons, William Clayton represents those who were absolutely convinced that the Civil War was the beginning of the apocalypse, but whose resilient faith weathered the storm of disillusionment with almost astonishing ease.

Though Mormon apocalyptic expectations were not unlike those of other contemporary millennialists, there were some important distinguishing elements. One was the Mormon assurance that the political Kingdom of God was already established among them, ready to take up the reins of government with the Savior when he came. Theoretically, the political kingdom (i.e., the Council of Fifty) had a separate identity from the spiritual Kingdom (the church), though the priesthood directed both. The Mormons also expected, after 1833, that the Saints (or at least a portion of them) would one day return to Jackson County, Missouri, there to build Zion, the New Jerusalem, from whence the Messiah would conduct his earthly reign.

Mormon millennialism was also distinguished by at least three periods of special intensity in the nineteenth century: the 1830s, when the Saints were first attempting to establish Zion in Missouri; the period of the Civil War; and the few years before 1890, when it was expected by many that the Lord would come either in 1890 or 1891. Those who accepted the 1890 date based it on a revelation to Joseph Smith that said, "Joseph, my son, if thou livest until thou are eighty-five years old, thou shalt see the face of the Son of Man; therefore let this suffice and trouble me no more."[6] Joseph would have been eighty-five on December 23, 1890. The year 1891, on the other hand, was pushed by those who took literally Joseph Smith's declaration of February 14, 1835, that "even fifty-six years should wind up the scene."[7] This meant that it would happen by February 14, 1891, and some even went so far as to set that as the exact date.[8] But the faith of most Mormon disciples was resilient enough that it could survive almost any apparent disconfirmation, and the failure of these expectations seemed to cause no turbulence at all in the mainstream of Mormon life. This chapter explores that resiliency with respect to William Clayton and the millennial expectations of the 1860s.

The coming of the Civil War was a powerful catalyst for the revival of Mormon apocalyptic commentaries. As early as 1832 Joseph Smith had prophesied a war between the states, beginning in South Carolina, which he said would "cause much bloodshed previous to the coming of the Son of Man." On April 13, 1844, William Clayton was at Joseph Smith's home and heard him prophesy "the entire overthrow of this nation in a few years."[9] The Latter-day Saints, therefore, were not in the least surprised when the South seceded. For many of them this was the beginning of the destruction of the United States, and that could only go hand in hand with their return to Jackson County. Equally important, the destruction was expected for two reasons: (1)

because of the general wickedness of the people, and (2) as punishment to the United States for the murder of the prophet Joseph Smith and for rejecting the Kingdom of God that had been established through him.

Such preaching began early, and William Clayton eagerly absorbed it all. In 1845 Brigham Young predicted that the temple in Jackson County would be built "in this generation."[10] Twelve years later, at the beginning of the so-called Utah War, he was angrily and openly predicting that the government of the United States would, through its own corruption, "go by the board" and that Mormonism would "take an almighty stride into influence and power, while our enemies will sink and become weaker and weaker, and be no more."[11] Then not long before the southern states began to secede, Brigham Young anticipated the coming national tragedy and added his own interpretation. "It is no more the Government of the United States," he told a group of Saints in October 1860, "but it is the broken Government of the once United States, and it will be forever so." In the same speech he told his listeners that most of them would live to return to Jackson County, though he warned them that this was no excuse for neglecting the development and beautification of the Great Basin, for those who did so would not be worthy to help build up Zion.[12]

With such clear expectations in the air that the government of America was doomed and that the return to Jackson County was scheduled for his generation, William Clayton's personal prophetic longings easily allowed him to build upon what his leaders said. By November 1860 the affairs of the states appeared so bleak, he told some business associates, that the Union "most assuredly" would be dissolved. Fearful scenes of blood and carnage would result among the people who had trampled the Constitution (which Mormons believed to be divinely inspired) under foot and must therefore pay the consequences.[13] He even warned his friends that anyone with money, property, or unsettled business in the states should get whatever was available without delay because "our fair Republic, about which poets and enthusiasts have sung and said so much, has now received its death stroke, and very soon will be amongst the things that were."[14] In December, eleven days before South Carolina became the first state to pass a secession ordinance, Clayton commented not only on the general political turmoil in the country but also on reports of natural disasters. "Verily the Lord has vexed the nation," he proclaimed, "and his judgements are being poured out upon the people without measure."[15] On the same day he wrote a long letter to George Q. Cannon who was in England, clearly revealing the source of his apocalyptic feelings. "From the spirit which now seems to operate much on President [Brigham] Young's mind," he reported, "*all* the Latter-day Saints will not stay here forever. *He talks much and frequently of Jackson County, Missouri.*" Then, bringing together in one significant letter all the prophetic feelings of the many disciples whose attitudes he no doubt reflected, Clayton colorfully portrayed their expectations on the eve of the Civil War:

> The nation that has cruelly banished the people of God from their midst, after coldly witnessing the martyrdom of two of the noblest and best men that ever lived, friends of God, of his Kingdom and of his people, and then to finish their catalogue of tyranny and persecution, sending a set of officers to coerce an innocent people at the mouth of the Cannon and point of the bayonet, (officers who were a disgrace to the name of men, but very fit representatives of the nation who sent them) with threats of utter extermination and annihilation,[16] I say that nation has got to drink the cup of bitterness to the dregs, which they tried to make the people of God swallow, but which was turned aside by a kind father in heaven: they have got to drink it, and woe! woe! woe to every son of Adam who is a bitter enemy to God and his Kingdom and has sought its overthrow. Some few of our intelligent men, say they think the overthrow of the United States is not so near at hand, because we as a people are not prepared for it. To this my only reply would be, that in the parable of the ten virgins, when at midnight there was a cry, "Behold the bridegroom cometh, go ye out to meet him," half the virgins were unprepared and had not oil in their lamps. Did the Saviour *wait* for them to get ready? No, he *came and the door was shut.* The parable is familiar to all the saints.[17]

On April 12, 1861, Fort Sumter, South Carolina, was fired upon and America's most tragic war began. On Sunday, April 21, William Clayton was called upon to stand up in the tabernacle and read the dispatch, received by pony express the night before, announcing the commencement of hostilities. Among the Mormons there was little apparent tendency to take sides. The general attitude, at least for the first year or two, seemed to be one of watchful waiting for the overthrow of all government in America and the establishment of the Kingdom. The expectation of at least some Mormon leaders was publicly expressed by President Brigham Young and by his counselor, Heber C. Kimball. "The whole Government is gone; it is as weak as water," said Brigham Young six days before Fort Sumter.[18] A month later he opined that God would allow neither North nor South to decide the fate of the war. Rather, since they had rejected the government of God, they would both continue to decline until "they have no rule, no authority, no gold, no silver, no power, nor anything that pertains to the earth and the saints." He predicted that neither the southern nor the northern states would remain united, but, rather,

> Bye and bye you will see a few of them divide up; they will separate by States one from the other. It will not be the South against the North, but the seceding parties will want an independent government for each of their respective states. Then bye and bye they will sever states asunder, and then it will be state against state. After that you will see the states boasting they have plenty of strength and power, and they will say we want a different kind of government, they will be divided among themselves, and become entirely disunited.
>
> As far as uniting any more, when once broken to pieces, they never will. But if they should unite for an hour or a day, they will again be dashed into fragments, when it will [be] impossible ever to gather them together again, for the principle of union will be taken from them.
>
> Now I suppose you will ask me how long this will be. Do you think they will be so divided as never more to come against us? I think we shall have to stand against them all, therefore gird on your armour.[19]

It was a curious dichotomy that Brigham Young predicted: the nation totally divided, yet each part strong enough to somehow threaten the Saints. Nevertheless, he assured his listeners, the wicked would be destroyed, and it would be the Saints who received knowledge and power.[20] In the same vein Heber C. Kimball preached that "ere long the whole face of the United States will be in commotion, fighting one against another, and they will destroy their nationality. . . . I have never prayed for the destruction of this Government, but I know that dissolution, sorrow, weeping, and distress are in store for the inhabitants of the United States, because of their conduct toward the people of God."[21]

Brigham Young was wise enough not to predict publicly exactly when he expected all this to culminate, though, on at least one private occasion, he speculated in an unusually precise manner. On August 22, 1862, he went to examine the foundation of the temple. He was having it rebuilt, he said, for he expected the temple to stand through the millennium. He then commented to the little group around him: "If we do not hurry with this I am afraid we shall not get it up until we have to go back to Jackson County, which I expect will be in seven years. I do not want to quite finish this Temple, for there will not be any Temple finished until the one is finished in Jackson County, Missouri." Then, as if concerned with what the Saints at large would think, he added, "Keep this a secret to yourselves, lest some may be discouraged."[22]

We must, of course, be cautious about what we read into all this. Though such statements were made, they were not made frequently. In addition, they probably, at times, reflected only momentary emotional and personal responses to particular situations, rather than considered efforts to pronounce official church doctrine. As Brigham Young spoke to various groups he sometimes emphasized different things, so that there was not total consistency even in his comments about future events. If on one occasion he tended to set a time for the return to Jackson County, on most others he was more cautious. In addition, his personal actions and preparations showed no inclination to leave Utah very soon—in spite of what he may have uttered at times. Many years earlier Joseph Smith had recognized that even church leaders could express opinions not necessarily dictated by revelation when he proclaimed that "a prophet was a prophet only when he was acting as such."[23] In that spirit, the fact that on occasion Brigham Young did not permit his own speeches to be published may have been a recognition of that same reality.[24] But whatever the case, the atmosphere in Utah at the beginning of the Civil War was charged with feelings against the government, and with the expectation that in some way the turmoil of the day was evidence of the cataclysm to come. With such assurances so widespread, William Clayton continued to pick them up and add to them.

In 1862 the people of Utah made their third unsuccessful attempt to gain entrance into the union as a sovereign state. This may have seemed incongruous to some if they believed that soon the government would be overthrown anyway. To others the attempt at statehood was merely evidence that the Mormons were still loyal to the Constitution. They also hoped for the benefits of state sovereignty and freedom from the domination of federally appointed officials. But Clayton had a different perspective. It seemed impossible to him that Utah would be admitted, for, he wrote with the famous prophecy of Daniel on his mind, "I cannot conceive the possibility of the '*Stone in mountains*' becoming a part of the '*Great Image*' before smiting it on its toes. . . . I do not think the Lord designs that his Kingdom shall ever become one of so corrupt a family as the States have proved themselves to be, nevertheless I can see the propriety of seeking and pleading for admission, in order that the United States may be left entirely without excuse when they strike their last blow at the Kingdom of God. They will justly deserve the consequence."[25] A year later he seemed even more certain that the quest for statehood was futile, for the time of the nation's final punishment had arrived: "I often told Bro. Hooper that Utah would never be admitted into the nation. He now believes it. It always looked to me impossible that the Lord would ever suffer his Kingdom to become a member of such a [corrupt?] and ungodly family of States, and hence I have never cherished the idea that we would be admitted for a moment. I have no doubt that like the brute beast that has received its death blow, the old nation will, in its expiring struggles, give one more desperate kick at the saints, but we have nothing to fear, and fear nothing, for we know in whom we trust."[26] Here, then, was a classic case of a disciple building upon a spirit displayed by his leaders, but taking its practical application much beyond what the leaders themselves would sanction. Brigham Young would hardly predict a failure in his quest for statehood.

William Clayton's apocalyptic expectations led him to become severely judgmental toward anyone who seemed to work against the Kingdom. (Or, at least, what may have been a natural tendency toward harsh judgment was enhanced by his immediate expectations.) As he read into the words of his leaders the possibility of immediate, dire consequences for an evil nation, he developed a hostile, colorful eloquence in his own writing that typifies the spirit of the times. When Stephen S. Harding was released as governor of Utah, Clayton wrote: "Old Pharaoh, alias S. S. Harding, is appointed U.S. consul at Valparaiso, Chile. The documents for his forward march are here, so that he can advance one step towards a warmer climate to which he is eminently entitled and qualified."[27]

Some of Clayton's most severe disapprobation was reserved for the federal troops who, under the command of Colonel Patrick Edward Connor, were stationed in Utah beginning in the fall of 1862. Not without cause, he berated them as among "that class of men who delight to prostitute weak-minded females, and draw ignorant men from the principles of truth to follow a golden phantom."[28] He was heartbroken that some of the Saints would befriend the soldiers. "To see our brethren barter their salvation and our sisters their honor and virtue for soldiers' greenbacks is too dark to think of," he lamented. Camp Douglas, after all, was being built only as "a nucleus for hell to gather round."[29]

So firm were Clayton's convictions and so dramatically did he state them that to read his letters of the Civil War period is literally to experience the feelings of a thoroughly devoted disciple who expected the Lord almost daily. His most speculative predictions were his own—based, to be sure, on what he heard from those he sustained as prophets, but also going beyond them in precise interpretations and immediate expectations. This speculative tendency, of course, was filled with certain spiritual dangers, for throughout his life it led Clayton to disappointment and potential disillusionment.

William Clayton's dismay with the governor, federal judges, and the soldiers was only a catalyst in the process of speeding up his millennial expectations. In January 1863 he predicted that it would be "but a few years more and the Saints can go back to Jackson County without fear of molestation."[30] By the end of the year he was convinced that war would soon break out in Europe "with as much virulence as that which has been destroying the land of Joseph [i.e., America] for the past three years." All this plus the discovery of gold and the opening of mines near the home of the Saints persuaded him that "our lease for the fair and peaceable valleys of Deseret is nearly expired for the time being, and soon the saints will again have to take to wagons and tents, and try camp life again." But, he wrote to George Q. Cannon, "be assured that the end of the trip will be Jackson County, Mo. It may however take seven years' travel to get there."[31]

By 1864 Clayton had arrived at the point where he could narrow down his expectations almost to the year—and act upon those expectations. Early in the year he began to make efforts to terminate his foreign collection agency, for, he wrote Cannon, "I do not think we can work much longer at this business." Then, anticipating his own preparations for the following year, he said mysteriously, "You will learn things that will surprise you before long. . . . The year '65 is big with the greatest events which has ever happened in the history of this church."[32] He urgently advised one of his missionary-collectors to "work while the day lasts," for the war and pestilence soon to come would never end until the people of the earth were thoroughly chastened. "The reflecting minds amongst the saints are watching the signs of the times, knowing the day is close at hand when the Kingdom will make a start for Jackson County, Mo. and before twelve months are past you will probably hear of exciting times in Utah."[33] For a time, at least, Clayton fully expected that before the end of the year 1865 the trek to Jackson County would begin.

As the new year got underway he did not lose this feeling, even though church leaders were not nearly as expectant as he. Clayton was nearly ready to refuse any more foreign collection business, and it was only Brigham Young's urging that persuaded him to continue. But in spite of the church president's lack of support for his views, he was almost certain that after 1865 "all such business will be ended, so far as the Saints in this country are concerned," and he was anxious to close up his foreign business activities "as speedily as possible."[34] Even as the hostilities of the Civil War drew to an end with the government still intact, Clayton was unmoved. As he wrote to William P. Nebeker,

> Some appear to think that since the surrender of Lee's army the war between north and south is virtually ended—that peace and prosperity will soon follow—that the union will be restored and things go on more swimmingly than ever. These seem to be the feelings of many of our people, but I do not so understand the designs of the Almighty . . . and I think the troubles of this country are but just fairly commenced, and I do not think it will be long before desolating war will step over the Atlantic and involve Europe as bad or worse than has been the case for four years on this continent. I know of no promise of a cessation of the judgements of our Father, until the nations have been made to bow and recognize him as the Supreme ruler and law giver. Do they do it now? No! I don't think a more wicked race ever lived on the earth than at present.[35]

It is clear that by this time Clayton's expectations were extreme, compared with those of the general community of the Saints. Somewhat arrogantly, perhaps, he assumed a special secret knowledge, and he was selective about whom he discussed it with. "I write free because you will keep this matter to yourself," he told Cannon in 1863.[36] Two years later he declared to Nebeker that he had foreseen the troubles he was lamenting three years before and that he "wrote and urged the brethren to hurry up all unsettled business as fast as possible and get everything clear while the door was open. Others did not understand matters as I did, and hence I am caught with much unsettled business on hand in Europe."[37]

Whether others agreed or not, and in spite of his effort to keep his feelings confidential, Clayton took at least one more step that demonstrated the integrity of his convictions. He actually began to make preparations for leaving Utah, and this even after the fighting between the states was over. "I am of the same mind I have been for years in regard to our having to move before the year '65 has passed away," he wrote George Hales on April 19, 1865. "I know the general opinion is far different, but each day now only confirms me more and more in the same views."[38] Satisfied in his own mind that many prominent people would be unable to remain in Utah another winter, he was attempting to purchase 400 or 500 bushels of wheat from Hales—not to be brought to Salt Lake City, but to be stored by Hales in southern Utah for the benefit of Clayton and his family when they began to move. "I think I have enough to do my family until we will be compelled to move. . . . Keep to yourself what I have said, and believe me."[39]

Clayton's expectations, then, were strong enough to compel him to action. He was cautious enough not to burn his bridges behind him, but he was covering all possibilities, and for him the march to Jackson County was a viable immediate prospect. On the same day that he wrote to Hales he also penned a letter to Miles Romney of Grafton, Utah, who was one of the architects of the St. George Temple. Here he vividly revealed just how serious he was and yet how cautious he felt he must be in making known his deepest concerns:

> I have for some months been reflecting on the propriety of writing you, to ask for some information of a personal and private character. I am well aware that your views correspond, in a great degree, with my own, in regard to the probable future, still, I do not think it would be wisdom for you to mention what I now write about. I am satisfied that the time is near at hand when many of us will have to leave this region and travel south to get

out of the way. There are many who I think will have to leave before another winter, and probably when we do leave we will have to go in a hurry. Now my family is pretty large and it would require a number of teams to move them all at once, more than I have means to furnish. If I could have a safe and secure place to store a load or two of surplus stuff, such as clothing, bedding, books &c, where it would be taken care of and not interfered with I would send it during the spring and summer when I could meet with a chance. Have you got a spare room where you could store and take care of such property for me, to the amount of, say, two loads or more, or what is your situation in regard to room &c? for I could feel safe if I could send my stuff to your care. And again, suppose I should be compelled to send my family at two different times for want of [teams?], what would be the chance of renting a house to put them in until I could get all together and come myself. Now I do not know that we will be under the necessity of moving this year, still it is very possible we may, and I would certainly like to feel my way before hand. You do not need to rejoice that you have got there before us. You will have to move on further. You are not far enough out of the way yet, as you will see when the big move commences.

I hope you will answer this fully and freely, and that you will not delay, for there are ominous signs in view which makes me anxious to do everything I can to be ready. Don't mention this to anyone, for I am sorry to say our people seem half asleep in regard to the signs of the times, and the great events constantly transpiring.[40]

Clayton's expectation that the year 1865 would see the beginning of the return to Jackson County was buttressed by more than the usual guesswork. By the early 1860s he had become intrigued with the "science" of astrology,[41] and it was partly on the basis of astrology that Clayton arrived at the date of 1865. He did not pretend to be an accomplished astrologer himself, but he read the journals, plotted astrological figures, and wrote frequently to those who were considered experts. As he told a friend in 1865, "I am no Astrologer nor ever have been, but I have a deep motive in view." That motive may well have been an effort to confirm his dating of the apocalypse, for in the same letter he went into great detail about the judgments of the Lord that were very near at hand.[42]

Though Clayton did not feel competent in interpreting astrological constructions, nevertheless he sometimes tried. On the basis of his own interpretations he was convinced that the "turning point" for starting the Kingdom on the road back to Jackson County was what he called "the end of the fifth seven years," or April 6, 1865.[43] This was just thirty-five years after the organization of the church, and somehow Clayton's astrology had helped him make the leap of faith that would date the beginning of the end on that significant anniversary.

But it was 1866, and the Saints were not on the march. Already the wheels of faithful accommodation were at work, and Clayton found an explanation for his mistaken judgment. "After the death of the prophet Joseph," he rationalized, "it took nearly two years before the church was fully on the way to the tops of the mountains, so it may be nearly two years now before the pressure is so great as to force us away from here." He looked at the predictions of the great astrologer Zadkeil concerning the restoration of Jerusalem in 1867 and commented, "But as the Kingdom of God is the head and leading principle, I look for a great change here before those very important changes can take place on the other half of the globe."[44]

Throughout the year 1866 Clayton maintained his slightly modified but still firm conviction that the end was just around the corner. "The prophet Joseph used to speak of the year '66 as being peculiarly a year of judgements and astounding events," he suddenly seemed to remember. "The Lord will not forget the redemption of Zion nor his promises to the saints, and hence, I look for events to transpire soon which will ultimately lead to that long looked for event."[45] It was the same language he had been using for six years, and still he kept it up with monumental self-assurance. In June he wrote to a missionary in England: "I suppose ere this slaughter has commenced, and if so destruction will be fearful. Well, it is the year 1866 and we must not be surprised at anything that takes place. I think it will drag France, England and the United States into the whirlpool, and if so I think the missionaries will have to flee to Zion for safety if nobody else does."[46]

But the conflagration did not come. The American government was not destroyed; war did not engulf Europe; the Saints were not driven out of Utah; and the return to Jackson County never came. Clayton's immediate prophetic expectations had failed. Therein lay an important test of discipleship, and one that has been faced time and time again by the followers of many prophetic movements, not only Mormons.

Clayton not only remained in the fold, but he also remained actively committed. Most observers of Mormonism would agree that this is no surprise, though various explanations might be offered. Some would pass it off as little more than accommodation under social pressure, observing how difficult it would be for a man like Clayton to bear the shame of admitting he was wrong all along. Others would call Clayton's faith mere blind faith—a stubborn but irrational determination to follow the leader no matter how discomforting the evidence against him was. For Latter-day Saints the answer is found in the concept of "testimony." The memory of his conversion experience, enhanced by his close association with the founding prophet, provided him the stamina to survive disappointments resulting from human failings and mistakes. Though the prophecy had failed of immediate fulfillment, his basic faith was still in the ultimate fulfillment of all the prophecies. If anyone, leader or follower, had made an error in calculating the time, this did not matter nearly so much as Clayton's basic testimony of the correctness of Mormonism as a whole. Though the records reveal no specific comments by Clayton, as it became clear to him that his immediate expectations were not to be, undoubtedly he would explain himself in much this way.

For those who seek more sophisticated explanations, research in the social sciences has provided some possibilities. In 1955 a study supported by the Laboratory for Research in Social Relations of the University of Minnesota was published under the title *When Prophecy Fails*, by Leon Festinger, Henry W. Riecken, and Stanley Schachter. After basic research on a modern apocalyptic group, the authors were able to establish a model for interpreting various historical movements that had survived the seeming disconfirmation of a basic prediction. Though some of their conclusions have since been challenged, the study is of interest here because of its possible application to the Mormon experience. If five essential conditions pertain, the authors hypothesized, then when disconfirmation occurs the result actually will be an increase in both conviction and proselyting activities. The five conditions are (1) a belief must be held with deep conviction; (2) the believer must have demonstrated his commitment by having taken some important action difficult to undo; (3) the belief must "be sufficiently concerned with the real world so that events may unequivocally refute the belief"; (4) the disconfirmation must be recognized by the individual holding the belief; (5) the believer must have social support—that is, he must be a member of a larger group who shares his expectations.

Clayton and others like him certainly met these criteria. His belief in the immediacy of the apocalypse was firm enough to compel him to action. After all, he had left his home at least twice for the sake of Mormonism, and in 1865, for the sake of an immediate expectation, he was planning another move. He could not help but recognize the failure of the Civil War predictions, and he certainly had refuge in numbers within the Mormon community around him.

When prophecy fails, the Festinger group concluded, the true believers often find reasonable and even ingenious explanations. Their rationalization thus reduces the dissonance somewhat, but to be fully effective the new explanation needs support from others. This, the researchers suggest, is the reason why proselyting often increases. "If the proselyting proves successful, then by gathering more adherents and effectively surrounding himself with supporters, the believer reduces dissonance to the point where he can live with [it]."[47] How far this might apply to Mormonism or to William Clayton is only speculative, but it is at least interesting to observe that in the five years following the Civil War the church sent out nearly twice as many missionaries as it had during the previous five years. The Mormons had disconfirmation (the end had not arrived), an explanation (human error, or prophets not speaking as prophets), and strength in growing numbers. They fit the Festinger model almost perfectly.

Clayton maintained his belief in the nearness of the apocalypse for the rest of his life, and he was still rather colorful in expressing it. He continued to see anti-Mormon activities of federal officers, as well as the election or appointment of certain people, as portents of the approaching storm. He continued to see "signs in the sun, earthquakes, hurricanes, storms, and floods and all kinds of calamities"[48] as testimony that the end was near. Though he was willing to admit that "it is difficult to tell what is in the future," and he refused to support an 1870 rumor that Salt Lake City would be "in ashes in less than twelve months,"[49] he remained confident that American officials would still try to destroy the Kingdom of God.[50] He also still believed that the overthrow of the nation would come because of its persecution of the Saints. In 1873 he wrote to William H. Hooper: "Solomon says, 'Whom the Gods would destroy, they first make mad,' and it certainly appears that the authorities are not merely mad, but insanely mad. If Solomon

was right, the signs are certainly very ominous. . . . Pharoah persecuted
Israel, but it brought destruction upon him and all his hosts."[51]

For Clayton, then, the years after the Civil War brought increased
rather than decreased times of foreboding, perhaps made even more
ominous by *not* knowing when the end would come. Stepped-up efforts of the gentiles in Utah to combat Mormon economic hegemony,
increased national efforts to combat polygamy and Mormon political
control in the territory, worsening financial problems in connection
with the panic of 1873, the efforts of the church to take defensive
economic measures, and the general apathy of the Saints all pressed
upon Clayton until he could say in 1874 that "these are the gloomiest
days I have ever seen since the martyrdom of our beloved prophet and
Patriarch, thirty years ago. . . . The end draws nigh, and it will not
come slowly and gradually, but like the 'whirlwind,' suddenly, when
the people are least expecting it. It is close at our doors."[52]

Clayton was not as willing in 1874 as he had been ten years earlier
to suggest when the Saints would begin their "big move," but as he
looked at the problems of 1875 he could not deny himself the luxury
of again suggesting that the time was perilously close. "Treachery is
all around us," he wrote to Francis M. Lyman, "and you don't know
who to trust. 'Except those days should be shortened there would be
no flesh saved.' How much they will be shortened I don't know, but
unless some great change takes place, before long it seems as tho there
will be few who will endure to the end."[53] Five years later Clayton
died, still clinging valiantly to his faith that all his millennial expectations were soon to be fulfilled.

At least two observations seem appropriate. To the scholar it is clear
that the Mormon experience with apocalyptic expectations is not
unique. But Clayton's experience is significant at least as a case study
of how these expectations affected the life of one representative Mormon disciple. Through him we glimpse the intense, emotional, and
self-assured longing for the coming of the final judgment that beat in
the hearts of many ordinary Saints. Through him we also observe the
marvelous resiliency that was an essential element of nineteenth-century Mormonism. Understanding that ability to adapt one's attitudes
to changing realities is essential to understanding the Mormon community itself.

Our final observation might be pointed more directly to those people
(the present writer included) who are active, committed members of

the Mormon community a hundred years later. Apocalyptic expectations are still with us, and will always remain, though the sense of immediacy is not nearly so great as in the days of William Clayton. We seem to have moved as a people toward a calmer attitude of continuing preparation without immediate expectation. At times, of course, we have our modern counterparts of William Clayton—those who see in certain signs some evidence that the Parousia is just around the corner and that most of us will live to see it. These people spread their wisdom as if they had special knowledge from sacred or authoritative sources, yet always the living prophets respond with the admonition that such statements are unauthorized and that no one knows the day or year. After Harold B. Lee was sustained as president of the church in 1972, the rumor became rampant that his patriarchal blessing implied that the Savior would come during his tenure. "Such a quotation is incorrect and without foundation," he declared, and in a strongly worded First Presidency message he reminded the Saints that any directions or guidance to the church as a whole must always come "by revelation, through the head."[54] But still the speculation persists, and even today we hear that the year 2,000, the end of the "sixth thousand years," is the time appointed for the winding up scenes to begin. No one knows, of course, and most faithful Mormons are reluctant to say "yea" or "nay" to such predictions. On the basis of their historical knowledge many will shrug off such talk as merely another in a long series of unauthorized and inauthentic apocalyptic enthusiasms. William Clayton undoubtedly would reply, using the 24th chapter of Matthew as his text, "Then be ye also ready, for in such an hour as ye think not the Son of Man cometh."[55]

NOTES

1. Clayton to Francis M. Lyman, 19 July 1874, Clayton Papers.
2. From 1830 on, the revelations through Joseph Smith established the tone of almost immediate millennial expectation: "For the hour is nigh, and that which was spoken by mine apostles must be fulfilled"; "I say unto you, that I come quickly"; "I say unto you, the time is soon at hand that I shall come in a cloud with power and great glory"; "The day soon cometh when ye shall see me, and know that I am"; "Labor ye in my vineyard for the last time"; "I am Jesus Christ, who cometh quickly, in an hour ye think not"; "Unto you it shall be given to know the signs of the times, and the signs of the

coming of the Son of Man" (Doctrine and Covenants 29:10; 33:18; 34:7; 43:28; 51:20; 68:11).

3. For excellent discussions of Mormon millennialism in the nineteenth century, see Louis G. Reinwand, "An Interpretive Study of Mormon Millennialism during the Nineteenth Century with Emphasis on Millennial Developments in Utah" (Master's thesis, Brigham Young University, 1971); Boyd L. Eddins, "The Mormons and the Civil War" (Master's thesis, Utah State University, 1966), chaps. 1–2; Earnest Lee Tuveson, *Redeemer Nation: The Idea of America's Millennial Role* (Chicago: University of Chicago Press, 1968), chap. 5, "Chosen Race . . . Chosen People"; Grant Underwood, "Seminal versus Sesquicentennial Saints: A Look at Mormon Millennialism," *Dialogue: A Journal of Mormon Thought* 14 (Spring 1981):32–44; Grant Underwood, "Early Mormon Millenarianism: Another Look," *Church History* 54 (June 1985):215–29; Grant R. Underwood, "Early Mormon Millennialism: Another Look" (Master's thesis, Brigham Young University, 1981); Stephen J. Stein, "Signs of Times: The Theological Functions of Early Mormon Apocalyptic," *Sunstone* 8 (Jan.–Apr. 1983):59–65. The Reinwand thesis is the most extensive study extant and must be consulted for a comparison of Mormon millennialism with the varieties of millennialism in the broader society.

4. I recognize the distinction between millenarianism (a belief in the physical return of the Savior to a righteous people) and millennialism suggested by Tuveson in *Redeemer Nation*, but Tuveson classes Mormons as millennialists, and I use the term here in its broadest possible sense.

5. For a brilliant analysis of medieval and reformation millennialism in Europe, see Norman Cohn, *The Pursuit of the Millennium* (New York: Harper & Row, 1961).

6. Doctrine and Covenants 130:14–15.

7. *History of the Church*, 2:182.

8. See Reinwand, "Interpretive Study of Mormon Millennialism," chap. 7, for a fine discussion of the 1890–91 enthusiasm. On page 140 Reinwand mistakenly says 14 March instead of 14 February, but on the following page he has an interesting quotation from Moses Thatcher, one of the Council of the Twelve, to the effect that the return to Jackson County would begin by 14 Feb. 1891.

9. Doctrine and Covenants 87; 130:12–17; Clayton, Nauvoo Journal, 13 Apr. 1844.

10. Transcript of conference held in Nauvoo, 6 Apr. 1845, in Thomas Bullock, "Record of Meetings, 1845–46," Bullock Papers.

11. *Journal of Discourses*, 5:229, 235. The tenor of the speeches Brigham Young gave on 13 Sept. 1857 included the idea that government officials were corrupt. He supported the form of government and the Constitution, but said that those who had sent troops to Utah were "as rotten as an old pumpkin that has been frozen seven times and then melted in a harvest sun. Come on with your thousands of illegally-ordered troops, and I will promise you, in the name of Israel's God, that you shall melt away as the snow before a July sun. . . . I am not speaking of the Government," he added, "but of the corrupt

administrators of the Government. They . . . can twist and turn in any and every way, to suit their hellish appetites" (ibid., 5:230, 235).

12. Brigham Young, Address at Pleasant Grove, Utah, 25 Oct. 1860, Brigham Young Papers. This seems to be the general tone of much of the preaching about the return to Jackson County. Evidently church leaders were dismayed that some Saints were using the expectation of the return to Missouri as an excuse for not working as hard as they could to build up the valleys of Utah. In 1856 Heber C. Kimball warned that no one would return to build up the holy city "until you learn to keep the commandments of God" (*Journal of Discourses*, 4:106), and in 1861 he warned the Saints that even though he and thousands of faithful should go, "we cannot go back until we have built some good houses" (ibid., 8:350). Brigham Young sustained this view in 1860 in a second speech in Pleasant Grove on the same day as the one previously cited. "Let the people make good improvements, and plant out nice orchards, and try to live here, and then you will have plenty to go back to Jackson County with." Building up Utah was a necessary preparation for building Zion in Missouri, for, as he said on another occasion, "we work every day for the kingdom to redeem and build up Zion here. And remember that our works here, point back to Jackson County Missouri, to put that land in the possession of the Saints, to build up the great Temple of God. Every hour we labor points to that." Speech at Centerville, Utah, 3 June 1861, Brigham Young Papers.

13. Clayton to Messers T. B. Peterson & Sons, 29 Nov. 1860.

14. Clayton to Elijah Thomas, 29 Nov. 1860.

15. Clayton to James C. Brown, Esq., 4 Dec. 1860.

16. Clayton was referring to the army sent to Utah by President James Buchanan in 1857. This quotation is a good example of the general Mormon attitude toward the Utah Expedition.

17. Clayton to George Q. Cannon, 4 Dec. 1860.

18. *Journal of Discourses*, 9:5.

19. Brigham Young, unpublished discourse, Salt Lake City, 5 May 1861, Brigham Young Papers.

20. *Journal of Discourses*, 9:5. See also unpublished discourse, 5 May 1861, Brigham Young Papers.

21. *Journal of Discourses*, 9:55.

22. Journal History, 22 Aug. 1862.

23. *History of the Church*, 5:265.

24. See unpublished discourse, Salt Lake City, 5 May 1861, Brigham Young Papers. Here President Young indicated specifically that although he would allow the speech to be written down, he was not sure he wanted to publish it to the world. This was one of the speeches in which he specifically predicted that the government would not survive the Civil War.

25. Clayton to Cannon, 22 Feb. 1862.

26. Clayton to Cannon, 22 Feb. 1863. Most of this letter was published in the *Deseret News*, but the portion quoted was judiciously omitted from the published version. See clipping in Journal History, 22 Feb. 1863.

27. Clayton to John Hooper, 27 May 1863.

28. Clayton to Jesse N. Smith, 28 Nov. 1863.

29. Clayton to Cannon, 17 Nov. 1863. See also Clayton to Smith, 18 Jan. 1864.

30. Clayton to Cannon, 18 Jan. 1863.

31. Clayton to Cannon, 11 Dec. 1863.

32. Clayton to Cannon, 27 Feb. 1864.

33. Clayton to William P. Nebeker, 18 June 1864. Nebeker was president of the Swiss, German, and Italian Mission. See also Clayton to Widerborg, president of the Scandinavian Mission, 21 July 1864. After dealing with strictly business affairs, he said, "I must take as much interest in hearing of the prosperity of the cause of truth as anyone can, and having closely watched the signs of the times for many years, now when the nations in Europe begin to be convulsed, and war, pestilence and famine begins to stalk around the land, I feel doubly interested in watching every move and every event which tends to the fulfillment of the predictions of the servants of God."

34. Clayton to Widerborg, 31 Mar. 1865.

35. Clayton to Nebeker, 12 Apr. 1865. This is probably a reflection of Clayton's literal interpretation of Joseph Smith's 1832 prophecy on war.

36. Clayton to Cannon, 11 Dec. 1863. "Don't think my views are wild," he added, "they are not so, but will prove to be stern reality. God bless you."

37. Clayton to Nebeker, 12 Apr. 1865.

38. Clayton to George Hales, 19 Apr. 1865.

39. Ibid. It is not clear exactly where Hales lived, but from the general context of the letter and the times, it appears that he was living somewhere in the southern part of the territory.

40. Clayton to Miles Romney, 19 Apr. 1865.

41. See Chapter 12 herein for a discussion of Clayton and the occult.

42. Clayton to Isaac Bullock, 3 Dec. 1865, William Clayton Letterbook, Church Archives. (This letterbook, not included in the Bancroft Collection, covers the period from 20 Apr. 1865 through March 1867.)

43. Clayton to John Sanderson, 3 Feb. 1866, ibid.

44. Ibid.

45. Clayton to Nebeker (salutation reads "Dear Brother Perry"), 4 Mar. 1866, ibid.

46. Clayton to Elder A. K. Thurber, 19 June 1866, ibid.

47. Leon Festinger, Henry W. Riecken, and Stanley Schachter, *When Prophecy Fails* (Minneapolis: University of Minnesota Press, 1956), 28.

48. Clayton to "Bro. Jesse" (Jesse N. Smith?), 23 Jan. 1870. See also William Clayton to Newel Clayton, 18 Oct. 1872. Here he looks at what seems to be impending suffering in England, and says, "But as these are among the calamities foretold by the Savior, we need not wonder that they increase in the earth." (See also his letter to Newel, 24 Nov. 1872.) "As to the people [of England] being unwilling to listen to Mormonism I am not surprised at that, for the English people have had a vast amount of preaching to. . . . Truth is not what this generation wants, but they are getting some pretty loud preaching from the Heavens, and altho' they will not acknowledge the hand of God in it, it is nevertheless true that the judgements are being rapidly poured upon

the nations. The severe storms on the coast of England, disease, and the very high price of meat and fuel, are severe afflictions on the people of England. The famine in Persia; the overflowing of the Po and the destruction of Chicago and Boston by fire, the cholera in different parts of Europe and Asia; the immense waste and destruction by fires, winds, floods, railroad disasters; the reckless regard of human life; and the dreadful increase in immorality among all the nations are, to me, prominent signs that the Lord is fulfilling the prophecies."

49. Clayton to Heber (Young?), 27 Mar. 1879.

50. Clayton to Peterson, 15 Feb. 1873.

51. Clayton to "Bro. Hooper" (William H. Hooper), 8 Feb. 1873.

52. Clayton to Lyman, 19 July 1874.

53. Clayton to Lyman, 20 Mar. 1875.

54. *Official Report of the One Hundred Forty-Second Semi-Annual Conference of The Church of Jesus Christ of Latter-day Saints*, October 1972 (Salt Lake City, [1972]), 125–26.

55. Matthew 24:44.

CHAPTER 12

The Esoteric Tendency

There was never a time in the life of William Clayton after his conversion to the church that he allowed circumstances or personal problems to shake his total commitment to the faith. At the same time, it is not surprising that Mormons such as he should rub shoulders with some of the more esoteric quasi-religious fads that ran to and fro in nineteenth-century America. Phrenology, astrology, alchemy, and spiritualism were all elements of the popular cultural climate, and at least some Utah Mormons were attracted to each of them.

William Clayton did not associate himself with such esoteric trends until after he arrived in Utah. He may have heard about them in England and in Nauvoo, but if he did they had little influence on him. Whatever he picked up in Utah was probably a reflection of what was happening in the broader popular culture of America, as well as the fact that at least some other people in Utah were beginning to show an interest.[1]

It may seem enigmatic that even a few devout Latter-day Saints should become involved in such movements that at least today seem far removed from acceptable Mormon practice. Perhaps no explanation is fully adequate, but a few thoughts might help bring into focus William Clayton's dabbling with astrology and alchemy. First, the proponents of both claimed scientific validity for their crafts, yet, they asserted, these crafts combined the world of nature with a transcendent mystical reality that could influence the soul of every person. In addition, both astrology and alchemy were authoritarian in nature—that is, the secrets could be discovered only by diligent study, so that laymen like Clayton relied on the interpretations of the masters rather than upon their own wisdom. It was not incompatible with the faith for a Mormon to look beyond the church for insight into matters about which the prophets said little or nothing. Furthermore, professors of both groups taught that their "science" was based in part on personal worthiness. William Lilly's *Introduction to Astrology*, published in 1647 and still popular over 200 years later, emphasized to students that they must "beware of pride and self-conceit," free themselves from sin, communicate daily with the heavens, and in every way strive to put themselves in favor with the Divine. "The more holy thou art, the more near to God, the purer judgement thou shalt give."[2] And the author of a 1907 text on alchemy had as a major theme the idea that true alchemists were not really concerned with transmuting base metals into gold. Rather, they were concerned with the soul and "sought the Highest Initiation or the Development of the Spiritual Nature in Man." The alchemists' power to preside over the transmutation of metals was only a result of the worthy transmutation of their own souls. The author even declared that true alchemists would have within themselves the "Magnetic Power" to attract and "coagulate" invisible elements, but that "this power is only possessed by those who are 'reborn in the spirit.' Those who do not know what this expression means are not 'reborn' (or initiated); and it cannot be explained to them."[3] Clayton's constant striving for perfection and his penchant for frequently reexamining his worthiness as a Saint may help account for his attraction to such mystical rhetoric.

Since ancient times astrology has appeared in many forms and places. But the form that eventually influenced Clayton came from nineteenth-century England.[4] It had flourished in the sixteenth and seventeenth centuries but languished to the point that a would-be practitioner had practically no sources to turn to. By the 1820s a revival was in progress, and one of its great popularizers was Robert Cross Smith, often referred to as the father of modern astrology. Like many leaders of his craft, he published under a symbolic pseudonym. His was "Raphael," and under this name he began a periodical called *The Prophetic Messenger*, the direct predecessor of the modern *Raphael's Almanac, Prophetic Messenger and Weather Guide*. Though the most dedicated astrologers fervently denied that theirs was a mere fortune-telling profession, Raphael wrote a number of books on both astrology and fortune-telling in general.

The next great English popularizer of astrology was "Zadkiel," otherwise known as Lieutenant Richard James Morrison of the British navy. Morrison left the navy in his twenties, became a follower of

Raphael, and soon began to publish his own annual magazine, *The Herald of Astrology* or, after 1848, *Zadkiel's Alamanac.* Zadkiel was a pretentious writer, apparently very appealing to the popular mind, and it was through him that Clayton obtained much of his astrological knowledge.

Though there was considerable interest in astrology earlier, it caught on most intensely in the United States late in the nineteenth century.[5] The Theosophical Society, one of the earliest American groups to promote astrology as well as other occult movements, was formed in 1875. Other societies followed around the turn of the century, and finally in 1926 the National Astrological Association was formed.

There were mixed feelings among the Mormons about the merits of astrology. Like many, if not most, Americans, they were readers of almanacs. These annual publications provided information about the rising and setting of the sun and moon throughout the year, information on the stars, advice for farmers, and a wide variety of helpful hints and newsy tidbits of interest to readers. They also contained the names and characters of the twelve signs of the zodiac, showing their relationship to the paths of the planets. Mormon apostle Orson Pratt published almanacs specifically for the interest of the Latter-day Saints from his office in New York City in 1845 and 1846. He had no sympathy, however, for the use astrologers would make of the zodiak. His 1846 almanac provided the usual listing but pointed out that it was only "according to the vulgar and erroneous ideas of the Ancients" that the signs governed "the different paths of the human system."[6]

In Utah prominent Mormon William W. Phelps published an annual almanac for about fifteen years, in the 1850s and 1860s. In 1852 he made it clear that he, like Orson Pratt, believed the influence of "signs, stars, &c., according to the wisdom of the world" was "unworthy of the confidence of saints."[7] Five years later, however, he was beginning to change his mind, possibly because Brigham Young had expressed a temporary interest. On June 28, 1857, the church leader asked Phelps if astrology were true. Phelps said he did not know, whereupon President Young replied that he thought it was.[8] The next day Phelps wrote a long letter to Brigham Young that showed he had been thinking about the matter for quite some time, and by 1860 he was apparently a believer.[9] In the meantime, Brigham Young gave it more serious consideration and determined that the Saints ought not to be involved in such things, and when people came to him asking for permission to establish schools of astrology he firmly turned them down.[10]

It was probably sometime before 1861 that William Clayton first told Brigham Young of his own interest in astrology. Thomas Job and a group of friends decided they would like to form an astrological school, and Clayton became interested.[11] Characteristically, however, Clayton hesitated to involve himself in something new without counseling with the prophet, and at his suggestion the group sought and was granted an interview with President Young. The matter, Clayton later recalled, "was pretty thoroughly talked over," but then the prophet asked that the school be dropped and that the brethren stop studying astrology.[12]

Suddenly Clayton found himself in a dilemma. It was not like him to ignore the advice of the prophet, and for a short while he may have complied. But what he was learning had become so intriguing that he was unable to stay away from it for long. He had asked permission and been denied it, but some of his friends were still involved and he could not keep his interest in check.

By 1862 Clayton was taking an active interest in what the stars had to say about the future. A Mormon friend, John Sanderson of Springville, was one local authority on the subject, and on April 26 Clayton wrote him an interesting letter. William H. Hooper, he explained, was on his way to Washington as a representative of the "State of Deseret," in an effort to obtain entrance into the Union. He was accompanied by C. W. West, who was going on a mission to England. It was exactly four minutes past 2:00 P.M. when they left, Clayton carefully informed his friend, which was a fact that astrologers might use in calculating the future trend of events. "If you have no objections," he said, "I would sincerely like your judgement upon three points." First, he wanted to know, would the trip to the states be prosperous? Second, would the travelers meet with any delay or trouble, either from Indians or white men? And, third, "what will probably be their success at Washington in striving to obtain the admission of the State of Deseret into the Union?" Then Clayton asked another question that demonstrated his belief that the astrologer could even obtain insight into important matters concerning the Kingdom. "I should also be much pleased to hear your judgement in regard to the probability of troops coming here this season," he wrote, "and any other matters in relation to the welfare of Zion which you may feel free to communicate."[13] Little wonder that Brigham Young had no use for astrology. It was, and still is, a fundamental tenet of Mormonism that any important matters "in relation to the welfare of Zion" will be revealed through the prophets, and certainly no astrologer could substitute in that respect.

We do not know what Sanderson replied, but whatever it was touched Clayton deeply. "Your very interesting letter of the 13th inst. has been received and read by me many times over," he wrote his friend, "and I can assure you the matters you have touched upon are of very deep interest to me. I only wish you had felt like writing a little more. However I am very grateful for so much."[14] Clayton was becoming more certain all the time that the quest for statehood would not succeed. Even before his first letter to Sanderson he had grave questions about it, and at least by the February following he was positive that "Utah would never be admitted to the union."[15] It would be misleading to suggest that astrology alone convinced him of this, but the evidence suggests that this occult "science" at least played a confirming role in William Clayton's mind.

It was possibly at this point that Clayton began to become personally acquainted with the literature and techniques of astrology. Sanderson had told him of a book on the subject, and sometime in May a mutual friend, Charlie Evans, left at Clayton's home *Zadkiel's Astronomical Ephemeris for 1862–3–4*. Evans said only to take care of the book until he returned,[16] but the curious Clayton would hardly pass up the opportunity to look at and learn from it. The following year he was writing to missionaries and others in London eagerly seeking several astrological works. "They are invaluable to me," he told a missionary friend, and he would explain why when the elder arrived home.[17]

Clayton continued to write to Sanderson and ask for his insight into both public and personal affairs. He heard that federal troops were being dispatched to Utah and that government officials, with the troops to back them, would begin to enforce the antibigamy law of 1862. Again he asked Sanderson for a prediction. "Will it be likely the officials can bring about a collision between the citizens and the troops," he asked, and "are the signs favorable for our enemies or against them?" He also wanted to know if the troops would really be likely to arrive.[18]

Though the Saints were not directly involved in the Civil War, its outcome was of great concern to Clayton, and it was the subject of many questions to Sanderson.[19] Clayton, after all, was getting ready to make some decision regarding his own future, and how he felt about the probable outcome of the war would affect those decisions. What about difficulties for the coming winter, he asked in August 1863. "Are the indications favorable for us or against us?" Would Colonel Connor have the power to bring about any mischief, and what information could the astrologer give relating to the movement of troops? Clayton saw in the war a way for the enemies of the church to wage battle against the Kingdom, and he looked to Sanderson for some confirmation or denial of his expectations. In 1865, convinced that the Saints could have no real peace for long in the Salt Lake Valley, he wrote his friend, "Five hundred families called to go to Dixie fulfils my prophecies for the past seven years."[20]

Even though popular astrologers claimed that almost anyone with average intelligence could learn to cast a horoscope, the task was complicated if done to perfection.[21] The astrologer needed as a minimum the date and place of the subject's birth. If the precise time of birth could be given, the "map" of the heavens could be more accurately constructed, and the horoscope presumably would be more accurate. The astrologer allegedly could draw character analysis, forecast life trends, portray tendencies toward weaknesses and disease, suggest remedies, and predict successes, failures, and other major events in his subject's life. He could also, on the basis of what he knew about leading individuals, forecast trends for nations and communities. Once Clayton believed, it made little difference whether he was concerned with the affairs of the nation, of Utah, or of his family; the heavens would provide information that could help him. So it was that when his two-year-old son Albert Cassius, child of Augusta Braddock, had been mysteriously ill for five months, Clayton sought the advice of Sanderson. He described all the symptoms, including his "frantic screaming both night and day," that no medicine seemed to help. He gave the exact time of the child's birth, July 3, 1862, at 2:55 A.M., then wrote: "And I believe if you can find the time you can tell me. What is the real cause and nature of his disease, and what is the best remedy?"[22]

Clayton also sought direction on business affairs. In the same letter, for example, he referred to the land warrant business. One of Clayton's vocations was attempting to obtain warrants on behalf of those to whom the government had promised land, and Sanderson was one such person. Clayton had been working with Judge John Kinney on the matter but now asked his astrologer, "What is your judgment in regard to them? Do you think they will come?" A year later he was asking more specifically for Sanderson's judgment on a figure he had raised for February 1 (i.e., he had plotted the position of the various heavenly bodies at a precise time for that day), for, he said, "it may be of importance to me in my business operations."[23] To cap it all, in the same letter he asked Sanderson for a copy of the "church figure."

By this time Clayton was beginning to study the literature for himself and could raise his own figures, if not interpret them. Before 1865 he obtained his books from London, but during the winter of 1864–65 the overland mails were suspended and Clayton became impatient. He wrote to California trying to obtain Zadkiel's 1865 almanac and ephemeris, for, he said, "I am anxious to get the books now." He also wanted the second volume of Zadkiel's *Handbook of Astrology*.[24] Clayton was studying the literature and had been caught up with its possibilities—it would be hard for him to stop.

Perhaps he temporarily forgot the conversation with Brigham Young of several years before. Whatever the case, it came as a a severe blow when he heard from a southern Utah friend in 1865 that Brigham Young had remarked, apparently with criticism, that Clayton had spent the past seven years in astrology. "I suppose from that," he wrote his leader, "that you certainly consider me an astrologer. This idea I beg leave respectfully to correct."[25]

Undoubtedly Clayton experienced a struggle with his conscience as he found himself on the horns of a harsh dilemma. He knew the prophet disapproved of something that he himself was intrigued with, yet he was devoted to the church and his whole relationship to it was, in part, dependent upon the confidence of the prophet. His explanation was, at best, equivocal—perhaps an effort to save his credibility with Brigham Young and at the same time salve his own conscience through a rationalization that might leave room for more than one interpretation. In any case, after referring to the meeting in the prophet's office years before, William wrote: "President Young I have not studied Astrology from that time to the present. I do not today know or understand even the first and most simple principles of it. I have never professed to understand it, and I am entirely innocent of all knowledge or practice of it."[26]

Technically, Clayton was not really an "astrologer," for he had not learned to cast horoscopes, he had not put himself in the business of advising others, and he still depended upon astrological experts to interpret for him. In that sense he was not a practitioner. But during

the past two or three years he had read some of the literature, he could
"raise a figure," he believed there was something to it, and he would
continue in his interest. This is not to say it was an all-consuming
passion, like the gospel. But he must have felt a continuing uncom-
fortableness whenever these two forces—his overwhelming devotion
to the church and his less consuming but real intrigue with astrology—
came in conflict.

Clayton's brush with the prophet's displeasure did not turn him
from his interest. For the rest of his life he subscribed to Zadkiel's
works[27] and continued to discuss the merits of astrology with his
friends. In 1869 he confided in a letter to John Royle that "I am kept
so much confined with business I have no time to study, or even to
raise a figure on the new and full moon, which is important to us."[28]
He referred his friend, who wanted some information, to Lilly's as-
trologically prestigious *Introduction to Astrology*, a work with which
he was clearly familiar. For a nonpractitioner, William Clayton's interest was lively.

The same letter suggests that at least to some degree Clayton realized
that astrologers could go too far. John Sanderson died in 1869, but by
this time Clayton believed his friend had begun to take their common
interest to extremes. "He got considerably reckless and led away by
unprincipled men," he wrote, "and I think it is well that the Lord
took him, or he might have apostatized." We are left uninformed as
to the specific difference Clayton had with Sanderson, but he commented that "men who get a little understanding of the science of
Astrology, act so unwisely, generally, that it takes those who are true
friends to the science, a great deal of time to counteract the influence
so foolishly created." The implication was that the "true friends" of
astrology within the church were those who, like Clayton, were not
on the verge of apostasy. Clayton did not stop to consider that maybe
he, too, was carrying his interest to extremes.

It is possible that some Mormons like Clayton were caught up with
astrology partly because the predictions of forthcoming calamities by
some popular astrologers were not unlike the predictions of the Mormons. Even the church-owned *Deseret News* recognized this in 1879,[29]
some six months before Clayton's death. The editor noted the receipt
of a pamphlet, written by "Prof. O. A. Grimmer" and published in
California, predicting a "long list of horrors" coming soon as a result
of stellar influences. The Saints were warned not to become excited

over such tidings of evil for the Lord himself had predicted them in the scriptures and yet had promised that his people should "stand in holy places and not be moved" when the scourging came.

The editor of the *News* warned his readers especially against those "star gazers" who fixed the hours, days, and seasons for impending events, though he added a polite bow to the astrologers. "We do not mean by this to cast any slur upon those who study the influences of the heavenly bodies," he wrote, for the Saints believed that the Lord had placed these bodies in their positions for certain purposes. The editor even considered the possible reality of "solar, lunar and stellar influences," including the possibility that heavenly bodies exerted both baneful and beneficial influences on the inhabitants of the earth. "But," he declared with a warning clearly intended to steer the Saints away from any serious dabbling in astrology, "the so-called science of astrology, particularly in these latter times, is so imperfect and unreliable that it forms no proper guide for the Latter-day Saints. Those who depend upon it are led apparently right for a time, but are generally switched off into error and difficulty. Some knowledge may perhaps be obtained in regard to planetary and zodiacal influences. But who among the astrological adepts of the nineteenth century knows anything of the higher governing bodies from which the sun receives its light, or the new conditions into which the whole solar system is passing?" In their ignorance of "higher and more powerful worlds" the astrologers could only create confusion. The "great tribulation" of the earth was approaching, but only the revealed word of God was needed to foresee and prepare for it. "What God reveals may be relied on. But what man adds to those divine communications is untrustworthy and to be viewed with caution if not with distrust and indifference." So much for the church's attitude, such as it was, toward the heavenly "science" in which Clayton was dabbling.

Clayton took no serious interest in other occult "sciences," except for a short flirtation with what seemed to be a form of alchemy. It does not appear that the secret society to which he attached himself was actually trying to turn base metal to gold (the traditional quest of the alchemist), but it did convince its members that through a secret process, which only the specially initiated could obtain, they could change the property of metal to make it more valuable. Why Clayton's faith allowed him to make this leap into the esoteric fringes is another enigma, but since there was often a bond between alchemists and astrologers[30] Clayton's interest may not have been so unusual.

The brief flirtation began and ended in 1864. A certain William Freeman of New York City had apparently combined in one mail-order business a variety of mystical opportunities for those who were so inclined. Someone loaned Clayton a copy of the guidebook *Cabala*, which evidently contained explanations of mysteries of Cabalism[31] as well as explanations and advertisements for other things. Clayton immediately placed an order for a copy of the guide *Cabala* (price $1), two "mysterious Electrical and Weird Rings, or Secret Talisman of the Ancient Hebrew and Egyptians" ($3 each), and one certificate of membership in the British Metallic Mutual Association ($1), which was apparently headed by Freeman. The balance of the $10 he sent was for a special (and magical?) fish bait, also advertised in *Cabala*. He even sent along two pieces of twine, cut to duplicate exactly the size of the fingers he wanted the "weird rings" to fit. He knew the association he was about to join was a secret society, for he said to Freeman, "In regard to membership, any requirements as to secrecy will be freely subscribed to by me as fast as known." Thus the mysticism of the Jews, the magic of the ancient Egyptians, the mysteries of metallic transposition, the obligations of a secret society, and the vicissitudes of angling were all a part of the strange and esoteric world that Clayton was falling into.[32]

Clayton's first brush with Freeman's movement drew him into its orbit almost immediately, even before he knew much about it. Only five days after writing his first letter, he ordered even more of the fantastic articles advertised. "I have full confidence in your publications," he wrote, "and in the reality of the wonderful things you promise." The order included the "chemical composition" or "sacred chain" composed of "twelve different chemical ingredients" ($3), a mysterious item he called a "String of the Civit Cat" ($7), a pair of "Electro Galvanic" women's shoes ($4), more special fish bait, with instructions ($3), and some special compound to make boots and shoes wear for five years ($3).[33]

Clayton was indeed eager to get going, possibly thinking of the larger project that involved changing the value of metals. Though the record is not clear, it may be that the "chemical composition" or "sacred chain" he wanted was something akin to the so-called Philosopher's Stone of the ancient alchemists—a substance that supposedly enabled the adept, when applied correctly, to transmute metals. It was also imagined that the Philosopher's Stone could be used to produce the "Elixir of Life," a universal medicine that had the mystical quality of renewing youth. Though Clayton never spoke specifically of these items, his apparent expectations of the British Metallic Mutual Association were not far from such occult promises. "I am yet rather ignorant how to go to work," he confessed to Freeman, but as soon as he had more information he would order a "complete outfit" for himself.[34] It was this outfit that would presumably provide the means to produce the fabled metallic changes.

It is difficult to piece the whole story together, but the record available suggests that as a hopeful initiate into a secret cult, Clayton was subjected to some of the trials often imposed upon novices as bait, though in the form of an apparent test of their true intentions. If Freeman was a conscious fraud (and the presumption here is that he was), his methods were indeed effective with people who had the will to believe. When Clayton's "weird rings" did not arrive after nearly two months, he wrote Freeman on April 28 inquiring about them. Three weeks later he wrote again assuring Freeman that he now knew the reason for the delay. It was Clayton's own worthiness to be let in on the secrets that must be investigated. "All is satisfactory to me in regard to the matter," the novice wrote, "and I have the consolation to know that you have the means to satisfy yourself in regard to the purity of my intentions; hence I have no anxiety. I am satisfied the rings will come in due time."[35] Such trusting disciples, when finally pronounced worthy, would indeed be willing buyers of even more occult books and paraphernalia.

Clayton was not the only one in Utah attracted to Freeman's association. On May 18 Clayton, his astrologer friend, John Sanderson, and Nicholas H. Groesbeck each ordered a "complete outfit with private instructions." "I know you are constantly communicating and forwarding outfits to *numbers* here," he commented.[36] Further, Clayton, Sanderson, and eleven others decided to form a branch of the British Metallic Mutual Association right in Salt Lake City. As might be expected, Clayton was appointed corresponding secretary. All thirteen signed a request to Freeman for a permit and the necessary instructions and sent, according to directions in *Cabala*, another $2 each.[37]

They had a problem obtaining their permit partly, as Clayton explained to Freeman, because they were all so "young in the knowledge of the science" and the organization that their procedures were irregular. They did not even know that it was necessary to sign and forward a special oath when applying for an outfit. He hoped, however, that with experience they would become "useful and worthy members" of the society. At the same time the optimistic Clayton presumed to make a suggestion to the eminent doctor. Why not organize Salt Lake as a central branch for the territory, authorized to represent all the branches in the territory? Then all the applications for membership and outfits could be handled through Clayton as corresponding secretary.[38] Whatever the merits of Clayton's new interest, he was still the willing workhorse for any group or institution to which he was committed. His willingness to serve as corresponding secretary was little different, in kind, from his willingness to serve as scribe, secretary, auditor, or treasurer in the other facets of his life.

As Clayton waited for the official permit to organize, he continued to order membership certificates for men whom he judged "worthy and desirous" of becoming members.[39] Finally in July, some two months after their first application, the coveted permit was received.[40] Clayton continued to act as corresponding secretary and even advanced money out of his own pocket to pay for postage and other expenses. As in so many other activities, willingness to serve meant at least a little economic sacrifice. "I find it causes me considerable trouble to keep track of all these little items which I advance for the brethren, especially when I have to wait so long before it is replaced," he complained to Sanderson.[41]

The Salt Lake chapter of the British Metallic Mutual Association started with at least twenty-six members.[42] They had paid their dues, ordered their outfits, signed their oaths of loyalty and secrecy, examined their own and each other's worthiness, and were ready to learn the secrets that would bring them, they hoped, both wisdom and wealth.

Meanwhile, Clayton continued to write Freeman about other mystical services and problems. The special fish bait did not work. "Perhaps," Clayton wrote, "I shall yet learn of some secret connected with it which would render it effective." His rings, on which he placed "inestimable value" beyond any financial consideration, never came. At first it appeared they were lost, but Clayton also continued to persuade himself that they were being withheld until his personal worthiness was proved. When, in July, Freeman gave him hope that he would yet receive a ring of his own, Clayton replied: "I hope you have some means of satisfying yourself as to my integrity and the purity of my motives." He welcomed a rigid inquiry into his "character, conduct and motives" and assured his New York mentor that "if, as I believe, you have the means to satisfy yourself, I have no doubt you will yet entrust me with that which is to be invaluable solely for my own personal protection and for no other purpose whatever."[43] Clayton seems to have accepted fully the notion that certain occult powers were dependent upon righteous living and personal integrity, and he was thus a ready target for being led along such paths.

Freeman even convinced Clayton and his associates that his occult devices had some mysterious healing powers. Clayton ordered, for example, a pair of metallic insoles for a woman afflicted with St. Vitus dance. He provided Freeman with a physical description and assured him that when the woman was informed what to do she would forward the money to cover all expenses. He sent money for metallic insoles for a man and wife who had a strange, longstanding malady somehow contracted while cleaning a bedstead, and on another occasion sent money for the healing of a woman with a stiff right hand and a swollen neck. In each case he forwarded a physical description of the afflicted, which suggests that Freeman had convinced his followers that he could do some kind of long-distance diagnosis and treatment in addition to sending metallic insoles.[44] There is no record that any of these people were helped.

But the big letdown as well as the greatest financial loss was the failure of the metallic outfit. Each outfit cost $30, cash in advance, in addition to the $6.50 to $9.50 express delivery charges.[45] The agreement was that after the new members had made $500 profit, they would be given additional outfits for $20.[46] We do not know what the outfit consisted of, but it is apparent that each contained a set of "private instructions," a piece of metal (possibly the base metal, lead?), and perhaps some special chemicals and working tools something akin to those of the alchemists. If the outfits did not produce, Clayton and his friends stood to lose at least $40 for each one ordered, counting the cost of returning the processed metal to Freeman.

As soon as the first outfits were received the ambitious group of novices began work. William Walker, who worked in metals by trade, built a small furnace at his home for "transmuting and working up the outfits for the members to the best possible advantage."[47] Clearly the "transmuting" process was designed to change the nature of the

metal and make it more valuable. The group expected, in fact, to make
it heavier and were convinced it would pass a certain test with acid,
all of which suggests that their process was akin to the ancient quest
for turning lead to gold. For every new effort, of course, a new outfit
must be ordered—and another $30 must be sent.

Sometime in July, Walker "worked up" the first five outfits. "Everything worked to a charm," reported Clayton, "with one very important
exception." The "growing properties" of the metal, which were supposed to become manifest after it was melted down, did not appear.
In other words, the process did not work at all. The instructions had
been followed to the letter for the entire complicated process. "The
metal was never suffered to chill, and it was attended to during the
three days' heat with the greatest punctuality," the disappointed Clayton wrote, "yet the metal is no heavier at the end of the three days
than it was immediately after melting." Nor did it pass the acid test
as they had expected. The successive failures, Clayton commented
sadly, "are a great disappointment to all the parties interested, but so
it is. We feel confident you will be able to inform us where the failure
arises."[48] He then packaged the five metal bars and returned them to
Freeman by mail for analysis and for payment of whatever money they
were worth. The payment, however, was not to be returned in cash
but rather in more outfits! Optimism still bloomed, and Clayton was
still certain that after Freeman's new instructions were received, they
would "be enabled to realize the full benefits enjoyed by others of
your numerous members and co-workers."[49]

What had gone wrong? Freeman never gave Clayton a satisfactory
answer. At first Clayton's loyalty to his new association made it impossible for him to think he had been bilked. It was part of a continuing
test of worthiness, he rationalized to a friend even after a sixth outfit
had failed. "We *think* Dr. Freeman has withheld some important ingredient until he assures himself of the purity and integrity of our
intentions which we consider would only be a natural act of cautionary
prudence." Nevertheless, he cautioned his friend, "as our labors, like
yours, have not been rewarded with the promised success, I would not
recommend you to send for any more outfits for the present."[50] Here
was the first note of pessimism. But if, as a result, Freeman sold no
more outfits or memberships at all in Utah, he had already made
hundreds of dollars from Clayton and his friends.

Four months later Clayton was ready to admit defeat and disillusionment. More recent correspondence with Freeman had convinced him that the five outfits were a "complete flop." "On account of extreme light weight and the fact it cracks when worked having fine red streaks running through it," Freeman had written him, the firm that usually purchased the processed metal could not use it. Though he planned to write Freeman again, Clayton's faith was practically gone. As he wrote to Charles Davis, who had also lost money on an outfit, "we have but little encouragement to hope for anything but entire loss," and even though he would write Freeman again he had "little hope of any better encouragement."[51] So far as the records reveal, the matter ended there.

Clayton had been duped, and for that he was probably mocked at as overly credulous and gullible. Many of today's readers may scoff the same way. But we must be cautious before casting stones, realizing that Clayton may not have been so unusual after all. Even today seemingly intelligent people are taken in by confidence rackets (including religious confidence games), miracle remedies, cults, and a variety of get-rich-quick schemes. It should not be wondered at that over a hundred years ago the populace who had no inkling of present-day scientific knowledge should be intrigued by similar notions. Clayton, furthermore, saw no conflict between his religion and his efforts to draw upon the mysterious forces of the universe to further his own well-being. In less than a year, however, his dabbling was over. Further, this particular esoteric tendency was only one facet of his total life—one, perhaps, that has been blown out of proportion here—but nevertheless one that demonstrates in a very interesting manner the varieties of Mormon experiences in the nineteenth century. We may react with some surprise because the William Clayton who indulged himself in this interest seems different, somehow, from the Clayton we have seen in other situations. On the other hand, Clayton's confrontation with spiritualism reveals again the man with whom we are more familiar: the dedicated, single-minded, sharp-tongued defender of the Kingdom.

Few things could be more abhorrent to William Clayton than either opposition to church leadership or apostasy, and for this reason the Godbeite movement came in for special denunciation from his ever-sharp tongue and pen. The intellectual roots of this movement went back as far as the 1850s when E. L. T. Harrison and Edward W. Tullidge were publishing speculative articles in the *Millennial Star*. A few years

later Amasa Lyman, who became the president of the Godbeite "Church
of Zion" in 1870, gave his first public sermon advancing rather unorthodox ideas at Dundee, Scotland. None of these incidents was linked
directly with the organization of the New Movement in 1868–69, but
they suggest that the unorthodoxy that resulted in the movement was
not a sudden thing.

An important element of the New Movement was an effort to reform
the church, particularly with reference to the influence of its leaders
in economic and political affairs. Church economic policy, in particular, came under attack. But hand in hand with these reform efforts
went an active commitment to spiritualism. As early as the fall of 1868
E. L. T. Harrison and William S. Godbe reported a series of seances
in New York at which early Mormon leaders as well as New Testament
apostles appeared and directed them in their attack on the Mormon
system. Others who subsequently joined the movement and became
important leaders included Edward W. Tullidge, prominent Utah historian and publisher, T. B. H. Stenhouse, another prominent Mormon
publisher, and his wife, Fanny (both of whom later published harsh
criticisms of the church, and particularly of plural marriage), Henry
W. Lawrence, Eli Kelsey, William H. Shearman, and Amasa Lyman, a
member of the Council of the Twelve Apostles. The official break came
in late 1869 when the leading dissenters were excommunicated from
the church and in December when the Church of Zion was organized.
On May 10, 1870, Amasa Lyman was excommunicated, and he soon
announced his acceptance of the presidency of the new church. As the
Godbeites continued in their criticism of church policy, they also promoted spiritualistic activities, including the use of mediums, participation in seances, and telling of the appearances of family members
and former church leaders. In September 1871 they were even granted
a charter by the National Convention of Spiritualists. The Godbeite
movement lasted about fifteen years before it dissipated.[52]

Though a few Mormons took a serious interest in spiritualism, even
outside the confines of the New Movement, in this instance William
Clayton was clearly within the mainstream and rejected spiritualism
with a vengeance. If, as Ronald Walker suggests, spiritualism had
enough in common with Mormonism that it offered the wavering Saint
"a warm and even familiar home" and if joining with the Godbeites
symbolized one's belief that the Mormon religious commonwealth had
failed,[53] then William Clayton could have no part of it. Godbeism

threatened the entire Mormon view of a theocratic society, and if all its economic, political, and religious ideals were adopted it would mean the dissolution of the Kingdom.

For Clayton the Kingdom was more important than any individual, and thus he even questioned the propriety of Brigham Young trying to save Stenhouse for the church. In October 1869 Stenhouse, Godbe, and Harrison were disfellowshipped, pending a trial for their membership. For reasons unexplained, Brigham Young dropped the charges against Stenhouse. Clayton had no faith that this "desperate effort to save him" would succeed because, he said, "when a man is led by a woman who is bitterly opposed to polygamy, I have no confidence in him." Though the prophet was merciful toward the apostates, Clayton was convinced that ultimately the church leader must "protect the church from overthrow, no matter who is hurt to accomplish it. A dead limb is best cut out and burned."[54]

Though such language appears harsh, Clayton meant it, for to him the challenge of the Godbeites was a challenge to his fundamental testimony: God speaks to and directs the Kingdom only through his chosen prophets, and to question their authority is to bore at the foundation of the Kingdom itself. By October of 1869 the Godbeite organ, the *Utah Magazine*, was stepping up its attacks on church policy, and by the end of the month Harrison and Godbe had been excommunicated. Apostasy was rampant, Clayton wrote to a friend, and during the trial of the church hundreds would probably go overboard, "and it will not be surprising if some big ones fall."[55] His expectations were exaggerated, for the movement never recruited enough members to create a major schism, but at least a number of prominent intellectuals and businessmen left the church during these trying months. Clayton was unsympathetic with all of them; they were merely biting the hand that had so long fed them: "Poor fools! Mormonism will rise triumphant, and shine gloriously as the Kingdom of God on the earth, when all traitors and enemies to it are forgotten."[56] The apostates were trying to "bore with a big augur," he said in December as he angrily described some of their meetings, and "it is useless ridiculing the movement, for they have all hell to back them."[57]

Though Clayton considered the Godbeites as little different from other spiritualists,[58] he also saw the economic implications of the growing heresy. He was deeply involved in the church's cooperative movement and saw the New Movement as a direct confrontation to it. In

November he wrote of the prosperity of the cooperative movement, and the increased unity it was bringing to the Saints. ZCMI, he noted, would soon open a wholesale drugstore "so that the saints will no longer be under the necessity of purchasing of an apostate Mormon."[59] He observed, however, that Godbe and his "associate apostates" were growing more bitter daily and that they would cry persecution.

As in all the other confrontations he was involved in, whether personal or public, Clayton had absolute faith that the Lord would use the threat to his Kingdom to good advantage. "One thing is certain," he wrote James McKean, "it seems as though hell is let loose, and the furies are darting their shafts against the Kingdom, but the Lord will overrule all things for good."[60] It was not impossible, in fact, that the Lord was using the apostates to purify the church. By May 1870 Clayton was pleased that the movement had not accomplished all its leaders wanted, but he declared that those who did join it were the kind the Kingdom of God was better off without. "I look for a great apostacy before long, for the church will be purified before Zion is redeemed."[61] Four months earlier he had expressed it almost poetically: "The saints feel well, the apostates feel hell, but all is in the hands of the Lord."[62]

In his own colorful style William Clayton was particularly harsh on the apostate leaders. Of Henry Lawrence he said, "The apostates here grow more bitter and fiendish every day. . . . You would scarcely know H. W. Lawrence. The spirit within him actually seems to turn his countenance black."[63] Fred A. Perris was "a big bug among the apostates,"[64] and the organizers of the Church of Zion were "poor fools."[65] The apostates, he told Francis M. Lyman, were the "Laws, Fosters and Higbees over again" (i.e., like the traitors to Joseph Smith), except that "these ignorant blockheads are led by the spiritual mediums."[66] When in January 1870 William Godbe told a New York merchant that he felt he had "the weight of a nation" on his shoulders, Clayton commented, "I think Godbe is actually becoming insane."[67]

In a way, Clayton's attitude toward individuals was like the delicate balancing of a scale. On the one side was his avid loyalty to the prophet and other church leaders, including his refusal to speak ill of any of them. On the other side was his utter disdain for apostates, and his seeming incapacity to find any virtue whatsoever in their motives and actions, except to the extent that they helped purge the church of its weaker elements. But could such a psyche maintain the balance if a trusted friend and church leader should suddenly cross over to the other side? That test came when Apostle Amasa Lyman joined the Church of Zion and became its leader.

In effect Clayton was part of the Lyman family, for he had married the apostle's daughter, Maria, as a plural wife. He had drawn close to his father-in-law and seemed to have great respect for his outstanding intelligence and capabilities, though he probably never fully understood Lyman's highly sophisticated theological speculations. When accusations began to circulate that Lyman was heretical and disloyal, Clayton could not believe them and came readily to his defense. In January 1867, for example, Lyman was called into account before the Twelve for denying the literal necessity of the atonement in a sermon he had given five years earlier in Scotland. Lyman signed a confession of error, though he never really abandoned the unorthodox views he had actually held for years. Clayton, meantime, interpreted the criticism as the result of jealousy and assured his father-in-law that "we shall outlive all jealousy bye and bye, and perhaps the true friends of Joseph will be remembered for their integrity."[68]

From this time on Lyman's association with the church was, at best, tenuous. In May 1867 the Quorum of the Twelve voted to drop him as a member, and this action was ratified at the following October conference. He was finally excommunicated on May 10, 1870.[69]

The strain for Clayton must have been difficult, and it appears that he was simply not willing to class Lyman with the apostates he had been so roundly criticizing. When anyone accused the former apostle of apostasy, in fact, Clayton became furious. About the end of July 1868 he was watching the organ being installed in the new tabernacle. Suddenly John Wardrobe came up and began to complain about the unpleasant circumstances of his son-in-law who lived in Beaver, for, said Wardrobe, there were only five Latter-day Saints in Beaver, the rest being followers of Amasa Lyman. "Too indignant to make any reply," Clayton held his tongue but he later wrote to a friend that he knew where Wardrobe got his information and, said he, "It strikes me as particularly unpleasant that Bp. Murdock is compelled to have such a spirit for his tithing clerk."[70] Clayton had no use for rumor-mongering when it involved his father-in-law. That same year he affectionately wrote Lyman, "You have many true and sincere friends who will never forget you, especially while you continue to follow the course you are doing and have done. By your wise policy your friends rejoice while your foes are defeated."[71]

The most abhorrent suggestion of all, so far as Clayton was concerned, was that Lyman might join the apostate Godbeites and even become their leader. Yet that is exactly what was being rumored late in 1869. "I have invariably ridiculed the idea that he would listen for a moment to any overtures from such a source," wrote Clayton to Francis M. Lyman, his brother-in-law, "and I am pleased to say, there are few indeed who think he could be influenced by any such contemptible spirit as possesses these apostates." But he heard the story again, and again wrote his brother-in-law, "I told him he was mistaken, for your father knew too much to associate himself with any such folly." When Lyman wrote back confirming Clayton's confidence the faithful disciple was relieved, but within a week he had heard more such rumors from someone apparently close to Amasa. A certain Dr. Taggart claimed to have had an interview with Lyman, who, he said, read him the sermon for which he had been dropped from the Quorum. "He makes no secret," Clayton wrote in distress, "of saying that your father is the man to take the lead of the apostate clique; that he is ready and expected to be the head of the apostate church. . . . I wish you would write at once and give me the facts, If there was an interview between your father and Taggart what was the topic . . . I shall have this report to meet and combat in various quarters and I would like facts to fight with, for that is what the enemy cannot stand."[72]

Exactly what happened in the next few months is not clear, except that sometime between December and May Clayton learned the truth—his father-in-law was, indeed, associated with the enemies of the Kingdom and would become their leader. Clayton was crushed. For him, however, there was only one course of action—to disassociate himself entirely from the man he had so admired yet never really understood. He felt betrayed as he saw his former friend and leader move so easily into the camp of the enemy and must have felt a vast emptiness in the thought that he had been deceived for so long. The sad but necessary result was that he would simply never speak to Lyman again.

Lyman, too, felt a sadness, but from his point of view he was only doing what he must. He wrote his wife Louisa on the day of his final excommunication from the church:

> The time has at length come when I shall again open mouth in the proclamation of the Gospel. This I have announced to br. Clayton and Marion [Francis Marion], the former of whom denounced me and declared it had made an Eternal separation be-

tween him and me all the charity he extended to me was his silence and permission to visit our *Maria* she dear soul said to me weeping that she never should forget her Father.

Marion was most deeply touched but said he should ever love and respect his Father. I did not ask him to indorse my views but act honestly up to the views he entertained and the future would give him light to see differently.[73]

How the actions of one person inevitably affect the lives of others, and especially of loved ones, is no better illustrated than in the story of Amasa Lyman. His son Francis Marion was disappointed but remained both loving toward his father and loyal to the church. In 1880 he became an apostle. Amasa's son-in-law William Clayton was horrified and openly turned against him, remaining, as Lyman described him, "cold and glum."[74] Amasa's daughter, Maria, was torn between two loves—one for her father and the other for her church and her marriage. Her decision was a long and probably agonizing one, but for over a year she stuck with Clayton. Her affection for him, however, seemed gradually to wane, especially as he continued to spurn her father. "I was very sorry to hear that Mr. Clayton would not speak to you," she wrote him in July, "but be assured it will never make me think any the less of my Father. I shall always love and honor my Father and do all I can to smooth off the rough edges of the trials he has to pass through in this life."[75] A year later she made her choice and left her husband, taking their son with her. Clayton was left to ponder the perplexities of discipleship and awesomeness of apostasy.

William Clayton's various confrontations with the esoteric fads of his day were only a minor part of his life, though in some way they had dramatic consequences. In terms of what they tell us about the Mormon community of nineteenth-century Utah, however, we hesitate to read too much into them, for Clayton was only one man among thousands. A few things are nevertheless suggested. Even though relatively few Mormons took up the "science" of astrology, that such a tenacious disciple as Clayton could take such a great interest in it suggests that his understanding of the gospel did not keep him from investigating a variety of possible sources of knowledge. That he did not drop the subject when told to do so suggests that he did not interpret Brigham Young's distaste for it as official church pronouncement. In a day when patent medicines, animal magnetism, metallic devices, and various other remedies were widely advertised and ac-

cepted, it is not surprising that at least some Mormons should dabble
in a variety of mysteries.

In Clayton's brush with alchemy, "weird rings," and the like, he
was even farther out of the Mormon mainstream, but it appears that
he dropped such diversions quickly.

In his attitude toward spiritualism, Clayton represented the main
current of Mormon discipleship, though his harsh reactions might be
analagous to the rocks and rapids in that current. What Mormon could
object to his denunciation of those who threatened the foundations
of the Kingdom, what Mormon would not applaud his call for support
of the living prophets, and them alone, as the only proper guides for
the Kingdom, and what Mormon would not understand when, in
disappointment, he broke all ties with a friend whom he felt had betrayed the Kingdom and embraced the enemy? His kind of discipleship
was perhaps summarized best in what he wrote to Francis Lyman
during the crisis over the Godbeites: "As to myself, there is nothing
in this world I care for, except that which is connected with Mormonism as it is and was."[76]

NOTES

1. Only in recent years have scholars begun to explore very deeply the
persistence of esoteric tendencies in America. Recent studies have demonstrated, however, that certain occult practices, including astrology, spiritualism, "white magic," and treasure hunting, were not uncommon in the eight-
eenth and nineteenth centuries, and that what we moderns might call the
"superstitious" was really a part of the folk culture even of respectable citizens.
One astute scholar, R. Laurence Moore, has cautioned us against too quickly
pinning pejorative labels on people of the past simply because their way of
looking at the universe was different from ours. "Our investigation calls for
caution because occultism was usually bandied about in the latter part of the
nineteenth century as a pejorative term. None of the groups I propose to
examine accepted for a moment the charge that it was occult (although each
vigorously directed the charge at the others). Historians can try to detach
themselves from the confused charges and countercharges that historical actors
made and use their own notion of what constitutes occult and esoteric belief
to settle the truth of those charges. But they cannot completely escape the
implication of the observation that superstition is a label for the other person's
religion. From somebody's point of view, all systems of thought . . . are tainted
with occult associations." R. Laurence Moore, "The Occult Connection? Mormonism, Christian Science, and Spiritualism," in Howard Kerr and Charles L.

Crow, eds., *The Occult in America: New Historical Perspectives* (Urbana: University of Illinois Press, 1983), 136. The entire book consists of several chapters that are each important contributions to a new interpretation of the occult in America. Especially see Jon Butler, "The Dark Ages of American Occultism, 1760–1848." The relationship of such esoteric tendencies to Mormonism has also only begun to be explored. For some excellent studies on treasure hunting in the time of Joseph Smith, for example, see the several articles in *BYU Studies* 24 (Spring 1984), and especially two by Ronald Walker: "The Persisting Idea of American Treasure Hunting," and "Joseph Smith: The Palmyra Seer." Though Clayton took up astrology and alchemy, there is no evidence that he showed any interest in treasure hunting or in another pseudoscience, phrenology, which some Mormons were curiously attracted to. For an interesting discussion of phrenology among the Mormons, see Davis Bitton and Gary L. Bunker, "Phrenology among the Mormons," *Dialogue: A Journal of Mormon Thought* 9 (Spring 1974):43–61.

2. William Lilly, *An Introduction to Astrology*, ed. Zadkiel (London: G. Bell and Sons, Limited, 1910), 10–12.

3. R. Swinburne Clymer, *Alchemy and the Alchemists*, 1 (Allentown, Pa.: Philosophical Publishing Co., 1907), title page, and 265–66.

4. For an interesting historical account and personal evaluation of astrology, see Christopher McIntosh, *The Astrologers and Their Creed* (New York: Frederick A. Praeger, 1969). Chapter 7 therein deals with the trends of the nineteenth century.

5. Ibid., 101.

6. Orson Pratt, *The Prophetic Almanac for 1846* (New York: "New York Messenger" Office, [1845]). I am indebted to David J. Whittaker for leading me to information relating to early Mormon almanacs. Dr. Whittaker's unpublished manuscript, "Almanacs and the New England Heritage of Mormonism," will prove useful for anyone wishing to read further.

7. W. W. Phelps, *Deseret Almanac for the Year of our Lord 1852 . . .* (Great Salt Lake City: W. Richards, Printer, 1852), 37.

8. *Wilford Woodruff's Journal*, 5:65 (28 June 1857).

9. W. W. Phelps to Brigham Young, 29 June 1857, Brigham Young Papers; W. W. Phelps, *Almanac for the Year 1860 . . .* (Great Salt Lake City: J. McKnight, 1860), 32. Here Phelps gave the following definition of an almanac: "The word ALMANAC is probably of Arabic origin and means a daily calculation for the rising, setting, and position of the sun, moon, planets, stars, constellations and phenomena of a year, in advance; *and anciently and modernly, contains many other matters of motion that may facilitate the business transactions of man.*

"A person without an Almanac is somewhat like a ship at sea, without a compass; he never knows what to do, nor when to do it;

"So Mormon, others, sect and Quaker;

"Buy Almanac, and pay the maker." (Italics added.)

10. In 1861, for example, he turned down a Salt Lake City tailor who came to him seeking permission to open a school of astrology. "Brigham Young Office Journal August 8, 1858 to September 30, 1863," 328–29 (30 Dec. 1861),

Church Archives. The entry reads: "Br. ———— a Tailor living in maine [sic]
St. called upon the President for the purpose of getting permission to open a
school to teach astrology. The Pres. referred him to Br. A. Carrington. President
Young remarked it would not do to favor Astrology—an effort was made in
the days of Joseph to establish astrology."

11. We make the assumption that this was not the 1861 incident cited in the
note above but rather occurred a year or so earlier. Clayton's 1865 letter, cited
below, says that Brigham Young had accused him of studying astrology for
the past seven years, and it seems that he began the study about the time he
asked permission to start the school.

12. Clayton to Brigham Young, 30 Oct. 1865, Brigham Young Papers.

13. Clayton to John Sanderson, 26 Apr. 1862.

14. Clayton to Sanderson, 30 May 1862.

15. Clayton to George Q. Cannon, 22 Feb. 1862, 22 Feb. 1863.

16. Clayton to Sanderson, 30 May 1862.

17. Clayton to Elder Richard Bently, 5 Dec. 1863. See also Clayton to Messers
A. S. Barnes and Burr, 20 Nov. 1863.

18. Clayton to Sanderson, 3 Sept. 1862.

19. See Chapter 11 herein for details on Clayton's concerns over the war.

20. Clayton to Sanderson, 8 Aug. 1863, 24 Feb. 1865.

21. For description of "how to do it," see Alan Leo, *Astrology for All Part
I* (London: Office of "Modern Astrology," 1908), and McIntosh, *Astrologers*,
chap. 11. Alan Leo was the pseudonym for William Frederick Allen, who in
the last part of the nineteenth century became one of the leading popular
astrologers in Europe. He probably reflected the type of astrology familiar to
Clayton and, says McIntosh, with the help of his manuals (all published after
Clayton's death), "it was possible for almost any dilettante to fancy himself
an expert caster of horoscopes" (ibid., 97).

22. Clayton to Sanderson, 6 Jan. 1864.

23. Clayton to Sanderson, 24 Feb. 1865.

24. Clayton to "Professor Cohen," 14 Feb. 1865. See also his order for books
in Clayton to James Linforth, Esq., 21 Mar. 1865.

25. Clayton to Young, 30 Oct. 1865, Brigham Young Papers.

26. Ibid.

27. See Clayton to Wm. Adamson, Esq., 18 Nov. 1872, and Clayton to S. W.
Ritter, 26 Nov. 1874.

28. Clayton to John Royle, 28 Nov. 1869.

29. See *Deseret Evening News*, 24 May 1879, "Astrology and 'The Great
Tribulation.'"

30. McIntosh, *Astrologers*, 117.

31. Cabalism is an ancient and secretive Jewish tradition that has some elements relating to astrology. Celestial influences, mystical numbers, and magical
powers are all part of the system.

32. Clayton to William Freeman, 2 Mar. 1864.

33. Clayton to Freeman, 7 Mar. 1864.

34. Ibid.

35. Clayton to Freeman, 18 May 1844.
36. Ibid.
37. Clayton et al. to Freeman, 14 May 1864.
38. Clayton to Freeman, 25 May 1864.
39. Clayton to Freeman, 13 June 1864.
40. Clayton to Freeman, 22 July 1864.
41. Clayton to Sanderson, 5 Aug. 1864.
42. At least twenty-six names can be identified in Clayton's correspondence, and there is a clear implication that there are others, not only in Salt Lake City but also throughout the territory.
43. Clayton to Freeman, 6, 13 June, 22 July 1864.
44. Clayton to Freeman, 14, 21 May, 6 June 1864.
45. Clayton to Freeman, 23 July 1864. Clayton to D. M. Thomas, 28 July 1864. Clayton originally sent only $20 for his first outfit, but he probably had to make up the difference later on.
46. Clayton to Thomas, 28 July 1864.
47. Clayton to Freeman, 22 July 1864.
48. Ibid.
49. Clayton to Freeman, 23 July 1864.
50. Clayton to Thomas, 28 July 1864.
51. Clayton to John Gerber, Sr., 5 Nov. 1864, and Clayton to Charles Davis, 5 Nov. 1864.
52. Spiritualism, the Godbeites, and Godbeite leaders have received considerable attention from scholars. For a fine general statement on spiritualism in Utah, see Davis Bitton, "Mormonism's Encounter with Spiritualism," *Journal of Mormon History* 1 (1974):39–50. For the best treatment of the Godbeite movement, which emphasizes the importance of spiritualism as part of the tradition of economic liberalism in Utah, see Ronald W. Walker, "The Godbeite Protest and the Making of Modern Utah" (Ph.D. diss., University of Utah, 1977). See also Ronald Walker's "The Stenhouses and the Making of the Mormon Image," *Journal of Mormon History* 1 (1974):51–72, and "The Commencement of the Godbeite Protest: Another View," *Utah Historical Quarterly* 42 (Summer 1974):216–44. For a recent and thorough study of Amasa Lyman, who was so important to Clayton's attitudes, see Loretta Hefner, "Amasa Lyman, the Mormon Universalist Apostle" (Master's thesis, University of Utah, 1977).
53. Walker, "Godbeite Protest," 173, 179.
54. Clayton to "Brother Jesse" (Jesse N. Smith?), 28 Nov. 1869.
55. Clayton to Heber Young, 14 Nov. 1869.
56. Clayton to Royle, 28 Nov. 1869.
57. Clayton to "Brother Jesse," 19 Dec. 1869.
58. Clayton to "Brother Jesse," 23 Jan. 1870.
59. Clayton to "Brother Jesse," 20 Nov. 1869.
60. Clayton to James McKean, 16 Jan. 1870.
61. Clayton to "Brother Jesse," 29 May 1870.
62. Clayton to McKean, 16 Jan. 1870.

63. Ibid.

64. Ibid.

65. Clayton to Heber Young, 23 Jan. 1870.

66. Clayton to F. M. Lyman, 4 Dec. 1869.

67. Clayton to "Brother Jesse," 23 Jan. 1870.

68. Clayton to Amasa Lyman, 13 Feb. 1867, Amasa Lyman Papers.

69. There is some confusion, perhaps, on this. Roberts, *Comprehensive History*, 5:271, indicates that he was excommunicated at the time he was dropped from the Quorum. Both Ronald Walker and Loretta Hefner, however, who have done the most recent studies on Lyman and the Godbeites, indicate that the excommunication was not finally acted upon until 1870.

70. Clayton to H. A. Skinner, 19 Aug. 1868, Clayton Papers.

71. Clayton to Amasa Lyman, 3 Dec. 1868, Amasa Lyman Papers.

72. Clayton to F. M. Lyman, 5, 8, 12, 16 Dec. 1869.

73. Amasa Lyman to Louisa Lyman, 10 May 1870, Amasa Lyman Papers.

74. A. Lyman to L. Lyman, 20 May 1870.

75. Maria Louisa Lyman Clayton to Amasa Lyman, 15 July 1870.

76. Clayton to F. M. Lyman, 5 Dec. 1869.

CHAPTER 13

How Not to get Rich in Pioneer Utah: The Economic Life of a Disciple

In a way, the title of this chapter is both misleading and facetious. It is misleading because in terms of income and apparent wealth William Clayton was probably among the top 5 percent of the family heads of the Territory of Utah. In 1870 he reported holding real property worth $5,000 and personal property worth $2,000, and his total tax assessment was nearly $4,000.[1] In comparison with most other heads of households, he looked very good, economically, on paper. But the facetious element in the title occurs because of William Clayton's unusual status. If his experience was any example, the way to avoid getting rich in pioneer Utah was to have nine wives and forty-two children. Even with a comparatively good income like his, a family of that size could drain it all—and in Clayton's case it apparently did.

In pioneer Utah religion and the concern for wealth were almost inseparable, for the exigencies of creating a new society in the Great Basin required the Mormons to emphasize economic ways and means. Accumulating wealth was necessary for building the Kingdom, and in Clayton's mind it was often just as important as preaching. "We cannot either eat or travel or build Temples or build up the Kingdom of God without money," he wrote to a missionary in 1863, "and it is just as right and honorable to collect from the nations that which is the just due of our brethren and sisters as it is to do any other good work."[2] Clayton's personal quest for economic well-being, successful at times and plagued with failure and disillusionment at other times, provides some telling insights into the nature of the Mormon community and the economic concerns of some of its disciples.[3]

None of Clayton's business endeavors made him wealthy, but they were characterized by at least three important revelations of his Mor-

mon value system: a strong sense of service, a high commitment to
ethical conduct, and thoroughness in detail. His methods of accounting
were precise and exact, and he demanded the same meticulous attention to detail from those who worked with him.[4] He was also prompt
to pay his debts. "My reputation," he wrote a Saint who owed him
money, "depends upon punctuality."[5] He was characterized by Orson
F. Whitney as "straitforward, methodical, and the soul of punctuality.
He kept his promises, and expected others to keep theirs. He had little
use for a man who would lightly break his word, even by tardiness in
keeping an appointment."[6] His collection business was, to him, as
much a public service as it was a source of income, and he was incensed
if he should be accused of gouging on his charges. "I am always willing
to do all I can to accomodate my brethren, and I am all the time using
my best efforts to collect their money and do them good, and much
of my time and services counts me nothing . . . but it is an injustice
to me to accuse me of charging exorbitant interest."[7]

Clayton often took time to evaluate his personal conduct, and he
was not loathe to admit it when he found himself falling short of his
own very rigid standards. Whatever weaknesses he observed within
himself he was impatient with and was constantly working to conquer.
Such an occasion came on September 5, 1847, when he was returning
to Winter Quarters. It was the Sabbath day, and the company he was
with had traveled twelve and a half miles. They camped near one of
the most important landmarks for western travelers, Independence
Rock. While some of the men killed a buffalo, Clayton walked over
to the imposing monolith and engaged in some deep and serious meditation. He prayed for his traveling companions, church leaders, family,
and himself, then he reflected on the matter of ethics. Experience had
taught him many maxims, he wrote in his journal, and he intended
to profit by them. "Be not hasty to promise, lest thy promise be considered worthless. Make not many promises without reflection, lest
thou fail to fulfill them and it dampen the confidence of thy friend.
If thou promise many things and regard not to fulfill them and it damp
the confidence of thy friend, then be assured that thy friends will
despise thy promises and have no dependence in them. Seek not to
speculate out of a good brother."[8] Clayton's Sabbath day introspection
might have been the lens through which he examined his personal
business ethics in years to come.

It has been said that one of Joseph Smith's weaknesses was a tendency to trust men too quickly. His disciple, William Clayton, had the same failing. This made him an easy mark for certain swindlers who would deliberately take advantage of trusting souls, as well as for some of his brethren who, however well intentioned, were unable promptly to repay what they borrowed from him. He was taken in by a mail-order alchemist,[9] was bilked out of $30 in a crooked lottery,[10] and was taken advantage of by business partners. But the best example of how his generosity and trusting nature hurt him economically is the story of young Henry Hanks.[11] In September 1869 Hanks, a British immigrant, wrote to Clayton from Brigham City explaining that important business compelled him to return to England and asking that Clayton cash a check for him. He would, of course, pay interest. William did not know the man, but when he appeared in Salt Lake City on October 9 he had so many good references that he was inclined to trust him. He went so far as to borrow $250, and gave it to Hanks in return for a check on a London bank for £50 sterling. This would result in about a $50 profit for Clayton, though he had to pay a monthly interest of 2 percent on the money he borrowed. He sent the check to his agent in London, H. Starr, Esq., and was twice informed that there were no funds to cover it. Young Henry, in fact, was not even in England.

Moneylending is always a calculated risk, but to lend money purely on the basis of paper credentials, with no tangible security, is not usually considered sound practice even when a substantial profit might result. But Henry Hanks was a Saint. He had been baptized in Box Elder County and appealed to Clayton on the basis of his brotherhood and the personal testimony of a few brethren whom Clayton trusted. The result was that the trusting moneylender was an extra $250 in debt.

The worried Clayton began to take action. Somehow he obtained the address of Hanks's father, the Reverend H. Hanks of Wollwich, England, and wrote him. He carefully explained the circumstances and then, appealing to the reverend's fatherly instincts, asked him to make the check good. He received a pathetic reply recounting a series of disappointments that the young man had brought into the life of his father. "Through his restless conduct," Clayton told a friend, "he has virtually broken his father's heart besides reducing him to nearly a state of beggary." Clayton was convinced that "if Henry Hanks is not an unprincipled scoundrel, he is so near it the difference is immaterial."

The father, nevertheless, offered to redeem his prodigal's debt and by June 1870 had sent half the money. Clayton was deeply touched, recognizing the burden this placed upon the good minister and the fact that he was in no way bound to pay. Yet, he told his London agent, if the father had heard the pleading of his son he could never think hard of Clayton for advancing the money. Even then Clayton displayed a remaining streak of credulity when he wrote the father on March 14, "When I reflect upon his expressions to me concerning you I am compelled to believe he is endeavoring to in some measure redeem himself before returning to the bosom of his family. I cannot think that all he said to me was deceitful and void of truth. . . . I would be very sorry to inspire you with hopes which may not be realized, but I still think there will be a satisfactory termination of the matter and that you will yet rejoice over the prodigal son." If possible, he told the minister, he would like to let him keep the money, but recent reverses had placed him so far in debt that he must have it. "It is a sorrowful matter on both sides . . . but we have neither of us a great many years to live, and I can only pray that the Lord in his infinite mercy may award you many happy days in this life and everlasting peace and glory in the world to come."

In June 1870 William suddenly learned that Henry Hanks was in New York City. Immediately he wrote a friend in that metropolis telling him of the affair and warning him to caution the Saints against Hanks, "for he will no doubt play the same game on some of them he did on me . . . he is a swindler and adventurer of the worst die." At the same time he asked his friend to collect the money due him, plus interest. He told him in confidence that the father had already paid £25, and of the distress it caused him to do it, but if he could get the whole amount from Henry he would refund the father's money. To have this privilege, he earnestly explained, "would do me more good than the receipt of the money."

The records do not reveal the outcome of the Hanks affair, but a simple comment to his London agent suggests his own rationalization for his bad judgment. He knew his weakness in trusting too readily, but "altho' such acts in men, tempts one never to trust his fellow man again, such a conclusion is contrary to my religious views, and whatever may be my ultimate loss in this, it will not hinder me from doing a kindness again as opportunity offers."

If Clayton was disappointed in the actions of apparent scoundrels such as Henry Hanks, he was equally or more concerned about the integrity of the Saints with whom he dealt each day. He had reason to be, for it was his business to collect debts, lend money, and buy and sell. "We believe in being honest," one of the Mormon Articles of Faith begins, and to William Clayton that meant not only telling the truth but also paying one's debts on time. As he dealt with those Saints who were slow to settle up, he sometimes pointedly preached to them of the jeopardy in which they placed their eternal salvation if they refused to change their ways.

Clayton was dismayed, for example, in 1863 when a brother to whom he gave twenty sacks for the purpose of returning them full of wheat did not return them but rather filled them and sent them to others. "I do not think it right," he wrote. "I will not say all I feel at such proceedings. If you will please bring the sacks home with good wheat in them (not *smutty*) all right; otherwise I shall expect pay for the sacks. Please ask yourself how you would feel if I had treated you in a similar manner."[12] To a customer who owed him money because of a billing error he wrote: "I know you will send the pay for it as soon as you get it. If all the brethren were as punctual and reliable as Bro. J. C. Wright we would enjoy universal confidence in each other, instead of almost universal distrust and doubt. It will be a happy day for Israel when a saints 'yea' means 'yea', and his 'nay' means 'nay.' "[13]

In 1872, when his personal economic kingdom seemed to be tumbling all around him, he became particularly irate with a brother who had engaged him to collect some money in England when all along the man knew that no money was actually due him. Clayton had put $45 of his own into the effort. "How long the church must be cursed by such men I do not know," he wrote a friend. "But *I do know* that no dishonest man can be exalted in Celestial glory. I am of the same opinion with President Young, that no dishonest man, who refuses or neglects to pay his just debts, when he is able to, ought to have a name and standing in the church. I have labored for the good of my brethren without compensation as much as anyone but I cannot give my time and pay expenses for the brethren too."[14] As a matter of last resort, he was ready to take the wayward Saint before the high council.

In 1873 Clayton wrote a member of the church who had borrowed money from another Saint ten years earlier in order to emigrate to Zion. Clayton was engaged to collect. "For your own sake," the collector wrote, "you are under the most sacred obligations" to pay. This was especially important for the tardy debtor was planning to enter into the "holy order of Celestial marriage [i.e., plural marriage], aiming for a fulness of Celestial glory." It is impossible, Clayton patiently explained, to attain this glory until we have paid our debts and atoned for our wrongs. "These little matters of right and wrong between brethren will have a much more serious effect upon our prospects hereafter, than many are aware of, and it is time that the Elders of Israel reflect, and cease to wrong each other, for all these wrongs must be righted. I fear it will yet be said to many, 'If ye have been unfaithful with the unrighteous mammon who will entrust to you the true riches.'" Clayton thought it much better to be wronged than to do wrong but was fearful that many Saints would sacrifice their Celestial glory for the sake of a few dollars. Then, reflecting again the deep disappointment he felt in the actions of some of them, he added:

> Bro. Crane, it is what I see and hear of daily of wrong done by brother against brother that has prompted me to write as I have. I sometimes feel as tho I could go through the Territory uttering the warning words "be honest with each other—be honest with your families—be honest with your God" for except our righteousness exceed that of sectarians we shall fail in our efforts for exaltation.
>
> In this matter of brother Jones', all I ask of you is to reflect seriously upon it to determine to do as you would be done by, and pay the debt honorably as fast as you can. You will make at least two persons feel well, yourself and brother Jones.[15]

Clayton's version of the Golden Rule, as expressed to another Saint, was simply "place yourself in my position and then do as you would be done by."[16]

The most interesting side of Clayton's collection business concerned debts owed to Saints who had immigrated from Europe without collecting them. When he began his international collection agency is not clear, but in 1863 he indicated to one of his agents that he had been at it for several years. Moreover, Clayton had more success than others who attempted to make such collections, and near the beginning of 1863 Brigham Young specifically assigned him to take care of all such matters in all countries of the world.[17]

Clayton went about his collection business in his usual methodical manner. He obtained the power of attorney from his clients and transferred it to his European agents. He demanded full information and was meticulous in keeping records of every phase of the transactions. At first he charged a fee of 10 percent for his services, though in 1865 he raised it to 15 percent.

On occasion Clayton performed an extra service that had the possibility of helping out both himself and his client. When he successfully completed one transaction in 1863, the client, Mrs. Hannah Low, was due to receive £72 sterling after Clayton's fee was deducted. This would amount to $349.20 American coin when it arrived in New York City. Clayton suggested to her, however, as he had done to others, that it would be expensive to forward the coin to Utah, but that he would be willing to pay her immediately in "legal tender notes" at a premium of 60 percent over face value. These notes were greenbacks issued by Congress during the Civil War under the Legal Tender Act of 1862, and the 60 percent premium undoubtedly reflected the highly inflated nature of such paper money. Clayton would take all the risk involved in transmitting the money from New York and would let his client draw the paper money whenever she wanted.[18] Her advantage was that she had the money then; Clayton's advantage was in speculating on the possible increase in value of the coin.

The international collection agency was, to Clayton, more than a personal business venture: it was also a religious calling. For that reason he had no hesitancy in calling upon the Mormon missionaries in Europe to act as his agents. He had missionary representatives in various countries, gave them power of attorney to act in behalf of his clients, and expected them to spend whatever time was necessary away from their missionary work to complete the collection business. Perhaps the most prestigious of these agents was Elder George Q. Cannon of the Council of the Twelve. From 1860 to 1864, with a brief interlude in Washington, D.C., Cannon lived in England and presided over the European mission.[19] Clayton endowed him with powers of attorney, sent many papers to him for action, and even though he realized it was taking up extra time continued to insist that it was a necessary venture.

The idea of doing business through church agents, and especially taking the time of missionaries for such mercenary concerns, was discomfiting to some Saints, and on occasion Clayton was forced to defend his system. He argued that what he was doing was really for the benefit of the Kingdom and that he had been assigned to do it by the prophet. When Elder William P. Nebeker wrote from Switzerland expressing some concern over the matter, Clayton took it up with the president of the church and then informed Nebeker that the prophet was desirous that this business be done through church agents. Even though it could be done through gentile bankers and solicitors very efficiently, the church leader simply did not want to depend on gentiles, and Clayton had the privilege of calling upon any elder whom he judged competent to perform the service. After all, he reminded his agent, "Much of the money collected abroad through my agency is used for church purposes, immigration &c., and the other portion is promptly paid to the parties here for whom the money is collected." He again assured the elder of the necessity of his work, for, he said, "I know of nothing that can be done toward the building up of the Kingdom without means. . . . Have no dubiety therefore about the propriety of your devoting both time and attention to these matters. It will be a good opportunity for you to qualify yourself for usefulness in other matters."[20] When Karl G. Maeser fell behind in his collection responsibilities in England, Clayton scolded him through the mails and complained that some missionaries seemed to forget "that temporal means are as much necessary as the spiritual, in building up the Kingdom of God."[21]

The religious mission of the collection agency, then, was to help provide the temporal means for building the Kingdom of God. It was also to provide practical business experience for the elders that would come in handy later. "Were it not that Prest. Young wishes the Elders to attend to such business in order to give them experience," he wrote in 1873, "I would prefer not to trouble them, but I respect his wishes and counsel in the matter."[22]

Clayton frequently showed some irritation with those who, for whatever reason, delayed in their collections. To George Q. Cannon he wrote, "I wish to [collect] . . . promptly and energetically, realizing that every year makes things worse, and leaves less and less prospect of the brethren obtaining that which is justly their due."[23] When money was slow in coming, his clients sometimes accused him of laxity, which irked him not a little. "The brethren think I have neglected their business," he complained, "which is not so. They should have their money collected for them . . . but I cannot do it, without some faithful Elder to work with me, and in order to work effectually he must consider it a part of his mission, which it really is."[24] To one elder who had

either neglected his duty or was holding the money for his own purposes he explained his own philosophy of promptness: "If I was to
hold money in my hands month after month, which I had collected
for my brethren, keeping the lawful owners out of it, without any
authority or permission whatever I should know at once I was dishonest and unworthy to be trusted with money belonging not to me,
but to my brethren. Whenever money comes into my hands for the
brethren I scarcely ever sleep until they are notified their money is
ready for them."[25]

Clayton continued his collection business until his death, though it
declined considerably between 1869 and 1871 while he served as secretary of ZCMI. During that time, in fact, the collections were virtually
taken over by non-Mormons, much to the dismay of Brigham Young
and other church authorities. As a result, when Clayton resigned from
ZCMI the authorities asked him to revive the business and promised
him their full support and influence in pursuing it.[26] He went into it
wholeheartedly, contacting new missionaries to act as agents and even
advertising his business in Utah in order to bring it up to its full
potential. After all, he wrote one agent, "It is of as much importance
to collect money for the saints as it is to preach the gospel."[27]

William Clayton was spared the trials of those Saints who in Ohio
and Missouri attempted unsuccessfully to inaugurate a new economic
order, the "Law of Consecration."[28] He accepted and lived the law of
tithing,[29] but it was a new church experience and a further test of his
discipleship when new efforts at economic cooperation were introduced in Utah.[30]

The first such effort to affect Clayton was the consecration movement of the 1850s.[31] Beginning in 1854, the Saints in Utah were asked
by Brigham Young and other church leaders to consecrate all their
properties to the church. The apparent hope was to marshal all the
economic resources of the Saints and use them more effectively in
building the Kingdom. The movement got underway in the April conference of 1854, and Clayton was among the first to subscribe. On April
9 the bishop of the Salt Lake City Seventeenth Ward called upon all
those willing to consecrate both themselves and their property to sign
a paper which the clerk would circulate. William Clayton was among
the forty-nine people who signed, indicating their desire to consecrate
property to the church.[32] But the consecration movement soon ended
with no practical economic results. Less than half the heads of house-

holds even filled out deeds of consecration, and none of these deeds was ever actually conveyed to the church. The proffered consecrations nevertheless symbolized a willingness to give all one possessed, if necessary, to create both spiritual and temporal unity in the Kingdom.

There were other such efforts among the Saints, and the 1860s saw the founding of numerous cooperative mercantile and manufacturing associations.[33] It appears that Clayton was not actively associated with them, however, until the organization of the most influential of all, Zion's Cooperative Mercantile Institution, better known as ZCMI.

William Clayton was intimately involved with ZCMI from the beginning. When it was decided that a cooperative merchandising establishment was necessary to the economic well-being of the territory, Clayton was among seventeen men sent out to preach its benefits in towns adjacent to Salt Lake City.[34] Then, when the new institution was officially organized in October 1868, Clayton was elected as its first secretary. He threw himself fully and enthusiastically into the work, which became so time-consuming that he was forced to give up nearly all his other business interests. Only his international collection agency remained intact, and even that suffered during the time he served "the Co-op." His work became increasingly heavy as ZCMI expanded its operations, and in less than a year after the parent store opened he wrote a friend that "you may be sure it is very difficult running 5 wholesale stores and carrying between $6 and 700,000 worth of goods."[35] According to his own estimates Clayton worked some seventy-two hours per week in 1870, and handled nearly $2 million annually.[36]

In spite of his willing devotion to the new cooperative effort, Clayton found in ZCMI another source of frustration and another trial to his discipleship. The long hours of confining work had a negative effect upon his already problematical health.[37] His wages were unsatisfactory, allowing him to make only about half his former earnings and forcing him by 1871 to go into the stock business to meet his needs.[38] He was soon disillusioned, furthermore, with what he considered to be unfair employment policies that presented the most serious challenge to his sense of propriety. He was particularly disappointed at what he considered to be inequities perpetuated by Horace S. Eldredge, one of the Seven Presidents of the Seventies and a member of ZCMI's board of directors, and Hiram B. Clawson, superintendent of ZCMI. A pointed letter to Eldredge in August 1870 contained Clayton's main indictment. Earlier he was able to earn some $5,000 or $6,000 dollars per year, but ZCMI had fixed his salary at $300 per month. At the same time Superintendent Clawson received $500 per month as well as "advantages, perquisites and presents worth over $100 per month." These advantages and perquisites included the fact that ZCMI kept Clawson's three sons and two teams constantly employed "all at good, liberal wages," and Clawson's three nephews were also regularly employed. But Clayton, after trying several times, could get no work for his own boys. Disappointed and disgruntled, he attacked Eldredge with perhaps the harshest words he ever allowed himself to write to a church leader:

> Now, what I would like to ask, is what has H.B.C. or H.S.B. ever done for the Kingdom that they should thus have its benefits and wealth stuffed into them at both ends, while others who have perhaps done as much for Israel and been as long tried and proved faithful can only have a menials position and menials pay compared with others. . . . When I was appointed Secretary I had made a business which was worth from five to six thousand dollars a year. This is all ruined and gone because I have not time to attend to it. Now, if you, as an Elder in Israel can see any justice or anything Godlike in such a distribution of public favors, you see different to what I do. I confess it has destroyed my confidence in men, very considerably.[39]

But even after all that, Clayton was determined not to remain bitter; said he, "Having once referred to it I shall let the matter drop believing there will be no such partial and unjust dealings in the next world. Praying that you may be blest and sustained in your present position and in all your future career. I remain as ever yours."

Nothing happened to relieve the disciple's burdens; if anything, they increased. A year later he complained again, this time to ZCMI's board of directors. His collection agency was almost defunct, his only income beyond his salary was the small territorial auditor's salary, and he performed the duties of that office mornings and evenings, before and after his regular work. His income was not enough to sustain his large family, and consequently, he reported, "I am gradually sinking deeper and deeper in debt, the thought of which destroys my peace of mind, causing me sleepless nights and comfortless days." He was receiving and paying out money at the rate of about $3 million annually, and he pointedly reminded the board of the responsibility and natural anxiety that attended such duties. Affirming that the business was prosperous and that it operated smoothly so far as his responsibilities were concerned, he pleaded with the board to "be kind enough to increase my compensation in an amount sufficient to free me from the harrassing thought that the harder I work the deeper I have to go in debt to live." Then, still demonstrating a remarkably accommodating spirit, the frustrated follower added, "I will rejoice in my position as Secretary, serve you as faithfully as in my power. Brethren will you kindly allow me enough for a comfortable living while I thus serve you."[40] Within less than three months, however, Brigham Young advised him, for the sake of his health, to resign. At this urging he stepped down from the co-op to try to rebuild his private business.[41]

In this case William Clayton's dilemma had nothing to do with whether or not he accepted the principles announced by his leaders: his acceptance of the co-op idea seemed wholehearted, and his devotion to his own responsibilities was exemplary. His problems lay with management policy and with his own inability to live on the salary paid him. But another form of church cooperation, the United Order, presented a more complex problem. What course should a faithful follower take if he disagrees with the announced policy of the church, and on what basis could he disagree with the policy promulgated by a prophet? Clayton did not fully solve the problem, but his concern over the United Order in 1874 has something to say about the problems of religious discipleship in every age.

The United Orders of Utah territory were part of Brigham Young's continuing effort to promote the economic independence of the Saints. Beginning in the winter of 1873–74, at least four different kinds of orders were established; some amounted to little more than traditional cooperative manufacturing or merchandising enterprises but at least one, Orderville, resulted in complete communal ownership of all means of production and distribution.[42]

In spite of his earlier willingness to consecrate his property, his acceptance of the principles upon which ZCMI operated, and his acceptance of Mormon church leaders as inspired prophets of God, Clayton found the establishment of the "New Order," as he called it, objectionable. In private correspondence to his close friend and confidant, Francis M. Lyman, he gave his reasons. First, he said, the "order of Heaven" could not be established unless everyone, from the highest church authorities down, entered into it. "A stream cannot rise higher than its fountain," he protested, and until all the top authorities were willing to lead out and join, the people as a whole could never be expected to adopt the order. Though it was "a pure and holy Celestial order," the Saints simply were not ready for it. Next, he observed that a federal law (i.e., the Anti-Bigamy Act of 1862) prohibited any church from holding more than $50,000 worth of property. This, he feared, would make any property consecrated to the church subject to federal confiscation.

Clayton's third argument was also legalistic, for he observed that a man who deeded all his property away would not be able to hold public office or sit on juries, for territorial laws provided that only householders and taxpayers could perform such functions. Since Clayton felt that the new movement should be promoted only if the church was prepared to have all the Saints involved, this would result in political control by the enemies of the church. "The right to vote, to hold office and to sit on juries, are too important, in these times, to be lightly thrown away."

Finally, Clayton gave his own interpretation of when the true Order of Enoch would be established. His reading of a revelation given to Joseph Smith on June 11, 1834,[43] convinced him that the Order of Enoch and the redemption of Zion would begin simultaneously. This could not come, he believed, until the church itself was purified from all its evils and the hearts of the Saints "turned in the depths of meekness and humility to the 'New and Everlasting Covenant,' even the covenant of Celestial marriage or plurality of wives, the most important principle ever revealed from the Heavens to man." He then undoubtedly reflected the great disappointment he so often felt in the actions of some Saints: "At present, we are far too worldly minded, too anxious to grasp and hoard up the riches of the earth, too covetous and illiberal in our dealings with each other, too fond of the pleasures and fashions and varities of the world, to successfully establish the Order of Enoch." Only after the judgments of the Lord had been poured out upon the earth would Zion be redeemed and the Order of Enoch be established. Clayton took some comfort, however, in the fact that since Brigham Young returned to Salt Lake City from his winter home in southern Utah, the principles he first preached had been "very materially" modified. The church president had begun to teach the new economic reform during his winter stay in St. George, but in Salt Lake City he was promoting merely a cooperation of trades and business—something quite different from the principle of consecration seemingly implied in other places.[44] Clayton wholeheartedly approved of that kind of cooperation, for it was "absolutely necessary to guard the people against being eat up by their enemies."[45]

In spite of his serious reservations, Clayton's kind of discipleship made it impossible for him to speak openly against the economic program of the church. He even hesitated to write his confidant, for as a follower who always wanted to be found on the right side of things, he had reconciled himself to the idea that opposition was the devil's tool and that his best course was to wait and watch but never openly oppose. His words were a classic statement of that kind of discipleship: "I cannot write in reference to that and many other subjects, with that confidence and enthusiasm, which many indulge in. I never *oppose* any measure started by the authorities, for in that neither I nor any member of the church can be justified. Opposition and division is the work of the enemy, and I trust never to be found on that side, in any degree. My course in regard to the 'new Order,' has been the same as it was when the principle of adoption was started in Nauvoo, and when the 'reformation' was started in 1857. *I wait and watch and say little. I will not oppose* my brethren in any thing."[46] The United Orders ultimately were short-lived, though not necessarily for the reasons Clayton outlined.

There were probably many who held reservations similar to Clayton's and had similar reasons for not speaking out in public. In Clayton's case, it was not a weak-minded fearfulness that caused him to remain silent, though to some degree his reticence was connected with his longing to stay in favor with his leaders. But more deeply, and more significantly, it was also a part of his genuine affection for the church and his concern for the spirit of unity in what he considered to be the most important of all missions—building the Kingdom. It was this that led him to conclude to his friend: "May the Lord bless and preserve you and me and everyone who desires to do right, that we may be enabled to stand true to the church and Kingdom of God under all circumstances."[47]

Brigham Young was not distressed when William Clayton resigned from ZCMI. Rather, he tried to help him reestablish his other businesses. The collection agency was one example, and another was Clayton's profession as a scribe and legal counselor. On November 10, 1873, President Young brought Clayton to the School of the Prophets, where he was unanimously admitted as a member. In introducing him, the church leader described him as "the most capable man in the community to make out Wills in strict conformity to law and recommended the brethren to avail themselves of his services."[48] President Young was clearly performing a dual service: wisely suggesting a necessary service to the members of the school and endorsing Clayton in such a way that it was bound to bring him business.

Clearly, however, the virtues of hard work, honesty, perseverance, and faith, even when they are combined, do not always produce great financial security. William Clayton's case was a prime example. The later years of his life were probably a time of testing such as he had never known before. He resigned from ZCMI in 1872 partly because he could not earn enough there to support his large family, but then, while suffering from ill health, he seemed to go from one financial reverse to another. Disappointing investments in mining enterprises, unfortunate loans made to friends, and unsuccessful business partnerships all were part of his frustrating final years.[49]

One notable disappointment was Clayton's partnership with C. W. Dotten. It began in 1865, when he dissolved his mercantile partnership with George Cronyn. Clayton's share of the remaining goods was valued at some $18,000, including $5,000 worth of "private family stores" such as tea, coffee, pepper, sugar, and various fabrics. All this was turned over to Dotten, who took it to Filmore and Beaver, Utah, in hopes of selling it. Clayton kept careful records of all he turned over and received information on what Dotten sold, but Clayton realized nothing from it. In addition, Clayton suddenly found himself held responsible for certain debts incurred by Dotten in the name of the partnership and was even the victim of a lawsuit in 1871 for one such debt. In some cases he borrowed money at high rates of interest to make Dotten's debts good. He was faced with a threat to bring him before a church high council as a result of Dotten's failure to deliver fifty-five bushels of wheat that Clayton had sold through the firm. "I am ready for the trial at any time," wrote the incensed Clayton, "because that will compel me to show up Dotten in his true colors."[50] Dotten, meantime, insisted that he owed Clayton nothing, and Clayton could only explain to his friends the nature of these and many other wrongs he felt Dotten had committed. "I have frequently been tempted to lay the whole matter before Prest. Young," he wrote, "but I do not wish to create a stink if I can help it."[51]

As if to add insult to injury, in 1872 Clayton was asked to take Dotten's personal note, payable in three installments without interest. He refused, of course. The Clayton papers reveal nothing more on the Dotten fiasco, but the whole incident only serves to illustrate the financial frustrations of a devoted disciple who tried in every way to conduct his business honorably, but who often was a too easy mark for those who would take advantage of him.[52]

In the middle of 1872 Clayton wrote a creditor that financially "I am worse cramped than I have been for years,"[53] though by the end of the year he could report to a friend that things seemed to be getting a little better.[54] During that year he tried a number of different ventures but with little success. He attempted to lease a foundry from Brigham Young, hoping to go into the business of manufacturing farm machinery with his brother.[55] He considered going into the business of selling steam engines, for the use of farmers and manufacturers in the territory.[56] He also began selling a "Band Cutter, Spreader, and Feeder," which he imported from the states.[57] He even attempted to become a book salesman and in May agreed with a Chicago publishing firm that he would circulate *Wonders of the World* in Utah territory. His commission was 40 percent, but by September he had decided he could not sell the book in the territory. It contained an anti-Mormon article that, after he read it, he pronounced a "tissue of falsehood from beginning to end." From then on, he said, he was unable to sell even one copy, though his son had canvassed Salt Lake City thoroughly.[58]

Clayton's financial condition did not improve, and the letters he wrote three and four years before his death are truly pathetic in their revelation of the financial frustrations of a faithful disciple. It was a tragic irony that the professional debt collector should find himself begging for relief from his own obligations. In December 1875 Clayton was asked for an immediate settlement of a note he had signed with someone else. Patiently he explained that the money had been borrowed by his client, with himself as co-signer, in full expectation that a collection being made in England would be available to repay the loan, but that the collection so far had failed. Clayton, however, simply could not pay at that time, and a forced collection would drive him to ruin and disgrace. He asked for time, and for a reduction of the interest, reminding his creditor that technically it was not his debt anyway. He also promised to sell a certain mine if he could or to borrow the money if necessary. "I have too much pride to ask the favor if I could help myself," he wrote, "but my circumstances are much worse than you have any idea of. The sacrifice of interest I respectfully ask you to make, you will never feel, but it would be of immense benefit to me."[59]

The year 1876 was especially difficult. On October 1 Clayton went so far as to request ZCMI to let him return stock, worth a little over $500, in exchange for winter provisions for his family. "I am over 62 years of age," he wrote, "and not as active as in years gone by. I do not recollect ever having entered into a winter under more discouraging circumstances than now surround me, hence my appeal to your generous and brotherly consideration."[60] That same month he wrote of his distress to a wealthy church member, John M. Horner, pleading for a substantial loan and suggesting that he might even lose his home if he could not come up with the money at that point. It must have been embarrassing to make such a plea, but as a faithful Saint Clayton also felt that he could call on the principle of brotherhood to support his plea. "Brother Horner," he wrote, "I appeal to your honor, as an Elder in Israel, to help me in this hour of deep distress," and in a later letter he pleaded: "The Lord has blessed you with abundance of this world's wealth, and I pray you in the name of my Father in Heaven to offer me that relief I so seriously need. Do not, I pray you as a brother, pass this letter by in silence."[61] The records do not reveal the result of this plea.

Clayton was not, of course, completely destitute for he had investments, property, and an income. But he also had heavy family expenses, financial commitments, and numerous bad debts owing him. His income simply was not adequate to meet the burdens all these thrust upon him. Economic abundance seemed always just beyond his grasp, though his personal integrity, perseverance, and will always to "do right" by those with whom he dealt remained characteristic of him to the end.

In 1879 William Clayton died intestate and almost insolvent. He left four living wives,[62] thirty-three living children, and one child on the way. His longstanding friend, Francis M. Lyman, was appointed executor of the estate.

The estate went to probate, and it took years to settle. The total value was estimated by Clayton's heirs to be less than $15,000,[63] but none was to go to any of them. His financial problems in the later years of his life had forced him to mortgage various portions of his property in order to pay outstanding debts. During the course of the probate, most of his property was sold to meet his remaining obligations. In the end, $365.10 was left on hand and this went to Lyman for his services and expenses as administrator. This may have seemed excessive, but Lyman was also keeping and paying for the education of Amasa Marion Clayton, the son of William's divorced wife, Maria Lyman.[64] The probate court discharged Lyman as executor on August 1, 1883, and so far as anyone suspected at the time that was the end. The estate was gone, but at least Clayton did not leave his family with unpayable debts.

Two years later something happened that would have warmed William Clayton's heart. When he died he held stock in the Wasatch Mining Company, and at the time of probate the stock was considered worthless—another of Clayton's frequent disappointments. But in 1885 it suddenly assumed value. The twenty-six-year-old Nephi Clayton, who had taken over many of his father's business activities, soon got the probate reopened, with himself appointed executor. With the permission of the court the stock was eventually sold for over $3,000, and in 1889 the proceeds were distributed to the family. After all expenses were paid, there remained enough to give each of the thirty-three children then living $59.14, and Clayton's first wife, Ruth, $658.58. Legally, nothing could be given to the other living wives, for they were not recognized as heirs by law, and whether Ruth shared with them is not known. But William Clayton, who had had so many business reverses and whose mining ventures were a special disappointment to him, could take some posthumous pleasure in having left not only a good name but at least some financial legacy for his family.

NOTES

1. Information on William Clayton's wealth was graciously provided to me by Larry T. Wimmer of the Economics Department at Brigham Young University who with Clayne Pope and James Kearl has conducted an important study on "Income and Wealth in Utah, 1850–1900."

2. Clayton to Paul A. Schettler, 27 Nov. 1863.

3. See Chapter 9 herein for a brief listing of Clayton's various occupations and business ventures.

4. Clayton to James Lewis, 10 Sept. 1863.

5. Clayton to Georg Todd, 3 Feb. 1877.

6. Orson F. Whitney, *History of Utah*, 4 vols. (Salt Lake City: George Q. Cannon and Sons Co., 1892–1904), 4:58.

7. Clayton to Rasmus Hansen, 16 Feb. 1864.

8. *William Clayton's Journal*, 358.

9. See Chapter 12 herein.

10. Clayton to J. M. Patee, 4 Mar. 1876. Clayton wrote this letter in an effort to recoup his losses from the swindler himself. In 1873 he had ordered twelve tickets from Patee, who had advertised a "Grand Gift Enterprise for Charitable purposes." In February 1874, he received notice that he had won a $200 prize, but the notice was accompanied by another circular calling for another $10. Clayton sent the additional money and asked that a parlor organ valued at $200 be sent him for the prize money. After getting no response he wrote to a friend in Chicago and found that Patee was in prison for swindling. In addition, Clayton had loaned another $10 to a friend who had then subscribed to the same lottery, and who still owed the money to Clayton. In 1876 Clayton had similar circulars from Laramie, and so he wrote this letter with a threat to sue. The papers do not reveal the outcome, but apparently Clayton lost a total of $30 in the swindle.

11. The story is reconstructed here on the basis of the following correspondence: Clayton to H. Starr, esqr, 8 Mar., 20 June 1870, to Rev. H. Hanks, 8 Jan., 14 Mar. 1870, to W. C. Staines, 26 June 1870.

12. Clayton to Arthur Stayner, 15 Aug. 1863.

13. Clayton to J. C. Wright, 11 May 1864.

14. Clayton to George C. Riser, 30 Apr. 1872.

15. Clayton to Thomas Crane, 7 Jan. 1873.

16. Clayton to Thomas Winn, 9 Apr. 1870.

17. Clayton to Schettler, 27 Nov. 1863, to William P. Nebeker, 22 Apr. 1864.

18. Clayton to Hannah Low and Sisters, 15 May 1864.

19. From December 1860 to May 1862 George Q. Cannon presided in conjunction with two other apostles, Charles C. Rich and Amasa M. Lyman. When the three men returned to America, Cannon went to Washington, D.C., for he had been elected delegate to Congress from the Territory of Utah. In July he returned to England.

20. Clayton to Nebeker, 22 Apr. 1863.

21. Clayton to Karl G. Maeser, 9 Jan. 1870. See also Clayton to Heber Young, 14 Nov. 1869, for further complaints about Maeser's slowness in paying attention to the collection business.

22. Clayton to Knud Petersen, 1 Jan. 1873.

23. Clayton to George Q. Cannon, 12 Oct. 1863.

24. Clayton to Heber Young, 14 Nov. 1869.

25. Clayton to Maeser, 9 Jan. 1870.

26. Clayton to Petersen, 11 Nov. 1871, and other letters in this time period.

27. Clayton to Petersen, 11 Nov. 1871.

28. For a discussion of this early economic system among the Mormons, see Arrington, "Early Mormon Communitarianism," 341–69.

29. Clayton's name appears regularly on the tithing rolls of the Salt Lake City Ward to which he belonged.

30. The best treatment of Mormon economic cooperation in Utah is Arrington, Fox, and May, *Building the City of God.*

31. See ibid., chap. 3.

32. Salt Lake City Seventeenth Ward, Historical Record, 9 Apr. 1854.

33. See Arrington, Fox, and May, *Building the City of God*, chap. 5.

34. Journal History, 10 Oct. 1868.

35. Clayton to McKean, 16 Jan. 1870.

36. Clayton to H. S. Eldredge, 21 Aug. 1870.

37. Clayton to Petersen, 11 Nov. 1871.

38. Clayton to George Peacock, 12 Feb. 1871.

39. Clayton to Eldredge, 21 Aug. 1870.

40. Clayton to the President and Directors of Zion's Mercantile Institution, 28 Aug.–9 Sept. 1871.

41. Clayton to Mrs. John R. Robbins, 7 Nov. 1871, to F. R. Kenner, 4 Nov. 1871.

42. See Arrington, Fox, and May, *Building the City of God*, chaps. 6-16, for the full story of the United Orders in Utah.

43. See Doctrine and Covenants 105.

44. Note that Arrington, Fox, and May explain this by demonstrating that there were actually a variety of United Orders designed to suit the special economic needs of particular kinds of communities. Clayton may well have been misinterpreting the broad picture. See Arrington, *Great Basin Kingdom*, chaps. 10 and 11, and Arrington, Fox, and May, *Building the City of God.*

45. Clayton to Francis M. Lyman, 19 July 1874.

46. Ibid.

47. Ibid.

48. Minutes of the School of the Prophets, Salt Lake City, Utah, 10 Nov. 1873.

49. Dahl, *William Clayton*, 191–95, deals briefly with Clayton's mining investments, and several of his letters in the 1870s in the Bancroft Collection reveal more details on this and other business ventures. In most cases Clayton seems to be very distressed with lack of success in these ventures, though he sometimes expresses optimism for the future.

50. Clayton to John R. Murdock, 6 Feb. 1871.

51. Ibid.

52. See Dahl, *William Clayton*, 190–91; Clayton to John R. Murdock, 6 Feb. 1871, to J. W. Christian, 27 Feb. 1872.

53. Clayton to A. W. White esq., 17 July 1872.

54. Clayton to F. M. Lyman, 13 Nov. 1872.

55. Clayton to Brigham Young, 7 Mar. 1872.

56. Clayton to Messers Owens, Lane, Dryer, & Co., 5 Apr. 1872.

57. Clayton to W. H. H. Young, esq., May 1872. Clayton notes in this letter that he and his co-workers had trouble assembling the machine after he got it.

58. Clayton to United States Publishing Co., 9 May, 2 Sept. 1872.

59. Clayton to A. W. White esq., 20 Dec. 1875.

60. Clayton to the President and Board of Directors of Zion's Cooperative Mercantile Institution, 1 Oct. 1876. In this letter Clayton indicates that he had stock worth $530. The ledger book of ZCMI shows that on 1 Sept. 1876 he had a stock balance of $508.31. The next volume shows no entry for Clayton, indicating that the company did as he requested, and thus he was divested of his stock. In a letter to Thomas R. Miller, 29 Oct. 1876, Clayton said that he had sold some coop stock at fifty cents on the dollar, but that he still needed more money for coal and winter clothes for the children.

61. Clayton to John M. Horner, 4, 29 Oct. 1876.

62. In addition, Alice Hardman, from whom he was divorced, was still living, but she did not appear in the probate records.

63. See Probate Court Record no. 678, County Clerk's Office, Salt Lake City, Utah. All the following information is in this record.

64. Francis M. Lyman Journal, 1 Aug. 1883, Church Archives.

"The Shaking between the Field and the Barn": The Clayton Allegory

An interesting perspective on the nature of discipleship was suggested toward the end of the nineteenth century by Josiah Royce, in his thoughtful introduction to John Fiske's *Outlines of Cosmic Philosophy*.[1] Royce was commenting on intellectual movements rather than organized religious bodies such as Mormonism, but some of his insights apply. He characterized two "sorts" of discipleship. One consisted of "the disciples pure and simple," those who fall under the spell of a leader or doctrine and spend their whole lives in expounding, defending, and warding off foes. Such disciples might be indispensable to the founding of a movement, but in the long run, Royce argued, they will hinder its growth. The second sort consists of those who take new concepts and give them expression in some novel way. They act, more or less independently, to build upon the doctrines of the founder, and they try to lead the thought they have accepted "to a truer expression. They force it beyond its earlier and cruder stages of development."

Under this criteria, William Clayton came closest to being a disciple of the first sort—the disciple "pure and simple." He was no innovator or formulator of new ideas, though he often came up with colorful and unique language with which to express traditional Mormon concepts. He saw himself as building and defending the Kingdom, but certainly not in the role of taking its doctrines to any further stage of development or even suggesting new ideas. To him, the doctrines were developed as far as they needed to be—anything not already revealed was simply not necessary for salvation and therefore was hardly worth speculating on. Even though the profound thought and speculative sermons of Orson Pratt (a disciple of the "second sort") in 1852 were interesting to Clayton, he was just as happy when they stopped, for such musings seemed of little value to the Kingdom.

William's brand of discipleship, however, was essential to the strength of early Mormonism. The church, after all, was more than the kind of intellectual movement Royce was concerned with, and it took more than unique ideas on the part of its disciples to make it survive. Joseph Smith, Brigham Young, Orson and Parley Pratt, and others provided the intellectual and spiritual leadership, but the Kingdom also needed soldiers who found pleasure in following the prophet with unquestioned loyalty, who were more concerned with spreading the doctrines they were taught than with casting them in new formulas, and who were so fiercely proud of their partisanship that they would stand anywhere to defend it. A revelation to Joseph Smith told the Saints to take upon themselves the "whole armor" of God—including the "breastplate of righteousness," the "shield of faith wherewith ye shall be able to quench all the fiery darts of the wicked," the "helmet of Salvation," and the "sword of my Spirit."[2] Disciples of Clayton's sort loved such imagery and happily saw themselves as building the fortifications, not planning them, and as following orders, not giving them.

Brigham H. Roberts, prominent Mormon intellectual, historian, and church leader early in this century, was deeply concerned that Mormonism should encourage more disciples of the "second sort."[3] They, after all, are the men of ideas and vision and are vital to the intellectual as well as the spiritual life of the church. He recognized that presenting new ideas and even recasting old ones carried potential for stress and strain, though he also spoke feelingly of the need to define the "essentials" of the faith narrowly, leaving room for wide-ranging opinion and discussion on the "nonessentials."[4] But Roberts lived in a different world than Clayton—a new age in which the challenge was no longer one of fighting the visible enemy but rather the more subtle one of dealing with new scientific and social thought, new methods of scriptural criticism, and new political alignments for the church. One wonders if a disciple like Clayton could be comfortable at all in the new age or would even have thought of Roberts's "essential" versus "nonessential" dichotomy. For him, whatever the prophet taught *was* essential. It was the disciple's role to accept and teach it, and Clayton's

brand of nineteenth-century discipleship helped make Mormonism a
force to be reckoned with.

The story of William Clayton was, in many respects, the story of
the Mormon community. He saw himself as first and foremost a disciple of Christ, but this meant that he also owed his devotion to those
prophets chosen to head Christ's earthly Kingdom. As a loyal follower
of both Joseph Smith and Brigham Young, therefore, his life was
wrapped up in building the Kingdom. This helps explain why thinking
and talking about the gospel was as routine to him as keeping accounts
or recording marks and brands. His last words before he died were of
the history of the church. As his son later reported, "Five minutes
previous to his death, he was conversing with Dr. Bernhisel about the
old days of Nauvoo, hence the uppermost thing in his mind was his
religion."[5]

Something William Clayton wrote early in his career may not have
been a literary masterpiece, but as an allegorical expression of Mormon
faith it was eloquent:

> I have often found that in the greatest seasons of suffering we
> have the greatest cause of rejoicing and so it has been with us for
> when we have thought impossible even then was our happiest
> moments. After all this I am aware that all we have suffered is
> scarce a beginning to our share of the tribulations of these last
> days. At the time of harvest men are sent to cut down the corn
> and then it is drawn to the barn, afterwards threshed and last of
> all sifted and so it is with the harvest of men. The Lord sent His
> servants to reap for he has declared that the harvest was fully ripe
> and we have been brought to the barn, but we have yet to be
> threshed and sifted and perhaps the sifting time will be the worst
> to endure. Then the chaff and tares will be separated from the
> pure grain and will be ready for burning. The kingdom of heaven
> is like unto a net cast into the sea, but not until it was drawn to
> shore was the separation of the good and bad. That grain which
> cannot endure the shaking between the field and the barn is in
> great danger of being lost in the journey and if once separated
> from the sheaf and care of the farmer it is in danger of being
> devoured by the fowls and other enemies. And they that hang
> down its head for fear of the toils of harvesting is of very little
> worth to the farmer. Those that come to this land must set their
> minds firm to come through all and not flinch if death should
> stare them in the face. The Lord calls for valiant hearted men who
> are not afraid to die.[6]

These words were penned in 1840 by William Clayton the eager young immigrant, who wanted his friends in England to know that being a Saint was no easy matter. They might just as well have been penned thirty-nine years later by William Clayton the ill and aging Saint, whose life had encompassed nearly all the joys and struggles that could come to a Mormon of his day. He had endured "the shaking between the field and the barn." The "field" was England where he was among the stalks of grain "white already to harvest" when Heber C. Kimball "thrust in his sickle with his might." The "barn" was the church—the Kingdom of God on Earth. There he had been subject to the "sifting and sorting" that separates the wheat from the tares, and he had endured. His threshing and winnowing did not come in questioning the truth of the Mormon gospel, the authority of the church, or the leadership of the living apostles and prophets. Rather, it came in surviving such challenges as outside persecution, the hard times associated with building new frontier communities, and the disappointments that sometimes befell him because of the actions of other people as well those of his own. Like most Saints, he was far from perfect, but at least he had not hung down his head for fear of the toils of harvesting. On December 4, 1879, he left the earthly "barn" to reap whatever reward the Farmer had for him in the eternal worlds.

Clayton was the kind of disciple who would look back on his life and say that it took suffering as well as testimony to strengthen him for his greatest challenges: preaching the gospel; raising eight families; providing economically for those families; bringing in money from abroad for the sake of both himself and the Kingdom; sending out missionaries; confronting gentiles economically through ZCMI; battling apostasy. Each of these brought him disappointment in one way or another, but it would be like him to say that his problems were only means of preparing him for the great "sifting." That his expectations were high is to be commended. That he had difficulty coping with disappointment is to be understood. That he was well equipped to make fresh assessments of his situation and renew his determined efforts to build the Kingdom is apparent from the story of his life. He summed up his own persistent lifetime attitudes on the plains of Iowa in 1846: "Gird up your loins, fresh courage take, Our God will never us forsake; And soon we'll have this tale to tell—All is well! All is well!"

William Clayton was not unprepared for death and even made preparations for his own funeral. In 1873 members of the School of the Prophets discussed death and decided to prepare individual statements concerning their own desires when that time should come. Clayton prefaced his note with a natural sentiment: "I desire to live as long as I can be useful to the Saints, and do good among my friends." He was in no hurry to get on to his reward. When he went, however, he wanted a casket made of any durable hardwood except redwood, which he feared would stain the white temple robes in which he would be buried. The Saints were concerned with sacred symbols, and the white robes represented the priesthood as well as the purity of the Kingdom of God. Neither a symbolic stain nor an actual one should be allowed on either. As a further symbol of the Kingdom, Clayton insisted that no black clothing be worn at his funeral by any of his family, for, he said, "I regard that emblematic of Satan's Kingdom, and the opposite of the uniform of Heaven." Finally, he wanted as little "ceremony and parade" as possible, evidently preferring something more symbolic of the peace he hoped to find beyond.[7]

Naturally he was concerned about how he might fare in the next life. If he could have listened to the church leaders who spoke at his funeral, he would have been comforted. "He was not without his faults in the flesh," said Apostle Joseph F. Smith,

But what were they? Were they such as partook of a deadly character? Did he ever deny the prophet Joseph, or did he deny the truth or prove unfaithful to his covenants or to his brethren? No, never! . . . But not withstanding his unflinching integrity, and his long life of fidelity and usefulness, let me say to you, that as for his faults, however, trivial, or important, he must answer. But he will be able to pay for his debts and to answer for his failings, and he will come forth, and all that has been pronounced upon his head by Joseph Smith and the Apostles will be confirmed upon him through all eternity. . . .

Then let me say to the family of our deceased brother, follow in the footsteps of your husband and father, excepting wherein he may have manifested the weaknesses of the flesh; imitate his staunch integrity to the cause of Zion, and his fidelity to his brethren; be true as he was true, be firm as he was firm, never flinching, never swerving from the truth as God has revealed it to us; and I will promise you, in the name of the Lord, that you will rise to meet your husband and father, in the morning of the first resurrection, clothed with glory, immortality and eternal lives.

In the same spirit the new leader of the church, John Taylor, sanctioned Elder Smith's remarks and added, "If there were any weaknesses in him pass them by, and live for God and for truth. He will be all right."[8]

NOTES

1. Josiah Royce, introduction to John Fiske, *Outlines of Cosmic Philosophy*, 13th ed. (Boston: Houghton, Mifflin and Company, 1892).

2. Doctrine and Covenants 27:15–18.

3. B. H. Roberts, "Book of Mormon Translated," *Improvement Era* 9 (1905–6):712–13.

4. B. H. Roberts, address in general conference of the Church, 5 Oct. 1912, as reported in *Eighty-Third Semi-Annual Conference of The Church of Jesus Christ of Latter-day Saints* (Salt Lake City: Deseret News, 1912), 30–35.

5. Nephi W. Clayton to "Bro. Reid," 9 Dec. 1879, Clayton Letterbook, Bancroft Collection.

6. Clayton to Edward Martin, 29 Nov. 1840, in *Heart Throbs*, 5:374.

7. Clayton to President Brigham Young and the Brethren in the Priesthood, n.d., Brigham Young Papers.

8. *Deseret Evening News*, 9 Dec. 1879.

INDEX

Adams, James, 136
Ainsworth, Elizabeth: marries Clayton, 205–6, 218n33
Alchemy, 323, 324, 331–37
Anointed Quorum. *See* "Quorum of the Anointed"
Apocalyptic expectations. *See* Millennialism
Astrology, 323–31

Backenstos, Jacob (sheriff), 104, 118
Beaman, Louisa (plural wife of Joseph Smith), 135
Bennett, John C.: denounces Mormon leaders, 138
Book of Mormon, 3–4
"Book of the Law of the Lord," 118
Booth, Ann, 21, 37
Booth, Robert, 21
Braddock, Augusta: marries Clayton, 204
Brannan, Samuel, 163; warns Brigham Young of efforts to stop Mormon exodus, 179–80
Bullock, Thomas, 228, 243; Clayton confides in, 290–91
Burnett, Peter: on Joseph Smith, 69
Butterfield, Justin, 90, 92

Cahoon, Reynolds, 111–12, 127–28
Cahoon, William F., 93
Calhoun, John C., 101, 103, 173
Carlin, Thomas, 87
Carrington, Albert, 231
Carthage, Ill., jail, 140, 158, 159
Church of Jesus Christ of Latter-day Saints, 4–8; membership in England, 1838–40, 18; opens missionary work in England, 16–17; plans for westward

movement, 176–81; social and religious attitudes in early Utah, 254
—Doctrines of, 3–4, 6–8, 23–24, 148n47; eternal progression, 122–23; eternal marriage, 123, 130–31; Godhead, 121–23; salvation for the dead, 75, 80n12, 123–24
Church of Zion. *See* Godbeite movement
Civil War, U.S.: and Clayton's millennial expectations, 303, 304–16; Joseph Smith's prophecy on, 304
Clawson, Hiram B., 358–59
Clay, Henry, 101, 103
Clayton, Amasa Marion (son of William and Maris Louisa), 208, 343, 366
Clayton, Ann Critchley (mother of William Clayton), 12, 19
Clayton, Daniel Adebert (first child of William and Margaret), 195
Clayton, Henrietta Lucretia (third child of William and Ruth), 74, 76
Clayton, Margaret (daughter of William and Ruth), 19, 47, 64n26
Clayton, Matthew, 206–7
Clayton, Moroni (first child of William and Diantha), 202, 214
Clayton, Nephi Willard (son of William and Augusta), 366
Clayton, Newell Horace (son of William and Ruth), 215
Clayton, Rachael Amelia (daughter of William and Diantha), 204, 214, 215
Clayton, Ruth Moon. *See* Moon, Ruth
Clayton, Sarah (daughter of William and Ruth), 18, 60, 47, 64n26
Clayton, Thomas (father of William Clayton), 12

Note on the Author

James B. Allen is professor of history and chair of the department at Brigham Young University, Provo, Utah, where he has taught since 1963. He was also assistant Church Historian for The Church of Jesus Christ of Latter-day Saints from 1972 to 1979. He is the author of numerous articles on western and Mormon history in such journals as *Utah Historical Quarterly, Dialogue: A Journal of Mormon Thought, BYU Studies,* and *Pacific Historical Review* as well as the following books: *The Company Town in the American West, Mormonism and American Culture* (with Marvin S. Hill), *Manchester Mormons: The Journal of William Clayton, 1840–1842* (with Thomas G. Alexander), and *The Story of the Latter-day Saints* (with Glen M. Leonard).